Building Soft Skills for Employability

This book is among the first of its kind to comprehensively examine the implementation of soft skills in universities in the developing country, Vietnam. The context is unique as the implementation is taking place within the distinctive socio-economic, cultural and political characteristics of the country, and amidst several simultaneously-executed educational reforms.

Tran lays down the foundation for discussion by providing readers with a comprehensive review of how soft skills implementation has come into existence in higher education across the globe, before diving into the implementation of soft skills in Vietnamese universities. He goes on to highlight the interesting differences in the conceptualization of soft skills between Vietnamese universities and those in the West.

The book depicts and compares how university leaders and managers tackle contextual factors, submit to constraints enforced by political forces, and how they use institutional advantages available for implementation. It goes further to examine how personal and contextual factors affect teachers' and students' engagement with the implementation, and highlights the role of work-integrated learning and extra-curricular activities in developing soft skills for students. Finally, the book investigates the contribution of external stakeholders, such as alumni, employers, skills experts, and local authorities to the implementation, and obstacles that prevent their participation.

This book will be a valuable reference for the implementation of soft skills in higher education around the world.

Tran Le Huu Nghia is currently teaching at the Faculty of Education, Monash University (Australia). He is also an honorary researcher at Ton Duc Thang University (Vietnam). He worked for eight years in the Vietnamese higher education sector prior to coming to Australia where he worked as a research fellow for Deakin University and Swinburne University of Technology. He completed the Master of Lifelong Learning: Policy and Management (2007–2009), a program coordinated by three prestigious European universities: Aarhus University (Denmark), Bilbao University (Spain), and the Institute of Education (the United Kingdom). Then as an Endeavour Postgraduate Awardee (2012–2016), he completed his PhD, with a focus on higher education studies, at the University of Melbourne, Australia. He has produced several research outputs, including articles in high impact journals such as *Higher Education, Teaching and Teacher Education, Teaching in Higher Education, Journal of Education and Work*, and *International Journal of Education Development*. His research interests include teaching and learning for employability, teacher education, international education, and teaching English as a second language.

Routledge Research in Higher Education

The Phenomenological Heart of Teaching and Learning
Theory, Research, and Practice in Higher Education
Katherine H. Greenberg, Brian K. Sohn, Neil B. Greenberg, Howard R. Pollio, Sandra P. Thomas, and John T. Smith

The Tenure-Track Process for Chicana and Latina Faculty
Experiences of Resisting and Persisting in the Academy
Edited by Patricia A. Pérez

Higher Education in Nepal
Policies and Perspectives
Edited by Krishna Bista, Shyam Sharma, and Rosalind Latiner Raby

Race, Law, and Higher Education in the Colorblind Era
Critical Investigations into Race-Related Supreme Court Disputes
Hoang Vu Tran

Post-Recession Community College Reform
A Decade of Experimentation
Chet Jordan and Anthony G. Picciano

Building Soft Skills for Employability
Challenges and Practices in Vietnam
Tran Le Huu Nghia

Life for the Academic in the Neoliberal University
Alpesh Maisuria and Svenja Helmes

The Doctorate Experience in Europe and Beyond
Supervision, Languages, Identities
Michael Byram and Maria Stoicheva

For more information about this series, please visit: www.routledge.com/Routledge-Research-in-Higher-Education/book-series/RRHE

Building Soft Skills for Employability
Challenges and Practices in Vietnam

Tran Le Huu Nghia

LONDON AND NEW YORK

First published 2020
by Routledge
2 Park Square, Milton Park, Abingdon, Oxon OX14 4RN

and by Routledge
52 Vanderbilt Avenue, New York, NY 10017

Routledge is an imprint of the Taylor & Francis Group, an informa business

© 2020 Tran Le Huu Nghia

The right of Tran Le Huu Nghia to be identified as author of this work has been asserted by him in accordance with sections 77 and 78 of the Copyright, Designs and Patents Act 1988.

All rights reserved. No part of this book may be reprinted or reproduced or utilised in any form or by any electronic, mechanical, or other means, now known or hereafter invented, including photocopying and recording, or in any information storage or retrieval system, without permission in writing from the publishers.

Trademark notice: Product or corporate names may be trademarks or registered trademarks, and are used only for identification and explanation without intent to infringe.

British Library Cataloguing in Publication Data
A catalogue record for this book is available from the British Library

Library of Congress Cataloging-in-Publication Data
A catalog record for this book has been requested

ISBN: 978-0-367-22703-6 (hbk)
ISBN: 978-0-429-27649-1 (ebk)

Typeset in Galliard
by Taylor & Francis Books

This book is dedicated to

Emeritus Professor Peter McPhee
The University of Melbourne, Australia

Professor Sophia Arkoudis
The University of Melbourne, Australia

Doctor Ryan Naylor
La Trobe University, Australia

Thank you for your guidance in my first steps into academia.

Contents

List of tables	viii
Acknowledgements	x
Introduction: Soft skills and graduate employability	xi

1	The surge in developing soft skills for students in higher education	1
2	Soft-skills implementation: A literature review	18
3	The context of soft-skills implementation in Vietnamese universities	41
4	Models for the development of soft skills for students in Vietnamese universities	61
5	Contextual factors and leadership for soft-skills policy implementation: Lessons from two Vietnamese universities	78
6	Teaching soft skills in Vietnamese universities: Teachers' beliefs, behaviors, and influential factors	96
7	Assessing soft skills: Practices and challenges	117
8	The contribution of internships to students' development of employability	135
9	Students' experience with developing soft skills via participation in extracurricular activities	154
10	External stakeholders' roles in developing soft skills in Vietnamese universities	173
11	Students' participation and engagement with soft-skills development	191
12	Building soft skills for employability: The way ahead	212

Index	233

Tables

1.1	Terms referring to soft skills in some countries	1
1.2	Different soft-skills frameworks for the 21st century	6
2.1	Top 10 soft skills selected by Australian university groups	23
2.2	Approaches to teaching generic graduate attributes	31
2.3	Levels of soft-skills implementation and respective tasks	36
3.1	Some indicators of the Vietnamese economy	42
3.2	Statistics of Vietnamese higher education from 2006–2017	48
4.1	A summary of participants	65
4.2	Soft-skills-implementation models in Vietnamese universities	71
5.1	Tasks involved in soft-skills implementation	79
5.2	Participants and universities	83
6.1	A summary of participants	102
6.2	Teachers' beliefs about teaching soft skills	109
6.3	Teachers' engagement with teaching soft skills	110
6.4	Factors influencing teachers' engagement with teaching soft skills	111
7.1	A summary of participants	122
9.1	Contribution of extra-curricular activities participation to students' employability skills	160
9.2	Frequency of organizing some types of extra-curricular activities and student engagement	167
10.1	A summary of participants and universities	177
10.2	Activities that alumni can participate in	184
10.3	Alumni's participation in soft-skills-development activities for current students	185
10.4	The influence of certain factors on alumni's participation intention	185
11.1	Participants' information	196
11.2	Students' perception of the importance of soft skills	197
11.3	Availability of soft-skills development activities in Vietnamese universities	199
11.4	Students' participation in soft-skills development activities	200

11.5 Student engagement with soft-skills development 202
11.6 Factors influencing student engagement with soft-skills development 204

Acknowledgements

This book is a combination of my doctoral dissertation and follow-up studies.

I cannot express enough thanks to my academic supervisors, academic committee, and researchers at the Centre for the Study of Higher Education (CSHE), University of Melbourne (Australia). I sincerely appreciate the learning opportunities provided by all of you.

My gratitude is also to the Australian Government's Department of Education and Training and the Department for Management of Science and Technology Development, Ton Duc Thang University (Vietnam). Without the Endeavour Postgraduate Award and your generous financial assistance, respectively, my doctoral dissertation and follow-up studies would not have been executed.

Foremost, this book project could not have been accomplished without the participants' kind support. Thank you for the time and useful data that you provided for the studies. All of your perspectives have been taken into account to generate insights into what is going on with developing soft skills for graduates' employability.

Finally, my heartfelt thanks are to my family, colleagues, friends and students. Thank you for standing by my side when the times got rough.

Introduction

Soft skills and graduate employability

Some decades ago, possessing a university credential could guarantee graduates a permanent job with which they could climb the career ladder. However, in our contemporary society, that scenario has completely changed. A university credential alone can no longer afford graduates a permanent job. This situation appears to have resulted from some key factors.

First, knowledge expansion and technological advancement have caused constant changes in skill demands in the labor market. It is estimated that knowledge doubled every century up to 1900; that time span reduced to 25 years after World War II, and nowadays, new knowledge doubles every 13 months, on average, with nanotechnology knowledge doubling every two years and clinical knowledge every 18 months (Dehkord, Samimi, Alivand, & Sani, 2017). The spread of the Internet is one of the major causes of the widespread distribution of knowledge (Schilling, 2010). Likewise, it is easy to observe that new technologies, equipment, and devices are being invented for the workplace at an unprecedented speed (Rossi, 2017; Susskind & Susskind, 2015). In such a climate, university curricula, which are usually framed within three to four academic years, cannot hope to include and impart all of the new knowledge and skills needed for the modern workplace. Even if universities could do so, graduates are unlikely to master all the knowledge and skills required for work by the time of their graduation, because their professional expertise needs time to grow within a community of practice. Unfortunately, employers want new employees to hit the ground running (Brunner, Zarkin, & Yates, 2018; McMurray, Dutton, McQuaid, & Richard, 2016; Stevens & Norman, 2016) so that they can spend less on training them (Lindorff, 2011; Tran, 2018). Consequently, only prospective employees who are able to demonstrate their capability, in addition to a university credential, can convince employers to offer them a job.

Second, the expansion of higher education (HE) has offered more learning opportunities for all who want a higher education, resulting in an increase in the number of graduates. For example, in a recent paper, Yang (2018) reported that in China the student HE enrollments increased from 936,690 in 1999 to 3,261,081 in 2009. By the end of this period, approximately 19 to 27% of graduates could not secure a job at their education level, despite a high economic growth rate in the country. In the same period, about 48% of four-year college graduates in the United States of America (USA) were not employed in jobs that require a degree (Vedder, Denhart, & Robe, 2013). The situation is no better in the United Kingdom (UK) either, where the Office for National Statistics reports that graduate underemployment has risen from 37% in 2001 to 47% in 2013 (cited in Mok & Jiang, 2018). In 2018, the graduate unemployment rate in Spain was 15.5%, France 9.2%, and Finland 7.6% (The Statistics Portal, 2018). Although graduate unemployment could be caused by economic recession, an over-supply of graduates appears to be the main cause because all of the mentioned countries have strong and relatively stable economies.

Third, labor-market realities now are characterized by constant changes with increasing complexities and career mobility. Permanent jobs are diminishing while precarious ones are increasing (Lewchuk, 2017; Maciejewska, Mrozowicki, & Piasna, 2016). For example, in 1976, the percentage of full-time employees in Australia and Canada was 85.4% and 87.5%, respectively; by 2015 the figures had dropped to 73.7% and 81.9%, respectively (Lewchuk, 2017). In Germany, between 2000 and 2010, the number of people with full-time jobs reduced by approximately 2.55 million, whereas the number of people with part-time jobs increased by 1.83 million (Lehndorff, 2016). Such a change in work arrangement means that graduates move from job to job or from one organization to another before they land a permanent employment position, possibly when their expertise is highly appraised. During the education-to-work and work-to-work transition periods, graduates need non-technical skills that enable them to navigate the world of work, identify employment opportunities relevant to their expertise, and demonstrate their capabilities to prospective employers before they can use their technical expertise for their work.

Fourth, the change in the nature of work and how work is carried out also reduces the value of university credentials. In our modern workplace, work is becoming more complex as it involves knowledge and skills from different disciplines (Bajada & Trayler, 2013; Ivanaj & Ivanaj, 2010). It is the norm that employees need to be capable of working individually and in a team to complete projects. Work outcomes are often the combination of the expertise of all people involved rather than reliant on individual expertise. All of this means that employees need both technical and non-technical skills and/or authentic work experience, not merely a university credential, to perform the job properly.

In response to these changes, HE institutions worldwide are investing in helping their students develop skills that enhance their employment and career-development prospects, creating a so-called employability agenda in HE. Employability skills are understood as "a set of achievements—skills, understanding and personal attributes—that makes graduates more likely to gain employment and be successful in their chosen occupations, which benefits themselves, the workforce, the community and the economy" (Yorke, 2006, p. 23). These skills help students "discern, acquire, adapt and continually enhance the skills, understandings and personal attributes that make them more likely to find and create meaningful paid and unpaid work that benefits themselves, the workforce, the community and the economy" (Oliver, 2015, p. 56). These snapshots of employability perspectives suggest that employability is not static but evolves throughout one's life. Therefore, graduates need to be able to adapt to all changes they are exposed to and learn continuously at work so that they can remain employable amidst the ups and downs of the labor market.

There are several proposed frameworks of graduate employability (for example, Clarke, 2017; Fugate, Kinicki, & Ashforth, 2004; McQuaid & Lindsay, 2005; Tomlinson, 2017) that comprise several types of capital, which can be developed via learning and work experience:

- **Human capital**: Specialized knowledge and skills, soft skills and attributes as well as socio-physical features such as gender, age, race, marital status, etc.
- **Social capital**: Social relationships, memberships and associations to people or organizations.
- **Cultural capital**: Understanding of cultures or practices in different contexts.
- **Psychological capital**: Psychological qualities beneficial for career development such as resilience, flexibility, self-efficacy, adaptability.
- **Identity capital**: Formation of work identities or personal investment in employment.

Despite being classified into several components, employability capital appears to be the combination of two sets of skills: technical and non-technical. The former includes skills distinctive to a discipline—i.e., specialized skills. The technical skills of a discipline can be homogenous between institutions in a country, or even across countries. The latter can be described as transferable, non-discipline-specific skills that may be achieved through learning and can be applied in study, work, and life contexts (Tertiary Education Quality and Standards Agency, 2013). They are also known as soft skills, generic skills, generic graduate attributes, and transferable skills (Bowman, 2010; Maria, 2016).

Looking back to the employability capital above, soft skills are dominantly composed of these types of capital. Thus, soft skills appear to be a significant determinant of employment outcomes. They help separate employable and unemployable job applicants or distinguish capable employees, who should be invested in for the future, from those who are less capable. Indeed, an abundance of studies indicate that employers are looking for soft skills in their prospective employees. For example, Brunner et al. (2018) analyzed the content of 199 entry-level employment advertisements posted to the Public Relations Society of America Job Center to find out what employers were looking for. They concluded that employers were not only looking for technical skills but also for soft skills, such as time management, deadline orientation, and collaboration. Using the same method, plus interviews and focus groups, Stevens and Norman (2016) analyzed 543 job advertisements in New Zealand to explore what capabilities employers needed from IT graduates. They found that employers were concerned about graduates' soft skills related to their ability to work in teams, serve customers, and function well in a business environment, and that employers often make recruitment decisions based on graduates' personal qualities. Framing their study within the context of the business discipline, McMurray et al. (2016) found that when recruiting graduates, employers paid attention to their personal attitudes, employability skills, relevant work experience, and degree results. They found that employers favored transferable skills such as trustworthiness, reliability, motivation, communication skills, and a willingness to learn.

Several studies also suggest that soft skills work to graduates' advantage when they apply for jobs, or in their career development once they are in a career. A study conducted by Stanford Research Institute and Carnegie Melon Foundation found that 75% of long-term job success depends on soft skills and only 25% on technical knowledge (Litecky, Arnett, & Prabhakar, 2004, p. 69). In another study conducted in the UK, Nickson, Warhurst, Commander, Hurrell, and Cullen (2012) surveyed 173 clothing, footwear, and leather retailers about what influenced their hiring decisions. The results showed that job applicants' personalities (79.7%) and appearance (68.2%) were much more important for their decisions than the applicants' work experience (41.1%) and qualifications (4.6%). Moving away from the contribution of soft skills to graduates' employment, Gayani Fernando, Amaratunga, and Haigh (2014) explored what contributed to women's career success. They found that although success can be affected by age and gender, it depended more on soft skills than technical skills. Shaping the study in an opposite direction, Eisner (2010) found that a lack of soft skills is the key reason for employees being fired.

Against numerous studies that support the importance of soft skills in one's career development, Groh, Krishnan, McKenzie, and Vishwanath (2016) found that training in soft skills, as part of the World Bank's Jordan NOW pilot programs, did not increase possibilities for Jordanian female youth to secure jobs. However, this training was delivered within 45 hours over a nine-day period, which is not meaningful for developing soft skills as these skills need time and practice to grow (Bowman, 2010; Gonczi, 2006). The study suggests that training students in soft skills must be conducted methodologically rather than adopting a rushed, practical approach only to help students get a job. It could also be that the soft skills training in the pilot programs was not localized enough to enable participants to meet local employers' expectations.

The literature on soft-skills training, which is mostly derived from the Western English-speaking context, shows a diversity of approaches, initiatives, and activities used to help students develop these skills, depending on institutional contexts. For example, soft skills can be imparted to students via add-on units at the beginning of a degree course, or they can be integrated into the curriculum and delivered simultaneously with technical skills (Al-Mahmood & Gruba, 2007; Barrie, Hughes, Smith, & Thomson, 2009). They can also be developed by work-integrated learning, community service, or extracurricular activities (ECAs) (Jackson, 2018; Osman, 2011; Tran, 2017a). However, research has consistently pointed out that universities have not invested enough, academics are disengaged, and students overlook developing soft skills (Barrie et al., 2009; de la Harpe & David, 2012; Jones, 2009; Tran, 2017a, 2017b). All of this means that, contrary to the increasing importance of soft skills in the labor market, the supply side (i.e., student, academic, and the university in general) has not developed these skills to meet the needs of the demand side.

In short, current labor-market realities are becoming complex and require graduates to possess more than credentials and technical knowledge and skills. Soft skills are largely found to contribute to graduates' success in securing a first job and to thrive in their careers. However, it seems that soft skills training in HE is fragmented and is often disregarded by some stakeholders. It is also suggested that the implementation of soft skills in HE depends on contextual factors. For these reasons, it is vital to examine how soft skills are developed to enhance students' employability within certain HE contexts.

The focus of this book

This book reports on how Vietnamese universities are developing soft skills as a strategy to build employability for their students and identify influencers of the implementation. In this book, soft skills are defined broadly as non-disciplinary skills that may be achieved through learning and be applied in study, work, and life contexts. As noted above, soft-skills implementation is context-dependent, but most studies related to soft-skills development in HE have been conducted in Western English-speaking countries. For this reason, Vietnam, a developing non-English-speaking country with a socioeconomic, cultural, and political context completely different from the West, provides an interesting case to expand the investigation of soft-skills implementation beyond the Western HE context.

Developing students' soft skills—as part of HE learning outcomes—has recently become a priority for Vietnamese universities. It is the response of Vietnamese universities to address the need of a skilled workforce as employers lament the shortage of soft skills in graduates (Bodewig & Badiani-Magnusson, 2014; Truong, Laura, & Shaw, 2018). Without a skilled workforce, the country will not be able to sustain its high socioeconomic growth rate (Anwar & Nguyen, 2014; Trinh & Doan, 2018) and compete in the process of regionalization in the Southeast Asian region (Jurje & Lavenex, 2015; Suci, Asmara, & Mulatsih, 2016; Tran & Nørlund, 2015). Their development of students' soft skills also derives from recent political initiatives regarding improving the quality of HE (Harman, Hayden, & Nghi, 2010; MOET, 2010, 2013).

Unfortunately, until now, there has been a lack of research examining how Vietnamese universities have been developing students' soft skills. Few studies have attempted to identify work skills that employers need, or assess graduates' attainment of these skills, and the perceived skills gaps, from the perspectives of employers, graduates, and students (Truong & Metzger, 2007; Tran, 2018; Tran, 2013; Tran & Swierczek, 2009). In other words, the existing studies seem to focus on output rather than process. Without investigating the process, it is difficult to identify the obstacles to remove so as to improve students' learning outcomes related to soft skills and to increase their employability throughout their career trajectories. Therefore, this book sets out to investigate the implementation of soft skills in Vietnamese universities using the perspectives and experiences of key agents of the implementation: university leaders and managers, academics, students and alumni—including employers. The book includes qualitative case studies conducted in six Vietnamese universities (named A, B, C, D, E, and F), which represent different institutional contexts, and quantitative studies whose data were collected from a range of Vietnamese universities across the country.

This book is unique because it captures a holistic implementation of soft skills in a non-Western HE context. It highlights a number of factors influencing soft-skills implementation that have not been found in Western HE, thus complementing the existing literature and expanding our insights into soft-skills implementation in different HE contexts. Although the book is framed within one country, its value lies in its holistic investigation of the implementation across all levels of the HE system. This holistic analysis is different from other edited books that snapshot aspects of the implementation in different countries and put them in a one-book volume. This book provides important implications for moving forward with developing soft skills at the HE level in Vietnam and in other countries so that graduates can successfully obtain their first job and remain employable throughout their career trajectory.

Organization of the book

The remainder of this book is organized into 12 chapters. The first three chapters set the background contexts and practices for soft-skills development in the world and in Vietnam; the next eight chapters report on practices and challenges associated with various tasks at different levels of soft-skills implementation. While focusing on presenting the findings relevant to the topic of each chapter, the author will also link these findings to the international context to highlight the differences and similarities in soft-skills implementation in Vietnam compared to other countries. The last chapter summarizes the main findings of the whole book and discusses ways to move forward with the implementation, not only for Vietnamese universities but also for others internationally. The main content for each chapter is as follows.

Chapter 1 reviews the literature to underline the importance of developing students' soft skills in the current changing landscape of HE across the globe. It also highlights the various initiatives used to develop university students' soft skills across different HE systems, institutions, and disciplines. It argues that soft skills are implemented differently across disciplines due to differences in disciplinary characteristics; between institutions due to discrepancies in institutional missions and visions; and between countries due to different sociocultural, economic, and political contexts and educational values.

Chapter 2 provides a comprehensive literature review on practices and challenges related to soft-skills implementation in HE contexts. Based on this literature review and theories related to education-policy implementation, the author presents a four-level conceptual framework for soft-skills implementation in HE:

- **National level**: The general context of soft-skills implementation
- **Institutional level**: All mechanisms and strategies for executing the soft-skills policy.

Introduction xvii

- **Curriculum level**: Setting soft skills learning objectives, teaching, and assessing these skills.
- **Extracurricular level**: The use of non-curricular activities for developing soft skills.

This framework will be used as a spine to link chapters in this book and guide the comparison of soft-skills implementation in Vietnamese universities with that of other countries.

Chapter 3 presents the context of soft-skills implementation in Vietnamese universities. It begins with depicting Vietnam as an emerging economy and a rapidly evolving society where there is a high demand for skilled workers to sustain its growth rate. Then it contradicts this picture by providing statistics about unemployment rates among university graduates and employers' complaints about the lack of soft skills in their employees. Against that national context, the chapter reports how Vietnamese universities are pressured by soft-skills-related policies issued by the central government, foremost the Ministry of Education and Training (MOET), employers' demands, and students' and the general public's expectations. The chapter concludes that it is time for Vietnamese universities to put forth efforts to develop students' soft skills by taking into account available institutional advantages and tackling contextual factors.

Chapter 4 reports an analysis of interviews with 28 top- and mid-level university leaders of six Vietnamese universities about how soft skills have been implemented in their institutions. The study shows that, despite choosing different soft skills to impart, they conceptualize the implementation as developing work-readiness skills for students, either on a school-wide or university-wide scale. Methodologically, the six universities develop work-readiness for students via skills subjects and ECAs. They also encourage disciplinary teachers to embed soft skills into specialized subjects and use work-integrated learning. The study suggests that university leaders make use of all possible institutional advantages for the implementation; nonetheless, they face several obstacles, such as lack of curriculum autonomy, inexperience in policy implementation, a shortage of qualified staff, and lack of connection with external stakeholders—essential elements for successful implementation of soft skills.

Chapter 5 features the influence of institutional leadership on the success of soft-skills implementation. Comparing the deployment of comparable implementation strategies in two universities, this chapter indicates that leadership skills are essential for soft-skills implementation, especially considering differences in institutional contexts and the competition of other institutional reforms. Leadership styles may affect teacher and student engagement with executing the soft-skills policy. This study also points out that to implement the policy successfully, Vietnamese universities need more autonomy, accountability, and proactiveness instead of relying on regulatory bodies such as MOET. It also points out that soft-skills implementation is context-dependent; thus, a copy-and-paste approach will not work.

In Chapter 6, the author will report on teachers' beliefs, engagement behaviors, and factors influencing their engagement in developing students' soft skills in Vietnamese universities. Using 41 interviews with teachers of Business Administration programs in six Vietnamese universities, and 147 responses to a survey of disciplinary teachers from 27 Vietnamese universities, the two studies in this chapter show that teachers hold different beliefs about teaching soft skills and demonstrate their engagement in different acts of teaching, and that both of these are affected by several contextual factors. Based on the findings, this chapter argues that leadership should be exercised to change teachers' beliefs about the relevance of teaching soft skills, prepare them for such a new role, incentivize them, and remove obstacles so that they can engage with teaching these skills with confidence.

Chapter 7 reports a study that explores the practices and challenges of assessing students' soft skills in the Business Administration programs of six Vietnamese universities. Content analysis of interviews with 41 teachers of skills subjects and specialized subjects reveals that teachers are organizing different formative and summative soft-skills-assessment activities. Unfortunately, the analysis indicates that their practices are fragmented across subjects in the curriculum. Teachers' beliefs regarding their roles in the university, expertise in assessments, and several contextual factors are found to influence their assessment practices. The chapter argues that leadership should be exercised more effectively in order to remove obstacles and engage teachers with assessing soft skills, which will yield a washback effect on students' learning of these skills.

Chapter 8 presents a study that examines the contribution of internship experience on students' development of employability, including soft skills. Using the perspectives of 28 student interns, the study reveals that internships can help students develop many soft skills and technical skills, as well as the professional understanding and attitudes necessary for their future employment. It also reports challenges that hinder the effectiveness of this form of work-integrated learning experience. Students' awareness of the importance of the internship(s), collaboration between the university and industry, the role of the mentor, student efforts, etc. are identified as factors that influence the effectiveness of internships. The chapter discusses ways to improve the effectiveness of organizing student internships.

Chapter 9 reports a mixed-methods study about the effectiveness of developing soft skills for students via ECAs. Using six interviews with leaders of the Youth Union and associates, which are primarily in charge of organizing ECAs for students in Vietnamese universities, 18 interviews with current students, and responses to a survey of 423 students, the study suggests that these activities can contribute to the development of soft skills. However, the effectiveness of this initiative appears to depend greatly on student engagement, which is found to be associated with: (i) their beliefs about the benefits of participating in ECAs; (ii) their ability to balance formal education activities, part-time work, and ECAs; (iii) the availability of information about these activities; and (iv) the professional organization of these activities.

Chapter 10 offers two complementary studies that explore the contribution of external stakeholders to students' soft-skills development. Using 69 university leaders' and teachers' perspectives, the qualitative study, with a focus on the Business Administration of six universities, reports that external stakeholders can take part in different tasks to impart soft skills to students. However, they find that the involvement of external stakeholders depends greatly on institutional leadership, existing industry networks, and these stakeholders' availability. The quantitative study, with participation of 154 alumni, shows that they are willing to help develop soft skills for current students in different activities. However, several factors prevent them from participating—most influentially, lack of time, not being invited by the university, fear of bureaucratic practices in the university, and a lack of experience in curriculum or program development for such activities. The chapter argues that Vietnamese university leaders need to approach external stakeholders more proactively in order to negotiate how they can help current students develop soft skills.

Chapter 11 features student engagement with soft-skills development. The analysis of 461 responses to a survey and 18 interviews with current students from six universities shows that students are highly aware of the importance of soft skills to their future work and life. They tend to develop soft skills via non-curricular activities more than curriculum-based activities. They also demonstrate a high level of cognitive engagement with developing soft skills, but this does not translate so much into concrete behaviors. The study reveals that their engagement was affected by: (i) personal beliefs about whether these activities related to their self-interest; (ii) controlling factors such as time, effort, and cost; and (iii) third-party encouragement. The chapter argues that Vietnamese universities should focus on organizing suitable soft-skills activities that meet students' interests rather than basing them on their own perspectives.

Chapter 12 accentuates lessons for soft-skills implementation learned from the case study of Vietnamese universities. It argues that contextual factors significantly shape the development of these skills. It summarizes the key challenges to implementation presented in the previous chapters. Based on the findings, it discusses a number of initiatives so that Vietnamese universities in particular, and universities across the globe in general, can consider advancing the implementation of soft skills in their institutions. The chapter also acknowledges some limitations of the book and some directions for future studies.

References

Al-Mahmood, R., & Gruba, P. (2007). Approaches to the implementation of generic graduate attributes in Australian ICT undergraduate education. *Computer Science Education*, 17(3), 171–185.

Anwar, S., & Nguyen, L. P. (2014). Is foreign direct investment productive? A case study of the regions of Vietnam. *Journal of Business Research*, 67(7), 1376–1387.

Bajada, C., & Trayler, R. (2013). Interdisciplinary business education: Curriculum through collaboration. *Education + Training*, 55(4/5), 385–402.

Barrie, S., Hughes, C., Smith, C., & Thomson, K. (2009). *The national graduate attributes project: Key issues to consider in the renewal of learning and teaching experiences to foster graduate attributes.* Sydney: The University of Sydney.

Bodewig, C., & Badiani-Magnusson, R. (2014). *Skilling up Vietnam: Preparing the workforce for a modern market economy.* Washington, DC: World Bank Publications.

Bowman, K. (2010). *Background paper for the AQF Council on generic skills.* Retrieved from: www.voced.edu.au/content/ngv%3A46853

Brunner, B. R., Zarkin, K., & Yates, B. L. (2018). What do employers want? What should faculty teach? A content analysis of entry-level employment ads in public relations. Retrieved from https://bit.ly/2BOJj4x

Clarke, M. (2017). Rethinking graduate employability: The role of capital, individual attributes and context. *Studies in Higher Education,* 43(11), 1923–1937.

de la Harpe, B., & David, C. (2012). Major influences on the teaching and assessment of graduate attributes. *Higher Education Research & Development,* 31(4), 493–510.

Dehkord, F. K., Samimi, M., Alivand, R., & Sani, E. A. (2017). An examination and assessment of knowledge management maturity in Karaj municipality. *Journal of Ecophysiology and Occupational Health,* 17(1–2), 34–39.

Eisner, S. (2010). Grave new world? Workplace skills for today's college graduates. *American Journal of Business Education,* 3(9), 27–50.

Fugate, M., Kinicki, A. J., & Ashforth, B. E. (2004). Employability: A psycho-social construct, its dimensions, and applications. *Journal of Vocational Behavior,* 65(1), 14–38.

Gayani Fernando, N., Amaratunga, D., & Haigh, R. (2014). The career advancement of the professional women in the UK construction industry: The career success factors. *Journal of Engineering, Design and Technology,* 12(1), 53–70.

Gonczi, A. (2006). The OECD: Its role in the key competencies debate and in the promotion of lifelong learning. In P. Hager & S. Holland (Eds.), *Graduate attributes, learning and employability* (pp. 105–124). Dordrecht: Springer.

Groh, M., Krishnan, N., McKenzie, D., & Vishwanath, T. (2016). The impact of soft skills training on female youth employment: Evidence from a randomized experiment in Jordan. *IZA Journal of Labor & Development,* 5(1). doi: 10.1186/s40175-016-0055-9

Harman, G., Hayden, M., & Nghi, P. T. (2010). *Higher education in Vietnam: Reform, challenges and priorities.* New York: Springer.

Ivanaj, V., & Ivanaj, S. (2010). The contribution of interdisciplinary skills to the sustainability of business: When artists, engineers, and managers work together to serve enterprises. In J. A. F. Stoner & C. Wankel (Eds.) *Global sustainability as a business imperative* (pp. 91–109). New York: Palgrave Macmillan.

Jackson, D. (2018). Developing graduate career readiness in Australia: Shifting from extra-curricular internships to work-integrated learning. *International Journal of Work-Integrated Learning,* 19(1), 23–35.

Jones, A. (2009). Generic attributes as espoused theory: The importance of context. *Higher Education,* 58(2), 175–191.

Jurje, F., & Lavenex, S. (2015). ASEAN Economic Community: What model for labour mobility? Working paper 2. NCCR–Swiss National Centre of Competence in Research. Retrieved from: www.wti.org/media/filer_public/24/f2/24f2c553-c4cc-4cc2-b670-6144e31d453c/nccr_working_paper_asean_jurje_lavenex__.pdf

Lehndorff, S. (2016). Internal devaluation and employment trends in Germany. In M. Myant, S. Theodoropoulou, & A. Piasna (Eds.), *Unemployment, internal devaluation and labour market deregulation in Europe* (pp. 169–196). Brussels: European Trade Union Institute (ETUI).

Lewchuk, W. (2017). Precarious jobs: Where are they, and how do they affect well-being? *The Economic and Labour Relations Review*, 28(3), 402–419.

Lindorff, M. (2011). Skills gaps in Australian firms. *Journal of Vocational Education and Training*, 63(2), 247–259.

Litecky, C. R., Arnett, K. P., & Prabhakar, B. (2004). The paradox of soft skills versus technical skills in IS hiring. *Journal of Computer Information Systems*, 45(1), 69–76.

Maciejewska, M., Mrozowicki, A., & Piasna, A. (2016). The silent and crawling crisis: International competition, labour market reforms and precarious jobs in Poland. In M. Myant, S. Theodoropoulou, & A. Piasna (Eds.), *Unemployment, internal devaluation and labour market deregulation in Europe* (pp. 229–254). Brussels: European Trade Union Institute (ETUI).

Maria, C. (2016). "Lost in translation": Soft skills development in European countries. *Tuning Journal for Higher Education*, 3(2), 389–427. doi: 10.18543/tjhe-3(2)-2016pp389-427

McMurray, S., Dutton, M., McQuaid, R., & Richard, A. (2016). Employer demands from business graduates. *Education + Training*, 58(1), 112–132.

McQuaid, R. W., & Lindsay, C. (2005). The concept of employability. *Urban Studies*, 42(2), 197–219.

MOET (2010). *Công văn 2916/ BGDĐT-GDĐH hướng dẫn xây dựng và công bố chuẩn đầu ra ngành đào tạo*. Retrieved from http://thuvienphapluat.vn/cong-van/Giao-duc/Cong-van-2196-BGDDT-GDDH-cong-bo-chuan-dau-ra-nganh-dao-tao-104676.aspx

MOET (2013). *Công văn 2435/BGDĐT-GDĐH về việc rà soát chuẩn đầu ra và biên soạn giáo trình*. Retrieved from http://thuvienphapluat.vn/cong-van/Giao-duc/Cong-van-2435-BGDDT-GDDH-ra-soat-chuan-dau-ra-va-bien-soan-giao-trinh-182111.aspx

Mok, K. H., & Jiang, J. (2018). Massification of higher education and challenges for graduate employment and social mobility: East Asian experiences and sociological reflections. *International Journal of Educational Development*, 63(Nov), 44–51.

Nickson, D., Warhurst, C., Commander, J., Hurrell, S. A., & Cullen, A. M. (2012). Soft skills and employability: Evidence from UK retail. *Economic and Industrial Democracy*, 33(1), 65–84.

Oliver, B. (2015). Redefining graduate employability and work-integrated learning: Proposals for effective higher education in disrupted economies. *Journal of Teaching and Learning for Graduate Employability*, 6(1), 56–65.

Osman, K. (2011). The inculcation of generic skills through service learning experience among science student teachers. *Procedia-Social and Behavioral Sciences*, 18, 148–153.

Rossi, B. (2017). Technology is ready to define the future of the workplace. *Information Age*. 18 April. Retrieved from www.information-age.com/technology-ready-define-future-workplace-123465776/

Schilling, M. A. (2010). *Strategic management of technological innovation*. New York: Tata McGraw-Hill Education.

Stevens, M., & Norman, R. (2016). Industry expectations of soft skills in IT graduates: A regional survey. Paper presented at the Proceedings of the Australasian Computer Science Week Multiconference, February 2–5, Canberra, Australia.

Suci, S. C., Asmara, A., & Mulatsih, S. (2016). The impact of globalization on economic growth in ASEAN. *Bisnis & Birokrasi Journal*, 22(2), 79–87.

Susskind, R. E., & Susskind, D. (2015). *The future of the professions: How technology will transform the work of human experts*. Oxford: Oxford University Press.

Tertiary Education Quality and Standards Agency (2013). *Australian qualifications framework*. Canberra: The Australian Qualifications Framework Council.

The Statistics Portal (2018). *Unemployment rate in member states of the European Union in June 2018.* Retrieved from www.statista.com/statistics/268830/unemployment-rate-in-eu-countries/

Tomlinson, M. (2017). Forms of graduate capital and their relationship to graduate employability. *Education + Training*, 59(4), 338–352.

Tran, A. N., & Nørlund, I. (2015). Globalization, industrialization, and labor markets in Vietnam. *Journal of the Asia Pacific Economy*, 20(1), 143–163.

Tran, L. H. N. (2017a). Developing employability skills via extra-curricular activities in Vietnamese universities: Student engagement and inhibitors of their engagement. *Journal of Education and Work*, 30(8), 854–867.

Tran, L. H. N. (2017b). What hinders teachers from translating their beliefs into teaching behaviors: The case of teaching generic skills in Vietnamese universities. *Teaching and Teacher Education*, 64(May), 105–114.

Tran, L. H. N. (2018). Game of blames: Higher education stakeholders' perceptions of causes of Vietnamese graduates' skills gap. *International Journal of Educational Development*, 62(Sep), 302–312.

Tran, T. T. (2013). Limitation on the development of skills in higher education in Vietnam. *Higher Education*, 65(5), 631–644.

Tran, Q. T., & Swierczek, F. W. (2009). Skills development in higher education in Vietnam. *Asia Pacific Business Review*, 15(4), 565–586.

Trinh, L. Q., & Doan, H. T. T. (2018). Internationalization and the growth of Vietnamese micro, small, and medium sized enterprises: Evidence from panel quantile regressions. *Journal of Asian Economics*, 55(April), 71–83.

Truong, T. T. H., Laura, R. S., & Shaw, K. (2018). The importance of developing soft skill sets for the employability of business graduates in Vietnam: A field study on selected business employers. *Journal of Education and Culture Studies*, 2(1), 32–45.

Truong, Q. D., & Metzger, C. (2007). Quality of business graduates in Vietnamese institutions: Multiple perspectives. *Journal of Management Development*, 26(7), 629–643.

Vedder, R., Denhart, C., & Robe, J. (2013). *Why are recent college graduates underemployed? University enrollments and labour-market realities.* Washington, DC: Center for College Affordability and Productivity.

Yang, L. (2018). Higher education expansion and post-college unemployment: Understanding the roles of fields of study in China. *International Journal of Educational Development*, 62(Sep), 62–74.

Yorke, M. (2006). *Employability in higher education: What it is, what it is not.* Retrieved from https://bit.ly/22VzZS0

1 The surge in developing soft skills for students in higher education

Up to now, we have known that soft skills are an important component of graduate employability. Before going further, it is important to understand what soft skills are, their nature and components. This will enable us to understand the various ways to implement soft skills in higher-education institutions across the globe.

What are soft skills?

It is not easy to have a consensus on a definition of soft skills, since these skills are conceptualized differently between disciplines, contexts, and countries (see Table 1.1). For example, in Australian HE, this set of skills is often referred to as "generic graduate attributes," "generic skills," "key competencies," "soft skills," and "employability skills." They are known as "key skills" or "core skills" in the UK; "essential skills" in New Zealand; or "necessary skills," and "workplace know-how" in the USA (Bowman, 2010; Hager & Holland, 2006). In Vietnam, these skills are referred to as "soft skills" (*kỹ năng mềm*) or "life skills" (*kỹ năng sống*). In this book, the term "soft skills" will be used as it is a common term in the literature of different disciplines and in Vietnam, the main context of this book.

Table 1.1 Terms referring to soft skills in some countries (Bowman, 2010; Cinque, 2016)

Countries	Equivalent names for soft skills
Australia	Generic graduate attributes, generic skills, key competencies, employability skills
UK	Key skills, core skills, life skills, key transferable skills, cross competencies
USA	Necessary skills, workplace know-how
New Zealand	Essential skills
Germany	Schlüsselkompetenzen (key competencies), Übergreifende kompetenzen (general competencies)
Denmark	Nøglekompetence (key competencies)
France	Compétences transversales (transversal competencies)
Spain	Competencias genéricas (general competencies)
Vietnam	Kỹ năng sống (life skills), kỹ năng mềm (soft skills)

Associated with different terms are a variety of definitions for soft skills. Some authors view soft skills in relation to whether these skills are innate abilities and are skeptical about whether students can be trained in them. For example, Heckman and Kautz (2012) define soft skills as personality traits, goals, motivations, and preferences that are valued in the labor market, in school, and in many other domains. Knight (2007) defines soft skills as wicked competences; others consider these skills as emotional intelligence (see Kyllonen, 2013; OECD, 2015) or non-cognitive skills, such as perseverance, sociability, and self-esteem (Heckman & Rubinstein, 2001). Non-cognitive skills and emotional skills have been found to "influence numerous measures of social outcomes, including better health, improved subjective well-being and reduced odds of engaging in conduct problems" (OECD, 2015, p. 3). Yet in reality, "soft skills include both social/interpersonal skills and […] the capacity to work on competences, to reframe and transfer them from one field to another, even from informal to formal learning" (Cinque, 2016, p. 394).

Some organizations define soft skills from administrative and management viewpoints, distinguishing soft skills from the remainder of learning outcomes of a certain level of education. For example, using the terms "generic graduate attributes," the Higher Education Council of Australia defined soft skills as "the skills, personal attributes and values which should be acquired by all graduates, regardless of their discipline or field of study" (Treleaven & Voola, 2008, p. 20). Likewise, Bowden et al. (2000) defined generic graduate attributes as:

> … the qualities, skills and understandings a university community agrees its students should develop during their time with the institution. These attributes include but go beyond the disciplinary expertise or technical knowledge that has traditionally formed the core of most university courses. They are qualities that also prepare graduates as agents of social good in an unknown future … (as cited in S. C. Barrie, 2007, p. 440).

In most cases, soft skills are defined in relation to technical skills. Technical skills are "those skills acquired through training and education or learned on the job and are specific to each work setting" while soft skills are "the cluster of personality traits, social graces, language skills, friendliness, and optimism that mark each one of us to varying degrees" (Litecky, Arnett, & Prabhakar, 2004, p. 69). Robles (2012) contrasted hard skills with soft skills, in which the former is the technical expertise and knowledge needed for a job, whereas the latter includes interpersonal skills and personal attributes. Davis and Muir (2004, p. 96) defined:

> … soft skills are attitudes and behaviors displayed in interactions among individuals that affect the outcomes of such encounters. These differ from hard skills, which are the technical knowledge and abilities required to perform specific job-related tasks more formally stated in job descriptions. (p. 96)

More conceptually, Weber, Finley, Crawford, and Rivera Jr (2009, p. 356) point out that soft skills are "interpersonal, human, people or behavioural skills needed to apply technical skills and knowledge in the workplace." Echoing this viewpoint, Laker and Powell (2011, p. 112) view soft skills as "intra-personal skills such as one's ability to manage oneself as well as interpersonal skills such as how one handles one's interactions with others."

It is also noted that some organizations or authors do not provide a concrete definition of soft skills but rather provide a list of examples of such skills for free interpretation. For example, the Malaysian Institute of Higher Learning interprets soft skills as non-academic skills such as communication, critical-thinking and problem-solving, leadership, teamwork, entrepreneurship skills, ethics and professional morals (Shakir, 2009). Mitchell, Skinner, and White (2010) consider that soft skills include leadership, self-management, conflict resolution, communication, emotional intelligence, and so on. Hager and Holland (2006) further explain that soft skills mostly cluster around human activities such as communication and working with each other, gathering and ordering information, and problem-solving (p. 2). They are seen as capable of enhancing work effectiveness, especially regarding the rapidly evolving and interconnected world we are living in now.

With the myriad terms used to refer to soft skills, as well as differences in the perspectives of researchers and governmental bodies, it is little wonder there has been a lack of consensus in coming up with a definition. Nevertheless, the importance of developing soft skills in HE as one way to enhance graduates' employability is acknowledged by all. Regardless of the availability of a definition of soft skills, it may not be applicable to the Vietnamese HE context, where some different terms have been used to refer to soft skills, albeit without any concrete definitions. Therefore, in this book, soft skills are defined broadly as non-disciplinary skills that may be achieved through learning and be applied in study, work, and life contexts. This definition allows some space to include various conceptualizations of soft skills, which could significantly influence their implementation.

Nature of soft skills

Understanding the nature of soft skills is vital for the successful implementation of these skills in a HE context. Despite there being few studies on the nature of soft skills, it seems that there is a consensus in this respect. Soft skills are found to be elusive, discipline-relating, and transferable between contexts. They cluster and complement each other. They require substantial time and practice to grow to a level where they can be used naturally.

Firstly, these skills are elusive. People have talked a lot about these skills and their importance in the modern workplace as well as in personal life. However, when it comes to providing a clear description of what they are, it is not easy at all (Knight, 2007). That partly explains why there are several definitions of soft skills, as reported above. People of different fields of study may describe these skills differently depending on which stance they hold. If they are more related to social values, they would consider these skills in terms of social benefits. Conversely, if people are business-oriented, they would view these skills in terms of socio-economic gain. This will be further illustrated by the cases of the Tuning

Educational Structures in Europe project (Tuning) and the Assessment of Higher Education Learning Outcomes (AHELO) project below. The elusive nature of soft skills causes many difficulties for the execution of soft skills policy in HE, as stakeholders do not have a consensus on what they should teach, as well as how to teach and assess these sorts of skills.

Secondly, despite the term "generic skills" used to denote soft skills, these skills are discipline-related in the sense that the importance and balance of these skills varies across disciplines (Barrie, Hughes, Smith, & Thomson, 2009; Jones, 2010). For example, written communication skills for students in social sciences may not be as technical and terminological as those for students in engineering. Communication and interpersonal skills are vital for journalism students, but they are less important for biotechnology students who spend most of their time working in the lab. This implies that soft skills should be taught within the disciplinary context. However, in practice, many prefer to treat soft skills as "generic" across disciplines and contexts of application possibly to ease the management of the implementation process. This may result in ineffective implementation of soft skills in educational contexts.

Thirdly, soft skills are transferable between learning and work contexts (Bridges, 1993; Hind, 1994). This characteristic reflects well the term "generic skills" in that in every learning and work context, these skills can be found. Once we master a soft skill within a particular setting, we can use it again in a different setting. For example, an IT technician can transfer problem-solving skills learned from his or her role in a bank to a textile manufacturer because most tasks would deal with computers and similar issues. However, in order to transfer these skills between the two work settings, he or she would need some time to adapt the skills to fit in with the "content" of a new work setting and focus. The problem-solving skills are the same, but the "material" on which these skills are applied is different, so they need modification. This characteristic of soft skills suggests that when developing these skills for students, activities need to be diverse so that they can flexibly practice these skills. This would enhance their ability to transfer soft skills across different work settings.

Fourthly, existing research suggests that soft skills exist as clusters of different but complementary skills which dynamically combine with each other differently in different contexts (Bowman, 2010; Gonczi, 2006; Hager & Holland, 2006; Tuning Educational Structures in Europe, 2019). Indeed, it is difficult to imagine how a businessperson can communicate effectively to his or her clients without interpersonal skills. Likewise, teamwork may not achieve expected outcomes if team members fail to communicate with each other to discuss, negotiate, and agree on solutions to solve the problems facing them. Problem-solving ability will not suffice if it does not involve critical thinking and/or creativity. This suggests that soft skills should not be imparted skill by skill; they must be taught and assessed together rather than by single skills, preferably within the context of a discipline (Ang, D'Alessandro, & Winzar, 2014).

Finally, soft skills take a great deal of time to develop, even one's entire life (Knight, 2007). That is why many soft skills are often classified under lifelong skills, which are essential for our modern life where knowledge is growing exponentially (Dehkord, Samimi, Alivand, & Sani, 2017). The Introduction discussed a study conducted by Groh, Krishnan, McKenzie, and Vishwanath (2016) where they tested the impact of short soft-skills training courses on young Jordanian women's employment outcomes. They did not find any correlations between them. Exposed for 45 hours over a nine-day period to several soft skills might have been enough time for these women to get a general idea about what these skills were, why they were sought after by employers, and how they might affect their job applications, but it was unlikely that these women could master these skills and put them into practice. Gonczi (2006) argued that soft skills need time and practice to grow. Indeed, it is easy to validate this claim. Just imagine public-speaking skills, which are important for most businesses. Although we may read several how-to books or watch YouTube videos to learn from those who have mastered these skills, we may still end up stuttering in front of a crowd, even if we have rehearsed several times. Without regular practice, soft skills may not stay with us or be summoned for effective use when needed. This essential nature of soft skills suggests that training courses must be organized within a long enough time span to offer students numerous chances to practice the skills in order to master them.

What soft skills are the most relevant for the 21st century?

Identifying a list of soft skills most relevant for the 21st century is not simple because, in our rapidly changing market realities, the skills needed constantly alter. However, reviewing the frameworks of soft skills that international organizations recommend, frameworks that are based on sound research, may give us a general view about what skills should be taught to young generations so that they can function well in the modern era.

Table 1.2 shows that there is no one definitive list of generic skills. Each list has been compiled under the influence of global, local, and organizational factors. For example, in the World Health Organization list, there are soft skills that enhance human well-being (coping with emotion, stress, and empathy), whereas other lists do not emphasize these. Likewise, the list of soft skills appears to change through time, taking into account the current essential elements of society. For example, the Institute for the Future list includes several skills to enhance our ability to work with information technology (new media literary, computational thinking, virtual collaboration), an essential element of our contemporary society. Regardless of disparities, these lists share some commonalities, which can be classified, with examples, as follows:

- **Basic skills**: Literacy, using numbers, using technology.
- **People-related skills**: Communication, interpersonal, teamwork, customer-service skills.

Table 1.2 Different soft-skills frameworks for the 21st century (Cinque, 2016)

Organization	Year	Name	Skills
World Health Organization (WHO)	1993	Life skills	<ul><li>Decision-making and problem-solving</li><li>Creative thinking and critical thinking</li><li>Communication and interpersonal skills</li><li>Self-awareness and empathy</li><li>Coping with emotions and coping with stress</li></ul>
Istituto per lo Sviluppo della Formazione Professionale dei Lavoratori	1994–1998	Transversal skills	Useful to:<ul><li>Diagnose the nature of the environment and task (mainly cognitive skills)</li><li>Relate to people and issues of a specific context (interpersonal or social skills, which is the emotional skill set, cognitive and behavioral styles, but also communication skills)</li><li>Address, that is to "face, cope, predispose to deal with the environment and the task, both mentally and emotionally ... take action on a problem with the best chance of solving it" (be able to set goals, to develop strategies, and to build and implement action plans)</li></ul>
Organization for Economic Co-operation and Development (OECD)	2003	Key competencies for a successful life and a well-functioning society	<ul><li>Using tools interactively, which includes the capacity to use language, symbols and texts interactively, use knowledge and information interactively, use technology interactively</li><li>Interacting in a socially homogenous group—i.e., relate well to others, cooperate, work in teams, manage and resolve conflicts</li><li>Acting autonomously, which includes key competencies that empower individuals to manage their lives in meaningful and responsible ways by exercising control over their living and working conditions (for example, form and conduct life plans and personal projects, defend and assert rights, interests, limits and needs)</li></ul>
European Union	2006	Key competences for lifelong learning	<ul><li>Communication in the mother tongue</li><li>Communication in foreign languages</li><li>Mathematical competence and basic competences in science and technology</li><li>Digital competence</li><li>Learning to learn</li><li>Social and civic competences</li><li>Sense of initiative and entrepreneurship</li><li>Cultural awareness and expression</li></ul>

Organization	Year	Name	Skills
Tuning Educational Structures	2008	Generic competences	• Instrumental competences—i.e., cognitive abilities, methodological abilities, technological abilities and linguistic abilities • Interpersonal competences—i.e., individual abilities such as social skills (social interaction and cooperation) • Systemic competences—i.e., abilities and skills concerning whole systems (combination of understanding, sensibility and knowledge; prior acquisition of instrumental and interpersonal competences required)
OECD	2009	21st century skills	• Information: "Information as source" (searching, selecting, evaluating and organizing) and "information as product" (restructuring and modelling of information and the development of own ideas/knowledge) • Communication: "Effective communication" (sharing and transmitting the results or outputs of information) and "collaboration and virtual interaction" (reflecting on others' work, creation of communities) • Ethics: "Social responsibility" (applying criteria for responsible use at personal and social levels)
Institute for the Future	2011	Future work skills 2020	• Sense making • Social intelligence • Novel and adaptive thinking • Cross-cultural competency • Computational thinking • New media literacy • Trans-disciplinarity • Design mindset • Cognitive load management • Virtual collaboration

This table is reproduced with written permission from the Managing Editor of *Tuning Journal for Higher Education* on 25 February 2019. The original work can be found in Cinque, M. (2016). "Lost in translation": Soft skills development in European countries. *Tuning Journal for Higher Education*, 3(2), 389–427.

- **Conceptual/thinking skills**: Collecting and organizing information, problem-solving, planning and organizing, learning-to-learn skills, critical thinking, creativity.
- **Personal skills and attributes**: Being responsible, resourceful, flexible, having self-esteem, management skills.
- **Skills related to the business world**: Innovation skills, enterprise skills.
- **Skills related to the community**: Civic or citizenship knowledge and skills.

Soft-skills-development initiatives in higher education worldwide

Recognizing the importance of soft skills in our modern life, international organizations, governments, and HE institutions worldwide have launched many initiatives to develop soft skills. These initiatives appear to be influenced by the socioeconomic, cultural, and political contexts of the country as well as the visions and missions of the institution.

International initiatives

On a global scale, a number of influential activities around soft-skills development have recently been initiated by supranational organizations, among which the Tuning and AHELO projects are most relevant to the HE context. Generally, despite the difference in purpose and scope, both projects highlight the importance and relevance of generic skills in current socioeconomic contexts. Furthermore, both projects take into account the differences in educational culture and tradition between education systems when tackling the issues related to HE learning outcomes in general and soft skills in particular.

In Europe, the Tuning project was implemented in 2000. It aimed to establish a measure to compare HE curricula across European countries (González & Wagenaar, 2003). It has now spread to other parts of the world, forming Tuning Latin America, Tuning Africa, Tuning China, etc. (Tuning Educational Structures in Europe, 2019). It introduced the concept of competences as the basis for the learning outcomes of HE programs for use in the European HE space. "Learning outcomes are statements of what a learner is expected to know, understand and/or be able to demonstrate after completion of learning" and "competences represent a dynamic combination of knowledge, understanding, skills and abilities [which] will be formed in various course units and assessed at different stages" (Tuning educational structures in Europe, 2019). The project also made clear technical and generic competences. While acknowledging the importance of technical competences as the basis for university-degree programs, Tuning emphasizes that generic competences (i.e., soft skills) are becoming more relevant for students' futures in terms of employability and citizenship. During Phase 1, the project also produced a list of most relevant generic skills for each field and across fields of study, based on consultation with graduates, employers, and academics. It is also interesting to note that while Tuning attempts to create compatibility and comparability across HE programs in Europe, it does not look for uniformity in the degree programs or curricula but simply looks for points of reference, convergence, and common understanding. Put differently, Tuning appears to protect the rich diversity of European education, appreciates the independence of academic and subject specialists, and respects local and national authority (Tuning Educational Structures in Europe, 2019). This notion suggests that the selection and development of subject-specific and generic competences vary across disciplines, institutions, and countries depending on the bounded contexts.

Taking a different approach, the AHELO project launched by the OECD attempted to create a new instrument to test students nearing the end of a bachelor's degree. The main rationale for the test was that current assessment methods were inadequate to meet the challenges posed by the technological changes in the 21st century (Coates & Richardson, 2012). The test focused on both soft and technical skills; however, for the trial, the project only focused on the economics and engineering disciplines. In terms of soft skills, the test was developed based on the adaptation of the US Collegiate Learning Assessment (Hardison & Vilamovska, 2009). Students taking this test needed to use critical thinking, analytic reasoning, problem-solving and written communication to answer several open-ended questions about a hypothetical but realistic situation and gather necessary evidence from different sources. The results were to be used for comparing students internationally regardless of language or cultural background in order to provide data of actual quality of learning and its relevance to the labor market. The AHELO project was expected to create an impact in the HE sector, just like the Program for International Student Assessment (PISA), which is a measure to test the skills and knowledge of students at 15 years of age. The AHELO project involved 10 HE institutions in each of the 15 participating countries across the globe, most of which are leading economies (Australia, Belgium, Columbia, Egypt, Finland, Italy, Japan, Korea, Kuwait, Mexico, the Netherlands, Norway, the Russian Federation, Sweden, and the USA). However, AHELO was critiqued to be unfit to all educational systems concerning cultural differences; thus, its reliability needed verifying (Tremblay, Lalancette, & Roseveare, 2012). Regardless of the failure of the AHELO project, assessing HE learning outcomes is still on the OECD's agenda: a new project that evaluates HE learning outcomes was reported to follow the AHELO project (Sharma, 2015).

Contrasting the two projects with regard to their perspective towards soft skills, AHELO is more concerned with the economic aspects of soft skills whereas Tuning, launched within the framework of lifelong learning, seeks both personal and social gain. The difference appears to relate to the role of the two organizations. The OECD is an organization promoting economic development; thus, it may appear more profit-inclined in most actions. Meanwhile, the European Union (EU) plays the role of moderator of its member states with respect to cultural diversity, political complexity, and social cohesion. Such a difference between the two projects indicates different intentions behind launching programs for soft-skills development, and these intentions need to be examined closely.

Despite the differences, both projects converge at two points. Firstly, both are interested in and concerned with generic-skills development for HE students. This suggests that generic skills have attracted policy makers on a global scale. Secondly, both organizations are aware of cultural differences between HE systems. The AHELO project did not succeed in making the test accepted across countries due to the feasibility of administering it and difficulties in validating the reliability of the test across all HE systems. The EU does not use competences as prescriptive elements to inform the curricula of programs in the European HE space but as references and comparative elements instead. Such cultural awareness suggests that soft skills may be selected, prioritized, and developed differently across HE systems.

National initiatives

Nationally, in many countries, developing soft skills for university students has become a major concern of policymakers, HE leaders, and academics, and seems to be driven by political factors. The UK, Australia, New Zealand, Malaysia, Thailand, Vietnam, Korea, Japan, Canada, Denmark, Switzerland, France, and South Africa have established national qualification frameworks, which specify the learning outcomes for all levels of education in each country. At the HE level, it is observed that soft skills are included as an integral part of the learning outcomes and are linked to quality-assurance and public-funding schemes (Danish Government, 2008; Quality Assurance Agency for Higher Education, 2008; Tertiary Education Quality and Standards Agency, 2013; Thai Government, 2006; The Quality Assurance Agency for Higher Education, 2014). The influence of political factors on elevating the role of soft skills in HE will be illustrated by the cases of British and Australian higher education, as follows.

Since the 1980s, the British Government and employers have articulated the need for training students in generic, transferrable skills as a key aspect of employability. However, soft skills were not a central issue in HE at the time. Not until the Dearing Report (published in 1997) were universities encouraged to develop program specifications with intended learning outcomes including knowledge and understanding, key skills, cognitive skills, and subject-specific skills (Atlay, 2006). Then the Framework for Higher Education Qualifications in England, Wales and Northern Ireland provided a more detailed description of knowledge, skills, and competencies that graduates of a British university should possess in terms of disciplinary knowledge and understanding, ability to apply the knowledge and understanding, communication and cognitive skills, qualities and transferable skills for employment purposes (Quality Assurance Agency for Higher Education, 2008). The Quality Assurance Agency for Higher Education (2014) in the UK has also passed the framework for HE qualifications and required degree-awarding bodies in the UK to comply with it.

In Australia, there have been many projects promoting the implementation of generic graduate attributes—an alternative term for soft skills in Australian HE—in recent decades. In 1992, the Mayer report (Mayer, 1992) encouraged tertiary institutions to develop seven competencies for students: collecting, analyzing and organizing information; communicating ideas and information; planning and organizing activities; working with others in teams; solving problems; using mathematical ideas and techniques; and using technology. The report appeared to influence the VET (Vocational Education and Training) sector and vocation-oriented universities significantly, but did not engage all Australian universities with soft-skills implementation due to the lack of a political mechanism. Then the National GAP project (2007–2008) was conducted to explore the progress and identify challenges to the implementation of soft skills in the Australian HE sector. The research team reported a slow and sporadic implementation across the HE system with numerous challenges along the way (Barrie, Hughes, & Smith, 2009). The researchers recommended linking soft-skills implementation with quality assurance to boost its progress (Barrie, Hughes, Smith, & Thomson, 2009). The Hunters and Gatherers project (2011–2013) was carried out by seven Australian universities to document the mapping of learning objectives related to soft skills in the curricula and evidence students' achievement of the objectives. This project was significant in that it urged the universities to explicitly include soft skills in the curriculum, deliver and assess them, and find ways to present their students' achievement of soft skills (Lawson et al., 2013). Most influentially, established in 2011, the Tertiary Education Quality and Standards Agency (TEQSA) issued the Australian Qualifications Framework (AQF) and Higher Education Standards Framework (HESF). TEQSA, as described on its website, "registers and assesses the performance of HE providers against the Higher Education Standards Framework." The "learning outcomes and assessment" section in the HESF strongly reflects the AQF, which includes soft skills as part of the HE learning outcomes. It is then possible to conclude that the arrival of the AQF and HESF has politically made soft skills an indispensable component of the Australian HE curricula.

It is also observed that the implementation of soft skills has been influenced by the socioeconomic, cultural, and political context of each country. For example, the Danish National Qualification Framework suggests that Denmark focuses on developing lifelong learning for students (Danish Government, 2008), which seems to derive from the need to better use the aging labor workforces and enhance the Danish flexicurity economic model (Bredgaard & Madsen, 2018; Klindt, Baadsgaard, & Jørgensen, 2017). In other words, characteristics of the labor workforce and economy may influence the selection of relevant soft skills for students to develop. Meanwhile, the Thai National Qualification Framework for Higher Education appears to require Thai universities to focus on developing moral and ethical qualities for students (Thai Government, 2006). This focus appears to be significantly influenced by Thailand being a Buddhist country and by the fact that the country is attempting to preserve "Thai wisdom" (Chaisinthop, 2014; Chansomsak & Vale, 2008; Ma Rhea, 2018; Pimpa, 2011). As such, prominent cultural values may be taken into consideration when identifying and developing soft skills for students. In other countries, such as China, political and citizenship education is one of the central missions of the education system (Banks, 2007; Kennedy, Fairbrother, & Zhao, 2013), suggesting that the political regime of a country also influences soft-skills implementation.

In short, the literature review suggests that while countries may engage in implementing similar initiatives for improving the quality of HE learning outcomes in general and soft skills in particular, the focus of these initiatives is influenced by the cultural, socioeconomic, and political contexts of each country.

Institutional level

Many universities publish the mission statements and learning outcomes of their institutions, including soft skills, on their websites. It is observed that the selected soft skills may look similar in terms of word choice; however, they diverge across institutions and reflect the underpinning characteristics of that institution. For example, years after the Mayer competences were encouraged for students, Pitman and Broomhall (2009) analyzed the statements of learning outcomes available on the websites of 38 Australian universities. The analysis revealed that communication, interpersonal skills, and problem-solving were most mentioned in the learning outcomes statements across the universities. The researchers also suggested differences in the selection of the intended soft-skills outcomes between groups of universities: Group of Eight (Go8), the Australian Technology Network (ATN), Innovative Research Universities Australia (IRU Australia), New Generation Universities (NGU), and the Unaligned Universities (UU). Such differences appeared to associate with the mission of each university. For example, the Go8 comprises Australia's oldest universities, which all have a strong liberal arts tradition; thus, 86% of the statements of this group have moral attributes compared with 50%, 67%, 56%, and 63%, respectively, in the other groups. Similarly, IRU Australia leads the other groups in terms of selecting "critical and analytical thinking" (100%) because they are more focused on innovation and research. These findings indicate that the discrepancy in soft-skills selection across universities of the same education system is likely to depend on the surrounding contexts as well as the defined missions and purpose of an institution.

In 2009, Barrie, Hughes, and Smith (2009) explored progress in implementing graduate attributes across the Australian HE sector. They found that soft skills were conceptualized differently depending on how a university viewed itself in relation to the external world. If it appreciated students' performance in the workplace, soft skills were defined more closely to the notion of employability skills; if it valued the graduates' future and their quality of life, soft skills were more about preparing the students for the unknown future; and finally if its mission was linked to and strongly influenced by professional bodies or accreditation agencies, soft skills were more about compliance with the qualities and skills determined by these organizations. Thus, it is possible to conclude that the selection of soft skills is different across HEIs contingent to their defined mission and vision or the perceived purpose of HE, which was raised by the B-HERT project a long time ago: "the contemporary focus on generic skills is really part of a bigger, as yet unresolved, debate about the purpose of university education and how to develop educated persons who are both employable and capable of contributing to civil society" (B-HERT, 2003, p. 6).

HE institutions are also observed to use different strategies and approaches for the implementation of soft skills. Universities can implement soft skills institution-wide (Fleming, Donovan, Beer, & Clark, 2010) or program-wide (O'Neill, 2010, Willcoxson, Wynder, & Laing, 2010). They can execute the implementation top-down, bottom-up, or a combination of both (Barrie, Hughes, Smith, & Thomson, 2009; James, Lefoe, & Hadi, 2004). Some institutions develop soft skills independently of disciplinary knowledge while some integrate them into the disciplinary curriculum (Al-Mahmood & Gruba, 2007; Barrie, Hughes, & Smith, 2009; Jääskelä, Nykänen, & Tynjälä, 2018). Pedagogically, soft skills are developed via problem-based learning (Hendriana, Johanto, & Sumarmo, 2018; Ibrahim, Al-Shahrani, Abdalla, Abubaker, & Mohamed, 2018; Vogler et al., 2018); community-service learning (Eike, Myers, & Sturges, 2018; Mak, Lau, & Wong, 2017; Payton, Barnes, Buch, Rorrer, & Zuo, 2015); online and distance learning (Brodie, 2011; Myers et al., 2014; Salleh, Tasir, & Shukor, 2012); and work-integrated learning (Losekoot, Lasten, Lawson, & Chen, 2018; Maelah, Aman, Mohamed, & Ramli, 2012; Tran & Nguyen, 2018). Finally, methods applied to soft-skills assessment also vary but mostly include capstone subject, (e)-portfolio, peer-assessment, and external assessment (in case of internship or work-placement) (Cranney et al., 2012; Hughes, Mylonas, & Ballantyne, 2017; Keller, Parker, & Chan, 2011; Palmer, Holt, Hall, & Ferguson, 2011). In an attempt to explain such discrepancy in the strategies and approaches to soft-skills implementation, Al-Mahmood and Gruba (2007) and S. C. Barrie (2007) suggest that such differences can be attributed to the underlying assumption and attitudes towards soft skills held by each institution and its stakeholders.

Thus, it is indicated that soft skills can be addressed differently across HE institutions based on stakeholders' perception and attitudes towards soft skills as well as institutional missions and visions. Initiatives for developing soft skills for students at the institutional level will be elaborated on in the next chapter.

Conclusion

In short, soft skills can be understood differently by individuals of different roles or organizations of different functions. It can be used as a general term to refer to non-technical skills. These skills are elusive, discipline-relating, and transferable between contexts. They cluster and complement each other and require substantial time and practice to grow to a level where they can be used naturally. Soft skills have become an essential part of HE curricula and developing soft skills for students has become a priority in the operation of HE institutions. Despite differences in approaches, the implementation of soft skills is commonly driven by political, socioeconomic, and cultural factors as well as a country's educational values. Most of the literature related to soft-skills development for enhancing graduates' employability derives from Western-developed and English-speaking countries. There has been a lack of similar research in developing, non-English-speaking countries whose politics, socioeconomic status, cultural features, and educational values may be different. It is useful to investigate the implementation of soft skills in these countries to complement existing literature in building soft skills for employability in HE so that our understanding about this issue can be extended.

References

Al-Mahmood, R., & Gruba, P. (2007). Approaches to the implementation of generic graduate attributes in Australian ICT undergraduate education. *Computer Science Education*, 17(3), 171–185.

Ang, L., D'Alessandro, S., & Winzar, H. (2014). A visual-based approach to the mapping of generic skills: its application to a marketing degree. *Higher Education Research & Development*, 33(2), 181–197.

Atlay, M. (2006). Skills development: Ten years of evolution from institutional specification to more student-centered approach. In P. Hager & S. Holland (Eds.), *Graduate attributes, learning and employability* (pp. 169–186). Dordrecht, The Netherlands: Springer.

B-HERT (2003). Developing generic skills: Examples of best practice. *B-HERT News*. Retrieved from https://bit.ly/2GAJ9QL

Banks, J. A. (2007). *Diversity and citizenship education: Global perspectives*. San Francisco, CA: Jossey-Bass.

Barrie, S., Hughes, C., & Smith, C. (2009). *The national graduate attributes project: Integration and assessment of graduate attributes in curriculum*. Sydney: Australian Learning and Teaching Council.

Barrie, S., Hughes, C., Smith, C., & Thomson, K. (2009). *The national graduate attributes project: Key issues to consider in the renewal of learning and teaching experiences to foster graduate attributes*. Sydney: The University of Sydney.

Barrie, S. C. (2007). A conceptual framework for the teaching and learning of generic graduate attributes. *Studies in Higher Education*, 32(4), 439–458.

Bowden, J., Hart, G., King, B., Trigwell, K., & Watts, O. (2000). *Generic capabilities of ATN university graduates*. Canberra: Australian Government Department of Education, Training and Youth Affairs.

Bowman, K. (2010). Background paper for the AQF Council on generic skills. Retrieved from www.voced.edu.au/content/ngv%3A46853

Bredgaard, T., & Madsen, P. K. (2018). Farewell flexicurity? Danish flexicurity and the crisis. *Transfer: European Review of Labour and Research*. doi: 10.1177/1024258918768613

Bridges, D. (1993). Transferable skills: A philosophical perspective. *Studies in Higher Education*, 18(1), 43–51.

Brodie, L. (2011). Delivering key graduate attributes via teams working in virtual space. *International Journal of Emerging Technologies in Learning (iJET)*, 6(3), 5–11.

Chaisinthop, N. (2014). Volunteering, Dana, and the cultivation of 'good people' in Thailand. *Anthropological Forum*, 24(4), 396–411. doi: 10.1080/00664677.2014.965129

Chansomsak, S., & Vale, B. (2008). The Buddhist approach to education: An alternative approach for sustainable education. *Asia Pacific Journal of Education*, 28(1), 35–50.

Cinque, M. (2016). "Lost in translation": Soft skills development in European countries. *Tuning Journal for Higher Education*, 3(2), 389–427. doi: 10.18543/tjhe-3(2)-2016pp389-427

Coates, H., & Richardson, S. (2012). An international assessment of bachelor degree graduates' learning outcomes. *Higher Education Management and Policy*, 23(3), 1–19.

Cranney, J., Kofod, M., Huon, G., Jensen, L., Levin, K., McAlpine, I., Scoufis, M., & Whitaker, N. (2012). Portfolio tools: Learning and teaching strategies to facilitate development of graduate attributes. Paper presented at the Australian Conference on Science and Mathematics Education (formerly UniServe Science Conference). Retrieved from: https://openjournals.library.sydney.edu.au/index.php/IISME/article/view/6431/7078

Danish Government (2008). *Qualifications framework for Danish higher education*. Retrieved from https://bit.ly/2URzxtC.

Davis, B. D., & Muir, C. (2004). Learning soft skills at work: An interview with Annalee Luhman. *Business Communication Quarterly*, 67(1), 95–101.

Dehkord, F. K., Samimi, M., Alivand, R., & Sani, E. A. (2017). An examination and assessment of knowledge management maturity in Karaj municipality. *Journal of Ecophysiology and Occupational Health*, 17(1–2), 34–39.

Eike, R. J., Myers, B., & Sturges, D. (2018). The impact of service-learning targeting apparel design majors: A qualitative analysis of learning growth. *Family and Consumer Sciences Research Journal*, 46(3), 267–281.

Fleming, J., Donovan, R., Beer, C., & Clark, D. (2013). A whole of university approach to embedding graduate attributes: A reflection. In J. Willems, B. Tynan, & R. James (Eds.), *Global challenges and perspectives in blended and distance learning* (pp. 246–257). Hershey, PA: IGI Global.

Gonczi, A. (2006). The OECD: Its role in the key competencies debate and in the promotion of lifelong learning. In P. Hager & S. Holland (Eds.), *Graduate attributes, learning and employability* (pp. 105–124). Dordrecht: Springer.

González, J., & Wagenaar, R. (2003). *Tuning educational structures in Europe*. Bilbao, Spain: University of Deusto.

Groh, M., Krishnan, N., McKenzie, D., & Vishwanath, T. (2016). The impact of soft skills training on female youth employment: Evidence from a randomized experiment in Jordan. *IZA Journal of Labor & Development*, 5(1). doi: 10.1186/s40175-016-0055-9

Hager, P., & Holland, S. (2006). *Graduate attributes, learning and employability (Vol. 6)*. Dordrecht, Netherlands: Springer Science & Business Media.

Hardison, C. M., & Vilamovska, A.-M. (2009). *The collegiate learning assessment: Setting standards for performance at a college or university*. Santa Monica, CA: Rand Corporation.

Heckman, J. J., & Kautz, T. (2012). Hard evidence on soft skills. *Labour Economics*, 19(4), 451–464.

Heckman, J. J., & Rubinstein, Y. (2001). The importance of noncognitive skills: Lessons from the GED testing program. *American Economic Review*, 91(2), 145–149.

Hendriana, H., Johanto, T., & Sumarmo, U. (2018). The role of problem-based learning to improve students' mathematical problem-solving ability and self-confidence. *Journal on Mathematics Education*, 9(2), 291–300.

Hind, D. W. (1994). *Transferable personal skills* (2nd edition). Tyne & Wear, UK: Business Education Publishers.

Hughes, K., Mylonas, A., & Ballantyne, R. (2017). Enhancing tourism graduates' soft skills: The importance of teaching reflective practice. In P. Benckendorff & A. Zehrer (Eds.), *Handbook of teaching and learning in tourism* (pp. 95–106). Northampton, MA: Edward Elgar.

Ibrahim, M. E., Al-Shahrani, A. M., Abdalla, M. E., Abubaker, I. M., & Mohamed, M. E. (2018). The effectiveness of problem-based learning in acquisition of knowledge, soft skills during basic and preclinical sciences: Medical students' points of view. *Acta Informatica Medica*, 26(2), 119–124.

Jääskelä, P., Nykänen, S., & Tynjälä, P. (2018). Models for the development of generic skills in Finnish higher education. *Journal of Further and Higher Education*, 42(1), 130–142.

James, B., Lefoe, G. E., & Hadi, M. N. (2004). Working 'through'graduate attributes: A bottom-up approach. Paper presented at the HERDSA International Conference, 4–7 July, Miri Sarawak, Milperra, New South Wales, Australia.

Jones, A. (2010). Generic attributes in accounting: The significance of the disciplinary context. *Accounting Education: An International Journal*, 19(1–2), 5–21.

Keller, S., Parker, C. M., & Chan, C. (2011). Employability skills: Student perceptions of an IS final year capstone subject. *Innovation in Teaching and Learning in Information and Computer Sciences*, 10(2), 4–15.

Kennedy, K. J., Fairbrother, G., & Zhao, Z. (2013). *Citizenship education in China: Preparing citizens for the "Chinese century"*. New York and London: Routledge.

Klindt, M. P., Baadsgaard, K., & Jørgensen, H. (2017). Beyond flexicurity: The shift towards work-first and its implications for street-level work in the Danish employment system. In K. Hogsbro & I. F. Shaw (Eds.), *Social work and research in advanced welfare states* (pp. 47–60). London and New York: Routledge.

Knight, P. (2007). *Fostering and assessing 'wicked' competences*. Retrieved from https://bit.ly/2E7bFHq

Kyllonen, P. C. (2013). Soft skills for the workplace. *Change: The Magazine of Higher Learning*, 45(6), 16–23.

Laker, D. R., & Powell, J. L. (2011). The differences between hard and soft skills and their relative impact on training transfer. *Human Resource Development Quarterly*, 22(1), 111–122.

Lawson, R., Taylor, T., Fallshaw, E., Summers, J., Kinash, S., French, E., & Angus-Leppan, T. (2013). *Hunters and gatherers: Strategies for curriculum mapping and data collection for assuring learning*. Retrieved from https://bit.ly/2DqAWgk

Litecky, C. R., Arnett, K. P., & Prabhakar, B. (2004). The paradox of soft skills versus technical skills in IS hiring. *Journal of Computer Information Systems*, 45(1), 69–76.

Losekoot, E., Lasten, E., Lawson, A., & Chen, B. (2018). The development of soft skills during internships: The hospitality student's voice. *Research in Hospitality Management*, 8(2), 155–159.

Ma Rhea, Z. (2018). Buddhist pedagogy in teacher education: Cultivating wisdom by skillful means. *Asia-Pacific Journal of Teacher Education*, 46(2), 199–216.

Maelah, R., Aman, A., Mohamed, Z. M., & Ramli, R. (2012). Enhancing soft skills of accounting undergraduates through industrial training. *Procedia-Social and Behavioral Sciences*, 59(Oct), 541–549.

Mak, B., Lau, C., & Wong, A. (2017). Effects of experiential learning on students: An ecotourism service-learning course. *Journal of Teaching in Travel & Tourism*, 17(2), 85–100.

Mayer, E. (1992). *Employment-related key competencies: A proposal for consultation*. Melbourne, Australia: Mayer Committee.

Mitchell, G. W., Skinner, L. B., & White, B. J. (2010). Essential soft skills for success in the twenty-first century workforce as perceived by business educators. *Delta Pi Epsilon Journal*, 52(1), 43–53.

Myers, T., Blackman, A., Andersen, T., Hay, R., Lee, I., & Gray, H. (2014). Cultivating ICT students' interpersonal soft skills in online learning environments using traditional active learning techniques. *Journal of Learning Design*, 7(3), 38–53.

O'Neill, G. (2010). A programme wide approach to assessment: A reflection on some curriculum mapping tools. Paper presented at the AISHE Conference, Dublin, Ireland. Retrieved from https://bit.ly/2Vhr16W

OECD (2015). *Skills for social progress: The power of social and emotional skills*. Retrieved from https://bit.ly/2qn2PMP

Palmer, S., Holt, D., Hall, W., & Ferguson, C. (2011). An evaluation of an online student portfolio for the development of engineering graduate attributes. *Computer Applications in Engineering Education*, 19(3), 447–456.

Payton, J., Barnes, T., Buch, K., Rorrer, A., & Zuo, H. (2015). The effects of integrating service learning into computer science: An inter-institutional longitudinal study. *Computer Science Education*, 25(3), 311–324.

Pimpa, N. (2011). Strategies for higher education reform in Thailand. In S. Marginson, S. Kaur, & E. Sawi (Eds.), *Higher Education in the Asia-Pacific* (pp. 273–289). New York, NY: Springer.

Pitman, T., & Broomhall, S. (2009). Australian universities, generic skills and lifelong learning. *International Journal of Lifelong Education*, 28(4), 439–458.

Quality Assurance Agency for Higher Education (2008). *The framework for higher education qualifications in England, Wales and Northern Ireland*. Quality Assurance Agency for Higher Education. Retrieved from: www.ncl.ac.uk/ltds/assets/documents/qsh-progapp-fheqsummary.pdf

Robles, M. M. (2012). Executive perceptions of the top 10 soft skills needed in today's workplace. *Business Communication Quarterly*, 75(4), 453–465.

Salleh, S. M., Tasir, Z., & Shukor, N. A. (2012). Web-based simulation learning framework to enhance students' critical thinking skills. *Procedia-Social and Behavioral Sciences*, 64 (Nov), 372–381.

Shakir, R. (2009). Soft skills at the Malaysian institutes of higher learning. *Asia Pacific Education Review*, 10(3), 309–315.

Sharma, Y. (2015). OECD to launch university outcomes benchmark system. *University World News*, 22 Oct. Retrieved from www.universityworldnews.com/article.php?story=20151015142742541

Tertiary Education Quality and Standards Agency (2013). *Australian qualifications framework*. The Australian Qualifications Framework Council. Retrieved from: https://bit.ly/2UxTUHm

Thai Government (2006). *National qualifications framework for higher education in Thailand*. Retrieved from: https://bit.ly/2DsbFSX

The Quality Assurance Agency for Higher Education (2014). *The frameworks for higher education qualifications of UK degree-awarding bodies*. Retrieved from: www.qaa.ac.uk/docs/qaa/quality-code/qualifications-frameworks.pdf

Tran, L. H. N., & Nguyen, T. M. D. (2018). Internship-related learning outcomes and their influential factors: The case of Vietnamese tourism and hospitality students. *Education + Training*, 60(1), 69–81.

Treleaven, L., & Voola, R. (2008). Integrating the development of graduate attributes through constructive alignment. *Journal of Marketing Education*, 30(2), 160–173.

Tremblay, K., Lalancette, D., & Roseveare, D. (2012). *Assessment of higher education learning outcomes*. OECD. Retrieved from: https://bit.ly/2IRTRnB

Tuning Educational Structures in Europe (2019). *Tuning methodology*. Retrieved from: www.unideusto.org/tuningeu/tuning-methodology.html

Vogler, J. S., Thompson, P., Davis, D. W., Mayfield, B. E., Finley, P. M., & Yasseri, D. (2018). The hard work of soft skills: Augmenting the project-based learning experience with interdisciplinary teamwork. *Instructional Science*, 46(3), 457–488.

Weber, M. R., Finley, D. A., Crawford, A., & Rivera Jr, D. (2009). An exploratory study identifying soft skill competencies in entry-level managers. *Tourism and Hospitality Research*, 9(4), 353–361.

Willcoxson, L., Wynder, M., & Laing, G. K. (2010). A whole-of-program approach to the development of generic and professional skills in a university accounting program. *Accounting Education: An International Journal*, 19(1–2), 65–91.

2 Soft-skills implementation
A literature review

Introduction

The previous chapter reviewed the international context of soft-skills implementation and highlighted that it was context-dependent. In that respect, it argued that Vietnam could provide an opportunity to expand our understanding of soft-skills implementation in a developing non-English-speaking country with different socioeconomic, cultural, and political aspects as well as higher education (HE) values. On that premise, this chapter will examine common practices for soft-skills implementation in HE and identify challenges facing the implementation in order to construct a conceptual framework on which subsequent chapters in this book will be developed. The literature review suggests that soft-skills implementation is diverse in terms of conceptualization, strategies, and activities involved, scale of implementation, and its impact. The implementation can be layered with different activities at the national, institutional, and subject levels and possibly supported by extracurricular or co-curricular activities.

Soft-skills implementation at the national level

As mentioned in Chapter 1, the socioeconomic and cultural characteristics of a country can influence soft-skills implementation. The characteristics of the labor workforce, young or old, skills sufficient or deficient, and the socioeconomic model may determine the level of need and relevant soft skills for HE students to develop so that they can survive and be competitive in the labor market (Bredgaard & Madsen, 2018; Danish Government, 2008). Likewise, cultural and educational values also determine what kinds of soft skills are selected for students to develop so that they can function well within that society and preserve cultural distinctiveness (Chaisinthop, 2014; Kennedy, Fairbrother, & Zhao, 2013). Therefore, these factors become national contextual factors that frame the implementation of soft skills in higher education.

However, it is recent political moves that have strongly driven HE institutions to comprehensively develop their students' soft skills. For example, in many countries a Ministry of Education (or equivalent) and associated quality-assurance agencies have been established to monitor the teaching and training activities of

HE institutions (Barrie, Hughes, Smith, & Thomson, 2009; El Hassan, 2013; Tang & Yi-Fang, 2014). These ministries have published a national qualification framework that defines learning outcomes for all levels of the education system (Danish Government, 2008; Tertiary Education Quality and Standards Agency, 2013; Thai Government, 2006; The Quality Assurance Agency for Higher Education, 2014). These agencies further specify the standards that HE institutions need to meet in their training and education activities (Tertiary Education Quality and Standards Agency, 2013). It is observed that soft skills have become one of the components of the learning outcomes defined in these national qualification frameworks and HE standards. Such drivers are intended to boost HE institutions' engagement with the implementation of soft skills (Barrie et al., 2009). However, not all countries in the world have established a HE quality-assurance agency, or it has not worked well, like in the case of Vietnam (Tang & Yi-Fang, 2014). In these countries, it is likely that soft-skills implementation relies on the aspirations of each HE institution. As the demand for graduates with adequate soft and technical skills increases, it is urgent that such drivers be established and enacted by their authority.

Also, under the umbrella of quality assurance and quality improvement, accreditation of professional bodies is found to influence soft-skills implementation. The literature indicates that professional bodies have a significant impact on the teaching and learning activities of vocation-oriented programs or institutions (Barrie et al., 2009; Carrivick, 2011; Sin, Jones, & Petocz, 2007). If these programs or institutions do not train students in accordance with the outcomes required by the professional bodies, they may be unaccredited, resulting in the termination of the program or institution. However, it seems that these professional accreditation bodies only specify the outcomes for HE institutions to comply with. They have not supported the institutions or programs with approaches, methods, or instruments that facilitate soft-skills implementation. This suggests that these vocation-oriented programs or institutions may be facing difficulties with implementing the specified soft skills. Equally important, while soft-skills implementation may be forcefully enacted in vocation-oriented programs such as engineering, accounting, or medicine, there are no professional accreditation bodies in the disciplines of the arts and sciences. Therefore, the implementation of soft skills in these disciplines is still a mystery.

In conclusion, soft-skills implementation is found to be closely associated with the socioeconomic, cultural, and political context of each country. Although there have been political drivers for soft-skills implementation, such as quality-assurance initiatives and accreditation of professional bodies, they may not forcefully engage HE institutions in developing soft skills for students. Their authority needs to be strengthened and soft skills should be included more observably in their framework, regulations, and operation.

Soft-skills implementation at the institutional level

This section reviews activities devoted to soft-skills implementation at the institutional level. Despite variance, major tasks include: (i) setting policies, incentives and drivers; (ii) developing an institutional implementation strategy; (iii) selecting soft skills outcomes; (iv) developing curriculum models; and (v) preparing resources and developing staff.

Setting policies, incentives, and drivers

HE institutions may have an organizational culture different from that of industrial businesses; however, more and more HE institutions are operating as business organizations (for example, Marek, 2012; Skoumpopoulou & Waring, 2017). Therefore, basic rules of change implementation, which are often applied in industry, have also been introduced in many HE institutions (Nguyen, Cornish, & Minichiello, 2014; Njue & Ongoto, 2018). According to organizational change-management theories, to introduce any change in the operation of an organization, the policy itself must clearly articulate to all stakeholders the necessity, purpose, and well-defined objectives of the change; the policy, accompanied by templates, step-by-step instructions for implementation, and implementation timelines, should be visible and recursively transmitted to stakeholders; and effective leadership, incentives, or management tools should also be in place to engage stakeholders with the implementation (Hayes, 2018; Lewis, 2019).

Explicitly developing students' soft skills marks a significant change in HE because teaching these skills was not the focus of the HE curriculum or the responsibility of academics. However, it is observed that policies related to soft-skills implementation are often hidden and not communicated with clarity to HE stakeholders. In most cases, the soft-skills policy is included in policies related to student learning outcomes rather than standing as an independent policy (Barrie et al., 2009). This reduces stakeholders' attention and engagement. Teachers continue to focus on doing research that is linked to funding and promotion opportunities (Barrie et al., 2009; Jones, 2009), and students continue to treat soft skills as secondary to technical knowledge and skills (Barrie et al., 2009; Tran, 2015).

In addition, incentives should be devised to make the implementation of soft skills in HE institutions progress faster. The necessity of implementing soft skills is often questioned, which is linked to unresolved debates about the purposes of our contemporary HE (B-HERT, 2003; Sin, Tavares, & Amaral, 2017; Star & Hammer, 2008). Without favorable rewarding schemes, HE institutions will not exert effort in implementing a soft-skills policy because they may have several priorities. Likewise, for teachers, without any additional benefits, why would they bother teaching these skills when their workload is already heavy?

Moreover, institutional management tools should be in place to ensure that stakeholders engage with the implementation. Unfortunately, management tools that can drive the implementation of soft skills in HE are not very effective. For example, curriculum audit and mapping are usually based on staff self-reports of what soft skills they teach and assess, sometimes with limited evidence collected from student surveys or other stakeholders (Barrie et al., 2009). Likewise, developing a set of professional skills aligned with skills standards set by external professional accreditation bodies has been used in many vocation-oriented disciplines but not in the arts or social science disciplines (Barrie et al., 2009).

Developing an institutional implementation strategy

Several institutional strategies have been adopted for soft-skills implementation, each with its own advantages and disadvantages. These strategies differ in terms of leadership approach, implementation scale, and key stakeholders responsible for the implementation.

HE institutions may execute a soft-skills policy using a bottom-up or top-down leadership approach or a combination of both. A bottom-up approach starts with academics' pro-activeness in imparting soft skills to students in the classroom, which builds academic ownership of the implementation, but it may not become widespread without institutional policies and incentives (Barrie et al., 2009). A top-down approach can enhance the implementation progress with active, and sometimes imposing, policies, incentives, resource preparation, and management tools, but it may face resistance from staff (Barrie et al., 2009; Nikitina & Furuoka, 2012). Thus, it may fail to establish academics' "buy-in" or may simply result in compliance. The effectiveness of the mixed approach may depend on how flexibly top-down and bottom-up elements are deployed. Barrie et al. (2009) argued that regardless of leadership approach, it should be visible across all levels of the institution and shared between all stakeholders, not just limited to vice-chancellors, deans, or course coordinators. They believed that the adopted leadership approach must meaningfully motivate and engage stakeholders to put effort into executing their soft-skills policy.

Soft-skills implementation strategies also appear to differ in terms of scale. Some universities execute the policy university-wide (Fleming, Donovan, Beer, & Clark, 2013; Nguyen, Truong, & Le, 2013) whereas many others choose to deploy it at a smaller scale, such as a faculty-wide (Frank, Strong, Sellens, & Clapham, 2013) or program-wide implementation (O'Neill, 2010). The university-wide approach may help the implementation advance in harmony across faculties and units of a HE institution. The difficulty may be associated with managing a harmonious implementation between faculties and ensuring the relevance of the soft skills selected for all disciplines. The other two implementation approaches may not yield a huge impact in teaching and learning soft skills, but it can preserve their distinctiveness within a disciplinary context as these skills appear to be discipline-related (Hager & Holland, 2006; Rychen & Salganik, 2003).

Also, implementation strategies vary in terms of principal conductors. Some universities rely completely on individual academics' discretion, without providing them with much support. This approach may be slow, but once it progresses, teachers develop a high level of "buy-in" because they already understand the meaning and have experienced some trials with teaching these skills (Barrie et al., 2009). Some universities have employed external experts to develop an "add-in" soft-skills curricula and deliver it independently or in cooperation with academics (Al-Mahmood & Gruba, 2007; Barrie et al., 2009). The risk of this approach is that it relies on the availability of soft-skills experts. It also causes a disconnect between soft skills and disciplinary skills, thus students' ability to transfer these soft skills into learning and work is often affected.

The differences in strategies suggest some hidden factors behind the adoption of these approaches. On the one hand, it seems that stakeholders' perception and attitudes toward soft skills affect the selection of implementation strategies (Barrie et al., 2009; Barrie, 2006, 2007). For example, if university leaders perceive that the central government is imposing soft skills, they are more likely to adopt a top-down approach to get it done accordingly. If they assume that soft skills are generic across disciplines, they may adopt university-wide implementation without preserving the disciplinary distinctiveness of soft skills. On the other hand, as the implementation requires changes in curriculum design, training pedagogical and assessment practices for staff, and linkages to industry (Al-Mahmood & Gruba, 2007; Fallows & Steven, 2000), the adoption of strategies must consider institutional factors, such as availability of resources, availability of soft-skills experts, academics' experience with curriculum innovation, and experience in change management. A careful analysis of these factors would decide a feasible implementation strategy to ensure the implementation results in the intended outcomes.

Selecting soft skills outcomes

On top of considering national contextual factors such as socioeconomic situation, cultural norms, educational values, and political practices, HE institutions also consider their institutional vision and mission in their selection of soft skills for their students to develop. For example, vocation-focused institutions tend to select soft skills that foster employability; elite universities favor skills that enhance students' academic abilities; and religious institutions may appreciate soft skills that encourage students' developing social attributes and values (Barrie et al., 2009; Pitman & Broomhall, 2009). A study by Pitman and Broomhall (2009) showed that Australian university groups selected different soft skills, ones that were closely related to their type of institution (Table 2.1). Accordingly, "behaving ethically" was adopted by Go8 universities more frequently than other university groups because the Go8 included Australia's oldest institutions, which have strong liberal arts traditions. The attribute of "awareness and respect of others" was selected by NGU more often than other groups possibly because they serviced more diverse student populations, including mature-age and international students, than did Go8 universities, whose student cohorts are often homogenous, high-achieving high school graduates. "Critical thinking" appeared in 100% and 86% of IRU and Go8 statements, respectively, much higher compared to the other groups because these two groups of universities focus more on developing academic ability and research skills in their students.

Rational selection of soft skills that align with institutional mission, vision, and context could enhance feasibility for soft-skills implementation. It may condition the possibility of linking these skills with technical knowledge and skills. However, this could limit the harmonious progress of soft-skills implementation across a HE system and cause difficulties for quality assurance activities, which usually operate based on a set of prescribed indicators or standards. It is possibly for this reason

Table 2.1 Top 10 soft skills selected by Australian university groups (adapted from Pitman & Broomhall, 2009)

Selected soft skills	Groups of Australian universities				
	Go8 (%)	ATN (%)	IRU (%)	NGU (%)	UU (%)
Communication skills	100	75	100	100	100
Interpersonal skills	86	50	83	78	100
Critical thinking	86	75	100	44	50
Behaving ethically	86	50	67	56	63
Problem-solving skills	71	75	67	56	88
Mastering of specific knowledge	71	100	67	56	75
Creative thinking	71	75	83	-	-
Technology literacy	57	-	-	-	-
Awareness and respect for others	57	75	50	89	75
Adaptability/transferability of knowledge	57	-	-	-	-
Lifelong learning	-	100	67	67	50
Professional skills	-	50	-	78	50
Leadership/community service	-	-	83	67	-
Information literacy	-	-	-	-	75

Note: Go8 = Group of Eight; ATN = Australian Technology Network; IRU = Innovative Research Universities Australia; NGU = New Generation Universities; UU = Unaligned Universities (universities that do not belong to any group).

that in quality assurance agency and government policies, soft skills are often treated as generic for all disciplines and institution types, such as in the national qualification frameworks of many countries, as mentioned in Chapter 1.

Furthermore, it is important that the selected soft skills should meet different HE stakeholders' expectations: academics, policymakers, employers, industries, students, students' parents, professional bodies, and HE regulatory agencies (Barrie et al., 2009). Each of these groups may have different viewpoints on which soft skills are relevant to graduates. Unfortunately, the current context of HE often leaves little space for dialogue and discussion between these groups (Barrie et al., 2009), resulting in clashes between different HE stakeholder groups over what soft skills are relevant (Cacciolatti, Lee, & Molinero, 2017). In most cases, employers' perspectives are consulted to enhance graduates' ability to secure employment opportunities (Callaghan & McManus, 2010; Taylor, 2016). Academics' perspectives are also taken the most seriously because they are the key implementers of the soft-skills policy (Taylor, 2016). HE institutions also take into account the perspectives of professional bodies or quality-assurance agencies because failing to do so may result in their accreditation or operation being terminated (Barrie et al., 2009; Carrivick, 2011). Interestingly, despite recent improvements (Chan & Fong, 2018; Taylor, 2016), the students who will be trained in these skills are often ignored in the consultation process and presumed to have an employment-focused perspective (Barrie et al., 2009). Hence, students may find several soft skills irrelevant to them, and disengage from developing these skills.

Developing curriculum models

HE institutions have developed different curricula models to impart the selected skills to students. This task is influenced by the underlying assumptions about the relevance of teaching soft skills in HE and the nexus between soft skills and disciplinary knowledge and/or skills (Al-Mahmood & Gruba, 2007; Barrie, 2007).

Barrie (2007) identified four assumptions that academics make about soft skills and their relevance in HE, namely *precursor, complementary, translation*, and *enabling*. Academics holding the first assumption expect students to obtain necessary soft skills prior to commencing university studies. The complementary perception views soft skills as part of the overall HE experience and as supporting elements of the acquisition of disciplinary knowledge. Academics with the translation perception view soft skills as separate from disciplinary knowledge but not independent of it; they include clusters of "personal attributes, cognitive abilities, and skills of application" (Barrie, 2006, p. 227). Finally, those holding the enabling assumption perceive soft skills as "the skeleton that provides both form and function to disciplinary knowledge and the learning of that knowledge" (Barrie, 2006, p. 229).

The National GAP Project (Barrie et al., 2009), which made inquiries into how generic graduate attributes (or soft skills) were implemented across Australian universities, categorized five types of soft-skills curriculum based on the assumptions of academics outlined above. These are:

- **Foundation curriculum/generalist degrees**: This includes aspects of a liberal arts model and is a prerequisite for entering disciplinary or professional degree programs. It explicitly focuses on developing broad intellectual capabilities to enhance students' learning outcomes when they start a degree program. This curriculum requires effort to assist students in linking their learning in the first degree to employment contexts as well as more contextual learning in subsequent studies of specialized curriculum.
- **Foundation curriculum**: The foundation curriculum is often delivered to students during their first year (rather than the first degree) at the university. It provides students with opportunities to broaden their perspectives and knowledge. Thus, it fosters students' transition in the first year, develops soft skills, and enhances their studies in subsequent years. However, the development of soft skills is limited due to time shortage and a lack of disciplinary context.
- **Co-curriculum**: Designed as soft-skills subjects for all students in a university or only for students of a specific discipline, it is delivered within the first year or throughout all years of a degree. It allows sequential development of complex soft skills but runs the risk of being isolated from the disciplinary curriculum, unless the two curricula are carefully designed to supplement each other. Internships or paid employment can be part of this curriculum.

However, while internships and paid employment can foster the growth of students' employment-related skills, they may discourage students from developing soft skills in class-based subjects. Likewise, teachers may disengage from teaching soft skills because they may assume that students are being trained in soft skills in the workplace.
- **Extra-curriculum**: This type of curriculum may include service learning, student exchanges, overseas study programs, memberships in clubs and societies, and student participation in staff members' research, governance, and public intellectual activities. Like the co-curriculum, it may discourage teachers and students from developing soft skills in the classroom. The biggest limitation is that it can only involve a limited number of students. This curriculum model is found to be effective with the use of portfolios, which document students' experiential learning.
- **Whole-of-program curriculum approach or integrated curriculum**: As the name suggests, it integrates soft skills into the disciplinary curriculum; thus, it is closer to the translation perception of soft skills. It allows the development of high-level, contextualized, and discipline-relevant soft skills. However, it is quite complicated to deliver such a curriculum. It requires an alignment between soft-skills concepts and teaching, learning, and assessment activities among all stakeholders. Also, teaching and learning of soft skills using this curriculum becomes less explicit and can be easily diverted by teachers and learners. Yet, this curriculum model is favored and adopted by many HE institutions.

The diversity of soft-skills curriculum models not only implies different assumptions about the nexus between soft skills and disciplinary skills but also suggests that HE institutions are purposefully designing a curriculum model suitable for their institutional or disciplinary context. For example, (Al-Mahmood & Gruba, 2007) presented a case where two ICT departments in a university used different curriculum approaches to deliver and assess soft skills. Based on the four assumptions about the relationship between disciplinary knowledge and soft skills identified by Barrie (2006), they sketched three soft-skills curriculum models named *dedicated, infused,* and *embedded,* corresponding with the precursor, complementary, and translation perceptions of soft skills, respectively. Elements of the enabling perspective could be found in all the models.

- **Dedicated curricula**: Experts design the curriculum, teach, and assess soft skills independently from disciplinary knowledge; it is taught as a one-off course or a series of units parallel with the disciplinary program throughout the academic years.
- **Infused curricula**: Soft-skills experts work in collaboration with academics that teach disciplinary knowledge, where applicable.
- **Embedded curricula**: The selected soft skills are mapped and allocated across the curriculum; therefore, soft skills are taught and assessed together with disciplinary knowledge.

The researchers found that while the dedicated curriculum model was simple and observable in the implementation, it was less effective because the soft skills were not taught in a disciplinary context, and there was not always adequate time for students to develop the skills. The infused approach fostered a connection between soft skills and disciplinary knowledge, but there was sometimes a lack of depth and specificity for the development of soft skills. The embedded curriculum model could address the nature of soft skills, but the implementation process was complicated. Academics usually resisted the embedded curriculum because they would have to teach disciplinary knowledge, technical skills, and soft skills, which would increase their workloads.

An interesting point in Al-Mahmood and Gruba's study is that the three models were applied in different departmental contexts and achieved different levels of success. The dedicated model was implemented in a small department where the teaching staff hesitated to teach soft skills, despite widespread institutional support. Thus, the soft skills were taught by skills experts, separate from the disciplinary curriculum. The implementation was successful since it was highly publicized, strongly supported by the academic staff, and made integral to the culture of the department. The infused model was applied in a research-focused department. Soft skills were taught together within a disciplinary context but as independent sessions. Owing to a shortage of time to impart both technical and soft skills, the department decided to change to using the embedded curriculum model. This change resulted in success, which was attributed to teaching soft skills through consultation with all key stakeholders (students, staff, and industry representatives), and with the support of senior academics. In short, the study indicated that a curriculum model that fits the institutional/departmental contexts and culture is a significant determinant for the success of soft-skills implementation.

Preparing resources and developing staff

To implement a new policy or change in an organization, it is important to prepare resources and develop stakeholders' expertise to achieve the intended change. In the case of soft-skills implementation, academics are key players who enact the soft-skills policy in their institution. Limited studies have documented strategies that HE institutions have made to prepare academics for such an implementation (Barrie et al., 2009). In contrast, research has identified academics' disengagement or compliant attitude as a challenge for the success of the implementation (de la Harpe & David, 2012; de la Harpe & Radloff, 2008; Jones, 2009). For example, A. Jones (2009, p. 188) notes that academics disengage or reject their role in teaching and assessing generic skills (an alternative term for soft skills) for several reasons:

- **Epistemological**: Generic skills are not considered to be part of disciplinary knowledge.
- **Cultural**: Generic skills are not seen as one of the central roles of the university teacher.

- **Intrinsic**: Generic skills are complex and difficult to define.
- **Pedagogical**: There is a lack of understanding regarding the nature of generic skills, and a lack of experience, or confidence, in teaching these attributes.
- **Structural**: These factors include large classes, the teaching of generic attributes not actively supported by departments, top-down implementation, lack of time, emphasis on research rather than teaching.

A number of studies about soft-skills implementation have suggested HE institutions should pay more attention to staff development with a focus on the following dimensions:

- **Enhancing staff members' perception of and attitudes towards soft-skills development**: Holding different beliefs about the relevance of soft skills, not all academics believe that they are important learning outcomes and so do not impart these skills to students in their subjects (de la Harpe & Radloff, 2008). Hence, HE institutional leaders need to patiently provide opportunities for these staff to change their beliefs about soft skills. They can do this by providing public discussions around the selected soft skills, involving them in developing faculty-relevant interpretations of the institutional statement, and inspiring debates on effective implementation strategies (Barrie et al., 2009). Leaders also need to change other stakeholders' perceptions and attitudes, such as management staff, librarians, career-development counselors, and students, because they all have a stake in the implementation and affect academics' work.
- **Developing practical skills to teach and assess soft skills**: The academic teaching job is usually defined as transferring disciplinary knowledge, with the teaching of soft skills only added lately (Jones, 2009). Academics have disengaged from teaching soft skills because they are not confident teaching these skills (de la Harpe & David, 2012; Jones, 2009). Therefore, it is important to train them in pedagogical practices conducive to imparting soft skills to students. In many Australian universities, academics can develop their soft-skills teaching expertise via different resources such as workshops on teaching techniques, web-based or text-based resources, or toolkits (Barrie et al., 2009). However, these activities only attract a small number of teachers. Situated academic-development strategies, such as teaching mentorship and co-teaching arrangements, are found to work better with respect to developing academics' soft-skills teaching ability.
- **Providing soft-skills teaching systems and structures**: Barrie et al. (2009) argued that providing efficient teaching systems and structures would enable the implementation of soft skills at the classroom level. They suggested providing templates for teachers to write learning outcomes or assessment statements, believing that such resources would encourage teachers to seek support with teaching and assessing soft skills. In addition, large class sizes, the arrangement in the classroom, and lack of time were identified as the most common inhibitors of effective soft-skills teaching. Therefore, these practicality barriers must be removed to enhance implementation.

- **Leadership in teaching soft skills**: Leadership is vital for accomplishing soft-skills-implementation objectives. Course coordinators, heads of department, deans and senior academics, and academics with soft-skills expertise in a department all need to be empowered to act as role models in teaching soft skills to motivate their colleagues. They can offer the "vital ingredient in creating a climate and culture in faculties that is conducive to staff members engaging in the teaching and curriculum development work that is required to achieve [soft skills]" (Barrie et al., 2009, p. 20).

Soft-skills implementation at the subject level

Three major tasks for soft-skills implementation at the subject level are setting learning objectives, teaching, and assessing. The latter two are observably still fragmented due to a lack of alignment of soft-skills learning objectives across subjects of a program, the elusive nature of soft skills, teacher disengagement, and poor student participation.

Setting learning objectives

In all levels of education, teachers usually set intended learning objectives for their subjects. With the emergence of quality-assurance activities, the intended learning objectives of subjects should align with those of other subjects and reflect the overall learning outcomes of the program. In the case of soft skills, if an HE institution chooses to develop soft skills for students using a curriculum separate from the disciplinary curriculum, skills experts are usually assigned to set soft-skills learning objectives. The learning objectives of this type of skills curriculum are often universal for all students, either university-wide or department-wide, depending on the scale of the implementation. In this case, the learning objectives may not complement students' studies in the disciplinary subjects and in their later work.

On the other hand, many universities choose to develop soft skills for students by integrating these skills into the disciplinary curriculum. Curriculum mapping has been used to map soft skills across subjects of a curriculum or a program (Ang, D'Alessandro, & Winzar, 2014; Holmes, Sheehan, Birks, & Smithson, 2018). Unfortunately, despite the investment of considerable resources, not all HE institutions are successful in this task (Barrie et al., 2009; Lawson et al., 2013). Ang et al. (2014) realized that mapping soft skills within the disciplinary curriculum is challenging for four reasons:

- There is a lack of shared meaning of soft skills across disciplines and groups of stakeholders, which hinders meaningful embedding of soft skills into different subjects of a program.
- Soft skills are most effectively developed within the context of a specific discipline. Therefore, embedding soft skills into the curriculum differs from program to program.

- Curriculum mapping requires a lot of work and cooperation from everyone involved in the delivery of a program. This may provoke resistance from academics because it increases their workloads.
- Current practices of curriculum mapping do not yield actionable insights. Whilst qualitative curriculum mapping may not be precise, the quantitative mapping process often consists of a simple frequency count of what soft skills are being taught, practiced, or assessed.

Despite the obstacles, mapping soft skills in a curriculum appears useful not only in aligning learning outcomes between subjects of a program but also in engaging stakeholders. Students may find a connection of soft-skills learning outcomes between subjects as one soft skill is taught in different subjects and its level is increased across the university years. Teachers are aware of what soft skills they are required to teach in their subjects, what level these skills should be taught at, and who is teaching those skills in other subjects. Without curriculum mapping, there would be inconsistency in soft-skills teaching to meet the declared learning objectives.

Analyzing good practices of curriculum mapping initiatives of many Australian universities under the Hunters and Gatherers Project, Romy Lawson et al. (2013) suggested that this task should be:

- **Holistic**: A whole-of-program approach would afford students opportunities to familiarize themselves with and develop these skills before they are asked to demonstrate soft skills in accordance with the standards they are expected to achieve by graduation.
- **Integrated**: Soft skills have to be embedded in the curriculum and become part of the assessment in order for academics and students to value these skills.
- **Collaborative**: The curriculum-mapping process must involve academics inclusively rather than being conducted as a top-down approach so they can engage in and recognize the importance of the process.
- **Sustainable**: Sustainability is important to ensure curriculum mapping is not reliant on specific individuals or resources.

Teaching soft skills

The student-centered pedagogical approach, with numerous teaching methods attached to it, is found to be conducive to students' soft-skills development. However, teaching these skills is challenged by teacher disengagement, student non-participation, and several teaching practicality issues.

Barrie (2007) found that pedagogical practices to train students in soft skills were associated with a teacher's perception of soft skills. Based on the four perceptions of soft skills mentioned earlier (precursor, complementary, translation, enabling), he also identified six ways that academics understand how students acquire soft skills:

- **Remedial**: Soft skills have already been developed in earlier education experience. The university only provides remedial teaching of soft skills for those who have not adequately developed these skills.
- **Associated**: Developing soft skills is part of the university's teaching role, but this for-all soft skills curriculum is additional and separate from the discipline curriculum.
- **Teaching content**: Soft skills are part of the discipline curriculum and are developed via teaching content of the discipline.
- **Teaching process**: Soft skills are not developed through content teaching but acquired through the teaching process of a usual university course.
- **Engagement**: Soft skills are not developed through the content taught, or the method used to teach, but through students' engagement in learning in their university course.
- **Participatory**: Soft skills are not developed through the way a student learns in a course but through participation in activities and the general learning experiences of broader university life.

Combining the academic's perceptions about soft skills and how students acquire them, he identified three approaches currently employed in the Australian HE context. These are outlined in Table 2.2.

In practice, several experiments with teaching methods under the framework of student-centeredness have proven the effectiveness of this approach in developing students' soft skills:

- Problem-based or project-based learning (Jollands, Jolly, & Molyneaux, 2012; Vogler et al., 2018).
- Community service learning (O'Connor, Lynch, & Owen, 2011; Shek & Chak, 2019).
- Online and distance learning (Brodie, 2011; Kim, Erdem, Byun, & Jeong, 2011).
- Work-integrated learning (Jackson, 2018; Leong & Kavanagh, 2013; Tran & Nguyen, 2018).

For example, Jollands et al. (2012) reported that problem-based learning contributed a great deal to graduates' development of skills such as project management, problem-solving, communication skills, research, and sustainability. Likewise, conducting a two-year study on the impact of project-based interdisciplinary teamwork, Vogler et al. (2018) concluded that it supported important aspects of students' learning, particularly improving their soft skills at first and then supporting both technical and soft skills in the later stage. A longitudinal study conducted by Brodie (2011) found that teamwork in the virtual space offered by a distance education course significantly increased engineering students' teamwork, communication, problem solving, and self-directed-learning skills. Shek and Chak (2019) examined the influence of service learning implemented at the Hong Kong Polytechnic University on students' learning outcomes and found that it enhanced

Table 2.2 Approaches to teaching generic graduate attributes (Barrie, 2007, p. 453)

Approach I: Generic graduate attributes as additive outcomes taught in a teacher-focused way in a supplementary curriculum

1. Generic graduate attributes are the basic prerequisite skills that students should already possess; they are only taught in remedial classes at university (precursor perspective)
2. Generic graduate attributes are skills and abilities that can complement, but not modify, disciplinary knowledge and are taught to all students as an unrelated add-on to the existing curriculum (complementary perspective)

Approach II: Generic graduate attributes as transformative outcomes taught in a teacher-focused way in an integrated curriculum

3. Generic graduate attributes make disciplinary knowledge relevant and are taught as part of discipline content (translation perspective)
4. Generic graduate attributes make disciplinary knowledge relevant and are taught through the process of teaching discipline content (translation perspective)

Approach III: Generic attributes as transformative outcomes taught in a learner-focused way in an integrated curriculum

5. Generic graduate attributes make disciplinary knowledge relevant and are learnt through the way students engage with the course (translation perspective)
6. Generic graduate attributes are complex abilities that infuse learning and knowledge and are learnt through the way students engage with the course (enabling perspective)
7. Generic graduate attributes are complex abilities that infuse learning and knowledge and are learnt through the way students engage with the university (enabling perspective)

their interpersonal effectiveness, team-building skills, problem-solving ability, and social responsibility. Smith and Worsfold (2015) found that work-integrated learning (WIL) had a huge impact on the development of students' professional readiness, self-efficacy and teamwork skills.

However, the literature also indicates that teacher disengagement, student non-participation, and several practicality issues hinder the effectiveness of teaching soft skills in HE. First, many teachers disengage from teaching soft skills because they find them irrelevant, do not feel confident teaching them (de la Harpe & David, 2012; de la Harpe & Radloff, 2008), or perceive that teaching them is not their responsibility (Jones, 2009). A lack of incentives, leadership, or management tools may also discourage them from including soft-skills-development activities in their subjects (Barrie et al., 2009). Second, student non-participation is another challenge with teaching soft skills. As student-centered pedagogies are often used to impart soft skills, students are expected to be able to self-regulate their learning of these skills. Unfortunately, many students solely study for a degree (James, Krause, & Jennings, 2009), favor technical knowledge and skills over soft skills (Tran, 2015), or are unaware of the importance of soft skills for their future life and work

(Barrie et al., 2009). Third, practicality issues (such as time, class sizes, teaching facilities and resources) are also found to hinder the effectiveness of soft-skills teaching (Barrie et al., 2009; Jones, 2009). In the integrated soft-skills curriculum model, teaching soft skills is usually considered a time-drainer and may be treated as of secondary importance compared to technical knowledge and skills. In other curriculum models, one-off courses may not help students attain the expected level of soft skills by the time they graduate. Large class sizes also make it hard for teachers to cater for individual students' learning needs and ability. Finally, effective student-centered teaching of soft skills requires adequate teaching facilities and resources, and these are often unaffordable for many universities in developing countries.

Assessing soft skills

Several skills-assessment tools and practices have been developed to increase students' awareness of their lack of soft skills, improve their engagement in soft-skills development, and provide evidence for the real assessment of soft skills. However, assessing soft skills is challenging due to the elusive nature of these skills, a lack of reliable assessment tools, and teacher and student disengagement.

A number of assessment initiatives have been used to help increase students' awareness of, and engagement in developing, soft skills. First, some tests are designed to help students self-evaluate their attainment of some important soft skills (Lawson et al., 2012; McMahon, Luca, & John, 2007; Quarrie, 2007). However, the tests often incorporate only skills that are easily measurable, excluding abstract, elusive skills. Many are skeptical of these test results as they heavily rely on students' confidence, honesty, and ability in self-evaluation (Jackson, 2014; Leach, 2012). Second, peer assessment provides students with opportunities to receive feedback from their friends about their skills (Gomes, Spandagou, & Ahmadi, 2008; Jones, Torezani, & Luca, 2012; Quarrie, 2007). Similar to self-assessment, peer assessment requires respectful and progressive attitudes among all students participating in the assessment activities (Heyman & Sailors, 2011; Kao, 2013). Third, course experience questionnaires provide students an opportunity to reflect on different aspects of the teaching and learning process throughout the course, including student and teacher engagement in developing soft skills (Talukdar, Aspland, & Datta, 2013; Yin, Lu, & Wang, 2014). However, coming at the end of the course, it is used primarily for monitoring teaching quality rather than increasing student engagement with soft-skills learning (Talukdar et al., 2013; Yin et al., 2014).

In addition, a number of assessment initiatives have been used to both increase student engagement and accumulate evidence for the formal assessment of students' attainment of soft skills. First, student portfolios, a purposeful collection of students' work, can be used to assess their efforts, progress, and achievements in one or more areas of the curriculum (Cranney et al., 2012; Palmer, Holt, Hall, & Ferguson, 2011; Rowley, Munday, & Polly, 2017). For instance, Deakin University's students remarked that the e-portfolio system was easy to use and helped them appreciate the skills and knowledge they had developed (Palmer et al., 2011). Similarly, capstone subjects are useful for improving student engagement and providing opportunities for formal assessment of soft skills (Keller, Parker, & Chan, 2011; Kilcommins, 2015). Capstone subjects are frequently offered in the final year of a university degree and can be in the form of a research project, work placement, internship, or service learning, providing students with opportunities to integrate, consolidate, or exhibit the acquired knowledge and skills to prepare them for work or further study (Keller et al., 2011; Kilcommins, 2015). Therefore, assessment of capstone subjects also involves assessment of soft skills. However, the weighting between generic and disciplinary skills is not clearly defined in capstone subject assessment. Also, who should do the assessing—students, academics, or supervisors? This is another issue that should be considered to ensure reliability of the assessment outcomes.

Moreover, some tools were ambitiously developed to evaluate students' performance of soft skills across multiple disciplines. The first example was the Australian Council for Educational Research (ACER) Graduate Skills Assessment (GSA), a standardized test proposed in the Nelson Report (Nelson, 2002). It is used to measure student performance on generic skills at the entrance and exit points of their degrees and is used as a proxy to monitor the "value add" to graduates' employability by Australian universities. However, the Victorian Language and Learning Network has questioned the validity of the GSA test concerning equity and cultural inclusiveness (Chanock, Clerehan, Moore, & Prince, 2004). The skills in the test were found not to complement psychometric testing and failed to capture the diversity of soft skills developed by universities of different missions and visions. Another example was the AHELO project (mentioned in Chapter 1), one of whose objectives was to assess soft skills across HE institutions. Although the test was reported to be reliable and valid, the project did not achieve its objectives because of the complexity of the skills and some practical issues (Tremblay, Lalancette, & Roseveare, 2012).

Furthermore, several factors have been identified to inhibit the assessment of soft skills. First, the elusive nature of soft skills challenges assessment practice. Soft skills are not discrete but are rather interrelated and context-specific (Gonczi, 2006; Hager & Holland, 2006; Jones, 2009). Thus, it would be unreliable if teachers were to test the level of each soft skill separately and without disciplinary context. The assessment activities become less reliable if there is a lack of shared perspective about what soft skills are and how to assess these skills among teachers. On top of that, teacher engagement with assessing soft skills is also critical for implementation at this level (de la Harpe & David, 2012; Hughes & Barrie, 2010). Those who do not teach soft skills will naturally ignore assessment of those skills. Those who do teach soft skills may feel diffident or have difficulty using new assessment practices that may require cooperation with other stakeholders, such as in the case of WIL (Barrie et al., 2009; de la Harpe & David, 2012). Consequently, students do not engage with learning soft skills because they generally study what teachers assess.

The National GAP Project report (Barrie et al., 2009) found that challenges to soft-skills assessment are caused by the following factors:

- A lack of consensus on what types of attributes or skills will be assessed, which may confuse teachers and students about what skills to develop.
- Teachers clinging to the existing assessment traditions rather than becoming involved in new assessment practices specific to soft skills.
- Requirement for an incremental approach, which consumes time and energy, which may result in superficial approaches.
- Relying too heavily on the professional body when assessing soft skills, which can result in developing (and assessing) some workplace skills and undermining other types of soft skills.
- Students not sufficiently involved in assessment practice, which limits material input for the assessment and the "washback" effects.

Soft-skills implementation via extracurricular or co-curricular activities

Extra-curriculum and co-curriculum were reported to be among curriculum models that HE institutions have adopted to develop soft skills for students (Barrie et al., 2009; Barrie, 2007). As the names suggest, these types of soft-skills curriculum stand separately from the disciplinary curriculum and only play a complementary role in consolidating students' knowledge and further developing skills via different kinds of social activities. Extracurricular or co-curricular activities may include taking part in volunteering programs (Khasanzyanova, 2017; Williamson, Wildbur, Bell, Tanner, & Matthews, 2018), travelling (Falk, Ballantyne, Packer, & Benckendorff, 2012; Scarinci & Pearce, 2012), or participating in unpaid work or internships that are not part of their studies (Grant-Smith & McDonald, 2018; Šuba, 2017).

Extracurricular or co-curricular activities have great potential for developing authentic soft skills for students. For example, Scarinci and Pearce (2012) studied 326 undergraduate business students at Northwood University (Florida, USA) to determine whether travel behaviors contribute to the development of their soft skills. The results showed that students improved 18 soft skills, including independence, open-mindedness, adaptability, and feeling comfortable around all types of people, with understanding and awareness as the most improved soft skills. Grant-Smith and McDonald (2018) found that unpaid work can help graduates develop professional and personal skills as well as enhance their employment prospects, especially for those in an education–employment transition phase.

Having recognized their benefits, many universities have included extracurricular or co-curricular activities into the strategies to improve students' levels of soft skills. For example, Universiti Malaysia Terengganu has incorporated these sorts of activities in campus life to improve students' employability advantage. Various co-curriculum activities are offered, including uniform, sports, cultural, leadership, and martial arts clubs. The researchers concluded that the assimilation of generic skills (especially leadership) through both curriculum- and co-curriculum-embedded programs provides the students with valuable added competencies (Yassin, Hasan, Amin, & Amiruddin, 2008). Likewise, under the employability programs, on the websites of most Australian universities now, there is information of several ECAs for students to participate in to prepare them for the future: student societies, sports clubs, a career consultation service, and volunteer activities. In Vietnam, the Youth Union and Associates (YUA) have been leading the youth to run community-engagement or community-development activities. For example, they organize the *Chiến dịch Mùa Hè Xanh* (Green Summer Campaign), where students go to rural areas to teach underprivileged children or help disadvantaged people, or they transfer knowledge and technologies to farmers. Recently, the YUA have been involved in training students in work skills, organizing career fairs, and offering career-consultation services.

However, extracurricular or co-curricular activities face many barriers. The first is associated with student participation. As it is called *extra*curricular, many students disregard the importance of such activities. For example, Vietnamese students appear to put great effort into obtaining specialized knowledge, or what is taught in class, rather than joining in such ECAs, which is also the expectation of their parents and teachers (Tran, 2015). The second challenge is that not all students would have the opportunity to participate in certain ECAs, such as being a research assistant, intern, or serving in a student committee where they may acquire and develop particular soft skills (Barrie et al., 2009). In most cases, students can only play the role of mere participants, in which they may not develop leadership or organization skills. Finally, as most ECAs are linked to the local community, the support of people, industries, or authorities is essential. Without their support, ECAs may only occur on campus, which hinders the meaningful development of soft skills.

Conclusion

This chapter has reviewed current practices and challenges of soft-skills implementation in HE across the globe. The chapter argued that, despite the many activities and efforts devoted to the implementation of soft skills at the national, institutional, and subject levels, implementation has not progressed much due to many personal and institutional factors, such as a lack of soft-skills policies and drivers, inadequate staff preparation, lack of consensus on perception of soft skills, and teacher/student disengagement, to name a few. Reviewing common practices for soft-skills implementation in the literature, this chapter has identified important tasks at different levels of the university. These tasks allow the development of the conceptual framework below, which will serve as a spine for this book, binding chapters together meaningfully.

Table 2.3 Levels of soft-skills implementation and respective tasks

Level of implementation	Implementation task
National level	• Socioeconomic, cultural, and political contexts of HE • Quality assurance • Accreditation • Learning outcomes assessment
Institutional level	• Policies, incentives, and drivers for soft-skills implementation • Approaches to soft-skills implementation • Selection of soft-skills outcomes and curriculum models • Staff and resources development
Subject level	• Setting soft-skills learning objectives • Teaching soft skills • Assessing soft skills
Extracurricular activities	• Social-engagement activities • Employment orientation and consultation • Skills classes • Political education

References

Al-Mahmood, R., & Gruba, P. (2007). Approaches to the implementation of generic graduate attributes in Australian ICT undergraduate education. *Computer Science Education*, 17(3), 171–185.

Ang, L., D'Alessandro, S., & Winzar, H. (2014). A visual-based approach to the mapping of generic skills: Its application to a Marketing degree. *Higher Education Research & Development*, 33(2), 181–197.

B-HERT (2003). Developing generic skills: Examples of best practice. *B-HERT News*. Retrieved from https://bit.ly/2GAJ9QL

Barrie, S., Hughes, C., Smith, C., & Thomson, K. (2009). *The national graduate attributes project: Key issues to consider in the renewal of learning and teaching experiences to foster graduate attributes*. Sydney: The University of Sydney.

Barrie, S. C. (2006). Understanding what we mean by the generic attributes of graduates. *Higher Education*, 51(2), 215–241.

Barrie, S. C. (2007). A conceptual framework for the teaching and learning of generic graduate attributes. *Studies in Higher Education*, 32(4), 439–458.

Bredgaard, T., & Madsen, P. K. (2018). Farewell flexicurity? Danish flexicurity and the crisis. *Transfer: European Review of Labour and Research*. doi: 10.1177/1024258918768613

Brodie, L. (2011). Delivering key graduate attributes via teams working in virtual space. *International Journal of Emerging Technologies in Learning (iJET)*, 6(3), 5–11.

Cacciolatti, L., Lee, S. H., & Molinero, C. M. (2017). Clashing institutional interests in skills between government and industry: An analysis of demand for technical and soft skills of graduates in the UK. *Technological Forecasting and Social Change*, 119(Jun), 139–153.

Callaghan, R., & McManus, J. (2010). Building the perfect graduate: What news employers want in new hires. *Asia Pacific Media Educator*, 20, 9–21.

Carrivick, J. L. (2011). Exploring the value of professional body accreditation for masters programmes. *Journal of Geography in Higher Education*, 35(4), 479–497.

Chaisinthop, N. (2014). Volunteering, Dana, and the cultivation of 'good people'in Thailand. *Anthropological Forum*, 24(4), 396–411. doi: 10.1080/00664677.2014.965129

Chan, C. K. Y., & Fong, E. T. Y. (2018). Disciplinary differences and implications for the development of generic skills: A study of engineering and business students' perceptions of generic skills. *European Journal of Engineering Education*, 43(6), 927–949. Retrieved from https://bit.ly/2Uy7JFE

Chanock, K., Clerehan, R., Moore, T., & Prince, A. (2004). Shaping university teaching towards measurement for accountability: Problems of the graduate skills assessment test. *Australian Universities' Review*, 47(1), 22–29.

Cranney, J., Kofod, M., Huon, G., Jensen, L., Levin, K., McAlpine, I., Scoufis, M., &Whitaker, N. (2012). *Portfolio tools: learning and teaching strategies to facilitate development of graduate attributes.* Retrieved from https://bit.ly/2KSckTE

Danish Government (2008). *Qualifications framework for Danish higher education.* Retrieved from https://bit.ly/2URzxtC

de la Harpe, B., & David, C. (2012). Major influences on the teaching and assessment of graduate attributes. *Higher Education Research & Development*, 31(4), 493–510.

de la Harpe, B., & Radloff, A. (2008). Developing graduate attributes for lifelong learning: How far have we got? Paper presented at the 5th International Lifelong Learning Conference, 16–19 June, Queensland, Australia.

El Hassan, K. (2013). Quality assurance in higher education in 20 MENA economies. *Higher Education Management and Policy*, 24(2), 73–84.

Falk, J. H., Ballantyne, R., Packer, J., & Benckendorff, P. (2012). Travel and learning: A neglected tourism research area. *Annals of Tourism Research*, 39(2), 908–927.

Fallows, S., & Steven, C. (2000). *Integrating key skills in higher education: employability, transferable skills and learning for life.* London: Kogan Page.

Fleming, J., Donovan, R., Beer, C., & Clark, D. (2013). A whole of university approach to embedding graduate attributes: A reflection. In J. Willems, B. Tynan, & R. James (Eds.), *Global challenges and perspectives in blended and distance learning* (pp. 246–257). Hershey, PA: IGI Global.

Frank, B., Strong, D., Sellens, R., & Clapham, L. (2013). Progress with the professional spine: A four-year engineering design and practice sequence. *Australasian Journal of Engineering Education*, 19(1), 63–74.

Gomes, V. G., Spandagou, I., & Ahmadi, M. (2008). Peer assessment in imparting graduate attributes. Retrieved from https://bit.ly/2ICscHU

Gonczi, A. (2006). The OECD: Its role in the key competencies debate and in the promotion of lifelong learning. In P. Hager & S. Holland (Eds.), *Graduate attributes, learning and employability* (pp. 105–124). Dordrecht, The Netherlands: Springer.

Grant-Smith, D., & McDonald, P. (2018). Planning to work for free: Building the graduate employability of planners through unpaid work. *Journal of Youth Studies*, 21(2), 161–177.

Hager, P., & Holland, S. (2006). *Graduate attributes, learning and employability (Vol. 6).* Dordrecht, Netherlands: Springer Science & Business Media.

Hayes, J. (2018). *The theory and practice of change management* (5th edn). London: Palgrave MacMillan.

Heyman, J. E., & Sailors, J. J. (2011). Peer assessment of class participation: Applying peer nomination to overcome rating inflation. *Assessment & Evaluation in Higher Education*, 36(5), 605–618.

Holmes, D. W., Sheehan, M., Birks, M., & Smithson, J. (2018). Development of a competency mapping tool for undergraduate professional degree programmes, using mechanical engineering as a case study. *European Journal of Engineering Education*, 43(1), 126–143.

Hughes, C., & Barrie, S. (2010). Influences on the assessment of graduate attributes in higher education. *Assessment & Evaluation in Higher Education*, 35(3), 325–334.

Jackson, D. (2014). Self-assessment of employability skill outcomes among undergraduates and alignment with academic ratings. *Assessment & Evaluation in Higher Education*, 39(1), 53–72.

Jackson, D. (2018). Developing graduate career readiness in Australia: Shifting from extra-curricular internships to work-integrated learning. *International Journal of Work-Integrated Learning*, 19(1), 23–35.

James, R., Krause, K.-L., & Jennings, C. (2009). *The first year experience in Australian universities: Findings from 1994 to 2009*. Retrieved from https://bit.ly/2KWCy7E

Jollands, M., Jolly, L., & Molyneaux, T. (2012). Project-based learning as a contributing factor to graduates' work readiness. *European Journal of Engineering Education*, 37(2), 143–154.

Jones, A. (2009). Generic attributes as espoused theory: The importance of context. *Higher Education*, 58(2), 175–191.

Jones, N., Torezani, S., & Luca, J. (2012). A peer-to-peer support model for developing graduate students' career and employability skills. *Intercultural Education*, 23(1), 51–62.

Kao, G. Y. M. (2013). Enhancing the quality of peer review by reducing student "free riding": Peer assessment with positive interdependence. *British Journal of Educational Technology*, 44(1), 112–124.

Keller, S., Parker, C. M., & Chan, C. (2011). Employability skills: Student perceptions of an IS final year capstone subject. *Innovation in Teaching and Learning in Information and Computer Sciences*, 10(2), 4–15.

Kennedy, K. J., Fairbrother, G., & Zhao, Z. (2013). *Citizenship education in China: Preparing citizens for the "Chinese century"*. New York and London: Routledge.

Khasanzyanova, A. (2017). How volunteering helps students to develop soft skills. *International Review of Education*, 63(3), 363–379.

Kilcommins, S. (2015). Capstone courses as a vehicle for integrative learning. In D. Blackshields, J. Cronin, B. Higgs, S. Kilcommins, M. McCarthy, & A. Ryan (Eds.), *Integrative learning: International research and practice* (pp. 143–156). Abingdon, UK: Routledge.

Kim, J., Erdem, M., Byun, J., & Jeong, H. (2011). Training soft skills via e-learning: International chain hotels. *International Journal of Contemporary Hospitality Management*, 23(6), 739–763.

Lawson, R., Taylor, T., Fallshaw, E., Summers, J., Kinash, S., French, E., & Angus-Leppan, T. (2013). *Hunters and gatherers: Strategies for curriculum mapping and data collection for assuring learning*. Retrieved from https://bit.ly/2DqAWgk

Lawson, R., Taylor, T., Thompson, D., Simpson, L., Freeman, M., Treleaven, L., & Rohde, F. (2012). Engaging with graduate attributes through encouraging accurate student self-assessment. *Asian Social Science*, 8(4), 3–12.

Leach, L. (2012). Optional self-assessment: Some tensions and dilemmas. *Assessment & Evaluation in Higher Education*, 37(2), 137–147.

Leong, R., & Kavanagh, M. (2013). A work integrated learning (WIL) framework to develop graduate skills and attributes in an Australian university's accounting program. *Asia-Pacific Journal of Cooperative Education*, 14(1), 1–14

Lewis, L. (2019). *Organizational change: Creating change through strategic communication* (2nd edn). Hoboken, NJ: Wiley-Blackwell.

Marek, K. (2012). *Knowledge production in European universities: States, markets, and academic entrepreneurialism (Vol. 3)*. Frankfurt: Peter Lang.

McMahon, M., Luca, J., & John, C. (2007). *A self-assessment tool to help learners develop teamwork skills*. Retrieved from https://bit.ly/2IPlHkh

Nelson, B. (2002). *Striving for quality: Learning, teaching and scholarship*. Canberra: Department of Education, Science and Training.

Nguyen, D. M., Truong, T. V., & Le, N. B. (2013). *Deployment of capstone projects in software engineering education at Duy Tan University as part of a university-wide project-based learning effort*. Retrieved from https://bit.ly/2UzJDKO

Nguyen, P. T. M., Cornish, L., & Minichiello, V. (2014). Management, leadership and change: Views from rectors, vice-rectors and academic staff in Vietnamese higher education institutions. *Asia Pacific Journal of Educational Development (APJED)*, 3(1), 69–77.

Nikitina, L., & Furuoka, F. (2012). Sharp focus on soft skills: A case study of Malaysian university students' educational expectations. *Educational Research for Policy and Practice*, 11(3), 207–224.

Njue, C., & Ongoto, H. (2018). Strategic management practices and change implementation in selected public universities in Kenya. *International Academic Journal of Human Resource and Business Administration*, 3(4), 124–149.

O'Connor, K., Lynch, K., & Owen, D. (2011). Student-community engagement and the development of graduate attributes. *Education + Training*, 53(2/3), 100–115.

O'Neill, G. (2010). *A programme wide approach to assessment: A reflection on some curriculum mapping tools*. Paper presented at the AISHE Conference, Dublin, Ireland. Retrieved from https://bit.ly/2Vhr16W

Palmer, S., Holt, D., Hall, W., & Ferguson, C. (2011). An evaluation of an online student portfolio for the development of engineering graduate attributes. *Computer Applications in Engineering Education*, 19(3), 447–456.

Pitman, T., & Broomhall, S. (2009). Australian universities, generic skills and lifelong learning. *International Journal of Lifelong Education*, 28(4), 439–458.

Quarrie, S. P. (2007). Student peer review as a tool for efficiently achieving subject-specific and generic learning outcomes: Examples in botany at the Faculty of Agriculture, University of Belgrade. *Higher Education in Europe*, 32(2–3), 203–212.

Rowley, J., Munday, J., & Polly, P. (2017). *Preparing future career ready professionals: A portfolio process to develop critical thinking using digital learning and teaching*. Retrieved from https://bit.ly/2vjLdpS

Rychen, D. S., & Salganik, L. H. (2003). *Key competencies for a successful life and well-functioning society*. Cambridge, MA: Hogrefe Publishing.

Scarinci, J., & Pearce, P. (2012). The perceived influence of travel experiences on learning generic skills. *Tourism Management*, 33(2), 380–386.

Shek, D. T., & Chak, Y. L. (2019). Perceived changes and benefits of a service-learning subject for underprivileged children in Shanghai: Views of university students. In D. T. L. Shek, G. Ngai, & S. C. F. Chan (Eds.), *Service-learning for youth leadership: The case of Hong Kong* (pp. 33–47). Singapore: Springer.

Sin, C., Tavares, O., & Amaral, A. (2017). Accepting employability as a purpose of higher education? Academics' perceptions and practices. *Studies in Higher Education*. doi: 10.1080/03075079.2017.1402174

Sin, S., Jones, A., & Petocz, P. (2007). Evaluating a method of integrating generic skills with accounting content based on a functional theory of meaning. *Accounting & Finance*, 47(1), 143–163.

Skoumpopoulou, D., & Waring, T. (2017). Cultural change through the implementation of an enterprise system: A UK university case study. *Journal of Enterprise Information Management*, 30(5), 809–830.

Smith, C., & Worsfold, K. (2015). Unpacking the learning–work nexus: 'Priming' as lever for high-quality learning outcomes in work-integrated learning curricula. *Studies in Higher Education*, 40(1), 22–42.

Star, C., & Hammer, S. (2008). Teaching generic skills: Eroding the higher purpose of universities, or an opportunity for renewal? *Oxford Review of Education*, 34(2), 237–251.

Šuba, P. (2017). Motives for young people to volunteer abroad: A case study of AIESEC interns from the perspective of volunteer tourism. *African Journal of Hospitality, Tourism and Leisure*, 6(3), 1–11.

Talukdar, J., Aspland, T., & Datta, P. (2013). Australian higher education and the course experience questionnaire: Insights, implications and recommendations. *Australian Universities' Review*, 55(1), 27–35.

Tang, T. T., & Yi-Fang, L. (2014). Stakeholders' perspectives on quality assurance in Vietnamese higher education. *Higher Education Evaluation and Development*, 8(2), 1–30. doi: 10.6197/HEED.2014.0802.01

Taylor, E. (2016). Investigating the perception of stakeholders on soft skills development of students: Evidence from South Africa. *Interdisciplinary Journal of e-Skills and Lifelong Learning*, 12(1), 1–18.

Tertiary Education Quality and Standards Agency (2013). *Australian qualifications framework*. Canberra: The Australian Qualifications Framework Council. Retrieved from https://bit.ly/2UxTUHm

Thai Government (2006). *National qualifications framework for higher education in Thailand*. Retrieved from https://bit.ly/2DsbFSX

The Quality Assurance Agency for Higher Education (2014). *The frameworks for higher education qualifications of UK degree-awarding bodies*. Retrieved from https://bit.ly/2W9jX9i

Tran, L. H. N., & Nguyen, T. M. D. (2018). Internship-related learning outcomes and their influential factors: The case of Vietnamese tourism and hospitality students. *Education + Training*, 60(1), 69–81.

Tran, T. T. (2015). Is graduate employability the 'whole-of-higher-education-issue'? *Journal of Education and Work*, 28(3), 207–227.

Tremblay, K., Lalancette, D., & Roseveare, D. (2012). *Assessment of higher education learning outcomes*. Retrieved from https://bit.ly/2IRTRnB

Vogler, J. S., Thompson, P., Davis, D. W., Mayfield, B. E., Finley, P. M., & Yasseri, D. (2018). The hard work of soft skills: Augmenting the project-based learning experience with interdisciplinary teamwork. *Instructional Science*, 46(3), 457–488.

Williamson, I., Wildbur, D., Bell, K., Tanner, J., & Matthews, H. (2018). Benefits to university students through volunteering in a health context: A new model. *British Journal of Educational Studies*, 66(3), 383–402.

Yassin, S., Hasan, F. A., Amin, W., & Amiruddin, N. (2008). *Implementation of generic skills in the curriculum*. Retrieved from https://bit.ly/2UQcQGh

Yin, H., Lu, G., & Wang, W. (2014). Unmasking the teaching quality of higher education: Students' course experience and approaches to learning in China. *Assessment & Evaluation in Higher Education*, 39(8), 949–970.

3 The context of soft-skills implementation in Vietnamese universities

Skills deficit in Vietnam: A hindrance to its future development

Vietnam: An emerging Asian dragon?

Vietnam is a developing country in Southeast Asia with a young population of approximately 95 million in 2017. There are 54 ethnic groups living across the country with the Kinh as the dominant group. According to the General Statistics Office of Vietnam (General Statistics Office of Vietnam, 2019a), in 2016, 34.4% of the population lived in cities and towns and the remaining 65.6% lived in the countryside. Approximately 48% of the population work in the agricultural sector, 22.9% in industry, and 35.2% in the service sector (Nordeatrade, 2019).

After nearly a thousand years under Chinese domination and a hundred years under colonization by France and the USA, the country gained back its independence in 1945 for the North and in 1975 for the South. Politically, Vietnam is one of the few socialist countries in the world still remaining after the fall of the Soviet Bloc. After a long time restricting its international relations to only socialist countries, at the National Congress VI in 1986, Vietnam introduced the Renovation Policy (the *Doi Moi*), which shifted the socialist planned economy to the so-called socialist-oriented market economy (Cao, 2000; Gates, 1995). This move has been reported to have saved the country from an imminent crisis and collapse and boosted its socioeconomic growth (Cao, 2000; Sanders, 2014; H.T. Tran & Santarelli, 2018; V.T. Tran, 2013). Vietnam now has established international relationships with most countries in the world, has joined international economic organizations such as the World Trade Organization (WTO), the ASEAN Economic Community, and Asia–Pacific Economic Cooperation, and has kept on building its image and prestige in the international arena.

Socioeconomically, after 1986, the country has successively experienced low unemployment rates, growing income, increasing foreign direct investment (FDI), and positive GDP growth (see Table 3.1). From a poor country that mostly relied on agricultural production and had to recover from the aftermath of terrifying wars, it has reduced poverty, set up industrial and service sectors, and begun exporting its products to other countries (Cao, 2000; Sanders, 2014; V.T. Tran, 2013). The government has committed to making Vietnam a strong economy in

Table 3.1 Some indicators of the Vietnamese economy (compiled from different sources)

Indicators	2010	2011	2012	2013	2014	2015	2016	2017
1. Unemployment rate (%)	2.64	2.02	1.77	1.95	1.87	2.12	2.10	2.05
2. Economic growth rate (%)	6.42	6.24	5.24	5.42	5.98	6.67	6.21	6.81
3. Gross national income (thousand USD)	1,250	1,360	1,530	1,710	1,860	1,950	2,060	2,170
4. Gross domestic product (billion USD)	115.9	135.5	155.8	171.2	186.2	193.2	205.3	223.9
5. Inflation rate (%)	8.86	18.68	9.09	6.59	4.71	0.88	3.24	3.52
6. Foreign direct investment, net inflows (billion USD/number of projects)	19.9 / 1,237	15.6 / 1,186	16.3 / 1,287	22.4 / 1,530	21.9 / 1,843	24.1 / 2,120	26.9 / 2,613	21.27 / 2,591

Notes

Indicator 1 is retrieved from https://bit.ly/2uQeA2N
Indicators 2, 3, 4 are retrieved from https://data.worldbank.org/country/vietnam
Indicator 5 is retrieved from https://bit.ly/2YOprZa
Indicator 6 is retrieved from https://bit.ly/2CZbgH8 and https://bit.ly/2CV5VRm

Southeast Asia. At each subsequent national congress since 1986, successes and failures have been discussed in order to set new socioeconomic development targets. The National Congress XI (Vietnamese Congress, 2011) and XII (Vietnamese Congress, 2016) set objectives to maintain the annual economic growth rate at 6.5% to 7.0%, increase the GDP per capita to USD 3200–3500 and achieve 85% of GDP from industrial and service sectors by 2020.

Table 3.1 summarizes some indicators of Vietnam's socioeconomic development from 2010 to 2017 (the latest statistics available), showing that Vietnam will most likely achieve its socioeconomic objectives soon. The unemployment rate has kept stably below 3% for almost a decade; the economic growth rate was above 5% in the same period. Although the inflation rate was quite high in 2011–2012, due to economic recession, in recent years the inflation rate has kept at approximately 3.0 to 3.5%. Foreign direct investment into Vietnam has been stable over the last decade, but with an increase in the number of projects. Citing a report from Vietnam's Foreign Investment Agency, *Vietnamnet* (2018) informs that there have been more than 27,350 foreign-invested projects in Vietnam so far with a total registered capital of $340 billion. South Korea was the leading source of FDI with $62.5 billion; Japan came second with $57 billion, followed by Singapore, Taiwan, British Virgin Islands, and Hong Kong. According to Nordeatrade (2019), the agricultural sector is dominated by cultivation and aquaculture, which contributes about 15.9% of GDP; industry accounts for 36.4% of GDP, with textiles, food processing, furniture, plastics, and paper the main industries, and vehicle-manufacturing, electronics, and computer technologies emerging ones; the services sector, which generates 45.5% of GDP, is mainly in tourism and telecommunication domains.

In terms of culture, the country is strongly influenced by Confucian values due to a cultural assimilation policy under the period of Chinese domination and the adoption of these values under successive Vietnamese feudal dynasties, especially under the Later Le (1428–1527) and Nguyen (1802–1883) dynasties (Ly, 2015). Confucianism was used as a guideline for political and educational practices and for many other aspects of life. As such, Confucian cultural heritages are deep-rooted in people's thinking and lifestyles, and define norms for social practices, including governance and leadership. For example, many rituals related to weddings and funerals can be tracked back to the Han traditions in China (Ly, 2015). Despite rapid changes in recent years, women are expected to follow the three "obediences" (*tam cương*)—obeying her father as a daughter, obeying her husband as a wife, and obeying her son as a widow—and the four virtues (*tứ đức*)—morality, proper speech, modest manner, and diligent work (Ly, 2015). Confucian heritages also strongly influence practices in education. For instance, under past Viet dynasties, examinations were used to recruit mandarins and officials for the rulers; that motive is still embedded in the mindsets and practices in Vietnam now. Teachers are highly respected due to the Confucian ranking of important people in society: king, teacher, father (*quân, sư, phụ*). This belief has resulted in teachers holding much power and potentially intimidating students by preventing them from critiquing what their teachers preach (L.T. Tran, Le, & Nguyen, 2014), which is a barrier to students' personal development and to social innovation. Although the Confucian cultural heritage is thought to hold back social development, it is useful in maintaining social order and tightening family and social bonds.

Vietnam also inherited some degree of Western lifestyle under the colonial periods (France and the US), and possesses relatively high levels of communist characteristics under the current socialist political regime (Huong & Fry, 2002, 2004; London, 2006). In recent years, under the process of globalization and regionalization, as well as the rapid development of the media, the youth are exposed to foreign cultures, especially Western ones, resulting in many changes in their worldview and lifestyles (Nguyen, 2015). Education at all levels is also influenced by foreign forces, with the presence of many international schools and institutions, imported programs and educational models, and languages of instruction (Kim & Mobrand, 2019; L.T. Tran & Marginson, 2018b), especially after Decision 86/2018/NĐ-CP on cooperation with foreign stakeholders in investing in education (Vietnamese Government, 2018). All of these factors have contributed to a Vietnam in transition, with cultural clashes occurring where younger people are found more open than their seniors.

With all of these remarkable achievements in the past 30 years and potential for further development, Vietnam has been regarded as one of the rising dragons in Asia (Irvin, 1995; Schaumburg-Müller & Chuong, 2010). However, as the world enters the era of the knowledge economy, a cheap labor force is no longer an advantage; the key to sustainable development is to be found in the hands of a skilled workforce (Hadad, 2017). Without successfully building up capable human resources, Vietnam will not be able to sustain its recent socioeconomic growth.

Current skills deficits in Vietnam

Since its fundamental policy change in 1986, Vietnam has been moving toward a middle-income country with the ambition of becoming a modernized and industrialized country. With economic development, the demand for highly skilled workers has also increased; however, research has consistently reported a shortage of skilled labor in Vietnam (Bodewig & Badiani-Magnusson, 2014; ManPowerGroup, 2011; Nguyen, Ngoc, & Montague, 2019; L.H.N. Tran, 2018b; World Bank, 2008). For example, the World Bank (2008) reported a survey by the Ministry of Labor, Invalids and Social Affairs (MOLISA) showing that only about 80% of the planned recruitment at the managerial level was implemented and that many firms needed to retrain HE graduates, especially those majoring in technology, business administration, and manufacturing and processing disciplines. The World Bank (2008) cited findings of a survey conducted by the MOLISA and Asian Development Bank, explaining that a key reason for not filling a certain position is that candidates do not meet the basic requirements of the position and lack practical skills (practical knowledge of the technology, work experience) and soft skills (written and spoken communication, communication skills in foreign languages, teamwork, creative thinking, etc.) rather than theoretical knowledge. The Bank called for Vietnamese HE institutions to improve soft skills for university graduates, considering it one of the crucial fields for the Vietnamese economy to sustainably grow. Unfortunately, six years later, in another report, the World Bank continued to detect a shortage of skilled labor in Vietnam, and a lack of workers with adequate soft skills is still a major challenge (Bodewig & Badiani-Magnusson, 2014). The Bank urged Vietnam to invest in skilling up the workforce to prepare for a modern economy.

A report by the ManpowerGroup (2011) revealed an acute shortage of skills in certain industries in Vietnam. Generally, the workers in food-processing, textile, healthcare, construction, transportation and logistics, and chemical and fertilizer industries all lacked technical expertise. In terms of soft skills, the ManpowerGroup survey also found a skills shortage applied to both management and blue-collar workers. About 25% of the participants responded that Vietnam's workforce was not quality-conscious enough and lacked communication skills. A slightly smaller percentage mentioned that Vietnamese workers fell short in adapting to new and changing situations, managing and completing tasks, and absorbing and applying new knowledge. There were also gaps in foreign language, computer and financial proficiency, innovation, and the ability to motivate others. Although the survey by ManpowerGroup is not specific to HE graduates, it does illustrate the shortage of skills in the labor market and the need to upgrade skills for the workforce, particularly soft skills.

In a recent study, L.H.N. Tran (2018b) asked 257 graduates and 525 final-year students to rate 37 work skills of their own and compare the ratings against the level of these skills needed in the workplace, as perceived by graduates. The study showed that the skills gap of final-year students and graduates in these skills ranged from 0.35 to 1.0 and 0.32 to 1.5, respectively, on a scale of 5. The study also found that these skills appeared not to improve even after graduates had been in the workplace for years. Most interestingly, the study showed that the skills gap of female graduates appeared to increase compared to the time they were at university. The author attributed such a phenomenon to the Confucian cultural heritage where men are favored over women regarding professional development, and women are expected to take care of their families rather than pursue careers.

The shortage of soft skills in Vietnamese graduates has also been reported in many media outlets. For example, Nguyen (2016) reported that employers are not impressed with the soft skills of Vietnamese graduates, citing the chairman of Vinapo Inc. who said that 90% of Vietnamese graduates did not possess the soft skills necessary for work. In another article, Nhan Viet Management Group reported that 94% of the employees in 500 enterprises in Ho Chi Minh City needed training organized by their employers prior to commencing work; among them, 61% needed training in soft skills, 53% in leadership skills, and 92% in technical skills (Anh, 2011). Ha (2015) reported a survey conducted by Jobstreet.com that revealed the top concern of employers in Vietnam when employing fresh graduates was the graduates' work skills—as opposed to salary rate, the chief concern of employers in Singapore and Malaysia. The surveyed employers revealed that fresh graduates in Vietnam were inexperienced and took too much time to learn the skills necessary for their job; therefore, employers preferred to hire candidates with existing experience.

All findings from the aforementioned studies and reports are consistent with the recent increase in unemployed graduates in Vietnam (Nguyen, 2016; Pham, 2013; Ha, 2015). A number of authors have attributed such a situation to the universities fundamentally transmitting specialized knowledge rather than training students in competencies or skills (L.T. Tran et al., 2014; T.T. Tran, 2015). Theory-laden curricula and a lack of connections with industries are critiqued to be the main causes of the graduate skills gap and unemployment, and students' passivity in planning and developing their career is another major reason (L.H.N. Tran, 2018a). Finally, constant changes in demands for skills in the labor market, as a consequence of rapid socio-economic development and foreign investment in the country, has also resulted in a mismatch between the skills that graduates possess and what employers need (L.H.N. Tran, 2018a).

With the inauguration of the ASEAN Economic Community in late 2015, the free flow of goods, services, investment, and skilled labor between ASEAN countries will quickly increase (Jurje & Lavenex, 2015). This means that Vietnamese graduates will have to compete with all ASEAN graduates for jobs. At the same time, they will also have opportunities to enter non-Vietnamese labor markets. As such, they will need skills that enable them to work effectively in that increased international environment, either in or outside Vietnam.

In sum, there is a severe shortage of skilled labor in Vietnam now. In the long run, this shortage may economically disadvantage Vietnam. Employers seem to increasingly demand that their employees work efficiently with each other using both technical and soft skills. Thus, Vietnamese universities need to improve the soft skills of their students so that, upon graduation, they can meet these demands and compete with candidates from other ASEAN countries. This is an essential task for Vietnamese universities now because low-cost labor, one of the competitive advantages of the Vietnamese economy in the past, will no longer be an advantage (Dien, 2014).

Developing soft skills in Vietnamese higher education

Contemporary Vietnamese higher education: An overview

Vietnamese higher education (HE) has a long history of development and possesses distinctive characteristics compared with its counterparts in many Western countries. Through its developmental stages, Vietnamese HE has been embedded with different values and heritage. Given that the first university was established in the 11th century under the influence of Chinese culture, it is no surprise that Confucianism, which stresses morality in maintaining social order (Cui, 2007; Ly, 2015), is embedded in the system (Huong & Fry, 2002, 2004). Through many feudal dynasties from the 11th to the 19th century, these Confucian values continued to grow, strongly thriving under the Later Le (1428–1527) and Nguyen (1802–1883) dynasties (Ly, 2015). Then, during the colonial period, it inherited some Western educational values, which appreciate new insights and application of knowledge (Huong & Fry, 2004). When Vietnam became a socialist country, the

HE system integrated socialist features. Although the Vietnamese HE model has been restructured toward the Western-style system lately (Harman, Hayden, & Nghi, 2010), in Vietnamese universities, instilling socialist thoughts and principles is as essential as developing intellectual ability: Marxist sciences and Ho Chi Minh thoughts make up a remarkable volume of the curricula and are taught as compulsory subjects (Doan, 2005; Huong & Fry, 2004; L.H.N. Tran, 2017). The Youth Union—a social-political organization under the umbrella of the Labor Party—have played a significant role in imparting socialist values to university students in Vietnam (L.H.N. Tran, 2017). Generally, together with the traditional norms mentioned previously, socialist morality is one of the prominent characteristics of Vietnamese HE. As such, Vietnamese HE has experienced the influence of several foreign influences; yet it seems to selectively adopt practices that suit its traditions (L.T. Tran, Ngo, Nguyen, & Dang, 2017).

In the current context, the Higher Education Law (Vietnamese Government, 2012) defines the purposes of Vietnamese HE as follows:

i   Train the workforce, uplift public education, nurture talents; produce new knowledge and products to meet the demands of socioeconomic development, assuring national security and defense, and integrating globally via doing scientific and technological research.
ii Produce graduates with a strong stance on politics and ethics; possess knowledge, professional skills, capability of R&D appropriate to educational level; possess good health, creativeness, responsibility in their jobs, good adaptability to the working environment, and a sense of community engagement.

Obviously, unlike many countries where pursuit of HE is for private return, personal development, liberal purposes, and/or social inclusion (Lagemann & Lewis, 2015), the purpose of Vietnamese HE is to produce human resources that possess knowledge, skills, and socialist political attributes in order to support national economic development, social inclusion, and construction of the political regime (Vietnamese Government, 2012).

Bound by the changing political and socioeconomic contexts of the country, the HE system in Vietnam has changed fundamentally since the *Doi Moi*. In terms of expansion and increasing training capacity, besides the public universities, new legislation in the 1990s allowed the establishment of private universities (Dao & Hayden, 2010; Huong & Fry, 2002). According to the latest statistics available from the General Statistics Office of Vietnam (2019b) in 2017, there were 235 universities across the HE system, and among these, 170 were public and 65 non-public institutions; the number of staff working for the HE institutions increased from 74,600 in 2010 to 93,500 in 2015; and graduates produced by the universities peaked in 2014 at 441,800 but dramatically dropped to 353,600 in the following year (see Table 3.2).

In terms of internationalization, Vietnam joined the WTO in 2007 and signed the General Agreement on Trade in Services (GATS). Under this agreement, Vietnamese HE started to compete with other HE providers. At present, there is a

Table 3.2 Statistics of Vietnamese higher education from 2006–2017

	2010	2011	2012	2013	2014	2015	2016	2017
HE institutions *	414	419	421	428	436	445	235	235
Public	334	337	340	343	347	357	170	170
Private	80	82	81	85	89	88	65	65
Teachers**	74.6	84.1	87.7	91.6	91.4	93.5	72.8	75.0
Public	63.3	70.4	73.9	75.2	74.1	76.1	57.6	59.3
Private	11.3	13.7	13.8	16.4	17.3	17.4	15.2	15.7
Students**	2,162.1	2,208.1	2,178.6	2,061.6	2,363.9	2,118.5	1,767.9	1,695.9
Public	1,828.2	1,873.1	1,855.2	1,792.0	2,050.3	1,847.1	1,523.9	1,432.6
Private	333.9	335	323.4	269.6	313.6	271.4	244	263.3
Graduates**	318.4	398.2	425.2	406.3	441.8	353.6	305.6	319.5
Public	278.3	334.5	357.2	350.6	377.9	308.7	268.4	282.0
Private	40.1	63.7	68.0	55.7	63.9	44.9	37.2	37.5

*unit: institution, **unit: thousand people; figures for 2016 and 2017 do not include colleges
Source: General Statistics Office of Vietnam (2019b)

foreign-owned university (Royal Melbourne Institute of Technology—RMIT) and a number of HE institutions established on the basis of collaboration between Vietnam and a foreign government (for example, the Viet-Germany University, Viet-France University, Fulbright Vietnam University, British University Vietnam). The aim is to make at least one of them a world-class university (Pham, 2014). In recent years, the system has also witnessed various programs offered on the basis of cooperation with foreign HE providers: 300 joint and twinning programs and 37 at-home internationalized programs (L.T. Tran & Marginson, 2018b). Multiple programs are also delivered in English to help students integrate into the global market (Nguyen, Walkinshaw, & Pham, 2017; L.T. Tran & Nguyen, 2018). All of these have diversified the HE system and catered for the need to increase international education in the country (L.T. Tran & Marginson, 2018a). Moreover, internationalization helps introduce new practices into the HE system, such as quality assurance and accreditation, credit-based curriculum, and student-centered pedagogies, to make the system more comparable with international practices (Do, Pham, & Nguyen, 2017; Le, Le, & Giang, 2017; L.H.N. Tran, Phan, & Tran, 2018). Furthermore, as a member of ASEAN, the universities in the system have had to adjust their programs to be more comparable with others, following the ASEAN Qualification Reference Framework (Menon & Melendez, 2017). All of these have exposed Vietnamese universities to opportunities for elevating themselves in the international arena of HE and at the same time require them to act and adapt to changes quickly or they will be left behind.

In the last decade, the Vietnamese HE system has been implementing the Higher Education Reform Agenda (HERA) to improve the quality of student learning outcomes and efficiency of university operation. This fundamental systemic reform agenda was approved by the government in 2005, including numerous ambitious targets for the HE system to achieve by 2020 (Harman et al., 2010). For example, the number of students enrolled in universities will triple compared to those in 2005; the number of staff with doctorate degrees will account for 40% of the total number of staff; the staff–student ratio will be 1:20 compared to the current 1:30; the curriculum will be renewed, restructured and internationalized; and the private sector will host 40% of total enrolments (Harman et al., 2010). There have not yet been any official reports on whether the targets have been met. However, a number of research studies indicate that HERA will face several challenges pursuing these ambitious targets. These include:

- **Financial constraints**: While the system is growing, the expenditure on HE is still low and lags behind other countries in the region; more critically, there is no hint of a workable strategy to finance the growth of the system and improve its quality (Harman et al., 2010).
- **Teaching and learning quality**: The quality of teaching and learning in Vietnamese HE is low because of the lack of formal preparation of academic staff for their teaching role, poor academic qualifications of the staff, low salary, the absence of a reward scheme to encourage quality teaching, a lack of curriculum autonomy, and inadequate learning materials (Harman & Bich,

2010; L.H.N. Tran et al., 2018). A lack of connection with industry also hinders producing graduates with qualities essential for the workplace (T.T. Tran, 2015).

- **Research and research commercialization**: Research activities in Vietnamese HE institutions are weak because of a lack of funding, heavy teaching workloads, lack of facilities and resources, and a developing research culture embedded in the system. Also, the linkage between the universities and broader society is not well-established, which hampers research commercialization activities to generate revenue for the universities (Fatseas, 2010; Harman & Le, 2010).
- **Governance, strategic planning and management**: The governance of HE in Vietnam is highly centralized. The lines of accountability between rectors and governing boards and their role in institutional governance are not clearly defined (Dao, 2015; Dao & Hayden, 2010). Institutional leadership and decision-making are seemingly in the hands of top-level university leaders (Nguyen, 2013). Recently, the Higher Education Law (Vietnamese Government, 2012) and the Higher Education Acts (MOET, 2014) have granted universities autonomy in curriculum and institutional operation to some extent; however, in practice, Vietnamese universities have not made good use of this autonomy.
- **Equity**: While the government is decentralizing financial autonomy to provincial and institutional levels, this may produce problems with equity access to HE. The provincial governments in impoverished areas cannot afford to support the colleges and universities in their regions, and the institutions have to charge for the provision of additional educational services. Thus, the underprivileged are unable to gain access to HE institutions (Evans & Rorris, 2010).
- **Quality accreditation**: The MOET is leading and regulating the universities to conduct some initiatives for quality assurance as well as linking these initiatives to the national university ranking (Vietnamese Government, 2015). Although these quality-assurance activities improve awareness of stakeholders about quality issues, they are progressing slowly and seem to be unable to compel universities to engage with them (Dao, 2015; Do et al., 2017; Tang & Yi-Fang, 2014).
- **Internationalization**: The current system is in a remarkable process of internationalization—increased number of Vietnamese international students, internationalized programs, international universities, staff exchange with a foreign institution, or short-term studies overseas for the university's staff (L.H.N. Tran, Hoang, & Vo, 2019; L.T. Tran & Marginson, 2018b). While these activities may contribute to improving the quality of HE, it may also increase "brain drain" and a tendency to rely on foreign ventures and partnerships (Welch, 2010). Other difficulties that it brings include an absence of national policy and support mechanisms, bureaucracy due to a top-down approach, and a lack of a holistic institutional approach to internationalization (L.T. Tran & Marginson, 2018a).

- **Privatization**: HERA proposed the private sector should account for 40% of enrolment by 2020, which means that a rapid expansion of the sector will occur in the next few years. However, incentives for this expansion are still not evident (Dao & Hayden, 2010), and practices of privatization are not clearly defined, resulting in twin privatization in public universities (Hoang, 2018).

At the institutional level, many universities in the system have paid attention to improving their positions in university-ranking leagues. In my personal search, I found that leaders of Can Tho University have been investing in building facilities and infrastructure, reforming pedagogical practice, upgrading the university's website, and training staff in order for it to have a better position in the leagues. Others, such as Ton Duc Thang University and Duy Tan University, are also moving in this direction, although they are focusing on becoming research-oriented institutions. All three mentioned universities have achieved remarkable results: from newly established universities or less-known universities in the system, they have become best Vietnamese universities in the QS World University Ranking or ARWU World University Ranking. This could be because university leaders have become aware of an increasing competition with universities in the region and in the world in terms of attracting prospective students. This could also be because MOET has launched a national scheme for ranking the universities in the system (Vietnamese Government, 2015) and will link this ranking with institutional privileges such as student enrolment quotas and institutional autonomy, as suggested by an official of the Department for Assessment and Quality Assurance in our personal conversation in late November 2015.

In conclusion, the literature indicates that in the contemporary socioeconomic, cultural, and political context, Vietnamese HE appears to possess the following characteristics:

- Various inherited education values—Confucian, Western, and socialist.
- A commitment to sustaining economic growth and the political regime.
- Operates under a fundamental reform agenda with ambitious targets.
- Centralized in terms of governance and management practices.
- A focus on teaching rather than research activities.
- Rapidly expanding but with poor teaching and learning quality.
- Lack of qualified staff.
- Lack of linkages with industry and society.
- Poor infrastructure and facilities.
- Weak quality-assurance activities.

The government's commitment to developing a skilled workforce

In the last decade, the government has demonstrated its commitment to improving the quantity and quality of the workforce. In several Vietnamese Government policies, decisions, and guidelines, education is the top national priority and developing a skilled labor workforce to meet socioeconomic objectives has always been key. Since the early 2000s, the government has clearly defined that developing a highly skilled workforce is the momentum of the industrialization and modernization of the nation as well as is key to social evolvement and rapid but sustainable economic development (Prime Minister, 2001). Likewise, the Educational Development Strategy for 2011–2020 sets out several objectives for the educational system in general and tertiary education in particular. Improving the quality of education appeared to be the focus of the strategy.

> ... educational quality will be improved comprehensively, including teaching ethics, life skills, creative ability, practice skills, foreign language competence and computer skills to meet the demand of the labor market, specially skilled labor for the industrialization and modernization of the country and building a knowledge economy ... (Prime Minister, 2012)

Specifically, for vocational and higher education, the Strategy elaborated the objectives, including:

- Complete the structure of vocational education and higher education.
- Adjust professional structure and educational levels.
- Improve education and training quality to meet the demand for socioeconomic development.
- Produce creative graduates with independent thinking, citizen responsibility, professional ethics, foreign-language competence, work discipline, industrial professionalism, ability to create jobs, adaptability to changes in the labor market, and ability to compete regionally and internationally.
- By 2020, all vocational schools will be able to enroll 30% of high school graduates, workers with tertiary education will account for 70% of the workforce, and there will be approximately 350–400 tertiary education students per 10,000 population.

Most recently, on 29 March 2018, in the capital city Hanoi, MOET in collaboration with the World Bank held a seminar to consult on the Higher Education Development Strategy for 2021–2030 and an extended vision to 2035. Although the Strategy is not yet available, the general objective is again placed on the importance of developing a skilled workforce for the knowledge economy, a workforce that can lead innovation and creativity in socioeconomic development and international integration (Q. Nguyen, 2018).

In practice, since the early 2000s, several initiatives have been developed to generate a strong and skillful workforce. Under the HERA, numerous reforms have been executed to improve the quality of HE, such as curriculum renewal, quality audit, adoption of active pedagogical practice, and improving English competence for teachers and students, to name a few (Do et al., 2017; Le et al., 2017; L.H.N. Tran et al., 2018). Likewise, new legislation has enabled the HE system to expand from 277 institutions in 2005 to 445 in 2015, an increase of almost 79%. Such extreme expansion obviously adds to the existing challenges of poor infrastructure, lack of facilities, and lack of staff, etc., as discussed earlier. Thus, it is unsurprising that while the number of HE graduates has increased, the quality of the workforce generally remains poor (Anh, 2011; Bodewig & Badiani-Magnusson, 2014; Nguyen, 2016; L.H.N. Tran, 2018b). In 2012, the then Prime Minister said of the quality of education and training between 2001 and 2010:

> Educational quality is still far behind the need for national development in the new era and compared to that of countries of advanced educational systems in the region and in the world. We have not resolved the puzzle of expansion in the quantity of students and the improvement of learning quality and professional expertise for students. Thus, graduates fail to adequately perform their work duties and there have been misbehaviors and inappropriate lifestyles in some student groups. (Prime Minister, 2012)

Therefore, MOET urged HE institutions to focus on developing students' soft skills, as employers lamented a lack of these skills in their employees, as reported earlier in this chapter. In early 2008, the then Minister of Education and Training required universities to engage in constructing and publishing the learning outcomes of their own institution by the end of 2008. He also emphasized that the enrolment quota would be allocated based on the quality of the learning outcomes of an institution: the better the quality provided, the higher the enrolment quota given.[1] However, not many of the universities responded to the recommendation. In 2010, MOET issued Guideline 2196/BGDĐT-GDĐH (MOET, 2010) commanding the HE institutions to write and publish the learning outcomes of each discipline offered in their institutions. The Guideline generally specified the expected learning outcomes of Vietnamese HE, outlined the steps toward creating and publishing the learning outcomes, and for the first time explicitly required universities to develop soft skills for their students in a national policy. According to the Guideline:

> ... learning outcomes are the specifications about the content of disciplinary knowledge; application skills, ability of technology comprehension and problem-solving; tasks that students can do upon graduation; and other specifications appropriate with levels and training disciplines ... (MOET, 2010)

The components of the HE outcomes specified in the Guidelines are:

- **Knowledge**: Disciplinary knowledge and professional capability.
- **Hard skills**: Specialized skills, profession-related application skills, problem-solving skills, situation-handling skills.
- **Soft skills**: Communication skills, teamwork skills, foreign-language skills, informatics skills.
- **Attitudes**: (i) Being aware of professional ethics and citizenship; (ii) being responsible and ethical, having a sense of professionalism, and a service attitude; (iii) self-study ability and creativeness at work.

Similar to the HE learning outcomes defined in the national qualification framework of other countries, the HE learning outcomes of Vietnamese universities comprise disciplinary knowledge, ability to apply specialized skills, and soft skills. However, Guideline 2196/BGDĐT-GDĐH did not provide any concrete definition of soft skills. Instead, it only gave a non-exhaustive list of soft skills that Vietnamese universities should develop for students. It is also interesting to note that MOET considered problem-solving skills and situation-handling skills as "hard skills," but studies often listed these two skills as soft skills. The soft skills recommended by MOET cover a range of work skills necessary in the workplace, attributes compatible with the socioeconomic, cultural, and political context of Vietnam, and skills that enable students to continue to learn throughout their life. The recommended soft skills in the Guideline suggest that MOET actually pays attention to solving the shortage of working skills in graduates currently entering the labor market, sustaining the system in the long term and anticipating the uncertain future of Vietnam. Because MOET only recommended a non-exhaustive list of soft skills, Vietnamese universities can choose to develop soft skills they perceive to be important for their students and relevant to their institutional context. This is an opportunity but at the same time a challenge for Vietnamese universities, particularly inexperienced ones, because they may struggle to implement a new aspect of the curriculum without detailed instruction from MOET. In addition, heavy teaching workloads, MOET's control over the curriculum, and centralized management structures, as discussed earlier, may present challenges for soft-skills implementation in each university.

In short, developing soft skills for students in Vietnamese universities has become a politically driven initiative, in addition to the socioeconomic pressure for skilled labor. In implementing MOET's soft-skills policy, Vietnamese universities may face challenges due to lack of experience as well as systemic and institutional barriers. The implementation may also be competing with other institutional priorities and reforms as the HE system was undergoing an unprecedented reform.

Responses of Vietnamese universities to skills demands

Prior to the issue of MOET's soft-skills policy, some studies related to the qualities of graduates were conducted using the perspectives of students, graduates, and employers (Nguyen, 2011; Trung & Swierczek, 2009; Truong & Metzger, 2007). The results generally suggested that graduates often lacked the sort of soft skills that employers needed and that there was a mismatch between the skills taught in the university and those demanded in the labor market. For example, Truong and Metzger (2007) surveyed 460 master's students, 153 employers, and 195 academics to establish quality indicators of business master's graduates in Vietnam. Despite differing opinions among the three groups of participants, the researchers found 19 variables for employability. Among them, the ability to apply knowledge in a work context, problem-solving skills, the "overall quality of work" (the final accomplishment of an assigned task), willingness to learn, enthusiasm, and self-motivation were the most important indicators. This study suggests skills that

Vietnamese business students should be trained in, but the researchers did not study the achievements of their graduates in these skills specifically.

Nguyen (2011) helped fill the research gap left by Truong and Metzger (2007) with a case study. He distributed a questionnaire to 120 employers/managers to investigate the competencies of the graduates in Ho Chi Minh International University, which was established with the goal of becoming a world-class university. The responses showed that the graduates were highly competent in most aspects in the workplace, except for those related to change leadership, networking, relationship building, and organizational and environment awareness. If even the graduates of such a well-supported university lacked soft skills, this suggests that graduates from "ordinary" universities would not possess adequate soft skills.

Slightly shifting the focus of the research from output to the process of skill delivery in HE, Trung and Swierczek (2009) sent mail surveys to 251 managers in private, state-owned, joint-venture and foreign-owned companies to collect their feedback about the skills of graduates from Vietnamese universities. They also surveyed 717 final-year students and 1,838 students of other years to explore their opinions about the delivery of competencies and skills in every course. The data from both surveys indicated that the delivery of skills and graduate competencies was below standard, especially interpersonal skills for effective teamwork.

After Guideline 2196/BGDĐT-GDĐH (MOET, 2010), research related to employability and/or soft-skills implementation in Vietnamese universities is scarce. T.T. Tran (2013) conducted a qualitative study to examine the interpretation and expectations of students, recent graduates, and employers regarding employability skills in Vietnam. She found that the majority of the students equated skills with knowledge; others sought to develop soft skills for themselves by attending skills classes outside the university. Even more negatively, many students simply let the situation go on without taking action. Meanwhile, employers preferred to employ graduates with a high level of soft skills and relevant work experience. The researcher argued that developing employability skills for students needed the collaboration of many HE stakeholders, but foremost the university, employers, and students. In addition, Truong, Laura, and Shaw (2016) interviewed 15 employers of large and well-known enterprises across Vietnam to explore the importance of soft skills in business success, identifying 19 soft skills essential for business programs. They called on business schools to integrate these skills into the curricula and argued that doing so would help advance the national and global economic interests of Vietnam. Moreover, (T.N. Nguyen, 2018) progressed further by reviewing relevant literature and proposing a model to develop soft skills for students in Vietnamese universities following the CDIO engineering education concept (for example, see Berggren et al., 2003). Although this paper addressed how to develop soft skills for students, it was only a literature review and conceptual paper. The only project that directly addresses how soft skills are delivered belongs to Vo, Berglund, and Daniels (2017). However, this project is underway and has no confirmed findings.

My personal search of Vietnamese universities' websites revealed that most programs offered by these universities have published the intended learning outcomes of which soft skills are a part. However, hardly any documents were found that showed how soft skills are developed for students, except for the Hanoi-based Vietnam National University. Nonetheless, on the website of each university, there are several announcements of soft-skills development courses organized for students as part of the curriculum or in cooperation with an external provider.

All of the studies above suggest that training soft skills for students is underway in Vietnamese universities. However, an absence of documentations and publications on this topic and responses of the universities to MOET's soft-skills policy suggests that developing soft skills for students could be overlooked because it occurs amidst many other institutional and systemic reforms. This lack of response also indicates that the universities could be facing challenges, which should be examined to provide timely support.

Conclusion

Vietnam is a developing country with the potential to have a strong economy. Its young population, abundance of natural resources, increased foreign investment, and proliferation in internationalization has helped the country experience a steady growth in all socioeconomic, cultural, and political aspects. However, it is experiencing a shortage in skilled workers, which the World Bank and local economists argue is the greatest hindrance to its future development. Since the early 2000s, the government has invested in reforming education, especially tertiary education, aiming to produce generations of skilled graduates who will serve the modernization and industrialization of the country. Despite remarkable achievements, HE graduates are reported not to be able to conduct work duties as well as expected. Employers keep lamenting a severe lack of soft skills in their employees. Thus, MOET encouraged and then commanded the universities to launch initiatives to equip students with soft skills to build their employability. A decade has passed since MOET's first attempts to require universities to develop these skills for students; however, there has been a lack of research into what is going on at the institutional level with regard to developing those skills. Vietnamese HE is a complex sector with characteristics different to its Western counterparts, and is under an unprecedented process of reform. This context presents a special case for investigating how soft skills for employability are being built in non-Western universities.

Note

1 In Vietnam, HE institutions are not allowed to enroll students as they wish; instead, they follow the quota annually allotted by MOET, as at the time this book is written.

References

Anh, H. (2011). 94% sinh viên ra trường phải đào tạo tiếp. *Thanh Nien Online*, 1 Dec. Retrieved from https://bit.ly/2W9Hcjy

Berggren, K.-F., Brodeur, D., Crawley, E. F., Ingemarsson, I., Litant, W. T., Malmqvist, J., & Östlund, S. (2003). CDIO: An international initiative for reforming engineering education. *World Transactions on Engineering and Technology Education*, 2(1), 49–52.

Bodewig, C., & Badiani-Magnusson, R. (2014). *Skilling up Vietnam: Preparing the workforce for a modern market economy*. Washington DC: World Bank Publications.

Cao, L. (2000). *Reflections on market reform in post-war, post-embargo Vietnam*. Retrieved from: https://scholarship.law.wm.edu/facpubs/145

Cui, D. (2007). A weakness in Confucianism: Private and public moralities. *Frontiers of Philosophy in China*, 2(4), 517–532.

Dao, K. V. (2015). Key challenges in the reform of governance, quality assurance, and finance in Vietnamese higher education: A case study. *Studies in Higher Education*, 40(5), 745–760.

Dao, V. K., & Hayden, M. (2010). Reforming the governance of higher education in Vietnam. In G. Harman, M. Hayden, & T. N. Pham (Eds.), *Reforming higher education in Vietnam* (pp. 129–142). New York, NY: Springer.

Dien, A. (2014). Vietnam's cheap labour may turn out to be a hard sell. *Thanh Nien News*, 5 March. Retrieved from https://bit.ly/2W10GXP

Do, Q. T., Pham, H. T., & Nguyen, K. D. (2017). Quality assurance in the Vietnamese higher education: A top-down approach and compliance-driven QA. In M. Shah & Q. T. N. Do (Eds.), *The rise of quality assurance in Asian higher education* (pp. 191–207). Cambridge, MA: Elsevier.

Doan, D. H. (2005). Moral education or political education in the Vietnamese educational system? *Journal of Moral Education*, 34(4), 451–463.

Evans, K., & Rorris, A. (2010). Optimising the impact of Vietnam's higher education sector on socio-economic development. In G. Harman, M. Hayden, & T. N. Pham (Eds.), *Reforming higher education in Vietnam* (pp. 167–181). New York, NY: Springer.

Fatseas, M. (2010). Research–industry cooperation supporting development in Vietnam: The challenge of translating policy into practice. In G. Harman, M. Hayden, & T. N. Pham (Eds.), *Reforming higher education in Vietnam* (pp. 103–115). New York, NY: Springer.

Gates, C. L. (1995). Enterprise reform and Vietnam's transformation to a market-oriented economy. *ASEAN Economic Bulletin*, 12(1), 29–52.

General Statistics Office of Vietnam (2019a). *Dân số trung bình phân theo giới tính và thành thị, nông thôn (Population ratio according to genders and living areas)*. Retrieved from www.gso.gov.vn/default.aspx?tabid=714

General Statistics Office of Vietnam (2019b). *Giáo dục đại học và cao đẳng (Higher education and vocational education)*. Retrieved from https://gso.gov.vn/default.aspx?tabid=722.

Ha, T. (2015). Businesses more concerned about human resources quality. *Vietnam Business Forum*, 13 August. Retrieved from http://vccinews.com/news_detail.asp?news_id=32452

Hadad, S. (2017). Knowledge economy: Characteristics and dimensions. *Management Dynamics in the Knowledge Economy*, 5(2), 203–225.

Harman, G., Hayden, M., & Nghi, P. T. (2010). *Higher education in Vietnam: Reform, challenges and priorities*. New York, NY: Springer.

Harman, G., & Le, T. B. N. (2010). The research role of Vietnam's universities. In G. Harman, M. Hayden, & T. N. Pham (Eds.), *Reforming higher education in Vietnam* (pp. 87–102). New York, NY: Springer.

Harman, K., & Bich, N. T. N. (2010). Reforming teaching and learning in Vietnam's higher education system. In G. Harman, M. Hayden, & P. T. Nghi (Eds.), *Reforming higher education in Vietnam: Challenges and priorities* (pp. 65–86). New York, NY: Springer.

Hoang, L. (2018). Twin privatization in Vietnam higher education: The emergence of private higher education and partial privatization of public universities. *Higher Education Policy.* doi: 10.1057/s41307-018-0086-8

Huong, P. L., & Fry, G. W. (2002). The emergence of private higher education in Vietnam: Challenges and opportunities. *Educational Research for Policy and Practice*, 1(1–2), 127–141.

Huong, P. L., & Fry, G. W. (2004). Education and economic, political, and social change in Vietnam. *Educational Research for Policy and Practice*, 3(3), 199–222.

Irvin, G. (1995). Vietnam: Assessing the achievements of Doi Moi. *The Journal of Development Studies*, 31(5), 725–750.

Jurje, F., & Lavenex, S. (2015). *ASEAN Economic Community: What model for labour mobility.* Retrieved from https://bit.ly/2vkoEBI.

Kim, H., & Mobrand, E. (2019). Stealth marketisation: How international school policy is quietly challenging education systems in Asia. *Globalisation, Societies and Education.* doi: 10.1080/14767724.2019.1571405.

Lagemann, E. C., & Lewis, H. (2015). *What is college for? The public purpose of higher education.* New York, NY: Teachers College Press.

Le, B. V., Le, H. M., & Giang, P. (2017). Implementing the credit-based education model in Vietnamese universities. *Tropicultura*, 34, 20–30. Retrieved from www.tropicultura.org/text/v34ns/20.pdf

London, J. D. (2006). Vietnam: The political economy of education in a "Socialist" periphery. *Asia Pacific Journal of Education*, 26(1), 1–20.

Ly, T. H. (2015). Confucian influences on Vietnamese culture. *Vietnam Social Sciences*, 5, 71–82. Retrieved from https://bit.ly/2Vkd4VB

ManPowerGroup (2011). *Building a high-skilled economy: A new Vietnam.* Retrieved from https://bit.ly/2XCRMjz

Menon, J., & Melendez, A. C. (2017). Realizing an Asean Economic Community: Progress and remaining challenge. *The Singapore Economic Review*, 62(3), 681–702.

MOET (2010). *Công văn 2916/ BGDĐT-GDĐH hướng dẫn xây dựng và công bố chuẩn đầu ra ngành đào tạo.* Retrieved from https://bit.ly/2VlKS4I

MOET (2014). *Quyết định số 70/2014/QĐ-TTg của Thủ tướng Chính phủ: Ban hành Điều lệ trường đại học.* Retrieved from https://bit.ly/2ID92lp

Nguyen, H. (2015). Globalization, consumerism, and the emergence of teens in contemporary Vietnam. *Journal of Social History*, 49(1), 4–19.

Nguyen, H. T., Walkinshaw, I., & Pham, H. H. (2017). EMI programs in a Vietnamese university: Language, pedagogy and policy issues. In B. Fenton-Smith, P. Humphreys, & I. Walkinshaw (Eds.), *English medium instruction in higher education in Asia-Pacific* (pp. 37–52). Cham, Switzerland: Springer.

Nguyen, M. T. (2011). Vietnamese students' employability skills. *International Education Studies*, 4(4), 175.

Nguyen, N. D., Ngoc, N. B., & Montague, A. (2019). Enhancing graduate work-readiness in Vietnam. In S. Dhakal, V. Prikshat, A. Nankervis, & J. Burgess (Eds.), *The Transition from graduation to work* (pp. 221–237). Singapore: Springer.

Nguyen, Q. (2018). Xây dựng Chiến lược tổng thể phát triển giáo dục đại học ở Việt Nam. *Nhân Dân*, 29 March. Retrieved from https://bit.ly/2GrRHbA

Nguyen, T. (2016,). Employers lament lack of soft skills in graduates. *University World News*, 22 Jan. Retrieved from https://bit.ly/2ZsVDRT

Nguyen, T. L. H. (2013). Middle-level academic management: A case study on the roles of the heads of department at a Vietnamese university. *Tertiary Education and Management*, 19(1). doi: 10.1080/13583883.2012.724704

Nguyen, T. N. (2018). Issues in soft skills development for Vietnamese students in current undergraduate programs. *Tạp chí Khoa học*, 15(7), 114–124.

Nordeatrade (2019). *The economic context of Vietnam*. Retrieved from https://bit.ly/2Uv58fW

Pham, H. (2013). Graduate unemployment and 'over-education' rising. *University World News*, 13 July. Retrieved from https://bit.ly/2IPY5w7

Pham, H. (2014). Vietnam: Aiming for at least one world-class university by 2020. *University World News*, 24 Jan. Retrieved from https://bit.ly/2IPZ8Mn

Prime Minister (2001). *Quyết định 201/2001/QĐ-TTg của Thủ tướng Chính Phủ phê duyệt Chiến lược phát triển giáo dục 2001–2010 (Prime Minister's decision 201/2001/QĐ-TTg on approval of the educational development strategy 2001–2010)*. Retrieved from https://bit.ly/2GD9QEA

Prime Minister (2012). *Quyết định 711/QĐ-TTg về việc phê duyệt chiến lược phát triển giáo dục 2011–2020 (Decision 711/QĐ-TTg on the approval of the educational development strategy for 2011–2020)*. Retrieved from https://bit.ly/2vhzkRg

Sanders, S. R. (2014). North versus south: The effects of foreign direct investment and historical legacies on poverty reduction in post-Đổi Mới Vietnam. *Journal of Vietnamese Studies*, 9(2), 46–67.

Schaumburg-Müller, H., & Chuong, P. H. (2010). *The new Asian dragon: Internationalization of firms in Vietnam*. Copenhagen: Copenhagen Business School Press.

Tang, T. T., & Yi-Fang, L. (2014). Stakeholders' perspectives on quality assurance in Vietnamese higher education. *Higher Education Evaluation and Development*, 8(2), 1–30. doi: 10.6197/HEED.2014.0802.01

Tran, H. T., & Santarelli, E. (2018). *Successful transition to a market economy in Vietnam: An interpretation from organizational ecology theory*. Retrieved from www.econstor.eu/bitstream/10419/174886/1/GLO-DP-0181.pdf

Tran, L. H. N. (2017). Developing employability skills via extra-curricular activities in Vietnamese universities: Student engagement and inhibitors of their engagement. *Journal of Education and Work*, 30(8), 854–867.

Tran, L. H. N. (2018a). Game of blames: Higher education stakeholders' perceptions of causes of Vietnamese graduates' skills gap. *International Journal of Educational Development*, 62(Sep), 302–312.

Tran, L. H. N. (2018b). The skills gap of Vietnamese graduates and final-year university students. *Journal of Education and Work*, 31(7–8), 579–594.

Tran, L. H. N., Hoang, T. G., & Vo, P. Q. (2019). At-home international education in Vietnamese universities: Impact on graduates' employability and career prospects. *Higher Education*. doi: 10.1007/s10734–10019–00372-w

Tran, L. H. N., Phan, T. N. P., & Tran, L. K. H. (2018). Implementing the student-centred teaching approach in Vietnamese universities: The influence of leadership and management practices on teacher engagement. *Educational Studies*. doi: 10.1080/03055698.2018.1555453

Tran, L. T., Le, T. T. T., & Nguyen, N. T. (2014). Curriculum and pedagogy. In *Higher education in Vietnam: Flexibility, mobility and practicality in the global knowledge economy* (pp. 86–107). London: Palgrave Macmillan.

Tran, L. T., & Marginson, S. (2018a). Internationalisation of Vietnamese higher education: An overview. In L. T. Tran & S. Marginson (Eds.), *Internationalisation in Vietnamese higher education* (pp. 1–16). Cham, Switzerland: Springer.

Tran, L. T., & Marginson, S. (2018b). Internationalisation of Vietnamese higher education: Possibilities, challenges and implications. In L. T. Tran & S. Marginson (Eds.), *Internationalisation in Vietnamese higher education* (pp. 253–257). Cham, Switzerland: Springer.

Tran, L. T., Ngo, M., Nguyen, N., & Dang, X. T. (2017). Hybridity in Vietnamese universities: An analysis of the interactions between Vietnamese traditions and foreign influences. *Studies in Higher Education*, 42(10), 1899–1916.

Tran, L. T., & Nguyen, H. T. (2018). Internationalisation of higher education in Vietnam through English Medium Instruction (EMI): Practices, tensions and implications for local language policies. In I. Liyanage (Ed.), *Multilingual education yearbook 2018* (pp. 91–106). Cham, Switzerland: Springer.

Tran, T. T. (2013). Limitation on the development of skills in higher education in Vietnam. *Higher Education*, 65(5), 631–644.

Tran, T. T. (2015). Is graduate employability the 'whole-of-higher-education-issue'? *Journal of Education and Work*, 28(3), 207–227.

Tran, V. T. (2013). Vietnamese economy at the crossroads: New doi moi for sustained growth. *Asian Economic Policy Review*, 8(1), 122–143.

Trung, T. Q., & Swiercek, F. W. (2009). Skills development in higher education in Vietnam. *Asia Pacific Business Review*, 15(4), 565–586.

Truong, H. T., Laura, R. S., & Shaw, K. (2016). New insights for soft skills development in Vietnamese business schools: Defining essential soft skills for maximizing graduates' career success. *International Journal of Social, Behavioral, Educational, Economic, Business and. Industrial Engineering*, 10(6), 1857–1863.

Truong, Q. D., & Metzger, C. (2007). Quality of business graduates in Vietnamese institutions: Multiple perspectives. *Journal of Management Development*, 26(7), 629–643.

Vietnamese Congress (2011). *Nghị quyết đại hội đại biểu toàn quốc lần thứ XI Đảng Cộng Sản Việt Nam*. Retrieved from https://bit.ly/2ZsfUXZ

Vietnamese Congress (2016). *Nghị quyết Đại hội lần thứ XII của Đảng*. Retrieved from https://bit.ly/2XG7R8h

Vietnamese Government (2012). *Luật giáo dục đại học*. Retrieved from https://bit.ly/2GNGV24

Vietnamese Government (2015). *Nghị định: Quy định tiêu chuẩn phân tầng, khung xếp hạng và tiêu chuẩn xếp hạng cơ sở giáo dục đại học (73/2015/NĐ-CP)*. Retrieved from https://bit.ly/2VnRgbJ

Vietnamese Government (2018). *Nghị định số 86/2018/NĐ-CP của Chính phủ : Quy định về hợp tác, đầu tư của nước ngoài trong lĩnh vực giáo dục (Government's Decision 86/2018/NĐ-CP on regulations on cooperation and investment in education with foreign stakeholders)*. Retrieved from https://bit.ly/2W53Qty

Vietnamnet (2018). Japan leads foreign investors in Vietnam in 2018. 29 Dec. Retrieved from: https://bit.ly/2WOskHc

Vo, H.-P., Berglund, A., & Daniels, M. (2017). A perspective from Vietnamese students on teaching of soft skills. Paper presented at the International Conference on Learning and Teaching in Computing and Engineering (LaTICE). Retrieved from https://ieeexplore.ieee.org/document/8064426

Welch, A. R. (2010). Internationalisation of Vietnamese higher education: Retrospect and prospect. In G. Harman, M. Hayden, & T. N. Pham (Eds.), *Reforming higher education in Vietnam* (pp. 197–213). New York, NY: Springer.

World Bank (2008). *Vietnam: Higher education and skills for growth*. Retrieved from https://openknowledge.worldbank.org/handle/10986/7814

4 Models for the development of soft skills for students in Vietnamese universities

Introduction

In recent years, there has been an increasing demand for graduates who can undertake work duties effectively (for example, Hurrell, 2016; Jones, Baldi, Phillips, & Waikar, 2017; Stevens & Norman, 2016). As a response, universities have paid more attention to deploying strategies to develop students' soft skills, in addition to professional expertise and academic abilities (Barrie, Hughes, Smith, & Thomson, 2009; Jääskelä, Nykänen, & Tynjälä, 2018; Kinash, Crane, Schulz, Dowling, & Knight, 2014; Tran, 2017). Soft skills are defined as non-discipline-specific skills that may be achieved through learning and can be applied to study, work, and life contexts (Tertiary Education Quality and Standards Agency, 2013). These skills may include communication, teamwork, and problem-solving skills, among many others. They have been found to increase graduates' employment outcomes and overall work performance, empower their lifelong learning abilities, prepare them for an unknown future, and enable them to act for the social good (Adnan, Daud, Alias, & Razali, 2017; Hager & Holland, 2006).

The literature, however, indicates that soft skills are implemented with different approaches, curriculum types, and pedagogical practices across HE systems and institutions. Such disparities were found to be associated with differences in the national context, institutional vision and mission, and stakeholders' underlying perceptions of soft skills (Al-Mahmood & Gruba, 2007; Barrie et al., 2009; Jääskelä et al., 2018). However, these implementation models are derived from the Western HE context, which may not be relevant to HE institutions in Eastern countries due to differences in educational values, sociocultural aspects, economic status, and even political regimes. Therefore, models for implementing a soft-skills policy in a non-Western context should be investigated to expand our understanding in this regard.

Complementing existing literature about how best to develop students' soft skills, this chapter reports on models that six Vietnamese universities developed. It will also analyze factors influencing the development of these models and discuss factors contributing to the effectiveness of each of these models. Content analysis of relevant documents and 69 interviews with key informants of the implementation reveal that despite selecting different soft skills, these universities shared similar conceptualization for executing their soft-skills policy: develop work-readiness for students. However, these universities translated the concept into practice differently, in terms of implementation scale, key players, and pedagogical practices to impart soft skills to students. The analysis showed that curriculum autonomy, university leadership, and connection with external stakeholders were pivotal for the adoption of these models. This chapter contributes to existing literature regarding the diversity of strategies that universities around the world are using to develop soft skills for students. The identified models would provide more options for universities with similar institutional contexts for the execution of the soft-skills policy in their institutions.

Context of soft-skills implementation in Vietnamese HE

Vietnam is a developing non-English-speaking country whose HE system possesses some different characteristics from those in the West. The contemporary HE is strongly characterized by a Confucian HE model (Marginson, 2011) infused with socialist ideologies, and it also possesses many Confucian morals and Western educational heritages (Harman, Hayden, & Nghi, 2010; Huong & Fry, 2011; Tran, Marginson, et al., 2014). The general aim of HE in Vietnam is to produce human resources with adequate skills and attributes to sustain the nation and to integrate it globally (Vietnamese Government, 2012).

Developing employability skills for university students has become an urgent mission for Vietnamese universities lately. Since *Doi Moi*, Vietnam has experienced a high economic growth rate for many successive years and is on target to become an industrialized and modernized country by 2020 (World Bank, 2008, 2018). Unfortunately, recent studies have showed that there is a lack of graduates with adequate levels of work skills, especially soft skills (Anh, 2011; Bodewig & Badiani-Magnusson, 2014; Tran, 2018; World Bank, 2008). After joining the World Trade Organization (WTO), signing the General Agreement on Trade Services (GATS) (Varghese, 2007), and becoming a member of the ASEAN Economic Community (International Labour Organisation and Asian Development Bank, 2014; Menon & Melendez, 2017), Vietnam is subjected to free labor flows in and out of the country. This indicates that without a skilled workforce, Vietnam will not be able to sustain its local labor market and compete in regional or global ones. Therefore, the HE system is expected to produce graduates who possess substantial specialized knowledge, technical skill, and soft skills to maintain competitiveness for Vietnam.

In that context, the Ministry of Education and Training (MOET) has committed to improving the quality of students' learning outcomes. The HE system has been undergoing unprecedented reforms since the early 2000s (Harman et al., 2010). One of the central targets of the reforms is to increase the quantity and quality of university graduates, following the advice of the World Bank's consultation on planning human resources development (Nghi & London, 2010). In 2010, MOET issued Guideline 2196/BGDĐT-GDĐH (MOET, 2010), which mandated Vietnamese universities develop soft skills for students. Examples of soft skills were listed as communication skills, teamwork skills, foreign-language skills, and informatics skills. Problem-solving and situation-handling skills were classified as hard skills. The Guideline also recommended developing students' attitudes, such as making them aware of professional ethics and citizenship, being responsible and ethical, having a sense of professionalism and service, and self-study ability and creativeness at work. This confirms that in different countries, the relevance of soft skills differs, as discussed in Chapter 1.

As such, on top of being aspirational for addressing socioeconomic demands, developing soft skills has become a politically driven initiative for all universities in Vietnam now. However, execution of a soft-skills policy faces numerous obstacles, including a lack of curriculum and institutional autonomy, inadequacy of qualified teachers, and insufficient resources, to name a few (Harman et al., 2010; Tran, Marginson, et al., 2014). Unfortunately, there have been very few studies that specifically investigate how the soft-skills policy has been realized in universities. Therefore, this aspect should be explored to provide universities with support where necessary.

Elements in soft-skills-implementation models

The term "soft-skills-implementation model" in this study refers to four elements associated with tasks in executing a soft-skills policy in a HE institution: the conceptualization of the implementation, the implementation scale, curriculum design, and pedagogical practices. The literature suggests that many factors are associated with these tasks, creating variances across the implementation models.

Conceptualization of the implementation: The concept that a university adopts for soft-skills implementation can shape the selection and delivery of soft skills (Al-Mahmood & Gruba, 2007; Barrie et al., 2009; Pitman & Broomhall, 2009). At the institutional level, HE institutions often adopt a concept with due attention to the characteristics of disciplines, institutional situation, and national context (Pitman & Broomhall, 2009). At the personal level, different groups of stakeholders may have different perspectives about relevant soft skills for students to develop (Barrie et al., 2009). Therefore, if universities favor a certain group of stakeholders' perspectives, that group will play a major role in shaping the content of the implementation. However, in the current context of HE, there is little space for dialogue and discussion between those groups (Barrie et al., 2009). In most cases, the perspectives of employers, academics, and professional bodies are often taken into account, but students' perspectives are often ignored or assumed to be employment-related.

Scale of the implementation: Universities can execute a soft-skills policy on a university-wide scale (Fleming, Donovan, Beer, & Clark, 2013), using a top-down leadership approach to ensure harmonious progress across disciplines and schools. However, it often fails to gain academics' buy-in because their perspectives are often not taken into account, which may result in compliant implementation rather than engagement. In contrast, some universities have put their soft-skills policy into practice on a program-wide scale (O'Neill, 2010; Willcoxson, Wynder,

& Laing, 2010). Barrie et al. (2009) observed that this approach starts with academic initiatives for training students in soft skills in the classroom. They argued that this leadership approach may engage teachers with teaching and assessing soft skills, but it may not be widespread without institutional policies and incentives.

Curriculum design: Some studies have reported curriculum types that universities design to impart soft skills to students (Al-Mahmood & Gruba, 2007; Barrie et al., 2009; Jääskelä et al., 2018). Generally, university leaders appear to design a soft-skills curriculum based on their viewpoint about the nexus between soft skills and discipline-specific skills. If they perceive that there is a close connection, the selected soft skills will be integrated and mapped across subjects of a curriculum as well as imparted within the context of a discipline by disciplinary teachers. This soft-skills curriculum design is often referred to as an embedded curriculum or integrated curriculum (Al-Mahmood & Gruba, 2007; Barrie et al., 2009; Jääskelä et al., 2018). The design can help students link soft skills with discipline-specific skills; however, it may make the implementation less visible and thus may cause people to gradually disengage. Also, mapping soft skills into the curriculum is complicated, and delivery of soft skills together with discipline-specific skills would multiply workloads for teachers; therefore, it may provoke resistance from teaching staff (Barrie et al., 2009).

In contrast, if they perceive that there is little or no connection between discipline-specific skills and soft skills, independent soft-skills subjects will be developed and imparted by skills experts to all students in the institution, regardless of their disciplines. These subjects are also organized as part of extra-curricular activities or foundational studies that facilitate students' transition into university life or from university to work (Al-Mahmood & Gruba, 2007; Barrie et al., 2009). While it is simpler to design and deliver such independent subjects, students may not be able to link these soft skills with discipline-specific skills. Such one-off soft-skills courses may not be long enough to help students attain a sufficient level of skill, if they do not engage to develop further on their own (Al-Mahmood & Gruba, 2007).

Pedagogical practices: The student-centered learning approach has been recognized to be conducive to developing soft skills for students. Many researchers have experimented and confirmed positive results of their teaching of soft skills using project or problem-based learning (Hendriana, Johanto, & Sumarmo, 2018; Ibrahim, Al-Shahrani, Abdalla, Abubaker, & Mohamed, 2018); community-service learning (Eike, Myers, & Sturges, 2018; Mak, Lau, & Wong, 2017); online and distance learning (Brodie, 2011; Myers et al., 2014); and work-integrated learning (WIL) (Losekoot, Lasten, Lawson, & Chen, 2018; Tran & Nguyen, 2018). The major obstacle for soft-skills implementation at the subject level is teacher engagement, which has been found to be associated with their perception of the relevance of soft skills in their subjects, their soft-skills expertise, institutional policy and incentives, student participation, and teaching practicalities (Barrie et al., 2009; de la Harpe & David, 2012; Jones, 2009). Therefore, to ensure a successful implementation of the soft-skills policy, it is important to develop teacher and institutional capacity, as well as consider a feasible pedagogical practice that fits well with the institutional context.

The present study

In 2013–2016, a study was conducted to investigate how soft-skills policies were executed in Vietnamese universities and identify influencers. Drawing from that project, this chapter will report the implementation models developed, analyze factors contributing to the development of such models, and discuss advantages and disadvantages of these models.

The study was conducted as a qualitative multiple case study, which provided an opportunity to investigate the implementation in depth and within its real context as well as compare the implementation across the cases (Yin, 2009). The study was narrowed down to the Business Administration program of six universities representing different institutional contexts. Based on the classification and history of universities, three public and three private universities were recruited for this study. Focusing on one program protected the disciplinary distinctiveness of soft-skills implementation (Jones, 2010). The Business Administration program was chosen because it is a popular program in Vietnamese universities and there is more evidence of soft-skills implementation in the School of Economics than in other schools.

The participants in each selected university were recruited using a snowball-sampling technique (Marcus, Weigelt, Hergert, Gurt, & Gelléri, 2017), which allowed the researcher to approach key informants of soft-skills implementation in a university based on the recommendation of another participant. In total, 69 university leaders, school leaders, disciplinary teachers,[1] and skills teachers,[2] as well as leaders[3] and staff members of the Youth Union and its associates (YUA),[3] were recruited (Table 4.1).

Data were collected by semi-structured interviews and relevant documents and policies that were either available on the university websites or provided by the participants. A qualitative content analysis was employed to analyze the data (Elo & Kyngäs, 2008). On a case-by-case basis, all relevant data were transcribed and repeatedly reviewed for content. Passages relevant to roles of external stakeholders in association with tasks in the analytical framework were highlighted and coded. Then, the codes across the cases were compared to find similarities and differences in external stakeholders' roles in soft-skills implementation across the universities. This step also involved evidence-based interpretation of factors influencing the

Table 4.1 A summary of participants

Universities	Participants
University A (public)	4 leaders, 7 teachers, 1 YUA leader, and 1 YUA staff member
University B (public)	4 leaders, 8 teachers, and 1 YUA leader
University C (public)	3 leaders, 9 teachers, and 1 YUA leader
University D (private)	4 leaders, 5 teachers, and 1 YUA staff member
University E (private)	3 leaders, 6 teachers, and 1 YUA staff member
University F (private)	3 leaders, 6 teachers, and 1 YUA staff member

Soft-skills implementation in the six universities

University A

Located in a regional city, University A is governed by MOET and the provincial authority in terms of academic affairs, finance, and administration. This structure is typical of public regional universities in Vietnam.

The School of Commerce and Business Administration first developed soft skills for students in 2002, with the twofold aim of increasing student engagement in their studies at the university and the graduates' employability. In 2009, following a university-wide curriculum renewal, soft-skills implementation in the school became more intensified. University and school leaders coordinated senior academics to select relevant soft skills and design skills subjects to impart learning and work-readiness skills to students. Due to MOET's regulation of credit numbers at that time (120–140 credits for an undergraduate program), the school could only add English, computer and communication skills subjects (7, 3, and 2 credits respectively, with a credit equivalent to 15 study periods of 45–50 minutes—as a conventional practice in Vietnamese universities) into the curriculum and leaves others as elective skills subjects. The skills subjects were taught by teachers in the school but were not connected to specialized subjects. Teachers outside of the School of Commerce and Business Administration taught foreign languages and computer skills. Disciplinary teachers of the Business Administration program had been encouraged to embed soft skills into their subjects where relevant, instead of being explicitly required to teach these skills. The interviewed teachers all stated that they used a student-centered teaching approach for delivering their subjects. In addition, students had to take a compulsory internship in the final year. The YUA also organized extracurricular activities (ECAs) to create more opportunities for students to engage in developing soft skills in conjunction with the main curricula. The YUA often invited skills experts and successful businesspeople to the university to organize skills classes or to share business experiences with students, respectively. They also led community-engagement activities so that students could develop social skills and service-oriented attitudes.

University B

Located in HCM City, a metropolitan city in Vietnam, University B is considered one of the *đại học trọng điểm* (key universities in the Vietnamese HE system). It has qualified academics plus an extensive network with industry, but unfortunately does not have curriculum autonomy. A prestigious institution without curriculum autonomy makes it a special case in this study.

University leaders suggested that before 2009, developing students' soft skills had primarily been the responsibility of the YUA. The university also required students to obtain a certificate in English and "soft-skills" as graduation requirements, which was provided by a recognized education provider in the city; thus, soft-skills implementation had relied heavily on external stakeholders. Aside from English and computer subjects (7 and 3 credits, respectively), which were taught to all students in the university regardless of their disciplines, there had been no subjects in the curriculum that specifically trained students in soft skills. The university leaders also suggested that they intentionally delayed executing MOET's soft-skills policy until 2015, when a number of institutional privileges came into effect, including curriculum autonomy. At the time of research, school leaders were directing teachers in the respective school to identify relevant soft skills, include them in the statement of learning outcomes, and prepare for the coming reform. In the School of Business Administration, a leader had identified and embedded the selected soft skills into a skills subject that aimed to enhance graduates' employment outcomes. Skills teachers would teach these skills subjects without direct connection to specialized subjects. Due to MOET's requirements for credit numbers, they prioritized soft skills that were more discipline-relevant in order to increase students' employment outcomes. Like in the School of Business Administration at University A, disciplinary teachers were encouraged to integrate soft skills into their subjects where relevant and feasible. They revealed that despite heavy teaching workloads, they attempted to use a student-centered learning approach in delivering their subjects. Students were required to take a compulsory internship in a relevant sector at the end of their study as a capstone subject. The YUA leader reported that they had organized diverse activities to help students develop soft skills, mostly community-engagement activities, charity work, and field trips to businesses.

University C

Located in an average-sized city, University C is considered one of the eight *đại học vùng* (the most important university in a geographical region). It is directly governed by MOET in terms of academic affairs, funding, and administration and is well known for its recent innovations in pedagogy and management practices.

Similar to University B, prior to 2013, University C focused on reforming its management practices and implementing student-centered pedagogy. It prioritized developing students' English skills (20 credits, and then cut down to 10 credits to fit with MOET's new curriculum structure of 120–140 credits per undergraduate program) and computer skills (3 credits). These skills subjects were taught to all students, regardless of their disciplines. In late 2013, university leaders decided to expand soft-skills implementation beyond English and computer skills to include those that would enable and encourage students to engage with their studies at the university and to obtain employment upon graduation. Therefore, they agreed that, in addition to ECAs, the YUA would coordinate at least one compulsory skills subject to all students in the university. At the same time, each school could design skills subjects to train students in soft skills that were relevant to the characteristics of the discipline, if applicable. The interviewed teachers of the School of Business all suggested that they had been trained in using student-centered pedagogies, so they felt confident using these practices in their teaching. Students were required to undertake a compulsory internship in the final year of their degree program. Finally, the YUA leader reported that they had organized several skills classes and some career fairs to develop work-readiness skills for students and led activities that enhanced students' social skills and service attitudes with the support of neighboring provincial authorities.

University D

Located in HCM City, University D was upgraded from a semi-public vocational college and is among 37 private universities established or upgraded after HERA was approved by MOET in 2005. University D is supervised by MOET but has been granted autonomy in curriculum and finance management. These privileges and the vocational education tradition make it a special case study.

Using curriculum autonomy, leaders of University D replaced the year-based curriculum with a credit-based curriculum in 2006 and started to focus on developing skills that would empower students with their learning and improve their chances of employment. In 2010, leaders of University D founded the Department for General Education to deliver a co-curriculum of skills to all students in the first two years at the university. This department coordinated nine skills subjects, and students were required to complete at least three out of the nine (9 credits). Students were also trained in English and computer skills (28 and 3 credits, respectively). The skills teachers consistently said that they were trained on, and required to use, a WIL approach to delivering their subjects. The disciplinary teachers also reported that they were required to train students in soft skills alongside disciplinary knowledge, using a WIL approach. In addition, students were required to work or take two compulsory internships, or to submit evidence of equivalent work experience in a local industry for exemption of the internships. Extracurricular activities were frequently organized by the YUA as an additional channel for students to develop soft skills. A special feature of ECAs at University D was that the agenda and the 20 clubs were established and operated by the students themselves, and YUA leaders only gave support when necessary.

University E

Located in a regional city, University E is among 37 private universities established or upgraded after HERA was approved by MOET in 2005. This university reports to MOET and does not have curriculum autonomy. It represents newly established private universities in Vietnam.

In spite of not having curriculum autonomy, University E uses a similar implementation model to that of University D. In 2008, university leaders founded the School for General Science and developed skills subjects to train all students in their first three years at the university. Like most universities in this study, they could only add communication skills, computer skills, and English skills (2, 3, and 24 credits, respectively) into the curriculum and left others as electives. Suggested by the rector and skills teachers, this skills curriculum aimed to train students in social values and skills that would enhance their learning and employment prospects. In the main curriculum, all disciplinary teachers were encouraged to train students in soft skills in conjunction with disciplinary knowledge. In addition, university leaders attempted to adopt WIL by employing successful, qualified people from industry to teach skills and disciplinary subjects. However, as suggested by most participants, due to being a newly established university and being located in a regional city, employment of qualified industry-based teachers like this was difficult and did not seem to help execute WIL very effectively. Business students in the university also had to take a compulsory internship in a local industry. Alternatively, they could submit evidence of equivalent work experience for internship exemption. Like the previous universities, the YUA in this university organized some seminars where local employers and recruiters shared business experiences and helped students with concerns about employment. The YUA also led some career fairs, charity work, and social-engagement activities.

University F

Located in HCM City, University F is one of 17 private universities in Vietnam that were established in the 1990s. The university is supervised by MOET primarily in terms of academic affairs. It represents the longest-established private universities in Vietnam.

At the time of research, English and computer subjects (4 and 10 credits, respectively) were taught to all students in the university. The university leaders suggested that they were finalizing the process to transfer its status from being a people-founded university to non-public. Therefore, as the rector stated, each school in the university was encouraged to execute the soft-skills policy in their own way, so that students' employability could be enhanced. In his opinion, that was why the university experienced different levels of progress in the implementation between the schools. At the School of Business Administration, disciplinary teachers all stated that they had recommended adding skills subjects into the curriculum to train students in skills that would enhance their engagement with studies and employment opportunities; unfortunately, the dean rejected it, explaining that the graduates' employability had already been high for many successive years. However, he encouraged disciplinary teachers to teach soft skills to students where they could. Both skills and disciplinary teachers suggested that they used a student-centered approach in their teaching. Students were required to take a compulsory internship as part of their study. The YUA leader stated that they had greatly contributed to developing soft skills for students in the school. Under YUA leadership, a variety of clubs were established, which not only helped advance students' discipline-specific knowledge and skills, but also nurtured their generic and social-engagement skills. The YUA also provided career-consultation services and connected students with employers by organizing career fairs, meetings with successful business people, and field trips to companies and enterprises.

Soft-skills-implementation models in Vietnamese universities

In this section, similarities and differences in the conceptualization, scale of the implementation, the channels, and pedagogical practices through which soft skills are imparted to students will be analyzed. The analysis will help identify models for executing a soft-skills policy in Vietnamese universities.

Conceptualization: Although there were slight differences in selecting relevant soft skills to develop for students, all six Vietnamese universities had at least one of two complementary goals when developing soft skills for students: (i) enhancing students' engagement with their university studies, and (ii) improving graduates' employability. The former could contribute to the latter by improving students' learning outcomes. Therefore, the main concept of soft-skills implementation in Vietnamese universities was equipping students with the skills to obtain a job and efficiently perform work duties—i.e., developing students' work readiness.

Implementation scale: The case studies showed that to translate the conceptualization into practice, top-level leaders of universities C, D, and E directly coordinated the implementation university-wide. In contrast, top-level leaders of universities A, B, and F allowed mid-level university leaders to put their soft-skills policy into practice in their respective school—i.e., a school-wide scale.

Imparting channels: Soft skills were imparted to students via two channels—curriculum-based and extracurricular. Via curriculum-based activities, soft skills were developed for students within skills subjects and specialized subjects if teachers wanted. However, this channel could not deliver all of the skills they intended to develop for students. Therefore, to make it up, the universities also imparted soft skills to students via ECAs organized by the YUA. The findings showed that universities A, B, C, and F used ECAs as the main channel whereas universities D and E used these activities as an additional channel through which students could develop soft skills.

Pedagogies: Participants from universities A, B, C, and F reported that they were using a student-centered approach to deliver their subjects, including skills subjects, to students, and a compulsory internship—a form of WIL—to train students in both soft skills and discipline-specific skills. In addition, universities D and E attempted to use a WIL approach in executing their soft-skills policy, both in the classroom and via internships.

Based on the differences and similarities in the four elements of the implementation, three soft-skills-implementation models in Vietnamese universities can be identified (Table 4.2).

The model that University C used was a variance of the model used by universities A, B, and F, as this university implemented its soft-skills policy on a university wide scale whereas the other three executed it on a school-wide scale. Universities D and E had a minor difference in the roles students played (leaders versus followers) in the YUA's extracurricular activities. However, this difference

Table 4.2 Soft-skills-implementation models in Vietnamese universities

Model	Description
School-wide, extracurriculum-based University A University B University F	• Implementation concept: developing work-readiness skills • Implementation scale: school-wide • Main channels to impart soft skills: ECAs and some stand-alone skills subjects, which were taught without connection to the disciplinary context • Pedagogical practice: complementing ECAs, the formal curriculum helped impart soft skills via the use of student-centered pedagogies and a compulsory internship (WIL). Soft skills were not explicitly taught and assessed in specialized subjects
University-wide, extracurriculum-based model University C	• Implementation concept: developing work-readiness skills • Implementation scale: university-wide • Main channels to impart soft skills: ECAs and some stand-alone skills subjects, which were taught without connection to the disciplinary context • Pedagogical practice: complementing ECAs, the formal curriculum complementarily developed soft skills for students via the use of student-centered pedagogies and a compulsory internship (WIL). Soft skills were not explicitly taught and assessed in specialized subjects
University-wide, curriculum-based model University E University D	• Implementation concept: developing work-readiness skills • Implementation scale: school-wide • Principal channel to develop soft skills: the formal curriculum; ECAs were a complementary channel • Pedagogical practice: WIL (both in the classroom and via internships) were used to develop soft skills for students. Several skills subjects were taught independently in the first two years but with a connection to specialized subjects. Soft skills were explicitly taught and assessed in all subjects

did not relate to the four major elements used to categorize the implementation models. Therefore, both of them are classified as using the same soft-skills implementation model.

Factors influencing Vietnamese universities' adoption of a soft-skills-development model

The purpose of Vietnamese HE as defined in HE Law (Vietnamese Government, 2012) appeared to influence the conceptualization of soft-skills implementation. All six Vietnamese universities consistently developed work readiness for students, which fit with the purpose of producing a qualified workforce for building the nation. They also chose soft skills recommended in Guideline 2196/BGDĐT-GDĐH (MOET, 2010): communication skills, teamwork skills, foreign-language skills, informatics skills, and others that they found relevant. This alignment between the soft-skills-implementation concept and the HE purpose supports the discussion at the B-HERT (2003) roundtable in Australia that soft-skills implementation was linked to the defined purpose of HE. This conceptualization also fit with Vietnamese universities' aspirations to address socioeconomic demands for skills in the labor market (Anh, 2011; Bodewig & Badiani-Magnusson, 2014; Tran, 2018; World Bank, 2008). In a country of Confucian heritage like Vietnam, students' learning is often dependent on teachers (Tran, Phan, & Tran, 2018; Tran, Le, & Nguyen, 2014). Therefore, when entering universities, they need support to develop adequate skills so that they can integrate into the academic environment of the university and better engage with their learning. Likewise, Vietnamese parents are overprotective of their children; therefore, most of them lack essential life skills and soft skills (Tran, 2013). For these reasons, developing work skills for university students has become urgent and critical in Vietnamese HE.

In addition, the scale of the implementation appeared to depend on the leadership of each university. It was evident from the six case studies that conventional top-down leadership and management (Marginson, 2011; Nguyen, 2013) was used to coordinate implementation tasks. However, it was exercised differently across the six case studies. In universities C, D, and E, top-level university leaders coordinated the implementation on an institution-wide scale. As explained by some participants and leaders from these universities, this leadership practice would allow the implementation to proceed consistently between different schools and programs. In this way, they prioritized a harmonious implementation without considering the connection between soft skills and specialized skills. In contrast, top-level leaders of universities A, B, and F agreed that mid-level university leaders should execute their soft-skills policy in their respective school in their own strategies—i.e., implementation on a school-wide scale. This leadership approach, as stated by two university leaders, was to make soft-skills implementation fit more successfully into the context of each discipline or school. These findings indicate that differences in perceptions of leaders of these six universities about the connection between soft skills and specialized skills could have influenced their choice of implementation scale.

Moreover, institutional contexts, including curriculum autonomy and the existence of the YUA, seemed to affect their adoption of these channels for realizing their soft-skills policy via curriculum-based or extracurricular activities. Firstly, aside from University D, university leaders reported that without curriculum autonomy, they had to comply with MOET's regulation of 120–140 credits per undergraduate program. Adding more skills subjects into the curriculum would mean having fewer credits available for specialized subjects. Therefore, they had to prioritize some soft-skills subjects and leave others as electives or rely on the YUA. University D had curriculum autonomy, so it was easier for it to modify the curricula to develop soft skills for students. Secondly, the YUA's extracurricular activities were involved in order to develop students' soft skills because the YUA had successfully led social-engagement activities in Vietnamese universities for decades. As reported in the case studies, the YUA developed soft skills for students via organizing classes for CV writing and job-interview skills, community-engagement activities, career fairs, and career-consultation services. These ECAs were aligned with the main concept of the implementation: developing students' work readiness. Extracurricular activities were the main channel to realize soft skills policy in universities A, B, C, and F, but were an additional channel in universities D and E. Findings related to soft-skills-imparting channels suggest three things: (i) curriculum autonomy was a major factor determining whether soft skills could be developed via curriculum-based activities; (ii) ECAs may be an alternative for soft-skills implementation in the context of crowded curricula; and (iii) if universities develop soft skills for students via combined channels, these channels must complement each other and align with the concept of the implementation.

Furthermore, soft skills were imparted by different pedagogical practices. Participants in universities A, B, C, and F reported that they were using a student-centered approach, including an internship, in delivering their subjects, including skills subjects, to students. The use of a "student-centered learning approach" in translating their soft-skills policy into practice is predictable because this approach has been found to be conducive to students' development of soft skills (Eike et al., 2018; Hendriana et al., 2018; Losekoot et al., 2018). Also, in recent years, MOET has launched several initiatives to help teachers in Vietnamese universities stay away from the traditional theory-based pedagogical practice to engaging with more active teaching–learning activities in the classroom (Harman & Bich, 2010; Tran et al., 2018). Under the student-centered approach, WIL in the form of a compulsory internship has long been used in Vietnamese universities. In participants' views, it was where students could develop the most relevant soft skills for their future career. In addition, universities D and E attempted to use a WIL approach in executing their soft-skills policy, both in the classroom and via an internship. For both universities, their institutional visions were to produce skilled graduates that met employers' demands. They recruited teachers with relevant industry experience and trained teachers in pedagogical practices to deploy the use of WIL. This pedagogical practice was innovative and also risky, considering not many Vietnamese universities had extensive connections and work experience with industry (Tran, 2009; Tran, 2016). As such, the adoption of pedagogical practices to impart soft skills to students appeared to depend on the teacher capacity and connections with industry a university had.

In short, factors influencing the adoption of implementation models in Vietnamese universities were:

- The defined purpose of the HE.
- Socioeconomic and cultural issues in the country.
- University leadership conventions.
- University leaders' perception of the nexus between soft skills and specialized skills.
- The level of curriculum autonomy that Vietnamese universities have.
- The roles of the YUA extracurricular activities in Vietnamese universities.
- Teacher capacity.
- Connections with industry.

The discussion in this section confirms the notion that there are diverse strategies and models that HE institutions develop to impart soft skills to their students (Al-Mahmood & Gruba, 2007; Barrie et al., 2009; Jääskelä et al., 2018). The development or adoption of these models depends much on contextual factors and personal perceptions about soft skills and their characteristics (Al-Mahmood & Gruba, 2007; Barrie et al., 2009).

Conclusion

This study found that soft-skills implementation in Vietnamese universities was conceptualized as developing work-readiness skills for student. The concept was translated into practice via both curriculum-based and extracurricular activities using a student-centered approach, which included work-integrated learning. The analysis showed that the adoption of soft-skills-implementation models in these universities was influenced by the socioeconomic and cultural context of the country, the HE purpose, university leaders' perceptions of the nexus between soft skills and specialized skills, university leadership conventions, the level of curriculum autonomy, as well as other institutional advantages that they had, which also created variances in the model across universities. The analysis also showed that curriculum autonomy, connections with external stakeholders, and effective leadership that could engage stakeholders and harness institutional advantages were the three major factors that could influence the effectiveness of the soft-skills-implementation model.

This study suggests that the soft-skills-implementation model cannot be copied but should be developed based on a careful examination of institutional context and larger socioeconomic, cultural, and political factors. Without such close examination, the model will not yield expected results. That said, although the study is most relevant to Vietnamese universities, the models can be useful references for any university operating in a similar context that needs to devise a suitable model. Likewise, ECAs appear to be useful in implementing the soft-skills policy, especially where HE institutions have little autonomy and the existing curricula are already crowded. Thus, they should be involved as an integral component of the institutional soft-skills-implementation model to maximize the benefits that they may bring.

Notes

1 Disciplinary teachers are teachers who teach specialized subjects in the Business Administration program.
2 Skills teachers are teachers who teach subjects that train students in certain soft skills, such as communication skills, computer skills, and English skills.
3 The Youth Union and associates is a socio-political organization established by Ho Chi Minh under the Communist Party. It is installed in each school and university in Vietnam and is in charge of political education and leading social-engagement activities.

References

Adnan, Y. M., Daud, M. N., Alias, A., & Razali, M. N. (2017). Importance of soft skills for graduates in the real estate programmes in Malaysia. *Journal of Surveying, Construction and Property*, 3(2). doi: https://doi.org/10.22452/jscp.vol3no2.4

Al-Mahmood, R., & Gruba, P. (2007). Approaches to the implementation of generic graduate attributes in Australian ICT undergraduate education. *Computer Science Education*, 17(3), 171–185.

Anh, H. (2011). 94% sinh viên ra trường phải đào tạo tiếp. *Thanh Nien Online*, 1 Dec. Retrieved from https://bit.ly/2W9Hcjy

Barrie, S., Hughes, C., Smith, C., & Thomson, K. (2009). *The national graduate attributes project: Key issues to consider in the renewal of learning and teaching experiences to foster graduate attributes.* Sydney, Australia: Australian Learning and Teaching Council.

Bodewig, C., & Badiani-Magnusson, R. (2014). *Skilling up Vietnam: Preparing the workforce for a modern market economy.* Washington DC: World Bank Publications.

Brodie, L. (2011). Delivering key graduate attributes via teams working in virtual space. *International Journal of Emerging Technologies in Learning (iJET)*, 6(3), 5–11.

de la Harpe, B., & David, C. (2012). Major influences on the teaching and assessment of graduate attributes. *Higher Education Research & Development*, 31(4), 493–510.

Eike, R. J., Myers, B., & Sturges, D. (2018). The impact of service-learning targeting apparel design majors: A qualitative analysis of learning growth. *Family and Consumer Sciences Research Journal*, 46(3), 267–281.

Elo, S., & Kyngäs, H. (2008). The qualitative content analysis process. *Journal of Advanced Nursing*, 62(1), 107–115.

Fleming, J., Donovan, R., Beer, C., & Clark, D. (2013). A whole of university approach to embedding graduate attributes: A reflection. In J. Willems, B. Tynan, & R. James (Eds.), *Global challenges and perspectives in blended and distance learning* (pp. 246–257). Hershey, PA: IGI Global.

Hager, P., & Holland, S. (2006). *Graduate attributes, learning and employability (Vol. 6).* Dordrecht, Netherlands: Springer Science & Business Media.

Harman, G., Hayden, M., & Nghi, P. T. (2010). *Higher education in Vietnam: Reform, challenges and priorities.* New York, NY: Springer.

Harman, K., & Bich, N. T. N. (2010). Reforming teaching and learning in Vietnam's higher education system. In G. Harman, M. Hayden, & P. T. Nghi (Eds.), *Reforming higher education in Vietnam: Challenges and priorities* (pp. 65–86). New York, NY: Springer.

Hendriana, H., Johanto, T., & Sumarmo, U. (2018). The role of problem-based learning to improve students' mathematical problem-solving ability and self-confidence. *Journal on Mathematics Education*, 9(2), 291–300.

Huong, P. L., & Fry, G. W. (2011). Vietnam as an outlier: Tradition and change in education. In C. Brock & L. P. Symaco (Eds.), *Education in South-East Asia* (pp. 221–243). Oxford, UK: Symposim Books

Hurrell, S. A. (2016). Rethinking the soft skills deficit blame game: Employers, skills withdrawal and the reporting of soft skills gaps. *Human Relations*, 69(3), 605–628.

Ibrahim, M. E., Al-Shahrani, A. M., Abdalla, M. E., Abubaker, I. M., & Mohamed, M. E. (2018). The effectiveness of problem-based learning in acquisition of knowledge, soft skills during basic and preclinical sciences: Medical students' points of view. *Acta Informatica Medica*, 26(2), 119–124.

International Labour Organisation and Asian Development Bank (2014). *ASEAN community 2015: Managing integration for better jobs and shared prosperity*. Retrieved from https://bit.ly/2GzAgpI

Jääskelä, P., Nykänen, S., & Tynjälä, P. (2018). Models for the development of generic skills in Finnish higher education. *Journal of Further and Higher Education*, 42(1), 130–142.

Jones, A. (2009). Generic attributes as espoused theory: The importance of context. *Higher Education*, 58(2), 175–191.

Jones, A. (2010). Generic attributes in accounting: The significance of the disciplinary context. *Accounting Education: An International Journal*, 19(1–2), 5–21.

Jones, M., Baldi, C., Phillips, C., & Waikar, A. (2017). The hard truth about soft skills: What recruiters look for in business graduates. *College Student Journal*, 50(3), 422–428.

Kinash, S., Crane, L., Schulz, M., Dowling, D., & Knight, C. (2014). *Improving graduate employability: Strategies from three universities*. Retrieved from https://bit.ly/2XG2juv

Losekoot, E., Lasten, E., Lawson, A., & Chen, B. (2018). The development of soft skills during internships: The hospitality student's voice. *Research in Hospitality Management*, 8(2), 155–159.

Mak, B., Lau, C., & Wong, A. (2017). Effects of experiential learning on students: An ecotourism service-learning course. *Journal of Teaching in Travel & Tourism*, 17(2), 85–100.

Marcus, B., Weigelt, O., Hergert, J., Gurt, J., & Melléri, P. (2017). The use of snowball sampling for multi source organizational research: Some cause for concern. *Personnel Psychology*, 70(3), 635–673.

Marginson, S. (2011). Higher education in East Asia and Singapore: Rise of the Confucian model. *Higher Education*, 61(5), 587–611.

Menon, J., & Melendez, A. C. (2017). Realizing an Asean Economic Community: Progress and remaining challenge. *The Singapore Economic Review*, 62(3), 681–702.

MOET (2010). *Công văn 2916/ BGDĐT-GDĐH hướng dẫn xây dựng và công bố chuẩn đầu ra ngành đào tạo*. Retrieved from https://bit.ly/2VlKS4I

Myers, T., Blackman, A., Andersen, T., Hay, R., Lee, I., & Gray, H. (2014). Cultivating ICT students' interpersonal soft skills in online learning environments using traditional active learning techniques. *Journal of Learning Design*, 7(3), 38–53.

Nghi, P. T., & London, J. D. (2010). The higher education reform agenda: A vision for 2020. In G. Harman, M. Hayden, & T. N. Pham (Eds.), *Reforming higher education in Vietnam* (pp. 51–64). New York, NY: Springer.

Nguyen, T. L. H. (2013). Middle-level academic management: A case study on the roles of the heads of department at a Vietnamese university. *Tertiary Education and Management*, 19(1). doi: 10.1080/13583883.2012.724704

O'Neill, G. (2010). A programme wide approach to assessment: A reflection on some curriculum mapping tools. Paper presented at the AISHE Conference, Dublin, Ireland. Retrieved from https://bit.ly/2Vhr16W

Pitman, T., & Broomhall, S. (2009). Australian universities, generic skills and lifelong learning. *International Journal of Lifelong Education*, 28(4), 439–458.

Stevens, M., & Norman, R. (2016). Industry expectations of soft skills in IT graduates: A regional survey. Paper presented at the Australasian Computer Science Week Multiconference, 2–5 February, Canberra, Australia.

Tertiary Education Quality and Standards Agency (2013). *Australian qualifications framework*. Canberra: The Australian Qualifications Framework Council.

Tran, L. H. N. (2017). Developing generic skills for students via extra-curricular activities in Vietnamese universities: Practices and influential factors. *Journal of Teaching and Learning for Graduate Employability*, 8(1), 22.

Tran, L. H. N. (2018). The skills gap of Vietnamese graduates and final-year university students. *Journal of Education and Work*, 31(7–8), 579–594.

Tran, L. H. N., & Nguyen, T. M. D. (2018). Internship-related learning outcomes and their influential factors: The case of Vietnamese tourism and hospitality students. *Education + Training*, 60(1), 69–81.

Tran, L. H. N., Phan, T. N. P., & Tran, L. K. H. (2018). Implementing the student-centred teaching approach in Vietnamese universities: The influence of leadership and management practices on teacher engagement. *Educational Studies*. doi: 10.1080/03055698.2018.1555453

Tran, L. T., Le, T. T. T., & Nguyen, N. T. (2014). Curriculum and pedagogy. In *Higher Education in Vietnam: Flexibility, Mobility and Practicality in the Global Knowledge Economy* (pp. 86–107). London: Palgrave Macmillan.

Tran, L. T., Marginson, S., Do, H. M., Do, Q. T. N., Le, T. T. T., Nguyen, N. T., ... Ho, T. T. H. (2014). *Higher education in Vietnam: Flexibility, mobility and practicality in the global knowledge economy*. New York, NY: Palgrave MacMillan.

Tran, N. C. (2009). Reaching out to society: Vietnamese universities in transition. *Science and Public Policy*, 36(2), 91–95.

Tran, N. T. (2013). *Vietnamese Parents' Attitudes Towards Western Parenting Behaviors and Interventions*. Nashville, TN: Vanderbilt University.

Tran, T. T. (2016). Building a close connection between higher education and industry for a better education outcome for Vietnam. *VNU Journal of Science*, 32(4), 36–43.

Varghese, N. (2007). *GATS and higher education: The need for regulatory policies*. Paris: International Institute for Educational Planning.

Vietnamese Government (2012). Lu⊠t giáo dục đại học. Retrieved from https://bit.ly/2GNGV24

Willcoxson, L., Wynder, M., & Laing, G. K. (2010). A whole-of-program approach to the development of generic and professional skills in a university accounting program. *Accounting Education: An International Journal*, 19(1–2), 65–91.

World Bank (2008). *Vietnam: Higher education and skills for growth*. Retrieved from https://openknowledge.worldbank.org/handle/10986/7814

World Bank (2018). *The World Bank in Vietnam*. www.worldbank.org/en/country/vietnam/overview

Yin, R. K. (2009). *Case Study Research, Design & Methods* (4th edn). Thousand Oaks, CA: Sage.

5 Contextual factors and leadership for soft-skills policy implementation

Lessons from two Vietnamese universities

Introduction

In the previous chapter, models for soft-skills development in Vietnamese universities were reported. The effectiveness of these models largely depends on institutional leadership and management practices. As noted by a number of researchers (Barrie, Hughes, Smith, & Thomson, 2009; de la Harpe & David, 2012; Jones, 2009), leadership and management appear to be important determinants of soft-skills implementation. Unfortunately, this seems to be one of the weakest points in the operation of Vietnamese universities.

Leadership, management, and governance in the Vietnamese higher education (HE) system are still highly centralized (Marginson, 2011). Most universities depend on the Ministry of Education and Training (MOET) or a central government regulatory body for their operation (Do & Do, 2014), resulting in little opportunity for the university itself to develop leadership and management capability (Dao, 2015). The curriculum is often controlled by MOET (Hayden & Lam, 2010; Tran, Le, & Nguyen, 2014), which reduces flexibility in designing university programs in a way that benefit students' learning and matches demands for skills in the labor market. Since 2013, Vietnamese universities have had autonomy in curriculum development and some institutional arrangements, as specified in the Higher Education Law (Vietnamese Government, 2012). However, in practice, MOET appears to maintain control over the operational activities of many Vietnamese universities, including curriculum development (Phuong, 2018). This causes many difficulties for universities because they cannot develop curricula to meet social demands and implement pedagogical and assessment changes (Harman & Bich, 2010). Universities hesitate to initiate something new, and often replicate what other universities have got away with.

Leadership and management activities in Vietnamese universities employ a top-down approach. Decisions are made from above by a group of powerful people, often members of the Communist party, while staff and student perspectives are hardly taken into account. Communication between groups of stakeholders within the university is often slow and lacks clarity, which results in delays in policy execution. Confucian educational heritage creates a strong hierarchy in social relationships between young and old, students and teachers, staff and leaders (see

Truong, Hallinger, & Sanga, 2017). This diplomatic and tactful culture (Nguyen, 2017; Pham, 2010) causes many difficulties with provision and reception of critical feedback, which are vital for implementing radical changes.

In such a context, to ensure successful soft-skills implementation, it is crucial that Vietnamese universities' leaders flexibly exercise their leadership and use management tools to coordinate the implementation. This chapter will compare the implementation of soft skills in two Vietnamese private universities, with a focus on the impact of their institutional leadership and management practices. Framed within Bourdieu's concepts of social field, habitus and capitals, the comparison reveals that despite using a similar implementation model, the implementation of soft skills in these two universities experienced different results. Differences in levels of curriculum autonomy, the deployment of leadership, connections with industry, and the use of extracurricular activities (ECAs) created disparate outcomes for the two universities. This chapter argues that to ensure success in soft-skills implementation, each university needs to analyze their institutional context, devise a feasible implementation strategy, and use effective leadership to implement tasks instead of replicating an implementation model reported to be successful somewhere else.

How soft skills are developed for students

Like policy implementation in other types of organizations, soft-skills implementation in HE institutions requires a substantial amount of investment, effective leadership, and management measures. A review of policy-implementation theories and recent empirical studies about soft-skills implementation suggests that HE leaders need to pay attention to the following tasks when executing a soft-skills policy in their institution (Table 5.1).

At the institutional level, four main leadership-related tasks should be exercised to prepare and manage the progress of soft-skills implementation. First, the soft-

Table 5.1 Tasks involved in soft-skills implementation

Level of implementation	Implementation task
Institutional level	• Policies, incentives, and drivers for soft-skills implementation • Approaches to soft-skills implementation • Selection of soft-skills outcomes and curriculum models • Staff and resources development
Subject level	• Setting soft-skills learning objectives • Teaching soft skills • Assessing soft skills
Extracurricular activities	• Social-engagement activities • Employment orientation and consultation • Skills classes • Political education

skills policy should clearly articulate the necessity for and purposes of the implementation to all intended stakeholders, as well as be accompanied by incentives and drivers to better engage stakeholders (Barrie et al., 2009; de la Harpe & David, 2012; Jones, 2009). Second, an implementation strategy suited to institutional or disciplinary characteristics, including a pedagogical approach, is communicated with clarity to stakeholders so that they understand their role and responsibility in the implementation (Al-Mahmood & Gruba, 2007; Barrie et al., 2009; de la Harpe & David, 2012; Jones, 2009). Third, selecting relevant soft skills and developing a curriculum model to impart these skills to students are essential because the former shapes the content of the implementation while the latter shapes the channels to deliver the content (Barrie et al., 2009). Together with the implementation strategy, the curriculum model also contributes to designating duties to stakeholders involved in the implementation. Finally, preparing resources and staff development must be considered a central task for the success of soft-skills implementation (Barrie et al., 2009). Changing teachers' attitudes about teaching soft skills in disciplinary courses, improving their pedagogical practice, supporting their teaching activities, and leading them to engage with developing soft skills for students are crucial but challenging (Barrie et al., 2009). This is a vital task because teachers are one of the key agents for translating the soft-skills policy into practice.

At the subject level, the first step is setting and aligning soft-skills learning objectives between subjects of a program, which is often achieved by mapping the curriculum (Ang, D'Alessandro, & Winzar, 2014; Robley, Whittle, & Murdoch-Eaton, 2005). In the second step, all teachers must be able to impart soft skills to students using a student-centered approach such as problem-based learning, community-service learning, or work-integrated learning (WIL) (Eike, Myers, & Sturges, 2018; Henderson & Trede, 2017; Hendriana, Johanto, & Sumarmo, 2018). Lastly, all teachers must be able to assess students' attainment in soft skills using the assessment tasks and prescribed criteria (Palmer, Holt, Hall, & Ferguson, 2011; Quarrie, 2007). Generally, teacher engagement and their ability to harmoniously teach and assess soft skills between subjects are key to the success of soft-skills implementation at the subject level.

In addition, many universities have been employing ECAs to create more opportunities for students to improve their soft skills (Barrie et al., 2009; Roulin & Bangerter, 2013). Therefore, ECAs are included to form another layer of the implementation in this study. Despite differences between universities, common ECAs are short skills development classes, community-service learning, internships, career fairs, or recreational activities. In Vietnam, these ECAs also include political education provided by the Youth Union and its associates (YUA).

The role of leadership and management for soft-skills implementation

Organizational culture is the collective values, beliefs and principles that members share (Camillo, 2015). Organizational culture stems from three sources: (i) founders' beliefs, values, and assumptions; (ii) the learning experiences of members as they grow; and (iii) new beliefs, values, and assumptions brought in by new members and leaders (Schein, 2004, p. 225). As such, leadership and management practices are meaningfully established and shape the culture of an organization. Organizational culture, or shared values and beliefs, affects the way people and groups interact with each other and with external stakeholders (Ravasi & Schultz, 2006).

The university also has its own culture, which is clustered around teaching-learning, research, and community engagement (Scott, 2006). Developing soft skills for students can be a major change in the teaching mission of many universities because traditionally it was not the academics' duty. Most academics are experts in their fields, but they may not have completed a teaching certificate and may not have experience in using active pedagogical practices to impart soft skills to students. Thus, they may feel intimidated when asked to teach and assess soft skills. They need effective leadership and considerable support to buy-in to the importance of soft skills and engage with delivering them (Barrie et al., 2009). Indeed, training teachers and providing ongoing support for teaching and assessing soft skills are crucial because these activities can help eliminate teachers' long-standing beliefs and routine behaviors that may block them from seeing the relevance of developing soft skills for students (Barrie et al., 2009). Both formal professional-development activities (e.g., workshops and seminars) and informal ones (e.g., communities of practice, peer learning, self-studies) should be organized to facilitate teachers' transition from transmitting content knowledge to training students in skills (Barrie et al., 2009). Through such activities, teachers can gain basic principles and teaching techniques to put into practice where they should be able to reflect and modify to best fit their teaching situations. Teacher engagement with soft-skills implementation would also be strengthened by generous incentive schemes and effective management tools (Barrie et al., 2009). Furthermore, it is obvious that learning resources, facilities, and student support services should be prepared well in advance to ensure the implementation of soft skills proceeds favorably.

In fact, using leadership to make changes in teaching conditions and teachers' expertise to enhance the transformation of their thinking and teaching behaviors can be explained by Bourdieu's concepts of social field, habitus and capital forms. A social field "consists of a set of objective historical relations between positions anchored in certain forms of power (or capital)" (Bourdieu & Wacquant, 1992, p. 16). Habitus is considered as "the learned set of preferences or dispositions by which a person orients to the social world" (Dumenden & English, 2013, p. 1080). For Bourdieu, the habitus and social field are connected to each other. Habitus entails the embodiment of social practices, the result of exposure to particular experiences within any given field (Bourdieu & Wacquant, 1992). However, habitus is changeable if it is conditioned appropriately (Hardy, 2009; James, Busher, & Suttill, 2015). In order for habitus to change, there must be a link between the "subjective habitus and the objective world of other people and things" (Bourdieu, 1977, p. 83). Habitus can also be formed based on different forms of capital that individuals can get access to and use in a social field to achieve certain goals. In Bourdieu's perspectives, cultural capital refers to the skills, knowledge, titles, and sensibilities people possess. It exists in connection to individuals in their general educated character such as accent, dispositions, and learning; in connection to objects such as books, qualifications, and learning resources; and in connection to institutions such as places of learning, universities, and libraries (Bourdieu, 1989, p. 21). Economic capital is defined as the access to material and financial resources (Bourdieu & Wacquant, 1992). Social capital encompasses the social assets arising from social memberships, networks, and relationships (Bourdieu & Wacquant, 1992; Siisiainen, 2003).

In the case of developing soft skills for students in HE, where traditional teaching methods have long been used, teachers would form the habit of teaching content rather than developing students' skills. If leaders want teachers to engage with teaching and assessing soft skills, they must exercise leadership and management to change the social field and supply appropriate forms of capital so that teachers can change their beliefs and teaching behaviors toward soft-skills implementation. Otherwise, the implementation of soft skills in Vietnamese universities will remain only rhetoric and never be materialized in concrete results.

The present study

In 2012–2016, six qualitative multiple case studies were conducted to identify factors influencing the implementation of soft-skills policy in the Business Administration programs of Vietnamese universities, using leaders' and academics' experiences with it. The Business Administration program was chosen because it is one of the most popular programs in Vietnamese universities, and the business schools appear to focus on developing soft skills for their students more than do other schools. Equally important, focusing on one program allowed deep analysis of the implementation and logical comparison of the implementation between different university contexts. The qualitative approach was chosen because it allowed the researcher to investigate and understand attitudes, behaviors, and experiences of individuals about soft-skills implementation within the context of their institution and did not eliminate or simplify what could not be discounted or simplified (Merriam, 2009; Yin, 2009).

Among these six cases, University D and University E, regardless of differences in institutional contexts, executed the policy using a similar implementation model. However, the former claimed to have succeeded whereas the latter did not. This chapter will compare soft-skills implementation, with a special focus on leadership and management issues, in these two Vietnamese universities to highlight the facilitators and inhibitors. Specifically, this chapter will answer the following question: What factors facilitated or inhibited soft-skills implementation in Vietnamese universities?

Participants in the selected universities were recruited using a snowball-sampling technique (Marcus, Weigelt, Hergert, Gurt, & Golléri, 2017). This helped the researcher approach potential participants based on the recommendation of another participant. The participants were selected purposefully to include viewpoints of different stakeholders involved in the implementation. For managerial staff, at the university level, the rector or deputy rector was interviewed. At the school level, the targeted participants were the dean, vice dean, and coordinator of the Business Administration program. Leaders of the YUA were also included because ECAs organized by them are essential for students' work-skills development. For academics, teachers who taught specialized subjects of the Business Administration program, and teachers participating in delivering a co-curriculum that trained students in communication skills, English skills, intercultural skills, and problem-solving skills, among others, were interviewed. In total, the researcher recruited and interviewed 20 participants who were involved in soft-skills implementation at the two universities. The demographic information is presented in Table 5.2. Participants were informed of the purpose of the study and how their identities would be protected, and asked to give consent for the researcher to use the information they provided for the purpose of the study.

Semi-structured interviews were used to collect data from participants. This method allowed the researcher to gather relevant data about soft-skills implementation tasks that have been identified, and simultaneously opened opportunities to clarify emergent issues throughout the interviews. Additionally, the researcher gathered policies, reports, minutes, and decisions available on websites of the universities, as well as from hard copies shared by the participants. These documents helped highlight the identity and institutional context, as well as provided additional data of

Table 5.2 Participants and universities

University	Institutional context	Participants
University D	University D had operated as a vocational college in a metropolitan city for more than 10 years before it was upgraded to a university. At the time of research, it was 22 years old and considered one of the best Vietnamese private universities. It is among 37 non-public universities established or upgraded after HERA was launched in 2005. University D is supervised by MOET, but it has been granted some degree of curriculum autonomy.	• Gender: 5 males, and 5 females • Work roles: 2 university leaders, 2 school leaders, 3 skills teachers, 2 disciplinary teachers, and 1 YUA organizer (also a disciplinary teacher) • Educational levels: 4 with a doctorate, and 6 with a master's degree
University E	University E is also among 37 non-public universities established or upgraded after HERA was launched in 2005. At the time of research, this university was 5 years old. As a newly established university in a regional city, it has very limited connections with local industry and qualified teachers. This university reports to the MOET mostly in terms of academic affairs; unlike University D, it does not have curriculum autonomy.	• Gender: 3 males, and 7 females • Work roles: 1 university leader, 2 school leaders, 3 skills teachers, 3 disciplinary teachers, and 1 YUA organizer • Educational levels: 1 with an undergraduate degree, and 9 with a master's degree

how the soft-skills policy was executed at the institutional and subject levels. It also allowed triangulation of data to improve the trustworthiness of the research findings.

A qualitative content analysis (Elo & Kyngäs, 2008) was employed to analyze the data. On a case-by-case basis, all interviews were transcribed and repeatedly reviewed for content. Passages relevant to soft-skills implementation, particularly facilitators and inhibitors of the implementation at each level, were highlighted and coded against implementation tasks in the analytical framework (Table 5.1). By doing this, the data were reduced and put into categories. Data that did not fit the tasks in the analytical framework were analyzed inductively to see whether they could form a subcategory of an existing category or develop a completely new one. This step also involved interpreting the data variations, if any, in consideration of the institutional contexts of each case. After this, facilitators and inhibitors of the implementation at institutional and subject levels were revealed for each case. Following this, comparing the coded data across the cases proceeded. This step illuminated the similarities and differences in soft-skills implementation between the universities. It also pointed out the most influential factors of the implementation in the Vietnamese context and distinctive influential factors compared with their Western counterparts. Finally, the results emerging from the analysis were organized into the final report.

Findings

Universities D and E used the same model to execute the soft-skills policy in their institutions. Both conceptualized the implementation of soft skills as developing work-readiness skills for students. They translated the concept into practice via three channels. First, skills subjects were designed and delivered by skills teachers from a Department of General Education (or equivalent) to all students in the first two years of their programs. These skills subjects, both compulsory and elective, generally helped students develop the soft skills necessary for their university learning and future work, such as English, communication, presentation, teamwork, problem-solving, and computer skills. Furthermore, soft skills were developed for students in specialized subjects using a WIL approach in the classroom and via internships. Finally, ECAs were organized to give students more opportunities to develop their soft skills, including political attributes, social-engagement skills, and CV-writing and job-interview skills. Despite using the same implementation model, they had different experiences with the implementation process and outcomes, as presented below.

University D

Participants consistently claimed that the university had successfully implemented the soft-skills policy. At the institutional level, the university leaders stated that the privilege of having curriculum autonomy helped them design and modify the curriculum to embed nine skills subjects (3 credits per subject[1]) that developed a variety of soft skills for students, on top of computer and English subjects (3 and

28 credits, respectively), which are considered soft skills in the Vietnamese HE context. According to the participants, soft skills in particular and the learning outcomes in general were selected based on the "core values of the university," "Vietnamese traditions" and the "globalized context," aiming to produce graduates who "would be capable of performing well in the workplace."

In leaders' and teachers' views, the success of soft-skills-policy implementation could be attributed to the strategy for building teacher capacity and the university's tradition of vocational education. Accordingly, the university used financial incentives to recruit only academics with a foreign degree or with authentic experiences in industry. The recruited teachers were trained in WIL-pedagogical practice to fit into the vocational education tradition of the university. As indicated by the interviewed leaders, this conditioned their engagement with teaching soft skills using WIL in specialized subjects.

> We have clear recruitment criteria to assess the competence of the staff: credentials, teaching experience, real experiences in relevant industries. […]. Teaching experience is for ensuring their ability to deliver the curricula, and practical experience in industries is for ensuring what they teach is reality-based. (Participant D10, top-level leader)

> Despite our experience, we still had to attend some pedagogy classes. The university supported us with this so that we have [satisfactory] teaching skills before teaching the students. Yes, the university has supportive policies on training staff to teach skills. (Participant D4, academic)

At the subject level, the interviewed teachers consistently reported that they knew what they were expected to teach students. This suggested that the soft-skills policy and implementation strategy could have been communicated with clarity to teachers in this university. Furthermore, they stated that they were confident about developing soft skills for students using a WIL approach because university leaders "always create good conditions" to support their teaching. They believed that existing facilities, as well as the management of these facilities, were supportive and good for their teaching of soft skills.

> Generally, teachers were aware of the importance of soft skills. […].They know that if they embed soft skills into their [disciplinary] subjects, the workload would increase and the teaching task would become more complex, but none of my colleagues has complained about teaching soft skills in their subjects. […]. Students and teachers are supported with good facilities such as computers, micros, whiteboards, projectors to increase student-teacher interaction for generic-skills development. (Participant D8, academic)

However, while acknowledging the university leaders' support to tackle barriers to the implementation, the interviewed disciplinary teachers suggested that they were facing some obstacles such as heavy teaching workloads, shortage of teachers, and students' superficial learning attitudes. The teachers suggested that class observations did not directly influence their engagement with teaching soft skills, but it drove them to use WIL in their teaching. For example, they used authentic teaching materials, linked the lessons to real-life business affairs, and invited successful business people to give a talk in their class.

Regarding student internships, the interviewed university and school leaders proudly reported that they could provide two internships for students throughout their studies should students prefer the university to do so. Otherwise, students could look for two internships or equivalent employment by themselves. This was because they had forged an extensive network with people in industry who were willing to receive and supervise their students. Consequently, all students in the school accumulated some authentic work experience and developed soft skills relevant to the Vietnamese work culture prior to their graduation.

Practices for assessing soft skills appeared to take place harmoniously among teacher groups, based on their claim. They reported that they assessed students' soft skills via group work, individual work, a midterm test, and a final examination, with an agreement among teachers about the weighting of these assessment tasks. However, in practice, it seemed that the teachers did not have concrete criteria for assessing students' soft skills but based it solely on personal experience.

Unlike at University E, the YUA of University D only "played the role of a supporter in organizing ECAs"—students themselves identified and organized ECAs to train themselves and their peers in these skills. The interviewed YUA staff member suggested that extensive connections with industry and proactive students helped establish more than 20 clubs to develop technical and soft skills. He mentioned that students did not know how to look for funding for their activities, although it is available in the university and partners of the university. He advised that students should analyze the procedure for applying for university funding and look for alternative resources from the available industry network.

> There are more than 20 clubs in this university founded by students. [...]. They tended to organize activities to develop technical skills and soft skills such as critical-thinking skills. (Participant D7, YUA leader and academic)

In short, despite limitations, participants from University D consistently suggested that soft-skills implementation progressed well or claimed that it was successful. The university and school leaders proved this by the fact that their graduates' employment outcomes were very high (from 75 to 90% for five successive years), and that in the latest survey, employers evaluated their graduates' work skills better than those of graduates from other institutions in the city.

University E

In our informal discussion, the rector of University E revealed that he coordinated the soft skills implementation following the model of a well-known university in the region, and that it was progressing well. From the experience of participants at University E, however, the implementation appeared not to have yielded positive results. At the institutional level, the interviewed university and school leaders stated that they planned to develop many soft skills for students, but they had difficulty adding skills subjects into the curriculum due to MOET's regulation of 120–140 credits for an undergraduate program. Therefore, following the rector's decision, they cut the credits of some existing subjects to save credits for new skills subjects. Even so, they could not integrate all the selected soft skills; thus, they prioritized English, computer, and communication skills (24, 3, and 2 credits, respectively), and left the others as electives (negotiation skills, problem-solving skills, teamwork, job-interview skills, etc.).

> The rector was influential in developing skills subjects. He had many experiences in industry, so he knew what skills to teach students. He suggested ideas, then people discussed, but the rector made the final decision. […]. there were not many debates around the skills proposed by the rector because people respected him. (Participant E2, mid-level leader)

Moreover, building teacher capacity appeared to be a big challenge in this university. Being a newly established university in a regional city, it could only attract early-career academics. The interviewed teachers admitted that they did not have authentic work experience in industry. They all agreed that university leaders paid much attention to improving teachers' qualifications and their teaching skills, even though many of these qualifications were not specifically related to teaching soft skills.

> When I started this job, I did not have a teaching certificate, […] the university provided me with some training courses before I sat an exam for the teaching certificate. I can improve my specialized knowledge and skills by myself, but the teaching methods courses helped me a lot. (Participant E3, mid-level leader and academic)

Similarly, the interviewed university and school leaders revealed that they deployed WIL by employing successful people from industry to teach some skills and specialized subjects on a part-time basis because these people could "impart authentic and industry-relevant skills." Unfortunately, limited connections with industries prevented them from employing those people with appropriate qualifications. Even after employing these industry-based academics, they had difficulties managing their teaching, as presented later.

> It is very difficult to find and employ skills teachers. […]. As we do not have enough skills teachers, we have to invite skills experts from industries and require young teachers to attend skills classes of these experts to learn how to teach skills. (Participant E3, mid-level leader and academic)

In the School of Business Administration, except for skills teachers, both full-time and part-time disciplinary teachers did not engage with teaching soft skills due to unclear communication of the policy and implementation strategy. The interviewed full-time disciplinary teachers justified that teaching soft skills was the responsibility of students and skills teachers. Despite being "encouraged" by university leaders, their main duty was to impart specialized knowledge and technical skills. They suggested that a lack of incentives and drivers made them disengage further with developing students' soft skills.

> Students must experience and accumulate soft skills via part-time jobs or observation of other behaviors or learn through the media. […] I taught a math subject, so it is not related to soft skills very much. (Participant E5, academic)
> Disciplinary teachers are not required to teach generic skills with a formal policy, so they are not fully engaged in teaching generic skills. (Participant E2, mid-level leader)

Moreover, these teachers seemed to hesitate to impart due to a lack of soft-skills teaching expertise, which was linked to some drawback of the teacher-training activities above. The interviewed leaders suggested that they expected full-time teachers to learn how to teach soft skills from part-time teachers, who were skills experts in industry. Regrettably, none of the interviewed teachers did so, making excuses in terms of "heavy teaching workloads," "ego," "avoiding causing troubles for a colleague," and a lack of institutional initiatives for this. On top of these issues, the interviewed teachers listed time shortage, large class sizes, and a lack of teaching resources as causes of their disengagement.

> In the classroom, desks and chairs are not moveable […] so it is impossible to organize effective group work. There are so many students in my class, so it is very noisy if I have to organize interactive learning activities. Teachers from other nearby classes complained, so I feel scared to organize such activities again. (Participant E6, academic)
> If we focused on disciplinary knowledge and technical skills, we lost generic skills. Otherwise, our lessons become fragmented. So, we have to make a balance. (Participant E6, academic)

Particularly, teachers reported that students' superficial learning disheartened them from imparting soft skills. They explained that most students in this non-public university had low academic competence and observed that students tended to study to pass exams and for credentials rather than for real competence.

> The students enrolled in this university are of low academic caliber, so their cognitive ability is low. They also lack authentic exposure to life, so they fail to satisfactorily solve real-life problems given to them. (Participant E7, academic)

Regarding the use of WIL, in teachers' observation, part-time teachers did not train students in soft skills, but only transmitted theoretical knowledge. The six teachers ascribed part-time teacher disengagement to a lack of clarity in communicating the soft-skills policy and their experience in WIL pedagogical practices.

> The university is employing people from local industries to teach some disciplinary subjects […]. Employing a bank director or a head of sale department is good in that they disseminate real experiences to students, but they do not teach soft skills. (Participant E6, academic)

The use of a compulsory student internship was limited also due to a lack of connections with industry. At the time of research, this initiative relied on students' efforts in searching for internship opportunities, as reported by the interviewed disciplinary teachers and school leaders.

> Unfortunately, the university does not have any service to support students with the internship […]. Students had to look for internship opportunities for themselves, but there are not many available. This issue is simply because enterprises do not want to receive interns, unless they are forced to do so, or have some benefits. (Participant E4, academic).

Students' soft-skills levels were assessed by skills teachers with a consensus on assessment methods and criteria. However, some disciplinary teachers completely ignored this task; others assessed informally based on their "observation" or "intuition" of students' observable behaviors. There was no adequate data on how part-time teachers assessed soft skills, but based on the interviewed teachers' perspectives, it seemed that these part-time teachers did not actually assess students' soft skills but assessed their understanding of these skills.

Regarding ECAs, the YUA staff member reported that, apart from developing political attributes, the YUA usually organized meetings with successful business people, career fairs, social-engagement activities, and contests on sports and arts to further train students in soft skills. The YUA did not organize skills classes because that was the responsibility of the School of General Sciences. He acknowledged that support of young academics and administrative staff facilitated their organization of ECAs. In addition, he revealed that a lack of funding, personnel, and connections with industry made them restrict ECAs within the campus. Students' superficial participation, in his opinion, could reduce the effectiveness of their work. He also observed that many students joined the YUA's extracurricular activities only to get "self-improvement" scores, which is used as a reference for granting scholarships and ranking of academic achievements, instead of improving their soft skills.

Discussion

This chapter compared soft-skills implementation in two Vietnamese universities that used a similar implementation model but experienced different outcomes. The findings suggested several factors, such as leadership, management, teacher engagement, a lack of connections to industries, etc., affected the outcomes of the implementation. In this section, these factors will be further analyzed through the lens of Bourdieu's concepts of social field, capital and habitus to see the connections among them.

The social field of University D could be characterized by its location in a socioeconomic, cultural, and educational hub of the country. Being a prestigious private university, it gained curriculum autonomy from the MOET. The university had invested in developing various forms of capital necessary for soft-skills implementation, including qualified teachers who have both academic competence and industry work experience, students with satisfactory academic competence, adequate facilities and resources, and an extensive connection with industry. In contrast, the social field of University E could be depicted as a newly-established institution located on the outskirts of a regional city and with a lack of curriculum autonomy. The capital available for soft-skills-policy implementation can be described in terms of a shortage of qualified teachers, poor student input, basic facilities and infrastructure, and a severe lack of connections with industry and the surrounding community. The social field and existing capital forms affected leadership of the two universities, and thus resulted in different levels of progress of the implementation.

First, the curriculum autonomy created marked differences in the experience with soft-skills implementation between the two universities. Together with the two national universities, University D was among the few institutions in the HE system that had curriculum autonomy at the time of research, although recent legislation has given Vietnamese universities such autonomy (Vietnamese Government, 2012). This added a powerful advantage to the social field that enabled the university to conveniently embark on developing soft skills for students. In fact, university leaders had renewed the curricula once prior to MOET's soft-skills policy embedded in Guideline 2196 /BGDĐT-GDĐH (MOET, 2010) and re-modified the curricula again following the Guideline to tailor the skills program and methodologically enhance the delivery of these skills subjects. Unlike University D, a lack of curriculum autonomy made it difficult for leaders of University E to modify the curricula. They could only add a couple of subjects to develop the most important soft skills in Vietnam such as English, computer skills, and communication skills for students by cutting down credits of other subjects in the same curriculum to comply with MOET's regulation of 120–140 credits per undergraduate program. Other skills were listed as electives, which in most cases students would not register to study because of their disengagement with learning (Tran, 2015).

Secondly, the social fields and different forms of capital also affected the leadership for building teacher capacity and engagement with soft-skills implementation. Using its reputation, institutional autonomy, convenient location, connection with people in industries, and financial incentives, leaders of University D successfully deployed a policy of recruiting teachers who had obtained at least a postgraduate degree from overseas and had worked in a relevant industry. They also used the vocational tradition, spent resources, and have these qualified teachers to provide ongoing professional development support and create a community of practice to upgrade teachers' teaching skills. Consequently, the teaching staff in this university had adequate capacity to execute a soft-skills policy following the model that the university leaders developed. In contrast, University E's new social status, narrow public recognition, location in a regional area, and lack of connection with industries restricted the rector's and university leaders' ambition to recruit qualified teachers and build a community of practice to enhance teacher capacity, as well as change teachers' beliefs and engagement with imparting soft skills to students. As a result, teachers, both full-time and part-time, did not methodologically develop soft skills for students or ignored them completely due to a lack of teaching expertise, unfavorable teaching conditions, and student disengagement.

Thirdly, leaders of both universities adopted the WIL approach to train their students in work readiness, their conceptualization of soft-skills implementation. However, a lack of economic, cultural, and social capital appeared to affect the use of WIL. In University D, teachers' academic capability and industry work experience and the long-standing vocational education of the university enabled teachers to engage with soft-skills implementation. Their teaching was supported by adequate learning resources and facilities. The student internship program was also supported by extensive connections with industries. Conversely, in University E, a lack of teacher capacity, even with part-time teachers (successful business people or industry-based trainers), caused difficulties for creating a community of practice where teachers could share experience in imparting and assessing soft-skills teaching. Their work was also hindered by inadequate facilities and resources. The shortage of connections with industry also negatively affected the student internship program, which mostly depended on students' own efforts in looking for internship opportunities.

Fourthly, the social field and capital also affected the way the YUA was involved in implementing the soft-skills policy. In both universities, the YUA was brought in as an extra channel to develop soft skills. However, University E involved the YUA as a compensation for a lack of room for adding skills subjects to the formal curricula caused by not having curriculum autonomy. University D included the YUA naturally as an additional channel for students to further develop the soft skills that they wanted. In University D, students were empowered to identify skills they wanted to develop, to organize activities and seek internal and external funding for their activities. By this, students could have developed skills relevant to their needs alongside leadership and organizational skills. In University E, in contrast, ECAs were led by the YUA leaders and students only played the role of participants. As such, students had fewer opportunities to develop organizational or leadership skills via such activities. Even worse, the findings showed that students participated in ECAs superficially only to get "self-improvement" scores, which was not the case at University D. Likewise, a lack of resources and connections to industry restricted their YUA activities on campus, making them less community-oriented than those at University D.

Moreover, the university leadership itself affected the progress of the implementation, as noted by (Barrie et al., 2009). Predictably, both universities, placed in a Confucian and socialist educational context (Marginson, 2011), used a top-down approach to coordinate implementation tasks. However, University D appeared to exercise their leadership better than did University E with regard to adding capital for the implementation. Evidence included clarity in communication of policy and implementation strategy to university stakeholders, efficiency in recruitment and building of teacher capacity, effective use of incentives and management tools to monitor teachers' work, and preparation and creation of good conditions for teaching and learning activities. Such leadership effectively changed teachers' beliefs and teaching behavior with regard to teaching and assessing soft skills, despite limitations. Consequently, teachers in University D engaged with developing soft skills for students. Conversely, as a newly established institution, University E's leaders might not have much experience in leadership and management, and they might have several objectives to complete compared to the long-standing University D. Therefore, such factors could have contributed to drawbacks in the leadership for soft-skills implementation: unclear communication, failure to build teacher capacity, underestimation of the importance of industrial linkages in deploying the WIL approach, copying a soft-skills implementation model without deeply examining their institutional context, etc. Therefore, despite the rector's strong will, great effort, and investment, most teachers did not engage with developing soft skills for students. Those who attempted to teach soft skills were restrained by issues related to learning resources, facilities, class sizes, student disengagement with learning, etc.

Conclusion

In conclusion, by comparing the implementation of a soft-skills policy in two Vietnamese universities that used a similar implementation strategy but experienced different levels of progress, three important factors for the success of implementation can be identified.

- First, curriculum autonomy appeared to be a prerequisite for the implementation. Without it as a favorable social field, universities could not appropriately modify the curriculum to include subjects that trained students in soft skills.
- Second, all forms of capital necessary for the implementation needed to be prepared well in advance to enable stakeholders to gradually engage with their tasks in the implementation.
- Third, university leadership should empower and engage teachers with teaching and assessing soft skills. Without convincingly engaging teachers, soft-skills implementation remains mere rhetoric or becomes fragmented due to a lack of harmony in teaching soft skills between teachers and between subjects.

Although this chapter only reports two case studies, it is evident that the success of soft-skills implementation is context-dependent. Therefore, applying an implementation model reported to be successful elsewhere into another institution without examining institutional capacity is risky. Rather, as noted in Al-Mahmood and Gruba (2007), each institution needs to analyze its institutional context, identify its strengths and limitations, and then devise a feasible implementation model and use effective leadership to coordinate tasks so that efforts and resources are not wasted.

Note

1 1 credit is equivalent to 15 face-to-face teaching sessions of 45 minutes for theoretical subjects.

References

Al-Mahmood, R., & Gruba, P. (2007). Approaches to the implementation of generic graduate attributes in Australian ICT undergraduate education. *Computer Science Education*, 17(3), 171–185.

Ang, L., D'Alessandro, S., & Winzar, H. (2014). A visual-based approach to the mapping of generic skills: Its application to a Marketing degree. *Higher Education Research & Development*, 33(2), 181–197.

Barrie, S., Hughes, C., Smith, C., & Thomson, K. (2009). *The national graduate attributes project: Key issues to consider in the renewal of learning and teaching experiences to foster graduate attributes*. Sydney: Australian Learning and Teaching Council.

Bourdieu, P. (1977). *Outline of a theory of practice (Vol. 16)*. New York: Cambridge University Press.

Bourdieu, P. (1989). Social space and symbolic power. *Sociological Theory*, 7(1), 14–25.

Bourdieu, P., & Wacquant, L. (1992). *An invitation to reflexive sociology*. Cambridge: Polity.

Camillo, A. A. (2015). *Handbook of research on global hospitality and tourism management*. Hershey, PA: IGI Global.

Dao, K. V. (2015). Key challenges in the reform of governance, quality assurance, and finance in Vietnamese higher education: A case study. *Studies in Higher Education*, 40(5), 745–760.

de la Harpe, B., & David, C. (2012). Major influences on the teaching and assessment of graduate attributes. *Higher Education Research & Development*, 31(4), 493–510.

Do, H. M., & Do, Q. T. N. (2014). Higher and tertiary education in Vietnam. In *Higher education in Vietnam: Flexibility, mobility and practicality in the global knowledge economy* (pp. 29–53). London: Palgrave Macmillan.

Dumenden, I. E., & English, R. (2013). Fish out of water: refugee and international students in mainstream Australian schools. *International Journal of Inclusive Education*, 17(10), 1078–1088.

Eike, R. J., Myers, B., & Sturges, D. (2018). The impact of service-learning targeting apparel design majors: A qualitative analysis of learning growth. *Family and Consumer Sciences Research Journal*, 46(3), 267–281.

Elo, S., & Kyngäs, H. (2008). The qualitative content analysis process. *Journal of Advanced Nursing*, 62(1), 107–115.

Hardy, I. (2009). Critiquing teacher professional development: Teacher learning within the field of teachers' work. *Critical Studies in Education*, 51(1), 71–84.

Harman, K., & Bich, N. T. N. (2010). Reforming teaching and learning in Vietnam's higher education system. In G. Harman, M. Hayden, & P. T. Nghi (Eds.), *Reforming higher education in Vietnam: Challenges and priorities* (pp. 65–86). New York, NY: Springer.

Hayden, M., & Lam, T. Q. (2010). Vietnam's higher education system. In G. Harman, M. Hayden, & N. T. Pham (Eds.), *Reforming higher education in Vietnam* (pp. 14–29). New York, NY: Springer.

Henderson, A., & Trede, F. (2017). Strengthening attainment of student learning outcomes during work-integrated learning: A collaborative governance framework across academia, industry and students. *Asia-Pacific Journal of Cooperative Education*, 18(1), 73–80.

Hendriana, H., Johanto, T., & Sumarmo, U. (2018). The role of problem-based learning to improve students' mathematical problem-solving ability and self-confidence. *Journal on Mathematics Education*, 9(2), 291–300.

James, N., Busher, H., & Suttill, B. (2015). Using habitus and field to explore Access to Higher Education students' learning identities. *Studies in the Education of Adults*, 47(1), 4–20.

Jones, A. (2009). Generic attributes as espoused theory: The importance of context. *Higher Education*, 58(2), 175–191.

Marcus, B., Weigelt, O., Hergert, J., Gurt, J., & Gelléri, P. (2017). The use of snowball sampling for multi-source organizational research: Some cause for concern. *Personnel Psychology*, 70(3), 635–673.

Marginson, S. (2011). Higher education in East Asia and Singapore: Rise of the Confucian model. *Higher Education*, 61(5), 587–611.

Merriam, S. B. (2009). *Qualitative research: A guide to design and implementation*. San Francisco, CA: Jossey-Bass.

MOET (2010). *Công văn 2916/ BGDĐT-GDĐH hướng dẫn xây dựng và công bố chuẩn đầu ra ngành đào tạo*. Retrieved from https://bit.ly/2VlKS4I

Nguyen, T. Q. T. (2017). Maintaining teachers' face in the context of change: Results from a study of Vietnamese college lecturers' perceptions of face. *Teachers and Teaching*, 23(1), 78–90.

Palmer, S., Holt, D., Hall, W., & Ferguson, C. (2011). An evaluation of an online student portfolio for the development of engineering graduate attributes. *Computer Applications in Engineering Education*, 19(3), 447–456.

Pham, T. H. T. (2010). Implementing a student-centered learning approach at Vietnamese higher education institutions: Barriers under layers of casual layered analysis. *Journal of Futures Studies*, 15(1), 21–38.

Phuong, H. (2018). Luật Giáo dục Đại học cản trở đổi mới. *Phap Luat*, 14 March. Retrieved from https://bit.ly/2UAomAL

Quarrie, S. P. (2007). Student peer review as a tool for efficiently achieving subject-specific and generic learning outcomes: Examples in botany at the Faculty of Agriculture, University of Belgrade. *Higher Education in Europe*, 32(2–3), 203–212.

Ravasi, D., & Schultz, M. (2006). Responding to organizational identity threats: Exploring the role of organizational culture. *Academy of Management Journal*, 49(3), 433–458.

Robley, W., Whittle, S., & Murdoch-Eaton, D. (2005). Mapping generic skills curricula: A recommended methodology. *Journal of Further and Higher Education*, 29(3), 221–231.

Roulin, N., & Bangerter, A. (2013). Students' use of extra-curricular activities for positional advantage in competitive job markets. *Journal of Education and Work*, 26(1), 21–47.

Schein, E. H. (2004). *Organizational culture and leadership*. San Francisco, CA: Jossey-Bass.

Scott, J. C. (2006). The mission of the university: Medieval to postmodern transformations. *The Journal of Higher Education*, 77(1), 1–39.

Siisiainen, M. (2003). Two concepts of social capital: Bourdieu vs. Putnam. *International Journal of Contemporary Sociology*, 40(2), 183–204.

Tran, L. T., Le, T. T. T., & Nguyen, N. T. (2014). Curriculum and pedagogy. In *Higher education in Vietnam: Flexibility, mobility and practicality in the global knowledge economy* (pp. 86–107). London: Palgrave Macmillan.

Tran, T. T. (2015). Is graduate employability the 'whole-of-higher-education-issue'? *Journal of Education and Work*, 28(3), 207–227.

Truong, T. D., Hallinger, P., & Sanga, K. (2017). Confucian values and school leadership in Vietnam: Exploring the influence of culture on principal decision making. *Educational Management Administration & Leadership*, 45(1), 77–100. doi: 10.1177/1741143215607877

Vietnamese Government (2012). *Luật giáo dục đại học*. Retrieved from https://bit.ly/2GNGV24

Yin, R. K. (2009). *Case study research, design & methods* (4th edn). Thousand Oaks, CA: Sage.

6 Teaching soft skills in Vietnamese universities

Teachers' beliefs, behaviors, and influential factors

Introduction

Soft skills, such as communication, interpersonal skills, teamwork, and critical thinking, have been found to enhance students' employability skills, help them learn autonomously throughout life, enable them to cope with an unknown future, and empower them to act for the social good (Adnan, Daud, Alias, & Razali, 2017; Hager & Holland, 2006). Therefore, teaching soft skills has recently become a central focus in many curricula in higher education (HE). The problem is that in the past teaching soft skills was not part of the academic profession, and thus, many university teachers do not seem to engage with it. Studies conducted in Western university contexts have found that their engagement with teaching soft skills seems to be associated with their personal beliefs about the relevance of teaching soft skills in HE (de la Harpe & David, 2012; Jones, 2009). A limited number of studies have argued that teachers' beliefs and behaviors could be improved if institutional leadership were more effective (Barrie, Hughes, & Smith, 2009; de la Harpe & David, 2012). However, there has been a lack of studies into teacher beliefs, their engagement, and factors influencing their engagement with teaching soft skills, especially in non-Western university contexts.

Therefore, to address the mentioned literature gaps, this chapter will report two complementary studies about the influence of different types of teacher beliefs on their engagement with teaching soft skills to Vietnamese university students. In these studies, the term "teacher beliefs" is defined as teachers' changeable awareness of and confidence in the importance of teaching soft skills to students. The first study involved 16 teachers of skills subjects and 25 teachers of specialized subjects of the Business Administration programs of six different Vietnamese universities. It showed that teacher beliefs were diverse and associated with the context where they were working. The analysis also showed that institutional leadership and teachers' personal motivation could strongly influence the translation of their beliefs into actual teaching behaviors. The second study, which involved 147 teachers from 27 Vietnamese universities, quantitatively measured the strengths of their beliefs and engagement and the influence of certain factors on their engagement. The studies reported in this chapter add value to existing literature about soft-skills teaching by using data from non-Western university contexts. Understanding teacher beliefs regarding the (ir)relevance of teaching soft skills and identifying factors affecting their beliefs and teaching behaviors of these skills have important implications for teacher professional development and help advance the implementation of a soft-skills policy in HE.

Teaching soft skills in higher education: Prospects and challenges

Teaching soft skills offers much potential to make changes in the university's operation. Firstly, teaching soft skills may help these institutions address various challenges exposed or introduced in the HE sector. Culturally, the expansion of the HE sector (Hayhoe, Li, Lin, & Zha, 2012), an increase in the number of full-fee-paying students on campus, and the introduction of the concept "students as customers in HE" (Star & Hammer, 2008) require universities to pay closer attention to students' learning needs and care for their students' employability. Socioeconomically, employers are complaining about graduates' ability to work (Hurrell, 2016), therefore universities have become aware of training students in skills that meet employers' demands. Politically, the increased influence of university rankings despite their flaws (Marginson, 2009; Soh, 2017), HE learning outcomes assessment (Coates & Richardson, 2012; Marginson, 2009), and linking soft-skills implementation to quality assurance and funding schemes (e.g. The Quality Assurance Agency for Higher Education, 2014) have convinced universities that developing soft skills for students is necessary.

In addition, soft-skills implementation creates opportunities for universities to improve the relevance of their roles in the contemporary context of HE (Star & Hammer, 2008). Traditionally, the university provided its education and research to the elites for a civic mission via formal, direct contact on campus (Temple, 2012). Such an operation appears less relevant in current contexts where employers and the larger society increasingly expect the university to produce employable graduates, to conduct applicable research, and to engage with surrounding communities rather than staying in their ivory tower. Teaching soft skills helps the university redesign the curriculum to embed, map and align market-relevant skills between subjects of a curriculum to produce graduates with sufficient work ability. Teaching soft skills also promotes work-integrated learning (WIL) activities, which may help tighten university-industry relationships and promote research collaboration as well as knowledge transfer.

Moreover, soft-skills implementation affords opportunities for improving academics' pedagogical use and assessment practices. The implementation of a soft-skills policy requires a radical shift away from using traditional teaching methods to embracing student-centered, more interactive ones. Pedagogical practices such as project-based learning (Hendriana, Johanto, & Sumarmo, 2018; Ibrahim, Al-Shahrani, Abdalla, Abubaker, & Mohamed, 2018), community-service learning (Eike, Myers, & Sturges, 2018; Payton, Barnes, Buch, Rorrer, & Zuo, 2015), online and distance learning (Myers et al., 2014), and work-integrated learning (Losekoot, Lasten, Lawson, & Chen, 2018; Tran & Nguyen, 2018) have been increasingly used because they are recognized to be effective in developing soft skills in students. Likewise, the implementation of soft skills also creates opportunities to reform assessment practices because soft-skills assessment requires constructive feedback from peers and the teacher, a higher level of student engagement, and collecting evidence for the assessment, such as a portfolio, rather than a single performance on a final test (Barrie, Hughes, Smith, & Thomson, 2009; Palmer, Holt, Hall, & Ferguson, 2011). Thus, soft-skills implementation encourages active teaching, deep learning, and student–student and student–teacher collaboration.

Unfortunately, teachers may not recognize the relevance of teaching these skills. Indeed, recent studies have identified many factors that prevent teachers from engaging with soft-skills teaching and assessment (de la Harpe & David, 2012; Jones, 2009; Palmer et al., 2011). Studies revealed that leadership-related, cultural, personal, and interpersonal factors influenced their teaching behaviors regarding training students in soft skills. For example, Jones (2009) found that while teachers believed that teaching soft skills was relevant, in practice, not many of them engaged with it in disciplinary subjects. She explained this in light of the espoused theory, positing that teachers did not teach soft skills because:

- They believe that soft skills are not part of disciplinary knowledge.
- They believe that teaching soft skills is not the central role of the university teacher.
- They find it hard to define soft skills as these skills are elusive and complex.
- They do not have adequate experience of, or confidence in, teaching these skills.
- They find that several obstacles hinder their teaching of soft skills, such as large classes, a lack of support by departments, a shortage of time, and a research-focused culture in the university.

In the same vein, de la Harpe and David (2012) found that instead of beliefs and expertise in teaching soft skills, it was teachers' willingness and confidence in teaching these skills that would engage them with the implementation. They argued that institutional leadership needs to be exercised to increase teachers' willingness, confidence, and beliefs about the relevance of teaching and assessing soft skills in HE.

Findings from the aforementioned studies about teacher engagement with teaching soft skills appear to reflect the theory of planned behavior (Ajzen, 1991). According to that theory, our intentions and actual behavior are generally guided by three kinds of beliefs: behavioral, normative, and control. Behavioral beliefs are our beliefs about the consequences of enacting a particular behavior. Such beliefs produce a positive or negative attitude toward the behavior based on our subjective evaluations of outcomes the behaviors may result in. Normative beliefs result from the expectations of others or social pressure about certain behaviors. They are a kind of belief imposed by others. Control beliefs are beliefs about the existence of contextual factors that may affect the performance of a specific behavior. When combined, they jointly lead to the formation of a behavioral intention, which may be translated into actual behaviors under suitable conditions. For example, if a teacher believes that teaching soft skills is important for improving students' future work and life (behavioral beliefs); if it is encouraged by the university leaders and coordinators (normative beliefs); and if it can be executed in the class conveniently due to the availability of facilities and teaching support services (control beliefs), then the teacher will most likely engage with imparting these skills to students.

Accordingly, although teacher beliefs may affect their engagement with imparting soft skills, such beliefs and their actual teaching behaviors may be influenced by contextual factors. It is because beliefs are formed and changed depending on experiences with the surrounding context (Assen, Meijers, Otting, & Poell, 2016; Ertmer, Ottenbreit-Leftwich, Sadik, Sendurur, & Sendurur, 2012; Tiwari, Das, & Sharma, 2015). When beliefs are altered, their teaching behaviors may change. Thus, it is important to examine teacher beliefs and engagement and the factors influencing these variables. This will help remove obstacles that impede teachers' engagement with imparting soft skills, contributing to the success of the implementation as teachers are key agents of soft-skills implementation.

Context of teaching soft skills in Vietnamese universities

Universities in Vietnam have recently been under a great deal of external pressure to develop soft skills for students. Employers are complaining that graduates are lacking practice in soft skills (written and spoken communication, communication skills in foreign languages, teamwork, creative thinking, etc.) and require substantial re-training at work (Anh, 2011; Bodewig & Badiani-Magnusson, 2014). This has resulted in a large number of unemployed university graduates, as many as 200,000 in 2018 (Linh, 2018). Citing a recent study conducted by the University of Social Sciences and Humanities, Professor Pham Minh Hac (former Minister of Education and Training) revealed that 26.2% of university graduates are unemployed, and 70.8% of them are employed in a job indirectly relevant to their discipline (Giao Duc Viet Nam, 2019). The lack of a skilled workforce will disadvantage Vietnam economically in the Southeast Asian region and globally, especially in this time of globalization and a knowledge-based economy. Therefore, in 2010, the Ministry of Education and Training (MOET) formally required universities to develop soft skills for students (MOET, 2010). Since then, teaching soft skills to students has been implemented. However, the progress and effectiveness of teaching–learning activities have not been investigated to identify and remove obstacles.

Undoubtedly, the current context of Vietnamese universities is challenging for soft-skills implementation. Unlike their Western counterparts, Vietnamese universities are more teaching- than research-oriented. Paradoxically, many teachers have not obtained qualifications and teaching experience to conduct their job satisfactorily at this level of education. The latest statistics published by MOET show that in 2017 there were 72,792 lecturers working in the HE sector, but only about 22.7% had completed their doctorate studies (Ministry of Education and Training, 2017). In this teaching-focused culture, teachers often use traditional teaching methods due to a lack of training on innovative teaching methods, a lack of resources, and other practicality issues (Harman & Bich, 2010; Tran, Phan, & Tran, 2018). Teachers often use assessments for summative rather than informative purposes (Tran, Le, & Nguyen, 2014), which reflects a traditional use of assessment. Limited connections and collaboration with industries may also hinder the use of WIL for the development of students' work readiness, causing a skills gap between what the universities develop and what employers need (Tran, 2018; Tran, 2016).

The teaching conditions in Vietnamese universities also disadvantage soft-skills implementation. Due to a large number of student enrolments (Harman & Bich, 2010), teachers often undertake an excessive teaching workload and deliver their lessons to overcrowded classes (Tran et al., 2018). Irrespective of recent investment, many Vietnamese universities generally have poor campus infrastructure, inadequate learning resources, and old facilities due to a lack of resources and limited funding (Dao, 2015). Most students depend on their teachers in their learning and superficially engage with learning only to pass subjects (Humphreys & Wyatt, 2013). The Confucian and socialist ideologies give teachers too much authority in the classroom while students are expected to accept what teachers deliver without questioning (Tran et al., 2018), which is not a favorable environment for students to develop soft skills.

In short, there has been a pressing need to train students in soft skills in Vietnamese universities. However, the current context of the universities appears unfavorable for the teaching and learning of these skills. Therefore, it is crucial to explore how teachers are implementing the soft-skills policy in the classroom and the obstacles facing them. Such a study will provide important implications for the advancement of soft-skills-policy implementation in Vietnamese universities and others with a similar context.

Research methods

This chapter will analyze teacher beliefs, engagement, and factors influencing their engagement with teaching soft skills in Vietnamese universities. It should be noted here that teacher beliefs, teacher engagement, and other possible influential factors are analyzed entirely based on teachers' self-report and their experiences with the implementation. The overall question that this chapter seeks to answer is: What factors influence teachers' engagement with teaching soft skills in Vietnamese universities?

To answer this question, two complementary studies were conducted and are reported in this chapter.

Study 1: A qualitative study

In 2012–2016, a qualitative multiple case study (Yin, 2009) was conducted to identify factors influencing soft-skills implementation in the Business Administration programs of three public and three private Vietnamese universities, which represented different institutional contexts in the HE system. Using a snowball-sampling technique (Browne, 2005), which allowed the researcher to approach key informants based on the recommendation of another participant, the researcher interviewed 69 university leaders, school leaders, teachers, and staff members of the Youth Union and Associates (YUA). However, for the purpose of this chapter, only 41 interviews with the teachers were used for the analysis. University leaders' perspectives were only included where they would be relevant to help clarify teachers' perspectives. Among these participants, 15 were male and 26 were female. Sixteen skills teachers were delivering subjects that trained students in soft skills, such as English, communication, CV writing, job interviews, cross-culture communication skills, and HE learning methods. Twenty-five were disciplinary teachers who taught disciplinary subjects for the Business Administration program. A summary of participants' demographic information is presented in Table 6.1.

Data were primarily collected by semi-structured interviews (Cohen, Manion, & Morison, 2018). All teachers were informed of the purpose of the study, their roles, and how their identities would be protected. In the interviews, they were invited to discuss: (i) reasons why they should or should not teach soft skills; (ii) activities they did to help students develop the skills; and (iii) factors influencing their teaching of these skills. The interviews lasted from 18 to 90 minutes depending on the level of experience each teacher had with teaching soft skills. All interviews were recorded and transcribed verbatim for analysis.

A qualitative content analysis (Elo & Kyngäs, 2008) was employed to analyze the data. Firstly, the researcher reviewed the transcripts to understand the perspectives and experiences of each teacher with respect to teaching soft skills. Teachers' beliefs were coded on a case-by-case basis, after which the codes were put together and classified with a particular focus on how teaching soft skills was relevant for students. Secondly, the researcher separated the transcripts of teachers by who did or did not teach soft skills. The first group was classified further, into skills teachers and disciplinary teachers. Self-reported teaching behaviors of the two groups of teachers were then analyzed, with a focus on how they developed these skills for students. Regarding influential factors, teachers' experiences with the implementation were analyzed with a focus on personal and organizational factors that may influence their beliefs and teaching behaviors.

Study 2: A quantitative study

In 2019, based on the major findings of Study 1, an online survey was designed to quantitatively analyze what teachers from different disciplines believe about the relevance of teaching soft skills, their engagement levels, and the influence of certain factors on their engagement. Apart from a demographic section, the survey had three main sections. Teachers were first asked to rate their agreement on reasons why they should teach soft skills to students and who they believed should be responsible for developing soft skills for students/graduates, using a 5-point Likert scale. Similarly, they were asked to indicate their engagement with certain soft-skills teaching behaviors, and to assess the influence of a variety of factors on their intention to teach soft skills, also using a 5-point Likert scale.

Data were collected using a snowball-sampling technique. The target participants were disciplinary teachers because the qualitative study above indicated that

Table 6.1 A summary of participants

Universities	Teachers				
	Gender	Qualification	Work duty	Seniority	Industry experience
A (public)	2 males 5 females	3 undergraduates 4 postgraduates	4 skills teachers 3 disciplinary teachers	3 early-career 4 mid or senior	4 yes 3 no
B (public)	5 males 3 females	1 undergraduate 7 postgraduates	1 skills teacher 7 disciplinary teachers	2 early-career 6 mid or senior	6 yes 2 no
C (public)	3 males 6 females	2 undergraduates 7 postgraduates	3 skills teachers 6 disciplinary teachers	2 early-career 7 mid or senior	4 yes 5 no
D (private)	1 male 4 females	0 undergraduates 5 postgraduates	3 skills teachers 2 disciplinary teachers	0 early-career 5 mid or senior	4 yes 1 no
E (private)	1 male 5 females	3 undergraduates 3 postgraduates	3 skills teachers 3 disciplinary teachers	3 early-career 3 mid or senior	1 yes 5 no
F (private)	3 males 3 females	1 undergraduate 5 postgraduates	2 skills teachers 4 disciplinary teachers	1 early-career 5 mid or senior	6 yes 0 no

this group of teachers was not engaged and held different beliefs toward teaching soft skills. The researcher sent the link of the survey to 10 colleagues who were working for 10 different Vietnamese universities in different fields of study, requesting them to complete the survey and forward it to their colleagues. The survey was open for a month (March 2019) and received 151 responses from 27 institutions. After removing incomplete responses, 147 responses were used for the analysis. Among them 38.8% were from males and 61.2% from females. Those who were working for a public institution and private institution accounted for 73.5% and 26.5%, respectively. In terms of work experience, 33.3% had worked for less than six years, 38.1% between six and 12 years, and 28.6% more than 12 years. The majority of them held a master's degree (81.6%) whereas only 7.5% and 10.9% held a bachelor or doctorate degree, respectively. In terms of disciplines, 45.6% were teaching subjects in the social sciences and humanities, 16.3% in economics and business, 15.6% in education, and 22.4% in natural sciences, technologies, health, and agriculture.

Data were analyzed using Statistical Package for the Social Sciences (SPSS) version 20. Only descriptive statistics were computed to generate results that complementarily illustrated the qualitative findings above. The mean scores (M) were interpreted using the framework below:

$1.0 < M \leq 1.8$	Very weak
$1.8 < M \leq 2.6$	Weak
$2.6 < M \leq 3.4$	Moderate
$3.4 < M \leq 4.2$	Strong
$4.2 < M \leq 5.0$	Very strong

Qualitative findings

Teacher beliefs about the relevance of teaching soft skills

At the time of research, all six universities had initiated activities to realize MOET's soft-skills policy; however, they were all at different stages of the implementation. Universities A and D had implemented the policy and were moving forward to evaluate the effectiveness of their soft-skills-development programs. Universities C, E, and F were struggling with imparting these skills to students via curriculum-based and extracurricular activities. University B had intentionally delayed the implementation of the soft-skills policy until 2015, at which point they were to launch a comprehensive institutional reform. However, all six universities had selected relevant soft skills for students to develop and had included them in published statements of learning outcomes. They had also assigned the responsibility of imparting soft skills to skills teachers, and either required or encouraged disciplinary teachers to further train students in soft skills in disciplinary subjects.

104 *Teaching soft skills*

The analysis showed that teacher engagement with teaching soft skills was associated with different types of beliefs.

Beliefs about the impact of teaching soft skills on students' futures

All of the interviewed teachers reached a consensus that it was relevant to teach soft skills to students in the contemporary context of Vietnamese HE. Firstly, consistent with the perspectives of several academics, such as Bridgstock (2009) and Hager and Holland (2006), more than three-quarters of the interviewed teachers believed that teaching soft skills would improve students' overall learning ability at the university. They stated that the majority of students lacked the skills and attributes necessary for them to engage with university learning; thus, it could influence the quality of their learning outcomes. In their opinion, students were "passive" and "timid," or "lacked confidence." Therefore, they needed to learn soft skills that would enable them to engage in university learning.

In addition, echoing findings in previous studies (e.g. Gayani Fernando, Amaratunga, & Haigh, 2014; Nickson, Warhurst, Commander, Hurrell, & Cullen, 2012), the teachers believed in developing soft skills for students because these skills would help students become more competitive for their future employment endeavors. With soft skills, they believed that students would be able to adapt to changes in the workplace, anticipate the future, and manage their career development. They also believed that training students in soft skills actually enhanced students' ability to better integrate into the social, cultural, and political context of Vietnam and globally. Their view is illustrated by the comments below:

> If they have soft skills, they will live more happily, confidently and become more self-controlled. Generally, […] they would have more ways to lead their lives. (Participant D6)
>
> I believe that soft skills are vital. They not only affect students' ability to develop professional expertise, they also affect their ability to interact with people, to communicate their ideas to employers, and to carry out assigned work duties. (Participant C12)

In short, all of these findings suggest that teachers had developed beliefs about the relevance of teaching students soft skills. They could see the contribution of their teaching of soft skills to the students' personal and professional development. These findings reflect the behavioral beliefs in the planned behavior theory developed by Ajzen (1991) where teachers are aware of the consequences of their engagement with teaching soft skills.

Beliefs about expectations of stakeholders regarding teaching soft skills

The interviewed teachers suggested that they should teach soft skills because external stakeholders such as students,[1] students' parents, employers, and the government expected them to equip students with these skills. Six teachers believed that teaching soft skills was relevant because students expected to be equipped with skills so that they could succeed in their future work and life. From their perspective, as students had to pay full tuition fees, universities should ensure that students could obtain a job and would be able to lead an independent life. Similarly, a senior disciplinary teacher from University A stated that universities needed to train students in soft skills because of employers' demands. She stressed that "when social demand changes, universities need to adapt their training accordingly." In the same vein, a disciplinary teacher attributed the relevance of teaching soft skills to MOET's policy. It was surprising because only one teacher mentioned MOET's policy whereas almost all university leaders mentioned it directly or indirectly. All of these reflect the fact that like their international counterparts, Vietnamese universities are under pressure caused by socio-economic, cultural, and political changes (see the Introduction of this book).

Almost half of the interviewed teachers believed that teaching soft skills was important because it was their university policy. All 16 skills teachers suggested that they trained students in soft skills because university or school leaders assigned that responsibility to them. Commonly across the six universities, skills teachers reported that they taught students how to write CVs, complete job applications and practice for job interviews, exercise teamwork, problem-solve, and communicate well, in addition to teaching them computer and English skills, which are treated as soft skills in MOET's policy (MOET, 2010). They all said that they were doing their best to complete their duties using various student-centered teaching techniques. Likewise, the disciplinary teachers from University D and one from University A admitted that teaching soft skills was their responsibility because the university leaders explicitly required them to teach and assess soft skills. Two from University D taught soft skills using a WIL approach, explaining that they had been trained to do so, and their university specified using this teaching method. Similarly, a senior disciplinary teacher from University A reported to have been teaching soft skills using student-centered methods because she was trained in those teaching methods. In the other universities, disciplinary teachers engaged with teaching such soft skills as communication, presentation, group work, problem-solving skills, critical thinking, and creativity to different extents. The majority of them stated that they "told students what the skills were" and "encouraged them to learn these skills," "shared experiences of how to learn soft skills," "showed video clips," or "introduced some materials" so that students could improve the skills at their own pace. A few of them gave constructive feedback or used peer evaluations on students' presentations, group work, or other types of classroom activities.

In short, teachers appeared to believe in the relevance of teaching soft skills to students under the influence of other stakeholders. This was in line with Ajzen's (1991) notion of normative beliefs, whereby the expectations of others or social pressure could influence teachers' attitudes to teaching students soft skills. However, the findings above indicate that not all teachers were clear about these expectations or social pressures. They suggested that there was miscommunication or unclear communication in

Beliefs about enablers of their teaching of soft skills

The majority of interviewed teachers admitted that they were not confident teaching soft skills, including some English teachers who mentioned that they believed in their ability to teach English skills, but other soft skills they were not so sure of. Most disciplinary teachers set soft skills as a secondary learning objective in their subjects, for various reasons, as reported below, but foremost due to a lack of experience in teaching soft skills.

> Now I mostly teach specialized knowledge and skills. […] I sometimes share with students soft skills based on my experience and intuition […]. Teachers need to have a shared understanding about soft skills, and ongoing professional training so that they understand, then impart these skills to students. That will be more effective. (Participant C7)

With the exception of University D, the analysis revealed that teachers had to consider several factors related to teaching practicalities such as student engagement, large class size, a shortage of time, and a lack of resources. Teachers repeatedly mentioned that in large classes, student-centered pedagogical practices could not work their magic in helping students develop soft skills. They believed that a lack of time also reduced the effectiveness of their teaching of soft skills because these skills needed time to be mastered. A heavy teaching workload also added more challenges to the shortage of time. Both skills and disciplinary teachers were disheartened because teaching soft skills involved new teaching techniques and assessment practices, which required them to spend more time preparing lesson plans and providing feedback to students who also disregarded learning soft skills. Finally, limited resources to support the teaching and learning activities, as noted in Dao (2015), also convinced teachers that they should not teach soft skills. If they did, they had to rely on online resources, which were in English and in most cases students failed to read these materials due to their low English proficiency level (e.g. Humphreys & Wyatt, 2013; Tran et al., 2018).

> You know, a teacher has to teach a class of hundreds of students. How can I manage them, and deliver my lessons effectively to them? (Participant E6)
> Throughout the four years, there is little room to teach generic skills. Programs have to go in accordance with the curriculum framework of MOET; it is impossible to go beyond the limit of credits. (Participant A3)
> If we focused on disciplinary knowledge and technical skills, we lost generic skills. Otherwise, our lessons become fragmented. So, we have to make a balance. (Participant E6)

> Some students only want to complete the program and graduate. They don't care about soft skills, no matter how much we emphasize the importance of these skills. (Participant C3)

In short, there were several contextual factors affecting teachers when they considered whether they should teach soft skills to students. As noted in the planned behavior theory (Ajzen, 1991), people would consider contextual factors that may interfere with their actions to decide whether they should behave in that way. Findings in this section indicate that teachers could hold such control beliefs in mind when they considered teaching soft skills to their students. Thus, issues related to teaching practicality must be removed so as to enhance teachers' control beliefs, thus increasing their engagement with teaching soft skills.

Teacher engagement with teaching soft skills and influential factors

The analysis showed that out of the 41 teachers participating in this study, 11 of them (26.8%) suggested that they did not teach soft skills, or only encouraged students to develop these skills on their own, rather than conducting any teaching activities to train students in soft skills. They explained that although teaching these skills to students was relevant, it was not their responsibility. Meanwhile, the other 30 teachers (73.2%) reported that they were engaging with developing soft skills for their students to different extents. Between the two groups of teachers, 100% of the skills teachers reported that they had been imparting soft skills to students, whereas only 56% of the disciplinary teachers had done so, as detailed in the section about teachers' beliefs about stakeholders' expectations.

The analysis revealed that leadership was a major factor influencing the translation of teacher beliefs into soft-skills teaching practices. Effective leadership helped teachers in University D, both skills and disciplinary teachers, engage with imparting these skills methodologically to their students (see Chapter 5). In the other five universities, depending on leadership, teachers engaged with it to various levels. The influence of leadership on teacher engagement can be demonstrated in four dimensions.

Firstly, with the exception of University D, the universities' soft-skills policy appeared not to be clearly communicated to teachers, making them confused about their responsibilities. Disciplinary teachers stated that teaching soft skills was the responsibility of the skills teachers and the YUA, and that they were "encouraged" to teach soft skills when applicable. However, the interviews with university leaders of these universities suggested that disciplinary teachers were expected to teach soft skills to the extent they could, rather than teaching the skills at their discretion. This miscommunication of the soft-skills policy resulted in disciplinary teachers not putting their beliefs regarding the relevance of teaching soft skills into practice at the subject level.

> Because teaching generic skills is not compulsory, teachers do not engage in it. […] I myself would not consider generic skills part of the curriculum. (Participant B5)

Secondly, a lack of incentives and management tools also influenced their teaching of soft skills. Many skills and disciplinary teachers believed that teaching soft skills was "hard" and "time and effort consuming." Thus, they deserved to be paid higher than other teachers; otherwise, they were not willing to teach soft skills. Likewise, excluding the interviewed teachers from University D, the others suggested that they did not teach soft skills because there was a lack of management tools that monitored their teaching of soft skills. Class observations and student course experience questionnaires were sometimes used, but these were not directly related to checking whether they were teaching soft skills. Consequently, many disciplinary teachers did not teach soft skills, even though they were capable of doing so.

> Salary for teachers is low and does not match our workload. So why should I enhance the quality of my work? If I work harder [in teaching skills to students], the salary will be the same. (Participant A4)
> There were no drivers for soft skills teaching, so teachers just do whatever they want. Gradually, they would not commit to developing soft skills for students. Why would they make themselves tired with more work? (Participant F6)

Thirdly, a lack of staff development also discouraged many skills and disciplinary teachers from teaching soft skills. For skills teachers, they reported that they could teach soft skills, thanks to their own experience, their attendance at previous skills-development classes, or their self-studies. Some disciplinary teachers taught soft skills based on their industry work experiences or from their motivation to help students learn and work more effectively. Except for the disciplinary teachers from University D, none of the disciplinary teachers related their teaching of soft skills to any forms of teacher-training activities provided by their respective institution. A disciplinary teacher expressed his opinion on this:

> Staff training is necessary! [...] Teachers may not understand and teach soft skills effectively [...] because compared with disciplinary knowledge and skills, imparting soft skills to students would need specific ways to successfully do so. (Participant C6)

This suggests that even when teachers have relevant soft-skills expertise, they still need further training in teaching methods to increase their confidence in imparting soft skills to students.

Lastly, as shown in the previous section on teachers' perspectives, most of the universities involved in this study did not prepare resources or remove obstacles related to soft-skills teaching and learning. Large class sizes, a lack of time allocated to soft skills and specialized subjects, a lack of teaching–learning resources and heavy teaching workloads all discouraged teachers from teaching soft skills even when they believed that it was their responsibility and it was relevant to teach these skills to students.

In short, teachers seemed to engage with developing soft skills for students to different extents depending on their beliefs about the relevance of teaching these skills. Institutional leadership appears to affect their beliefs and teaching behaviors. Clarity in policy and implementation strategy communication, development and employment of effective management tools, use of attractive incentives, adequate preparation of resources, provision of staff training, and removal of teaching practicality issues were important leadership-related tasks that would enhance their engagement.

Quantitative findings

Teachers' beliefs

Descriptive statistical analysis results showed that teachers held very strong beliefs about the relevance of developing soft skills for students. Among the six reasons surveyed, all participants (N = 147) rated that teaching soft skills would enhance students'/graduates' job prospects the highest (M = 4.50, SD = 0.74), followed by helping students integrate globally (M = 4.40, SD = 0.72), and maintain students'/graduates' competitiveness in the labor market (M = 4.37, SD = 0.75), which was rated almost as high as facilitating students to transition to university education (M = 4.36, SD = 0.66). The other two reasons, enhancing students' learning quality (M = 4.30, SD = 0.68) and helping students/graduates integrate into Vietnamese society (M = 4.30, SD = 0.72) were equally rated, but with some slight variance in their ratings (Table 6.2).

Likewise, when asked about who should be responsible for developing soft skills for students, teachers ascribed that responsibility to students the most (M = 4.28,

Table 6.2 Teachers' beliefs about teaching soft skills

Teachers' beliefs	M	SD
Why should soft skills be taught to students?		
Enhance students' learning quality	4.30	0.68
Facilitate students to transition to university education	4.36	0.66
Enhance students'/graduates' job prospects	4.50	0.74
Maintain students'/graduates' competitiveness in the labor market	4.37	0.75
Help students/graduates integrate into Vietnamese society	4.30	0.72
Help students integrate globally	4.40	0.72
Who should be responsible for developing soft skills for students?		
Skills teacher	3.37	0.97
Disciplinary teacher	3.19	0.92
The Youth Union and its associates	3.33	0.95
Students' family	3.52	0.90
The whole society	3.29	0.90
Students themselves	4.28	0.70
Employers	2.88	0.91

110 *Teaching soft skills*

SD = 0.70), remarkably higher than the other stakeholders. In contrast, teachers believed that they bore the responsibility the second least (M = 3.19, SD = 0.92), after employers (M = 2.88, SD = 0.91). Consistent with the findings in the qualitative study above, teachers in this study also believed that the YUA (M = 3.33, SD = 0.95) and skills teachers (M = 3.37, SD = 0.97) should be more responsible for imparting soft skills to students than the disciplinary teachers. Teachers also believed that students' families (M = 3.52, SD = 0.90) and the whole society (M = 3.29, SD = 0.90) should share the responsibility of developing soft skills for students. Generally, disciplinary teachers largely rejected being responsible for imparting soft skills to students (Table 6.2).

Teachers' engagement behaviors

The results (Table 6.3) showed that disciplinary teachers engaged with teaching soft skills at a strong or just moderate level. Among the six teaching behaviors surveyed, teachers rated "organizing activities for students to develop soft skills (without assessment)" (M = 3.52, SD = 1.01) the highest, followed by telling students the importance of soft skills for their future work and life (M = 3.44, SD = 0.96). They also reported that they gave a bonus score if students demonstrated great soft skills during the course (M = 3.37, SD = 1.06), and gave impulsive feedback, where applicable, so that some students could improve soft skills on their own (M = 3.39, SD = 0.90). Although it could be a simple teaching-related behaviour, it was surprising to find that the teachers sometimes showed soft-skills-development learning resources to their students (M = 3.11, SD = 3.37). This could be because most of such resources are in English, which, as mentioned in the previous study, was of no use to students due to their lack of English skills, as revealed by teachers in Study 1 above. Finally, teachers rated their engagement with teaching and assessing soft skills methodologically the lowest (M = 2.76, SD = 1.26), noticeably lower than the other five teaching behaviors. This indicated that teachers seemed to have problems with teaching expertise, rather than with a lack of soft skills. The high standard-deviation values also signified that while some groups of teachers could do this well, others could not.

Table 6.3 Teachers' engagement with teaching soft skills

How do they teach soft skills?	N	M	SD
Telling the importance of soft skills	147	3.44	0.96
Showing learning resources where you can self-teach soft skills	143	3.11	0.94
Giving encouraging mark	146	3.37	1.06
Giving feedback on students' soft skills for them to improve	147	3.39	0.90
Organizing activities for students to develop soft skills where possible	145	3.52	1.01
Teaching and assessing students' soft skills methodologically	127	2.76	1.26

Table 6.4 Factors influencing teachers' engagement with teaching soft skills

Why don't they teach soft skills?	M	SD
The university does not have a policy requiring me to teach soft skills	3.10	1.20
The university does not have any tools to manage my teaching of soft skills	3.00	1.19
The university does not incentivize me to teach soft skills	3.01	1.26
I believe that teaching soft skills is not as important as teaching technical skills	2.91	1.24
I believe that teaching soft skills is not my duty (but someone else's)	3.22	1.19
I am not confident in my soft skills, thus ignore teaching these skills	3.12	1.19
I am not confident using teaching methods to impart those skills	3.20	1.05
There is a lack of facilities and resources for imparting soft skills	3.37	1.15
Large classes cause difficulties for teaching soft skills	3.48	1.07
I do not have enough time to teach soft skills due to huge workloads	3.35	1.15

The influence of certain factors on teachers' engagement

The results (Table 6.4) showed that practicality issues such as class sizes, a shortage of time, and a lack of resources were the most influential factors on teachers' engagement with imparting soft skills. Accordingly, class sizes (M = 3.48, SD = 1.07) influenced their intention to teach soft skills at a strong level, followed by a lack of facilities and resources (M = 3.37, SD = 1.15) and a shortage of time (M = 3.35, SD = 1.15) at a moderate level.

The group of factors related to teachers' beliefs and their expertise appeared to affect teachers' intentions to teach soft skills a little lower than practicality issues. Among them, the belief that teaching soft skills was someone else's responsibility seemed to cause teachers to disengage the most (M = 3.22, SD = 1.19). The belief that soft skills are less important than technical skills was reported to have the least effect on their teaching intention (M = 2.91, SD = 1.24). Their lack of confidence in their own soft skills also moderately affected their teaching intention (M = 3.12, SD = 1.19), but its influence was less than their lack of confidence in the teaching expertise required for delivering these skills to students (M = 3.20, SD = 1.05).

Finally, factors related to the presence of policy, incentives, and management tools moderately influenced their intention to teach, with the absence of a soft-skills policy affecting their teaching intention the most (M = 3.10, SD = 1.20), followed by a lack of incentives (M = 3.00, SD = 1.19) and lack of a management tool (M = 3.01, SD = 1.26).

Discussion and conclusion

The two studies reported in this chapter found that teachers held different beliefs about the relevance of teaching soft skills to students in the contemporary context of Vietnamese universities. It appears that their beliefs were associated with their recognition of the benefits to students if they taught soft skills, stakeholders' expectations of them teaching soft skills, and the existence of conditions that support their task of imparting these skills. The three mentioned dimensions of their beliefs toward teaching soft skills are reflective of the planned behavior theory developed by Ajzen (1991). They also confirm the notion that teacher beliefs are multi-faceted and appear to be shaped by their professional expertise, life experiences, and working environments, as noted in several studies (Assen et al., 2016; Ertmer et al., 2012; Tiwari et al., 2015).

In addition, the analysis revealed that despite a high level of belief in the importance of teaching soft skills to students, in practice disciplinary teachers (as opposed to skills teachers who were appointed specifically to teach soft skills) often disengaged from teaching these skills. Evidenced by quantitative results, they believed that it was largely students' own responsibility, or that of someone else, not theirs. Such a belief has been found in previous studies conducted in the West and was the major reason why developing soft skills in a disciplinary context was patchy (Barrie et al., 2009; de la Harpe & David, 2012; Jones, 2009). However, in Vietnamese universities, disciplinary teachers reported that they had helped to impart soft skills in different actions such as telling students about the importance of soft skills, directing them to resources available, giving bonus scores to encourage students to develop soft skills, or organizing certain activities where possible. The biggest obstacle appeared to be their lack of confidence in delivering the skills due to their lack of teaching experience in imparting such skills.

For this reason, teacher motivations alone appeared inadequate to help all teachers translate their beliefs into soft-skills teaching behaviors. They were discouraged by several institutional factors, including large class sizes, heavy teaching workloads, time shortages, insufficient resources allocated to soft-skills teaching, a lack of incentives for soft-skills teaching, and students' disengagement, even when they had soft-skills expertise. In that institutional context, institutional leadership appeared to powerfully help teachers to translate their beliefs into behaviors, which is consistent with findings from de la Harpe and David (2012) and Simon Barrie et al. (2009). As shown in the qualitative study, effective leadership must be associated with: (i) clarity in communication of the soft-skills policy and teacher responsibilities; (ii) effective incentives and management tools for implementation; (iii) ongoing teacher capacity development; and (iv) preparation of good conditions for implementation (resources, teaching facilities, class sizes, etc.). Thanks to effective leadership, teachers in University D engaged with their teaching whereas teachers from the other five universities implemented teaching of soft skills at their discretion, resulting in a fragmented implementation at the subject level. In Vietnamese universities, where leadership and management is highly centralized, teachers do not have as much autonomy as their counterparts in the West (Marginson, 2011), and thus they depend on their leaders' decisions and direction. The quantitative study confirmed this notion. A lack of leadership and management—demonstrated by absence of policy (possibly due to unclear communication), incentives and management tools, insufficient teacher preparation, and several teaching practicality issues—affected teacher engagement with teaching soft skills from a moderate to strong level.

Based on the findings, it is recommended that if university leaders would like to implement a new pedagogical practice or a curriculum-related reform, they not only need to make teachers believe in the relevance of that practice or reform, but must also motivate teachers to translate their beliefs into concrete teaching activities. At the same time, they should exercise leadership in order to remove obstacles and harness advantageous conditions to facilitate that translation process and gradually engage their teachers in the implementation.

It is noted that this study has some limitations. First, it investigated teachers' beliefs and teaching behaviors entirely based on teachers' self-reports, without any classroom observation to identify disparities between what they stated and acted. Second, this study would have been more complete if there had been both teacher beliefs and disbeliefs in the relevance of teaching soft skills. Third, quantitative data was collected for the purpose of illustrating qualitative findings, but did not test the correlation between teacher beliefs, engagement, and influential factors. Future studies should tackle these limitations to generate more insights, thereby contributing to the success of soft-skills implementation.

Note

Part of this chapter is reproduced with the written permission of the publisher from the following journal article: Tran, L. H. N. (2017). What hinders teachers from translating their beliefs into teaching behaviors: The case of teaching generic skills in Vietnamese universities. *Teaching and Teacher Education, 64*(May), 105–114.

Note

1 Students are classified as external stakeholders because they only stay with the university for a limited time and are not involved in the internal affairs of the university, except those related to their learning.

References

Adnan, Y. M., Daud, M. N., Alias, A., & Razali, M. N. (2017). Importance of soft skills for graduates in the real estate programmes in Malaysia. *Journal of Surveying, Construction and Property*, 3(2). doi: 10.22452/jscp.vol3no2.4

Ajzen, I. (1991). The theory of planned behavior. *Organizational Behavior and Human Decision Processes*, 50(2), 179–211.

Anh, H. (2011). *94% sinh viên ra trường phải đào tạo tiếp*. Thanh Nien Online, 1 Dec. Retrieved from https://bit.ly/2W9Hcjy

Assen, J., Meijers, F., Otting, H., & Poell, R. (2016). Explaining discrepancies between teacher beliefs and teacher interventions in a problem-based learning environment: A mixed methods study. *Teaching and Teacher Education*, 60, 12–23.

Barrie, S., Hughes, C., & Smith, C. (2009). *The national graduate attributes project: Integration and assessment of graduate attributes in curriculum*. Sydney: Australian Learning and Teaching Council.

Barrie, S., Hughes, C., Smith, C., & Thomson, K. (2009). *The national graduate attributes project: Key issues to consider in the renewal of learning and teaching experiences to foster graduate attributes.* Sydney: Australian Learning and Teaching Council.

Bodewig, C., & Badiani-Magnusson, R. (2014). *Skilling up Vietnam: Preparing the workforce for a modern market economy.* Washington, DC: World Bank Publications.

Bridgstock, R. (2009). The graduate attributes we've overlooked: Enhancing graduate employability through career management skills. *Higher Education Research & Development,* 28(1), 31–44.

Browne, K. (2005). Snowball sampling: Using social networks to research non-heterosexual women. *International Journal of Social Research Methodology,* 8(1), 47–60.

Coates, H., & Richardson, S. (2012). An international assessment of bachelor degree graduates' learning outcomes. *Higher Education Management and Policy,* 23(3), 1–19.

Cohen, L., Manion, L., & Morison, K. (2018). *Research methods in education.* New York, NY: Routledge.

Dao, K. V. (2015). Key challenges in the reform of governance, quality assurance, and finance in Vietnamese higher education: A case study. *Studies in Higher Education,* 40(5), 745–760.

de la Harpe, B., & David, C. (2012). Major influences on the teaching and assessment of graduate attributes. *Higher Education Research & Development,* 31(4), 493–510.

Eike, R. J., Myers, B., & Sturges, D. (2018). The impact of service-learning targeting apparel design majors: A qualitative analysis of learning growth. *Family and Consumer Sciences Research Journal,* 46(3), 267–281.

Elo, S., & Kyngäs, H. (2008). The qualitative content analysis process. *Journal of Advanced Nursing,* 62(1), 107–115.

Ertmer, P. A., Ottenbreit-Leftwich, A. T., Sadik, O., Sendurur, E., & Sendurur, P. (2012). Teacher beliefs and technology integration practices: A critical relationship. *Computers & Education,* 59(2), 423–435.

Gayani Fernando, N., Amaratunga, D., & Haigh, R. (2014). The career advancement of the professional women in the UK construction industry: The career success factors. *Journal of Engineering, Design and Technology,* 12(1), 53–70.

Giao Duc Viet Nam (2019). *63% sinh viên thất nghiệp khi ra trường.* Retrieved from https://bit.ly/2Z19sqD

Hager, P., & Holland, S. (2006). *Graduate attributes, learning and employability* (Vol. 6). Dordrecht, Netherlands: Springer Science & Business Media.

Harman, K., & Bich, N. T. N. (2010). Reforming teaching and learning in Vietnam's higher education system. In G. Harman, M. Hayden, & P. T. Nghi (Eds.), *Reforming higher education in Vietnam: Challenges and priorities* (pp. 65–86). New York, NY: Springer.

Hayhoe, R., Li, J., Lin, J., & Zha, Q. (2012). *Portraits of 21st century Chinese universities: In the move to mass higher education (Vol. 30).* Dordrecht, Netherlands: Springer Science & Business Media.

Hendriana, H., Johanto, T., & Sumarmo, U. (2018). The role of problem-based learning to improve students' mathematical problem-solving ability and self-confidence. *Journal on Mathematics Education,* 9(2), 291–300.

Humphreys, G., & Wyatt, M. (2013). Helping Vietnamese university learners to become more autonomous. *ELT Journal,* 68(1), 52–63.

Hurrell, S. A. (2016). Rethinking the soft skills deficit blame game: Employers, skills withdrawal and the reporting of soft skills gaps. *Human Relations,* 69(3), 605–628.

Ibrahim, M. E., Al Shahrani, A. M., Abdalla, M. E., Abubaker, I. M., & Mohamed, M. E. (2018). The effectiveness of problem-based learning in acquisition of knowledge, soft skills during basic and preclinical sciences: Medical students' points of view. *Acta Informatica Medica*, 26(2), 119–124.

Jones, A. (2009). Generic attributes as espoused theory: The importance of context. *Higher Education*, 58(2), 175–191.

Linh, T. (2018). Nước ta đang có 5 triệu lao động trình độ đại học, 200 ngàn thất nghiệp. *Giao Duc*, 2 August. Retrieved from https://bit.ly/2ToWIep

Losekoot, E., Lasten, E., Lawson, A., & Chen, B. (2018). The development of soft skills during internships: The hospitality student's voice. *Research in Hospitality Management*, 8(2), 155–159.

Marginson, S. (2009). The knowledge economy and higher education: Rankings and classifications, research metrics and learning outcomes measures as a system for regulating the value of knowledge. *Higher Education Management and Policy*, 21(1), 1–15.

Marginson, S. (2011). Higher education in East Asia and Singapore: Rise of the Confucian model. *Higher Education*, 61(5), 587–611.

Ministry of Education and Training (2017). Số liệu chung về đại học năm học 2015–2016 và 2016–2017. Ha Noi, Vietnam: Ministry of Education and Training.

MOET (2010). *Công văn 2916/ BGDĐT-GDĐH hướng dẫn xây dựng và công bố chuẩn đầu ra ngành đào tạo*. Retrieved from https://bit.ly/2VlKS4I

Myers, T., Blackman, A., Andersen, T., Hay, R., Lee, I., & Gray, H. (2014). Cultivating ICT students' interpersonal soft skills in online learning environments using traditional active learning techniques. *Journal of Learning Design*, 7(3), 38–53.

Nickson, D., Warhurst, C., Commander, J., Hurrell, S. A., & Cullen, A. M. (2012). Soft skills and employability: Evidence from UK retail. *Economic and Industrial Democracy*, 33(1), 65–84.

Palmer, S., Holt, D., Hall, W., & Ferguson, C. (2011). An evaluation of an online student portfolio for the development of engineering graduate attributes. *Computer Applications in Engineering Education*, 19(3), 447–456.

Payton, J., Barnes, T., Buch, K., Rorrer, A., & Zuo, H. (2015). The effects of integrating service learning into computer science: An inter-institutional longitudinal study. *Computer Science Education*, 25(3), 311–324.

Soh, K. (2017). The seven deadly sins of world university ranking: A summary from several papers. *Journal of Higher Education Policy and Management*, 39(1), 104–115.

Star, C., & Hammer, S. (2008). Teaching generic skills: Eroding the higher purpose of universities, or an opportunity for renewal? *Oxford Review of Education*, 34(2), 237–251.

Temple, P. (2012). *Universities in the knowledge economy: Higher education organisation and global change*. New York: Routledge.

The Quality Assurance Agency for Higher Education (2014). The frameworks for higher education qualifications of UK degree-awarding bodies. Retrieved from: www.qaa.ac.uk/docs/qaa/quality-code/qualifications-frameworks.pdf

Tiwari, A., Das, A., & Sharma, M. (2015). Inclusive education a "rhetoric" or "reality"? Teachers' perspectives and beliefs. *Teaching and Teacher Education*, 52, 128–136.

Tran, L. H. N. (2018). Game of blames: Higher education stakeholders' perceptions of causes of Vietnamese graduates' skills gap. *International Journal of Educational Development*, 62(Sep), 302–312.

Tran, L. H. N., & Nguyen, T. M. D. (2018). Internship-related learning outcomes and their influential factors: The case of Vietnamese tourism and hospitality students. *Education + Training*, 60(1), 69–81.

Tran, L. H. N., Phan, T. N. P., & Tran, L. K. H. (2018). Implementing the student-centred teaching approach in Vietnamese universities: The influence of leadership and management practices on teacher engagement. *Educational Studies*. doi: 10.1080/03055698.2018.1555453

Tran, L. T., Le, T. T. T., & Nguyen, N. T. (2014). Curriculum and pedagogy. In *Higher education in Vietnam: flexibility, mobility and practicality in the global knowledge economy* (pp. 86–107). London: Palgrave Macmillan.

Tran, T. T. (2016). Building a close connection between higher education and industry for a better education outcome for Vietnam. *VNU Journal of Science*, 32(4), 36–43.

Yin, R. K. (2009). *Case study research, design & methods* (4th edn). Thousand Oaks, CA: Sage.

7 Assessing soft skills
Practices and challenges

Introduction

Soft skills are non-discipline-specific skills that can be found across disciplines and can be transferred between study, work and life contexts (Tertiary Education Quality and Standards Agency, 2013). Some examples of these skills are communication, presentation, teamwork and problem solving. These skills have been found to enhance students' employability skills, support their independent learning throughout life, enable them to cope with an unknown future and empower them to act for the social good (Hager & Holland, 2006). Therefore, teaching and assessing soft skills has recently become more relevant in many curricula in HE (Bunney, Sharplin, & Howitt, 2015). Existing literature, mostly from the West, suggests that despite recent progress in teaching soft skills, assessment of these skills has faced many challenges associated with teacher and institutional capacity (Barrie, Hughes, Smith, & Thomson, 2009; Bunney et al., 2015; Jackson, 2014; Tremblay, Lalancette, & Roseveare, 2012).

In the case of Vietnam, a developing non-English speaking country located in Southeast Asia, the Ministry of Education and Training (MOET) has recently issued a policy that requires universities to develop soft skills for students (MOET, 2010). This is because there has been a shortage of labourers with sufficient skill levels against the rapid socio-economic growth rate of the country (Bodewig & Badiani-Magnusson, 2014; ManPowerGroup, 2011; Nguyen, Ngoc, & Montague, 2019; Tran, 2018; World Bank, 2008). Without a skilled workforce, Vietnam would not be able to sustain its economic growth, achieve socio-economic objectives, and compete internationally. Therefore, developing soft skills for students, as part of their employability, has become a focus among many curriculum reforms that have taken place in the HE system within the last ten years. However, how the policy is implemented—particularly how the skills are assessed—has not yet been studied. As such, Vietnamese universities can serve as a unique testing ground to investigate current practices and challenges for assessing students' soft skills.

Complementing Chapter 6, which focused on depicting how soft skills were teaching in Vietnamese universities and related obstacles, this chapter will report soft skills assessment practices and associated challenges in Vietnamese universities. The study does not frame the analysis of soft skills assessment challenges within the classroom but links them to institutional leadership and the wider institutional contexts.

Overall, by recoding soft skills assessment practices and challenges associated with them, the study will provide important implications for teacher professional development regarding assessing soft skills and for soft skills implementation.

Literature review

Assessment is often defined as a series of activities organized at the end of a course to measure students' attainment of skills or a body of knowledge, which is known as summative assessment (Burke, 2010). It can also include ongoing activities that teachers use throughout a course in order to provide students with feedback that will improve their learning, which is referred to as formative assessment (Burke, 2010). However, it is often difficult to make a clear distinction between formative and summative assessment (Hernández, 2012); therefore, in this study, assessment refers to both formative and summative assessment.

Assessment practices have been found to have a washback effect on both teachers' and students' respective teaching and learning activities. Therefore, effective assessment practices would help improve the quality of teaching–learning activities and would in turn increase the quality of students' learning outcomes (Musekamp & Pearce, 2015). However, conducting truly effective assessments is not an easy task, especially when it comes to evaluating such abstract learning outcomes as soft skills.

It is observed that some soft skills assessment initiatives have recently been carried out in HE around the world (Chanock, Clerehan, Moore, & Prince, 2004; Jackson, 2014; Tremblay et al., 2012). They are used to encourage students to develop soft skills for themselves, to produce tangible evidence for the evaluation of students' attainment of soft skills, and to compare students' mastery levels of these skills across different universities. However, the effectiveness of these initiatives is still questioned. This section will report on these soft skills assessment initiatives and challenges associated with them.

Several assessment activities have been used to help students become aware of their level of soft skills and to engage in the development of those skills. Firstly, self-assessment activities are often used to provide students with opportunities to personally evaluate their attainment of important soft skills (Lawson et al., 2012; McMahon, Luca, & John, 2007). The difficulty with this type of assessment is that it can only incorporate a limited number of skills that are easily measured, and excludes abstract, more elusive skills; and its effectiveness relies heavily on students' confidence, honesty, and ability to self-evaluate (Jackson, 2014). Secondly, peer assessment activities are used for students to receive feedback from their fellow students about their skills (Lai, 2016; Quarrie, 2007). To be effective, peer assessment requires respectful and open-minded attitudes among all students participating in the assessment activities (Kao, 2013). Thirdly, course experience questionnaires also give students opportunities for soft skills assessment (Ng, Kiang, & Cheung, 2016; Yin, Lu, & Wang, 2014). These are usually provided at the end of a course and ask students to reflect on different aspects of the teaching and learning process throughout the course, including student and teacher engagement in developing soft skills. Unfortunately, this assessment activity is primarily used for monitoring teaching quality rather than increasing student engagement with soft skills learning (Yin et al., 2014). Although there is usually a section asking students about their engagement and their teachers' commitment to soft skills development, the section appears to be lost among many other aspects of the questionnaire.

In addition, some assessment initiatives have been used to both improve students' learning of soft skills and provide concrete evidence for the formal assessment of these skills. For example, portfolio or e-portfolio has been frequently used to compile students' work and exhibit their efforts, progress and achievements in developing soft skills (Cranney et al., 2012; Palmer, Holt, Hall, & Ferguson, 2011; Rowley, Munday, & Polly, 2017). Students reported that this tool helps them engage with the learning process, as well as easily track their development through the course or program (Palmer et al., 2011). Likewise, capstone subjects are also used to provide opportunities for students to develop soft skills and for teachers to assess their students' skills (Keller, Parker, & Chan, 2011). Capstone subjects are frequently offered toward the end of a university degree, often in the form of work placement, internships, service learning or research projects (Holdsworth, Watty, & Davies, 2009). Capstones require students to integrate, consolidate or exhibit the acquired knowledge and skills in practical work situations (Holdsworth et al., 2009; Keller et al., 2011). Therefore, assessment of capstone subjects also involves the assessment of soft skills. In many situations, an industry-based mentor will give feedback and evaluate students' work performance based on his or her personal experience or intuition. The difficulty with this practice is that experience and intuition are both highly personal and subjective, and the assessment result is usually a combination of both disciplinary and soft skills. Therefore, the weighting between generic and disciplinary skills should be clearly defined, so this type of soft skills assessment activity can become more transparent to students.

Moreover, some assessment tools were ambitiously developed to evaluate and compare students' levels of soft skills across multiple disciplines. The first example is the Graduate Skills Assessment (GSA) in Australia, a standardized test that was proposed in the Nelson Report (Nelson, 2002) to measure students' soft skills at the entry and exit points of their degrees. This test was targeted to monitor the 'value added' in terms of skills that universities provide to enhance graduates' employability. However, the validity of the test was questioned on grounds of equity and cultural inclusiveness (Chanock et al., 2004). The test was also criticized for leaving out many skills that universities were developing for their students. Another example is the AHELO project, which aimed to assess soft skills across HE institutions. Although the test was reported to be reliable and valid, the project did not achieve its objectives because of the complexity of the skills and practical issues related to the handling of the assessment (Tremblay et al., 2012).

Regardless of recent progress, the literature suggests that soft skills assessment is facing some challenges. Primarily, the elusive nature of soft skills creates confusion while designing soft skills assessment activities, developing methods and defining criteria. Soft skills are not discrete but are instead interrelated and context-specific (Hager & Holland, 2006; Jones, 2010). Therefore, it would not be reliable if teachers were to test their students' levels of soft skills without disciplinary context. Assessment activities would become even less reliable if there were a lack of consensus on what soft skills are, which soft skills should be assessed and how to assess them. Also, teacher disengagement with assessing soft skills is an obstacle to executing soft skills policy (de la Harpe & David, 2012; Hughes & Barrie, 2010). Because many academics do not believe that teaching soft skills is their duty (Jones, 2010), those who do not teach these skills also do not assess these skills. For those who teach and assess soft skills, they are restrained by conventional assessment practices in their institution or may face challenges using new pedagogical practices intended for teaching and assessing soft skills, which may involve cooperation with other stakeholders and require even more time and effort (Barrie et al., 2009). Therefore, despite having soft skills expertise, teachers may not teach or assess the skills if they are not confident and willing to do so (de la Harpe & David, 2012). Last but not least, student engagement with soft skills assessment activities is also important (Palmer et al., 2011; Ya-hui & Li-yia, 2008). For example, Ya-hui and Li-yia (2008) argued that:

> the lack of emphasis on students' engagement could lead to mistakenly selecting as important for the focus of assessment, simply the acquisition of skills, knowledge or dispositions, rather than the holistic connection of these to their application in the workforce. (p.1)

Perhaps it is for this reason that many soft skills assessment activities aimed to increase students' awareness of the importance of soft skills, providing them with feedback and guidance so they could develop these skills further and engage with such activities, as mentioned earlier.

In conclusion, soft skills assessment is an important part in the process of developing these skills for students; unfortunately, there are many obstacles preventing teachers from effectively organising these assessment activities. As concluded by Barrie et al. (2009), it is caused by the following factors:

- There has not yet been a consensus on what type of soft skills will be assessed, which may confuse teachers and students about which soft skills to teach and learn.
- Teachers cling to the existing assessment tradition of the discipline, rather than becoming involved with new types of assessment tasks which would be more compatible with soft skills assessment (work-integrated, internship, or portfolio, for instance).
- The effectiveness of soft skills assessment involves an incremental approach, which is time- and energy-consuming; consequently, this may result in superficial approaches to soft skills assessment.
- Some profession-oriented disciplines rely too heavily on the professional body when assessing soft skills. Such reliance may result in developing and assessing some workplace skills and undermining transformational aspirations, which form the soft skills philosophy of many universities.

- Students are not sufficiently involved in the practice of soft skills assessment, which limits the input of material for the assessment and the washback effects.

Therefore, institutional leadership should be exercised effectively in order to develop teacher capacity, increase their engagement and remove obstacles so that teachers can conduct soft skills assessment tasks to the best of their ability (Barrie et al., 2009; de la Harpe & David, 2012; Jones, 2009).

Methods

In 2013–2014, a qualitative multiple case study (Yin, 2009) was conducted to investigate factors influencing soft skills implementation in the Business Administration programs of Vietnamese universities. The qualitative method was chosen because it can effectively investigate participants' attitudes, behaviours, and experiences regarding a phenomenon in their own setting (Merriam, 2009). In addition, a multiple case study was chosen because it allows researchers to investigate an issue "in depth and within its real context" (Yin, 2009, p. 18) and several case studies would help improve the trustworthiness of the findings (Merriam, 2009).

A maximum variation sampling principle (Merriam, 2009) was employed to select the universities of different institutional contexts. Primarily based on differences in institutional types (public versus private), locations (metropolitan versus regional city-based), and their history of establishment and development, three public and three private universities were recruited for this study.

The participants from each selected university were recruited using a snowball sampling technique (Browne, 2005), which allowed the researcher to approach key informants of soft skills implementation of an institution based on the recommendation of another participant. In total, 69 participants were interviewed, including university leaders, school leaders, teachers and staff members of the Youth Union and its associates (YUA).[1]

However, this chapter only reports the practices, challenges, and factors influencing teachers' conduct of assessing soft skills. This chapter will answer the following two questions:

- How do teachers in Vietnamese universities assess students' soft skills in their subjects?
- What factors influence the conduct of assessing these skills in their subjects?

Data from 41 interviews with teachers were used for the analysis to find answers to the research questions. Among these participants, 15 were male and 26 were female. Sixteen of them were assigned to teach subjects that developed students' soft skills, such as English, communication, CV writing, job interviews, cross-culture communication skills, and HE learning methods. The other 25 teachers were those involved in teaching specialized subjects for the Business Administration programs of the six universities. A summary of participants' key demographic information is presented in Table 7.1.

Data were primarily collected by semi-structured interviews (Horton, Macve, & Struyven, 2004) with the participants. All participants were informed of the purpose of the study, their roles and measures to protect their identities. In the interviews, the researcher invited the teachers to discuss: (i) the relevance of developing soft skills for students in the current context of Vietnamese HE; (ii) their actions to help students develop the skills; (iii) factors that would facilitate or impede their teaching and assessing of these skills. The interviews lasted from 18 to 90 minutes, depending on the experience each teacher had with teaching soft skills. The interviews were recorded and transcribed verbatim for the analysis.

A qualitative content analysis (Elo & Kyngäs, 2008) was employed to analyze the 41 interviews with teachers. For the purpose of this chapter, the analysis focused on sections where interviewees discussed soft skills assessment activities and associated challenges. Occasionally, relevant documents, test samples and perspectives of university leaders would be taken into account to highlight important issues related to teachers' viewpoints. The researcher read the transcripts several times to understand the perspectives and experience of each teacher regarding teaching soft skills. Teachers' practices of assessing soft skills and

Table 7.1 A summary of participants

Universities	Teachers				
	Gender	Qualification	Work duty	Seniority	Industrial experience
A (public)	2 males 5 females	3 undergraduates 4 postgraduates	4 skills teachers 3 disciplinary teachers	3 early career 4 mid or senior	4 yes 3 no
B (public)	5 males 3 females	1 undergraduate 7 postgraduates	1 skills teacher 7 disciplinary teachers	2 early career 6 mid or senior	6 yes 2 no
C (public)	3 males 6 females	2 undergraduates 7 postgraduates	3 skills teachers 6 disciplinary teachers	2 early career 7 mid or senior	4 yes 5 no
D (private)	1 male 4 females	0 undergraduates 5 postgraduates	3 skills teachers 2 disciplinary teachers	0 early career 5 mid or senior	4 yes 1 no
E (private)	1 male 5 females	3 undergraduates 3 postgraduates	3 skills teachers 3 disciplinary teachers	3 early career 3 mid or senior	1 yes 5 no
F (private)	3 males 3 females	1 undergraduate 5 postgraduates	2 skills teachers 4 disciplinary teachers	1 early career 5 mid or senior	6 yes 0 no

challenges they faced with the practice were coded teacher by teacher. Then these codes were compared and grouped based on their similarities and differences. The codes of all 41 interviews with teachers were then put together and classified with a focus on personal and organisational factors. Finally, these findings were incorporated in the final report.

Findings

At the time of research, all six universities had initiated activities to execute the MOET's soft skills policy. Generally, they conceptualized the implementation of soft skills as developing work-readiness for students. They also commonly developed soft skills subjects to impart university learning methods, communication, presentation, teamwork, problem solving, CV writing, and job interview skills to students. English and computer skills continued to be taught to students more intensively, as these two skills are considered "soft skills" by the MOET (MOET 2010). The analysis of the curriculum of the Business Administration programs showed that the universities reserved from 12 to 40 credits[2] out of 120–140 credits of the curriculum, as regulated by the MOET, for these soft skills development subjects. University D stood out from the others with 27 credits for soft skills subjects—9 of which were compulsory, 28 credits for English subjects and 3 credits for computer subjects. These skills subjects were not treated as a co-curriculum, but part of the disciplinary curriculum of the Business Administration program. In addition to these skills subjects, the university leaders either required or encouraged other teachers to further train students in soft skills in specialized subjects. They also had the YUA organize extra-curricular activities to offer students more opportunities to develop soft skills.

However, the universities were found to be at different stages of progress in executing the soft skills policy. Specifically, University D reported to have successfully implemented the policy and was moving forward to evaluating the effectiveness of their soft skills development programs. Meanwhile, universities A, C and E were struggling with how to successfully impart these skills to students via the curriculum and extra-curricular activities. University B intentionally delayed the implementation of soft skills policy until 2015, at which point they could launch a comprehensive institutional reform. The Dean of the School of Business Administration of University F refused to implement soft skills policy. However, teachers in these two universities were encouraged to teach and assess soft skills.

Practices of assessing students' soft skills

Based on teachers' self-reports, seven teachers (17.1%) who taught specialized subjects of the Business Administration program completely ignored assessing students' soft skills, whereas the other 34 teachers (82.9%) conducted and engaged with assessing these skills to various extents. They reported that they had been assessing students' soft skills via different types of activities.

First, all 16 teachers of skills subjects and 18 teachers of specialized subjects consistently reported that they had used peer assessments to help students assess soft skills. They often assigned students to group projects and then would randomly invite a few groups to report their work to the entire class. After each presentation, the students in the class were asked to evaluate that group's performance in terms of the content of the presentation, the way group members collaborated, the way each member presented, language use, body language and confidence. Teachers commented that feedback from their peers helped students recognize strengths to further develop and weaknesses to improve. Teachers also noted that students were timid at first, but they became gradually more assertive, confident and analytical in giving feedback on their peers' performances.

Second, all teachers of skills subjects and eight teachers of specialized subjects reported that they often used self-assessment for students to develop some soft skills in simple assignments. After teachers had given general instruction, students were required to assess their own work against the criteria that the teachers had provided. The teachers hoped that this type of assessment would help students develop reflective learning skills. However, several teachers complained that students tended to disregard such assessment activities because they had already been given the answers and the results of their assignments, and thus did not independently take time to reflect on their performance in the assignment.

Third, three soft skills subject teachers from University A reported that they had used teamwork log sheets to help students develop soft skills and generate evidence to assess their soft skills. In these soft skills subjects, teachers often assigned groups of students to project work, which would be evaluated for midterm exams. The teacher provided each group with a log sheet on which students were required to record and assess their own and others' contributions to the project by percentage, along with an explanation. Based on the group's assessment and comments, combined with the quality of the project, the average score for each group member would be calculated. One teacher explained that this practice was used to develop students' teamwork skills, management skills, leadership, and a spirit of responsibility, and simultaneously identify students who relied on others to pass the midterm exam. However, samples of the log sheet that a teacher showed the researcher suggested that students focused on indicating the percentage of their contribution to the group project, but there was little information of how the project was completed and who contributed what to it. Thus, this assessment tool only provided information for the teacher to assign scores to students rather than drove students to develop soft skills as the teachers expected. Another teacher further commented that this assessment practice was disheartening because it required a great deal of time and effort for both teachers and students.

Fourth, a soft skills subject teacher from University D required students to build a portfolio of materials they had read, along with their journal writings, as evidence for the assessment of their progress in the subject. This teacher suggested that the practice required work from both the students and teachers, and the final evaluation was a substantial endeavour for teachers. Portfolios were also used for exemption of the compulsory internship in Universities D and E. According to policies in these two universities, students had to undertake a compulsory internship (two, at University D) as capstone subjects, which were purposefully used to develop both technical and soft skills for students. If they could provide evidence of full-time employment equivalent to the length of time required for the internship, they would receive an exemption from the internship. Therefore, students had to accumulate evidence of their employment records for the exemption. A school committee would evaluate their portfolios and would then make the final decision on whether students met the requirements for exemption.

Fifth, in all six universities, students' soft skills were also assessed during the capstone internship. During the internship, an experienced employee would mentor student interns to develop professional and soft skills. A disciplinary teacher from their school would mediate when students faced difficulties in the workplace, as well as supervise students as they wrote the internship report. At the end of the internship, teachers evaluated students' performance and soft skills via the internship reports and an evaluation form completed by the mentor. Specialized subject teachers consistently noted that their assessment mostly relied on mentors' feedback, primarily because heavy teaching workloads at the university prevented them from closely supervising their students throughout the internship.

Sixth, all teachers mentioned the use of student course experience questionnaires in their universities. In the literature, this questionnaire is believed to offer students an opportunity to reflect on how much they developed soft skills in a certain subject, thus increasing their awareness of the importance of developing soft skills (Ng, Kiang, and Cheung 2016; Yin, Lu, and Wang 2014). However, participants consistently suggested that the questionnaire was only used as an administrative tool to collect students' feedback about teachers' overall work performance. Consistent with their comments, the samples of the students' course experience questionnaires showed that there were virtually no questions that allowed students to reflect on their achievement of the learning objectives of a subject by completing the questionnaire.

The analysis revealed that teachers conducted soft skills assessment activities inconsistently across subjects. In all six universities, there was a lack of consensus on soft skills assessment criteria and methods. The documents collected from the interviewed participants and on the university websites only provided descriptions of soft skills development subjects, but there was no information about soft skills assessment methods and criteria. This was consistent with skills subject teachers' suggestions that they had agreed on which soft skills to assess, but they did not agree on common assessment methods and assessment criteria. For example, a soft skills subject teacher in University A commented on this as below:

> The [assessment] criteria are still not in consensus and are very much subjective dependent on each assessor. For example, in assessing problem-solving skills, it greatly relates to the assessor's knowledge, experience, and their reasoning philosophy. (Participant A5)

The situation was worse in specialized subjects because it relied entirely on teachers' discretion. There was hardly any agreement on what soft skills were to be assessed, the assessment methods to be used, assessment criteria and weighting of these skills in the total score of a subject. In most of the cases, teachers reported that they would save around 10–20% for soft skills in the total score of their subjects:

> The weighting for soft skills is not high, just around 20% [...]. I not only assess their disciplinary knowledge, but also the way they present and interact with their peers. All of these were announced to students in advance. (Participant A8)

Eighteen teachers of specialized subjects reported that they assessed students' soft skills based on their intuition, observation, or personal experience, all of which seemed to vary between teachers. This can be illustrated by how two specialized subject teachers assessed presentation skills as below:

> Their presentation is assessed based on their manners, their style of dress, the content, and creativity, which reflect the "respect for diversity" core value of the university. (Participant D4)

> The presentation must demonstrate their skills in writing the report, researching information, and organizing information as well as how they collaborate with each other. (Participant D5)

About one-third of these teachers did not assess soft skills explicitly but awarded scores to students who showed that they possessed a high level of soft skills when they worked in groups, presented assignments, or reported on group projects. They explained that they did it as an incentive to motivate students' active participation in the subjects.

In short, teachers of skills subjects and specialized subjects in the six Vietnamese universities had been using different forms of assessment to help students become aware of the importance of soft skills, provide feedback so that students could improve their level of soft skills, and evaluate students' attainment of soft skills. However, not all teachers were engaged in assessing students' soft skills. They seemed to organize these soft skills assessment activities based on their discretion, instead of a consensus on which soft skills would be assessed, assessment methods and assessment criteria. These findings suggested that there were multiple factors influencing their involvement in or conduct of soft skills assessment activities.

Challenges of assessing students' soft skills

The analysis pointed out three major difficulties of conducting soft skills assessment activities, as presented below.

Teachers' beliefs about their duties: All teachers of skills subjects believed that it was their duty to teach and assess students' soft skills because university leaders assigned them to teach such subjects. The seven teachers of specialized subjects who did not assess students' soft skills felt that it was not their duty but was the responsibility of teachers of skills subjects and the YUA. They believed that they were solely responsible for delivering specialized knowledge and technical skills. As they did not teach soft skills, they also did not need to assess them.

> I do not assess students' soft skills as part of the final assessment because it would be unfair for them: I do not teach them these skills explicitly, so I can't assess the skills explicitly. But I would rather use it as an incentive. (Participant B7)

It turned out that the belief of these specialized subject teachers stemmed from unclear communication of soft skills policy and implementation strategy. Except for teachers from University D, teachers of specialized subjects from other universities often cited the word "encourage" that university leaders used to justify their not teaching and assessing soft skills. However, interviews with university leaders helped clarify that these leaders expected teachers to develop soft skills for students to the best of their ability rather than choosing whether to develop soft skills or not.

Most specialized subject teachers, except those from University D, thought that assessing students' soft skills was secondary to imparting discipline-specific skills and knowledge. It was also interesting to note that four teachers of specialized subjects assessed students' soft skills even though they did not teach any of these skills in their subjects. Those teachers explained that as soft skills had been taught in skills subjects, they expected students to apply these skills into their learning of specialized subjects. Therefore, these four teachers always reserved a small portion of the overall score for assessing students' soft skills.

Teachers' expertise: The English teachers all suggested that they confidently trained students in English skills because they had been professionally trained to teach English as a foreign language and often attended conferences and seminars organized in their regions and their own universities. However, teachers of soft skills subjects and specialized subjects, including those from University D, admitted that they sometimes felt confused when conducting other soft skills assessment activities. As soft skills were abstract, they believed that teaching these skills was difficult, assessing these skills was even more difficult, and would need specific methods. Unfortunately, unlike English teachers, most of them consistently reported that a lack of training in methods for assessing students' soft skills hindered them from effectively conducting soft skills assessments. In their opinions, although the universities organized pedagogical training sessions prior to their commencement of academic teaching, these training sessions focused on general teaching and assessment methods, mostly theories; therefore, when it came to assessing soft skills specifically, they were confused and were not able to confidently assess these skills.

Contextual factors: Many organisational factors were found to inhibit teachers' abilities to conduct soft skills assessments. Most teachers complained that assessing soft skills was disheartening because it required substantial effort and was very time-consuming. Because soft skills assessment activities were organized throughout the course to give students feedback on how they could improve their soft skills, the workloads proliferated in large class sizes. Even so, teachers were not incentivized to effectively execute the job. Nor did the universities manage teachers regarding their teaching and assessing soft skills. Two teachers commented on these issues as below:

> Large class size is one of the obstacles of our teaching of soft skills [...]. There are over 50 students in the class. Thirty students are already too many. I am unable to observe all of them. (Participant A5)

> There were no drivers for soft skills teaching, so teachers just do whatever they want. Gradually, they would not commit to developing soft skills for students. Why would they make themselves tired with more work? (Participant F6)

It was relatively common to hear from both groups of teachers that they or their colleagues reduced the number of formative assessment activities as well as the complexity of assessment tasks to alleviate their workload. These behaviours could have affected the quality of soft skills assessment activities and students' generic learning outcomes.

In addition, teachers in Universities E and F stated that the assessment convention in their universities reduced the effectiveness of assessing students' soft skills. They pointed out that in both skills and specialized subjects, teachers could only organize formative soft skills assessment activities and evaluate students' learning outcomes with one midterm exam, which was worth approximately 30 to 40% of the total score. For specialized subjects, this 30 to 40% included specialized knowledge, technical skills and soft skills. The remainder was reserved for the final exam, which was organized university-wide on the same day for all students studying the same subject. In their opinion, in most of the cases, the final exams focused only on testing students' content knowledge and specific technical skills, rather than soft skills. Consequently, students disregarded participating in soft skills development activities that teachers organized in class—including skills subjects—and appeared to only participate when teachers forced them to do so or when these activities were assessed for grades. A teacher commented on student disengagement as below:

> Students only want to complete the program and graduate. They don't care about soft skills, no matter how we emphasize the importance of these skills. (Participant C3)

In summary, assessing soft skills was challenging because teachers did not believe that teaching and assessing soft skills was their responsibility in HE. It was also difficult because most teachers did not have adequate experience with teaching and assessing these skills. Even when they attempted to do so, several contextual factors hampered their efforts.

Discussion and conclusion

This study investigated activities that teachers in Vietnamese universities used to assess their students' soft skills and factors influencing their assessment practices.

The study found that teachers used various activities to assess their students' soft skills, just like their counterparts in Western universities: self-assessment, peer-assessment, portfolios, teamwork log sheets, and capstone internships (Keller et al., 2011; Lai, 2016; Lawson et al., 2012; Palmer et al., 2011). All of these were used for formative and/or summative assessment purposes. However, the study indicated that teachers inconsistently used or disengaged with these assessment practices due to several factors. This section will further discuss and highlight the relationship between these factors.

Consistent with existing literature (de la Harpe & David, 2012; Hughes & Barrie, 2010), teacher beliefs about their roles in higher education was the primary factor that decided whether a teacher would become involved in assessing soft skills. As reported in the Findings section, all teachers of skills subjects assessed soft skills because they were formally appointed in that role. Meanwhile, seven specialized subject teachers ignored assessing soft skills completely; and the remaining teachers, aside from those at University D, occasionally organized formative soft skills assessment activities because there was a lack of clarity in communicating soft skills policy and soft skills development responsibilities to them. This made many of them believe that teaching and assessing soft skills were primarily the responsibility of teachers of skills subjects and the YUA, while their responsibilities were teaching and assessing specialized knowledge and technical skills. This suggests that clarity in communicating soft skills development duties and initiatives to increase teachers' belief in this role are prerequisites for teachers to begin to engage with assessing soft skills.

If teachers believed that developing soft skills for students was their responsibility, their lack of expertise in assessing these skills was another obstacle. This lack of expertise initially seemed to stem from the fact that soft skills are elusive, cluster together and are often associated with the nature of each discipline (Gonczi, 2006). Assessing soft skills is thus not as simple as marking a right or wrong answer to a question. Rather, it requires a teacher to possess these skills and accumulate experience in recognition and judgement of students' behaviours in tasks that involve the use of these skills. However, many teachers in Vietnamese universities did not have authentic work experience in industries nor did they have opportunities to develop expertise in soft skills teaching and assessment. In this study, English teachers could perform their teaching and assessment activities satisfactorily, possibly because English had been taught as an important subject in the HE curricula and teacher professional development activities had been frequently organized (Duong & Chua, 2016). In contrast, other soft skills subjects had just been added into the curricula, closely following the MOET's soft skills policy in 2010. Likewise, specialized subject teachers were used to transmitting theoretical knowledge to students and assessing this knowledge rather than training students in soft skills (Harman & Bich, 2010). Consequently, when it came to assessing soft skills, they were confused by new approaches to soft skills assessment, many of which they had not used before, such as portfolio or teamwork log sheets, or co-assessment with an industry-based mentor in the case of internships. At the time of research, most of them reported conducting soft skills assessment based on their observations or intuition, without concrete assessment criteria. The problem is that it is difficult to determine the reliability of teachers' observations or intuition. These issues suggest that it is essential for the universities to train teachers in using soft skills assessment practices so that they could embark on and engage with the duty. Unfortunately, this study revealed that aside from University D, the other Vietnamese universities did not provide training that specifically developed teacher capacity in assessing soft skills. As previously mentioned, leaders of Vietnamese universities were focusing on other reforms that were simultaneously taking place (Harman, Hayden, & Nghi, 2010), so they often left soft skills teaching and assessment to the teachers' discretion instead of investing in developing teacher capacity for teaching and assessing soft skills.

Without institutional leadership, on top of a lack of expertise, teachers also faced several contextual factors that hindered them from effectively conducting soft skills assessment activities. Large class sizes multiplied teachers' workloads because assessing soft skills required a great deal of effort and time. Teachers reported that they could not efficiently organize formative soft skills assessment activities, which requires giving constructive feedback to each student. Many of them attempted to use self and peer assessment as a compensation, but it relied heavily on students' engagement with these activities. The existing assessment practice also reduced their chances to effectively assess and evaluate students' soft skills. A common exam organized at the end of the semester meant that teachers could only assess and evaluate their students' soft skills for the midterm exam, which often accounted for 30–40% of the total score of a subject, and included soft skills, specialized knowledge and technical skills. Therefore, this situation did not compel students to get involved in soft skills development activities, including formative soft skills assessment activities, which further discouraged teachers. Regrettably, as mentioned earlier, instead of removing these contextual barriers and giving incentives for teachers to engage with soft skills assessment, Vietnamese university leaders were prioritizing other reforms that were concurrently taking place in their institutions (Harman et al., 2010). As such, even when teachers put forth the effort to assess soft skills, their effort would not succeed if obstacles, e.g. large class sizes, student disengagement with developing soft skills, and inertia of conventional assessment practices, were not removed.

All the obstacles discussed above could have been removed by effective leadership, which can be evidenced by the case of University D. Leaders of this university exercised effective leadership to strategically build teacher expertise and support teachers with practicality issues for their teaching and assessment activities, and used incentives and management tools to engage teachers with teaching and soft skills assessment activities; thus, the university experienced success in the implementation of soft skills policy. In contrast, a lack of effective leadership created challenges for teachers to organize soft skills assessment activities. Teachers in universities A, B and E faced difficulties because leaders paid more attention to other institutional reforms. Soft skills teaching and assessment in universities B and F were almost completely halted by leadership decisions, relying heavily on teachers' discretion. Teachers in universities aside from University D were not trained to develop soft skills expertise, nor were they supported or incentivized when they attempted to teach and assess soft skills. As such, many of them felt discouraged and withdrew from the implementation. In this way, the case of Vietnamese universities confirmed that leadership is pivotal for engaging teachers with soft skills teaching and assessment activities, just as Barrie et al. (2009) argued in their study.

In short, this study found that teachers were using different soft skills assessment activities to increase students' awareness of the importance of these skills, giving constructive feedback so that students could further develop them, and measuring students' levels of soft skills. However, soft skills assessment activities were not conducted consistently across the subjects of a program. Some teachers disengaged from assessing soft skills because they believed that it was not their duty, as well as unclear communication of teacher responsibilities by university leaders. Others did not assess soft skills because of their lack of expertise, large class sizes, a lack of incentives and management tools, and existing practices of assessment in the institution. These factors appeared to stem from a lack of leadership exercised for soft skills teaching and assessment, which was linked to the fact that university leaders prioritized other important reforms simultaneously taking place. As such, if universities wish to compel their teachers to conduct soft skills assessment activities, which will contribute to the success of the implementation of soft skills policy, university leadership should be leveraged more effectively to inform teachers of their roles and responsibilities, to encourage teacher engagement by incentives and management tools, to train them in soft skills assessment methods, and create favourable conditions for them to conduct these assessment activities. Finally, it should be noted that this study relied on teachers' self-report, and did not include class observation to witness how teachers conducted soft skills assessment activities in the classroom. Therefore, findings should be interpreted carefully. Future studies should include different sources of data, including teachers' self-report, class observations and students' reports, so that teachers' soft skills assessment practices and influential factors can be examined more thoroughly.

Note

This chapter is reproduced from the following journal article with the permission from Taylor and Francis: Tran, L. H. N. (2017). "It is complicated!": Practices and challenges of generic skills assessment in Vietnamese universities. *Educational Studies, 44*(2), 230–224. doi: 10.1080/03055698.2017.1347496. There is minor adaptation to make it fit into the context of this book.

Notes

1 The YUA are socio-political organisations under the Communist Party of Vietnam that are installed in each school and university, primarily in charge of political education and leading social engagement activities.
2 At the time of research, the MOET regulated that an undergraduate program should be organised within 120–140 credits, where a credit is equivalent to 15 sessions of 45–50 minute face-to-face teaching–learning.

References

Barrie, S., Hughes, C., Smith, C., & Thomson, K. (2009). *The national graduate attributes project: Key issues to consider in the renewal of learning and teaching experiences to foster graduate attributes*. Sydney: Australian Learning and Teaching Council.

Bodewig, C., & Badiani-Magnusson, R. (2014). *Skilling up Vietnam: Preparing the workforce for a modern market economy*. Washington, DC: World Bank Publications.

Browne, K. (2005). Snowball sampling: Using social networks to research non-heterosexual women. *International Journal of Social Research Methodology*, 8(1), 47–60.

Bunney, D., Sharplin, E., & Howitt, C. (2015). Generic skills for graduate accountants: The bigger picture, a social and economic imperative in the new knowledge economy. *Higher Education Research & Development*, 34(2), 256–269.

Burke, K. (2010). *Balanced assessment from formative to summative (Vol. 25)*. Portland, OR: Ringgold Inc.

Chanock, K., Clerehan, R., Moore, T., & Prince, A. (2004). Shaping university teaching towards measurement for accountability: Problems of the graduate skills assessment test. *Australian Universities' Review*, 47(1), 22–29.

Cranney, J., Kofod, M., Huon, G., Jensen, L., Levin, K., McAlpine, I., Scoufis, M., & Whitaker, N. (2012). Portfolio tools: Learning and teaching strategies to facilitate development of graduate attributes. Paper presented at the Proceedings of The Australian Conference on Science and Mathematics Education (formerly UniServe Science Conference). Retrieved from: https://bit.ly/2KSckTE

de la Harpe, B., & David, C. (2012). Major influences on the teaching and assessment of graduate attributes. *Higher Education Research & Development*, 31(4), 493–510.

Duong, V. A., & Chua, C. S. (2016). English as a symbol of internationalization in higher education: A case study of Vietnam. *Higher Education Research & Development*, 35(4), 669–683.

Elo, S., & Kyngäs, H. (2008). The qualitative content analysis process. *Journal of Advanced Nursing*, 62(1), 107–115.

Gonczi, A. (2006). The OECD: Its role in the key competencies debate and in the promotion of lifelong learning. In P. Hager & S. Holland (Eds.), *Graduate attributes, learning and employability* (pp. 105–124). Dordrecht, Netherlands: Springer.

Hager, P., & Holland, S. (2006). *Graduate attributes, learning and employability (Vol. 6)*. Dordrecht, Netherlands: Springer.

Harman, G., Hayden, M., & Nghi, P. T. (2010). *Higher education in Vietnam: Reform, challenges and priorities*. New York, NY: Springer.

Harman, K., & Bich, N. T. N. (2010). Reforming teaching and learning in Vietnam's higher education system. In G. Harman, M. Hayden, & P. T. Nghi (Eds.), *Reforming higher education in Vietnam: Challenges and priorities* (pp. 65–86). New York, NY: Springer.

Hernández, R. (2012). Does continuous assessment in higher education support student learning? *Higher Education*, 64(4), 489–502.

Holdsworth, A., Watty, K., & Davies, M. (2009). *Developing capstone experiences*. Melbourne: Centre for the Study of Higher Education, University of Melbourne.

Horton, J., Macve, R., & Struyven, G. (2004). Qualitative research: Experiences in using semi-structured interviews. In C. Humphrey & B. Lee (Eds.), *The real life guide to accounting research: a behind-the-scenes view of using qualitative research methods* (pp. 339–357). Oxford, UK: Elsevier.

Hughes, C., & Barrie, S. (2010). Influences on the assessment of graduate attributes in higher education. *Assessment & Evaluation in Higher Education*, 35(3), 325–334.

Jackson, D. (2014). Self-assessment of employability skill outcomes among undergraduates and alignment with academic ratings. *Assessment & Evaluation in Higher Education*, 39(1), 53–72.
Jones, A. (2009). Generic attributes as espoused theory: The importance of context. *Higher Education*, 58(2), 175–191.
Jones, A. (2010). Generic attributes in accounting: The significance of the disciplinary context. *Accounting Education: An International Journal*, 19(1–2), 5–21.
Kao, G. Y. M. (2013). Enhancing the quality of peer review by reducing student "free riding": Peer assessment with positive interdependence. *British Journal of Educational Technology*, 44(1), 112–124.
Keller, S., Parker, C. M., & Chan, C. (2011). Employability skills: Student perceptions of an IS final year capstone subject. *Innovation in Teaching and Learning in Information and Computer Sciences*, 10(2), 4–15.
Lai, C.-Y. (2016). Training nursing students' communication skills with online video peer assessment. *Computers & Education*, 97, 21–30.
Lawson, R., Taylor, T., Thompson, D., Simpson, L., Freeman, M., Treleaven, L., & Rohde, F. (2012). Engaging with graduate attributes through encouraging accurate student self-assessment. *Asian Social Science*, 8(4), 3–12.
ManPowerGroup (2011). *Building a high-skilled economy: A new Vietnam*. Retrieved from https://bit.ly/2XCRMjz
McMahon, M., Luca, J., & John, C. (2007). A self-assessment tool to help learners develop teamwork skills. Paper presented at EdMedia: World Conference on Educational Media and Technology. Retrieved from: https://ro.ecu.edu.au/ecuworks/1609/
Merriam, S. B. (2009). *Qualitative research: A guide to design and implementation*. San Francisco, CA: Jossey-Bass.
MOET (2010). *Công văn 2916/ BGDĐT-GDĐH hướng dẫn xây dựng và công bố chuẩn đầu ra ngành đào tạo*. Retrieved from https://bit.ly/2VlKS4I
Musekamp, F., & Pearce, J. (2015). Assessing engineering competencies: The conditions for educational improvement. *Studies in Higher Education*, 40(3), 505–524.
Nelson, B. (2002). *Striving for quality: Learning, teaching and scholarship*. Canberra: Department of Education, Science and Training.
Ng, A. K.-L., Kiang, K.-M., & Cheung, D. H.-C. (2016). Assessing students' attainment in learning outcomes: A comparison of course-end evaluation and entry-exit surveys. *World Journal of Education*, 6(3), 56–65.
Nguyen, N. D., Ngoc, N. B., & Montague, A. (2019). Enhancing graduate work-readiness in Vietnam. In S. Dhakal, V. Prikshat, A. Nankervis, & J. Burgess (Eds.), *The transition from graduation to work* (pp. 221–237). Singapore: Springer.
Palmer, S., Holt, D., Hall, W., & Ferguson, C. (2011). An evaluation of an online student portfolio for the development of engineering graduate attributes. *Computer Applications in Engineering Education*, 19(3), 447–456.
Quarrie, S. P. (2007). Student peer review as a tool for efficiently achieving subject-specific and generic learning outcomes: Examples in botany at the Faculty of Agriculture, University of Belgrade. *Higher Education in Europe*, 32(2–3), 203–212.
Rowley, J., Munday, J., & Polly, P. (2017). Preparing future career ready professionals: A portfolio process to develop critical thinking using digital learning and teaching. Paper presented at the International Conference on Interactive Collaborative Learning, 27–29 Sep, Budapest, Hungary.
Tertiary Education Quality and Standards Agency (2013). *Australian qualifications framework*. Canberra, Australia: The Australian Qualifications Framework Council.

Tran, L. H. N. (2018). The skills gap of Vietnamese graduates and final-year university students. *Journal of Education and Work*, 31(7–8), 579–594.

Tremblay, K., Lalancette, D., & Roseveare, D. (2012). Assessment of higher education learning outcomes. Feasibility study report. OECD. Retrieved from: https://bit.ly/2IRTRnB

World Bank (2008). *Vietnam: Higher education and skills for growth*. Retrieved from https://openknowledge.worldbank.org/handle/10986/7814

Ya-hui, S., & Li-yia, F. (2008). Assessing graduate attributes for employability in the context of lifelong learning: The holistic approach. *US–China Education Review*, 5(11). Retrieved from: https://files.eric.ed.gov/fulltext/ED503876.pdf

Yin, H., Lu, G., & Wang, W. (2014). Unmasking the teaching quality of higher education: Students' course experience and approaches to learning in China. *Assessment & Evaluation in Higher Education*, 39(8), 949–970.

Yin, R. K. (2009). *Case study research, design & methods* (4th edn). Thousand Oaks, CA: Sage.

8 The contribution of internships to students' development of employability

Introduction

Internships, also referred to as cooperative education or work placement (Gault, Leach, & Duey, 2010), are "a term-length placement of an enrolled student in an organization—sometimes with pay, sometimes without pay—with a faculty supervisor, a company supervisor and some academic credit earned toward the degree" (Narayanan, Olk, & Fukami, 2010, p. 61). Higher education (HE) institutions have lately been using this mode of training more intensively to expose their students to the real workplace, develop their professional skills, and enhance their career prospects. This is possibly because competition for jobs between university graduates is becoming more intense (Li, Whalley, & Xing, 2014; Wu, 2011).

Existing studies reveal that internships can positively contribute to graduates' career prospects by helping them develop relevant professional skills and soft skills, connect with professionals, become acclimated to the workplace, and enhance employment competitiveness (Gault et al., 2010; Khalil, 2015; Nunley, Pugh, Romero, & Seals Jr, 2016; Simiyu, Okaka, & Omondi, 2015). Conversely, studies also point out the negative impact of internships on career development, such as causing the interns to feel stressed or burnt out, to doubt their competencies, and to feel confused about their career-path choices (Odio, Sagas, & Kerwin, 2014). These mixed results require further investigation because students' experiences with internships may be affected by different personal factors, such as their beliefs about the importance of the internship and their engagement with it, as well as influence from stakeholders involved in the internship.

This chapter will report a qualitative study that explored students' internship experience, with a focus on soft-skills development, and factors influencing their learning experience throughout the internship. The analyses of 28 in-depth interviews with student interns in Tourism and Hospitality, Business Administration and Information Technology of two Vietnamese universities revealed that internships helped students consolidate and develop professional knowledge and skills, identify their career paths, expand their professional network, and change their learning attitudes and behaviors. Students' beliefs and engagement, collaboration between the university and industry, and knowledge and skill gaps between what the university delivers and what industry needs were important factors influencing students' learning experiences. This chapter recommends that students' meta-cognition of their learning process and university–industry collaboration should be enhanced so that students' internship experiences are more positive, which in turn benefits them in developing employability capital, including soft skills.

Employability, employability capital, and employment outcomes

Employability is often understood as "a set of achievements—skills, understanding and personal attributes—that makes graduates more likely to gain employment and be successful in their chosen occupations, which benefits themselves, the workforce, the community and the economy" (Yorke, 2006, p. 23). It enables graduates to find and create jobs that benefit them and the people around them (Oliver, 2015). As a growing idea, employability not only comprises human capital but also involves students' psychological attributes, social networks, and sense of belonging (Clarke, 2017; Fugate, Kinicki, & Ashforth, 2004; Tomlinson, 2017).

Resembling McQuaid and Lindsay's (2005) employability framework, Fugate et al.'s (2004) human capital refers to a range of factors that "influence a person's career advancement variables such as age and education, work experience and training, job performance and organization tenure, emotional intelligence, cognitive ability and KSAOs"[1] (p. 24). They are closely associated with occupational expertise and high-order thinking skills such as teamwork, problem-solving, and critical-thinking skills, and link to career identity, especially in highly specialized disciplines such as medicine and teaching (Clarke, 2017).

Social capital encompasses the social assets arising from social memberships, networks, and relationships (Bourdieu & Wacquant, 1992). Likewise, Tomlinson (2017, p. 342) considers social capital as "the sum of social relationships and networks that help mobilize graduates' existing human capital and bring them closer to the labor market and its opportunity structures". A large network with influential members would enhance graduates' awareness of employment opportunities and give them a higher chance of finding employment (Fugate et al., 2004; Tomlinson, 2017).

In Bourdieu's perspective, cultural capital refers to the skills, knowledge, titles, and sensibilities people possess (Bourdieu, 1989, p. 21). However, in this chapter, this perspective is not used as it appears to resemble the concept of human capital of other authors. Instead, in this chapter cultural capital is "the formation of culturally valued knowledge, dispositions and behaviours that are aligned to the workplaces that graduates seek to enter" (Tomlinson, 2017, p. 333). This capital is often connected to students' experience of mobility, or mobility capital (King, Findlay, & Ahrens, 2010).

Career identity "provides a compass for the individual, thereby offering a motivational component to employability" (Fugate et al., 2004, p. 20), "provides a frame through which they may be able to channel their experiences and profiles" (Tomlinson, 2017, p. 345), or "diffuse[s] career experiences and aspirations" (Fugate et al., 2004, p. 19). It defines who graduates will be or become, and may include goals, hopes, fears, personal traits, values, and beliefs.

Personal adaptability refers to the changing of personal knowledge, skills, and attitudes to meet the demands of the situation (Clarke, 2017; Fugate et al., 2004).

Optimism to challenges, propensity to learn, openness to changes and new experiences, internal locus of control, and generalized self-efficacy are five aspects of personal adaptability (Fugate et al., 2004). Likewise, adaptability, self-efficacy, and resilience are essential elements of psychological capital that may enhance graduate employability (Tomlinson, 2017).

It is recognised that most of the employability capital above belongs to the domain of soft skills, except part of the human capital. Soft skills may include different domains such as emotional intelligence, personalities, psychological attributes, personal and interpersonal skills, and non-cognitive skills. Therefore, soft skills constitute a significant part of graduates' employability.

It is also noted that employability is not equal to employment outcomes. Graduates may possess employability capital, which makes them employable, but their employment outcomes still depend much on the extent to which the labour market needs their capital as well as how they get access to job information and demonstrate their capital to prospective employers. Provided that graduates have a similar set of specialized skills, soft skills would distinguish between "right" and "not so right" candidates for a job vacancy in an employer's perception.

Internship experience and the development of students' employability

Large volumes of internship-related studies have been conducted and consistently point out that internships bring benefits to students. First, internships can help students apply the acquired knowledge and skills as well as develop new knowledge and relevant professional skills (Gilbert, Banks, Houser, Rhodes, & Lees, 2014; Khalil, 2015; Simiyu et al., 2015). For example, using paired T-tests to analyze students' self-ratings, Gilbert et al. (2014) found that interns of life and health sciences at Indiana University–Purdue University, Indianapolis could increase their awareness and use of appropriate methodology as well as proficiency in their area of expertise just six months after entry into the internship. The study also revealed that by the end of the internship, students could significantly improve their written communication skills, ability to apply classroom knowledge, and knowledge of topic areas. Likewise, investigating students' experiences with the internship program of business students at Kuwait University, Khalil (2015) found that the internship strongly enhanced students' adaptability to the workplace, improved their ability to work in teams and to behave professionally, and it improved computer skills as well as communication skills.

Second, internships can afford students an opportunity to navigate the world of work. Studies conducted by Simiyu et al. (2015) and Schmidt (2017) indicated that internships offered students opportunities to connect with employers and professionals in the industry they were targeting. The researchers also found that interns learned to acclimate to workplace settings and explore different career paths via their own experience or the guidance of professionals and mentors. Some studies also documented that most interns grew confident in developing their career within the industry in which they undertook the internship (Odio et al.,

2014; Rothman & Sisman, 2016). In their qualitative longitudinal study, Odio et al. (2014) also found that internships can confuse many students of sport and event management regarding their career paths. These studies suggest that students' authentic experiences with the internship are significant for their career decisions: they can be as much encouraging as they are discouraging, which needs further investigation.

Third, graduates who have undertaken internships often have better employment opportunities. They can usually find higher-paid positions, and often have a higher level of job satisfaction (Gault et al., 2010; Khalil, 2015; Nunley et al., 2016; Simiyu et al., 2015). For example, results of a study by Gault et al. (2010) indicated that undergraduates with internship experience are more likely to obtain full-time employment opportunities—and often with higher starting salaries—than those who did not participate in internships, even average-performing interns. Similarly, a study by Nunley et al. (2016) revealed that graduates with internship experience could increase their job interview rate by 14%, and this rate was even more significant for those who had high academic achievements and had completed a non-business degree.

Fourth, despite limited research in this area, internships have been found to enhance students' learning. A large-scale study conducted by Binder, Baguley, Crook, and Miller (2015) led to the conclusion that internships could improve students' learning; however, these academic benefits appeared to be associated with aspects of the non-academic environment where internships took place. Tran and Nguyen (2018) also found that internships could help change students' attitudes toward learning. It could be that in the internship environment, interns were exposed to workplace diversity, affected by authentic connections with peers or community, frequently received performance feedback from mentors or professionals, and engaged in self-reflection, all of which encourage students to develop their reflective learning ability.

Factors influencing students' experience with the internship

Research also indicates that students' experience with internships depends on several factors. Student engagement may be an important determinant that can contribute to positive internship learning outcomes. Students must possess a sufficient level of professional knowledge and skills to satisfactorily complete assigned tasks in the internship, in which they can also consolidate their knowledge, polish existing skills, and develop new skills (Jackson, 2015; Narayanan et al., 2010). Likewise, their meta-cognition and attitudes toward the internship can also determine the level of benefits they may get from the internship. For example, students without adequate awareness of the importance of internships may overlook these learning opportunities; students from regions of low unemployment rates may not value the internship or exert as much effort during the internship as their counterparts in regions of high unemployment rates. According to the community of practice and situated learning theories (Lave & Wenger, 1991; Wenger, 2010), if interns do not deeply participate in tasks assigned during the internship, they may not develop their professional knowledge and skills as much as they should. Similarly, several studies have found correlations between one's beliefs and behaviors (Borghetti & Beaven, 2017; Montano & Kasprzyk, 2015) or with interference of contextual factors (Navarro & Thornton, 2011). Therefore, students' beliefs about the importance of the internship may also direct their behaviors during the internship, or engagement, which in turn affect the internship outcomes.

Moreover, the extent to which students are involved in tasks during the internship, quality supervision and feedback can also affect the benefits interns may receive via undertaking the internship (Lam & Ching, 2007; Narayanan et al., 2010; Odio et al., 2014; Read et al., 2017). For example, Lam and Ching (2007) examined 307 interns in Hong Kong and found that the supervisor, team spirit and involvement, autonomy, and help from the supervisor led to the students' overall satisfaction with the internship. Another study with 119 student coaches conducted by Read et al. (2017) also showed that while internships provided worthwhile experiences and facilitated skills development, the effectiveness appeared to heavily depend on mentoring, especially on the clearly defined responsibilities of internship providers and interns.

In short, existing literature suggests that internships can bring students many benefits; however, these benefits appear to depend on several factors related to interns, involved stakeholders, and the contexts in which they take the internship. Therefore, it is worth investigating students' internship experiences and influential factors so as to help improve their learning experience with this valuable work-integrated learning opportunity.

The present study

The study reported in this chapter aims to explore students' learning experiences with the internships, with a special focus on how their soft skills are developed throughout the internship, as well as identify factors influencing their learning experiences. Specifically, it aims to find answers to the following research questions:

- In what ways do internships benefit students in terms of building their employability?
- What factors influence their internship learning outcomes?

The study was carried out as a qualitative study because the qualitative method can investigate and understand attitudes, behaviors, and experiences of individuals regarding a phenomenon in their own setting (Merriam, 2009).

An invitation for an in-depth interview was sent via email to all fourth-year students of Tourism and Hospitality, Business Administration and Information Technology, who had just completed an internship within the last three months. These three programs were offered by three different universities located in the south of Vietnam: two public and one private. The email explained to students the objectives of the study, their roles in the interview process, and how their identity would be protected. A total of 28 students agreed to join the interview: 12

students of Tourism and Hospitality, eight of Business Administration, and eight of Information Technology. Among them, 16 were male and 12 were female. All of them were between 21 and 23 years of age at the time of research.

Prior to the interview, the participants were informed of the study purpose again and the measures to protect their identity and were asked for their consent. In the interview, each student was asked to discuss: (i) their beliefs about the importance of the internship that they held before they actually undertook it; (ii) how they engaged with the internship; (iii) their experience with the internship; and (iv) the influence of the internship experience on their career intention. The interviews were recorded and transcribed verbatim.

Qualitative data were analyzed using a content-analysis approach (Elo & Kyngäs, 2008). On a case-by-case basis, the researcher openly coded the transcript. Then the codes were grouped based on their similarities to form themes of internship benefits and influencing factors. The four major themes were: (i) students' beliefs about the importance of the internship before they actually undertook it; (ii) their engagement during the internship; (iii) perceived benefits of the internship with regard to their employability development; and (iv) factors influencing their internship learning experience.

Students' beliefs about the importance of internships

All students believed that the internship was either "important" or "very important" for their studies. They believed that it was an opportunity for them to face reality, to put their knowledge and skills into practice, and to prepare for their future career. The following comment was common among them:

> Internships are extremely important. Undertaking them, students can improve knowledge and understanding about the profession in its real context, have opportunities to polish their work skills and adaptability to the business environment, have chances to establish a new relationship with professionals, as well as enhance students' confidence and readiness to enter the labor market. (Participant 4—Tourism and Hospitality)

However, students held different beliefs about the influence of their internship experience on future employment outcomes. They commonly suggested several factors can contribute to the success of a job applicant, such as professional knowledge and skills, credentials from a prestigious institution, and relevant work experience. Most students also mentioned that social relationships, either forged by them, or their family members and friends, were essential determinants of employment outcomes in Vietnam. Their perspectives can be illustrated by the comments below:

> A job application has many elements, such as university degree, certificate of foreign language, certificate of computer skills, and portfolio that shows our competence. [...] So, internships can be learning opportunities rather than an

important determinant of employment outcomes. (Participant 1—Tourism and Hospitality)

I think it depends on where you undertake the internship and what you are involved in doing in that company. Like, many of my friends applied for software development internship, but they ended up working as Internet technicians. I believe that their internship did not contribute to relevant employment outcomes. (Participant 22—Information Technology)

Students' engagement with internships

Students' engagement with the internship can be demonstrated via different dimensions. First, while most students looked for a company or a position where they would like to undertake the internship, about a quarter of participants relied on their universities, family members, or teachers for the internship.

> I looked for internship opportunities through the website internship.edu.vn. I applied everywhere and finally got three offers, but I accepted the offer from [name of the organization] because I would like to have a high score for my internship unit. (Participant 16—Business Administration)

> It is difficult to get an internship opportunity relevant to our study, so I relied on my university to find one relevant for me. (Participant 19—Business Administration)

Just over half of them mentioned that they learned about the company and the position they were about to undertake during the internship. These students also prepared for their internship by reviewing the knowledge that they believed would be useful for the work role.

> It is good to get to know about the company, such as the work culture, their strength and expertise, so that we can focus on reviewing knowledge in that respect. Also, getting to know the company will create an advantage during the interview for the internship and working with colleagues later. (Participant 18—Information Technology)

Throughout the internship, the majority reported that they invested a great deal of effort into all of the assigned tasks. Several reported that they looked for opportunities to be involved in specific tasks so that they could develop skills they wanted to improve, or just to network with professionals.

> Although I had to undertake the internship in a company far from my home, I managed to be on time every day. […] Because they did not have enough employees, I was assigned a lot of things to do and I tried to complete all. Some days I stayed late until 6pm. I generally asked my colleagues all the things that I did not know to learn from them. (Participant 20—Business Administration)

> I tried my best during the internship to gain as much experience as possible, as well as leaving good impressions with the employer so that I could apply for a job there later. (Participant 11—Tourism and Hospitality)

Nevertheless, a number of students confessed that they just completed the internship as required, or to access the database in the company, collecting data for their undergraduate thesis rather than engaging with it. Others admitted that they did not try hard enough during the internship or that they passively relied on their mentor to assign tasks rather than proactively working on tasks within their work role.

> I did not try my best during the internship. Personally, I did not prepare adequate professional knowledge, and was not confident enough. I did not have good health, either, to join in all of the activities with tourists. (Participant 1—Tourism and Hospitality)

Others disengaged with the internship because they were not involved enough in the daily work life of the company or were assigned to do tasks irrelevant to their expertise or had to carry out tasks misaligned with their expectation before the internship.

> My mentor told me that I did not need to come to the company. When there were tourists, he would call me in. […] I think I was involved in tasks too little. My classmates who undertook the internship in other companies were involved in many tasks. (Participant 7—Tourism and Hospitality)
> My friend chose to accept the internship offered by [name of the company], but when he was there, he did not have anything big to do. They gave him some side jobs rather than being involved in the real project there, which I believe was not useful for his skills development. (Participant 22—Information Technology)

These results suggested that students appreciated the possible benefits that internships might bring them. However, their engagement with the internship appeared to depend on their beliefs and attitudes towards it and how they were involved in tasks during that internship. Their engagement was also demonstrated in various ways, not always in observable behaviors.

Contribution of internships to students' employability

The analysis showed that the internships helped students develop different types of employability capital that could enhance their chances of getting a job upon graduation and their career development. Soft skills were found to constitute a major part of the employability capital in addition to technical knowledge and skills.

Human capital

Consistent with the findings in many previous studies, such as Gilbert et al. (2014), Khalil (2015), Simiyu et al. (2015) and Schmidt (2017), this study found that the internships helped students develop more professional expertise. They recognized that the internship afforded them opportunities to consolidate existing knowledge and apply it to assigned tasks. Through trial and error, they admitted that they gradually improved these essential professional skills. Simultaneously, they could identify the gaps between their existing knowledge and what was required to perform the tasks well.

> I learned a lot from that internship via my observation and experience working in particular tasks. After four months, I understood many things in marketing practices in the sales industry: how it is operated, how people build a trademark, etc. (Participant 16—Business Administration)
> I could apply skills that I learned about programming and databases to work on the real database of the company ... Compared with what I learned from my formal studies, what I learned from the internship is newer and more practical. (Participant 21—Information Technology)

Students also suggested that the internship put them in situations that forced them to acquire these new skills. They confirmed that despite initial embarrassment, they could gradually carry out the assigned tasks with confidence. The internship also helped them develop soft skills to the next level and within real-life situations.

> When I first came to the office, I did not know how to use the fax machine, search for potential customers, and market our tours to them, because these skills were not taught at the university. [...] Similarly, there were situations that required our flexibility, such as guests requesting to change their rooms, handling fee discrepancies when a kid accompanies an adult guest. So, I think I developed my problem-solving skills the most in the internship. (Participant 8—Tourism and Hospitality)
> In the company, I learned more about new technologies and developed different soft skills like communication, especially communication in English, communication with my superiors, with colleagues or my subordinates. (Participant 23—Information Technology)

As a result of the situated learning experience (Lave & Wenger, 1991) throughout the internship, several students changed their attitudes toward their learning awareness and behaviors, which is consistent with findings in Binder et al. (2015). For example, they recognized the importance of some subjects that they had previously disregarded and affirmed that they would read the materials of these subjects again to fill in the knowledge gap. They recognized the negative consequences of learning for scores or passing the subject and affirmed that they would learn for their future career development. This change in attitude would enhance the development of their human capital.

Social capital

Students suggested that they expanded their professional network. All of them agreed that their mentor connected them with colleagues in the organization or with other stakeholders in the industry, apart from providing constructive feedback on professional skills development. This finding confirmed the important role of mentors in constructing students' learning experiences during the internship in previous studies (Lam & Ching, 2007; Narayanan et al., 2010; Odio et al., 2014; Read et al., 2017).

> My mentor enthusiastically instructed me on how to make the bed, arrange the room, pick up guests from the airport and shared with me all the stuff necessary for being a tour guide. Especially when I did something unsatisfactorily, he gave me feedback and suggested ways to improve. He taught me everything. He even oriented me to some job possibilities. (Participant 1—Tourism and Hospitality)

Some of them also made new friends and business contacts. A Tourism and Hospitality student also revealed that she had made acquaintances with some potential business partners, whom she may cooperate with to develop a business in the future.

> When I worked as an intern in a restaurant-hotel, I got to know some team leaders and managers. They helped me a lot. We chatted and they promised that they would help me when I graduate, and we can collaborate to do some business. (Participant 9—Tourism and Hospitality)
> My mentor connected me with colleagues in other departments of the company, but he was still the one who helped me the most. (Participant 13—Business Administration)

Half of the students also reported that they maintained good relationships with professionals they met or worked with during the internship. The internship allowed students to establish a network with professionals in the industry, something that was difficult to do when they had only studied at the university.

Cultural capital

Students perceived that the internship allowed them to acquire new knowledge on the world of work. Resembling finding in Gilbert et al. (2014), students in this study reported that they began to understand and adapt to operational principles of the industry, organizational rules and regulations, as well as maintaining relationships between colleagues. One of them commented on this below:

> My first duty was to learn about departments and services in the hotel under the instruction of senior colleagues. [...] I gradually got used to the work environment there, polished my skills and working attitudes before they

assigned me to more important tasks. (Participant 3—Tourism and Hospitality)

The internship also helped many students recognize their unprofessional behavior. From there, they adjusted their behaviors to become more professional and aligned to the practice in an industry. Such adaptability to a work culture is an essential element of cultural capital.

> I developed professionalism, like being more responsible. I used to be careless: I often completed my job and left there without reporting to anyone, so my colleagues critiqued and advised me to report my work progress so that people can know and work harmoniously. [...] I recognize that I have changed a lot even in my replies to email, texting or making phone calls, very different compared to before. (Participant 15—Business Administration)

Consequently, students became more acclimated to the work culture of their industry, which reflected other studies about student internships in other countries such as Khalil (2015).

Psychological capital

The internships provided an opportunity for students to test their psychological attributes and mindset. Many students faced difficulties during their internship because they had never been exposed to work before. In the Confucian culture of Vietnam, children and young adults often do not go to work until they graduate from tertiary education. Therefore, the sudden shift in daily routines, with more tasks to do and responsibilities to bear, confused students. As such, the internship served as a test site of their will and determination. For example, a Business student narrated his initial experience with the internship and how he overcame it:

> I believe that students' psychological factor is important for the success of the internship. I lost motivation in the first week of the internship because [...] I had to work from 8am to 5pm, [...] mostly sit at the desk working with the computer. After that week, when I had to write a reflective report, I felt like no I have to change. If I cannot adapt to this, many consequences may happen. By orienting myself and changing my attitudes to the internship more positively, I could adapt to that work culture more quickly. (Participant 13—Business Administration)

Likewise, all Tourism and Hospitality students commented that they had to maintain an attitude of good service toward their customers, even when customers were demanding. At times, they were about to get furious, but as they stated, they pulled themselves back because if they got angry, that would not only affect the host business but also affect their internship results. However, after being exposed to such a work environment for long enough (these students had to undertake two compulsory internships), they became more patient and flexible in dealing with difficult customers.

For the Information Technology student group, the difficulty they faced in the workplace was the knowledge and skills gap because the IT industry progresses much faster than what the university could prepare them for. As a result, many students struggled, but they did not give up, noting that they learned on the job and got used to the fast-pace changes of the industry and formed continuous learning attitudes, which would benefit them in the long term in this industry.

> The knowledge that we learned at the university is just basic. When we graduate, we may have to learn all over again because information technology is constantly growing. So, we must be able to learn by ourselves, a high level of self-study skills is needed. (Participant 26—Information Technology)

As a result, students developed psychological attributes beneficial to their career development such as confidence, patience, resilience, and flexibility. These findings are aligned with findings in previous studies such as Khalil (2015), Odio et al. (2014) and Rothman and Sisman (2016).

Career identity

Consistent with findings of previous studies (Odio et al., 2014; Rothman & Sisman, 2016), the majority of students also stated that the internship helped them envision their career paths. Most decided to enter the industry upon graduation because they recognized that they liked to work in that field, felt they belonged, or simply felt confident in their expertise for jobs in the industry. The evaluation of others on their performance during the internship also appeared important for their career decision, as illustrated in the comment below.

> My mentor complimented me for my disciplined attitude as well as the way I worked with guests during the internship. The guests themselves did not complain about me, were very satisfied even. So, after this internship, I am glad to develop my career in this industry. (Participant 9—Tourism and Hospitality)

About one-fifth of the students proudly revealed that they received a job offer in the company where they undertook the internship. However, it seemed to depend on the personnel needs of the company.

> Yes, I got a job offer [after completion of the internship]. Most companies would recruit us interns to be employees if they see that we are the right ones. But many only provide internship opportunities, no subsequent employment. [...] About one-third of my cohort got a job after the internship. (Participant 26—Information Technology)

However, the internship experience intimidated some students, especially Tourism and Hospitality students, from entering the industry, as pointed out in Odio et al. (2014). Four of them identified some unsolvable difficulties and recognized that they would be incapable of working toward being a tour guide or waiter/waitress and had started to consider new career paths away from tourism and hospitality.

> The most difficult issue for me is that the female tour guide had to share a room with a male driver overnight [...]. Nobody had told us this at the university. I think that I may quit working as a tour guide. (Participant 8—Tourism and Hospitality)
> I aspired to work as a tour guide, but after the internship, I found that I did not love the job very much. [...] I feel stressed due to time pressures and I will not be able to manage my family matters if I have to lead a tour for several days. (Participant 12—Tourism and Hospitality)

This does not mean that the internship failed to develop a career identity for students. Rather, it suggested that the internship helped students to adjust their career aspiration to better fit into their personal expectations and circumstances. This adjustment is vital for students to develop a successful career upon graduation.

Influential factors in Vietnamese students' internship experience

Knowledge and skills gap

According to situated learning theory and community of practice (Lave & Wenger, 1991; Wenger, 2010), internships exposed students to a community of practice where they could learn about the industry they were about to enter and develop relevant knowledge and skills for their future profession. However, students would need to have some foundational knowledge and skills prior to undertaking their industry internships. Consistent with a finding in Jackson (2015) and Narayanan et al. (2010), in many interviews, students, especially students of Information Technology, reported that there was a discrepancy between the knowledge and skills that the university delivered and what the industry needed. This caused many difficulties for them in carrying out assigned tasks. This situation was predictable because Vietnamese higher education is notorious for being theory-based (Tran, 2018a). The curriculum is developed mostly based on academic and educational leaders' perspectives rather than on industry needs. It is infrequently updated and delivered as content teaching rather than skills development. As a result, students often possess a substantial body of technical knowledge but lack practice and soft skills (Tran, 2018a, 2018b).

On the other hand, the knowledge and skills gap provided students with opportunities to adapt to the authentic work environment to fill the gap, although this appeared to depend on students' attitudes and ability to self-direct their learning. Those who could reflect and self-assess their learning could turn this disadvantage into an advantage for their professional development. Difficulties caused by the skills and knowledge gap also forced students to decide whether they wanted to complete the internship. Through this, students could develop qualities and attributes such as resilience, patience, and flexibility, which are essential for career development (Fugate et al., 2004; Tomlinson, 2017).

Students' beliefs and engagement

The relationship between one's beliefs and behaviors has long been examined. Although there have been conflicting findings about this relationship, it seems that more empirical studies have confirmed this relationship rather than rejected it (Borghetti & Beaven, 2017; Montano & Kasprzyk, 2015; Navarro & Thornton, 2011). Consistent with these studies, this study suggests that students' beliefs influence their experience with the internship. As reported earlier, all students believed that the internship was an important element of their studies and served as a bridge between their education and the workplace. However, they held different beliefs about the influence of internship experience on their employment outcomes. It appears that such beliefs oriented the students differently with respect to the extent to which they looked for, prepared for, and engaged with the internship. Those who believed it could positively influence their employment outcomes seemed to invest more effort and time into their internships and were more likely to ask to be involved in different tasks as well as ask for advice and feedback on their work performance through which they could accumulate more employability capital. Conversely, the data showed that those who did not believe in the positive effect of the internship on their employment outcomes did not actively engage with it, relying instead on their mentor to assign tasks and give feedback.

Such a lack of confidence in the power of internships on employment outcomes could have resulted from recruitment and hiring practices in Vietnam. It has been reported that in Vietnam several employers make their hiring decisions based on their personal relationships with job applicants or bribery instead of the applicants' competencies, especially in public organizations (Son, 2015; Tuoi Tre News, 2012). Although it is not widely depicted in the literature, this practice is popular and many people, including students, know of it, as illustrated by Participant 1 above. In addition, such beliefs could have resulted from a lack of communication about the importance of internships on the part of the university. Students seemed to view undertaking internships as meeting graduation requirements instead of a valuable learning experience and a chance to present themselves to potential employers.

The analysis also showed that student engagement could influence their employability in two respects. First, their engagement facilitated the development of knowledge, skills, and networks for their future profession. The evidence for this was that self-reported engaging students seemed to more proactively look for opportunities to put knowledge and skills into practice, identify their knowledge and skills gaps, and develop new and relevant professional skills. All of these were consistent with the theory about situated learning (Lave & Wenger, 1991) and the theory of community of practice (Wenger, 2010), which is that active participation or interaction with professionals in the community of practice can foster the development of interns' professional knowledge and skills. Second, student engagement can influence interns' career choices after experiencing the internship. The data analysis revealed that engaged students appeared to explore, get involved in different tasks, consult professionals, and self-assess whether they could fit in the industry, and make better-informed decisions about their career, as reported earlier.

Unfortunately, the study revealed that many interns did not engage or noticeably engage with the internship. The evidence for this was that many of them reported depending on mentors' instructions rather than their own initiative during the internship. Although this could be linked to their beliefs about the importance of the internship, it could also be associated with the work culture in Vietnam, where mentors/seniors often hold great power over interns/subordinates. Such a hierarchical social relationship and imbalance in authority at work can restrict students from learning opportunities throughout the internship and thus diminish their learning outcomes.

Those findings suggest that students need to be trained in meta-cognition about the internship and of their learning process. Without appropriate attitudes about the importance of the internship and without knowledge about how their learning should be managed throughout the internships, students will not be able to make the best used of the internship opportunities to create employment advantage for themselves.

Industry–university collaboration

Another factor that affected students' experiences with the internships emerging from the data was a lack of collaboration between the university and industry. Students of Tourism and Hospitality reported that they had to look for internship opportunities by themselves; students of Business reported that they often had to look for one although the student support service provided some help; students of Information Technology could look for one or wait until their faculty invited an IT company to come interview them and recruit interns, working as unpaid employees. Although Vietnamese universities invested in supporting students, they had difficulties organizing the internships due to a lack of connection with industry (Tran, 2018a) and a large number of students in their institutions (see also Chapters 4 and 5 of this book on this issue). This practice of arranging internships on the one hand allowed active students to look for internships relevant to their studies in companies that they wanted to work for. Thus, it helped them develop employability capital and offered them a chance to present themselves to their desired employers. However, on the other hand, many students looked for internships that were the most convenient for them in terms of meeting the completion requirements rather than for a rewarding learning experience. For example, they chose internship offers that were close to their home, easy to complete even if less relevant to their studies, or in a company that contained members of their family.

In addition, there has been a lack of collaboration between academic supervisors and industry mentors in helping structure students' learning experiences. From the data, in all three universities, the academic supervisor played the role of an advisor who worked from a distance and of an assessor at the end of the internship by marking students' internship reports, project work (often in the form of an undergraduate thesis), and industry mentor's feedback on students' work performance. Due to heavy teaching workloads, many of them did not visit the workplace to see how their students were experiencing the internship. This could affect their evaluation later because everything was based on text instead of students' actual performance, in which many students might face difficulties in written language expression. Also, the industry mentor only guided students through the internship by assigning tasks, managing students' work performance, providing feedback or advice when necessary, and providing brief feedback on students' work performance to the academic supervisor. It seemed that there was no agreement between the university and the mentor about what knowledge and skills students should obtain by the end of the internship. Vaguely defined roles, responsibilities, and students' expected learning outcomes, on top of their responsibilities for carrying out their work, would hinder their engagement with mentoring the students, especially providing relevant feedback, an essential element for a positive internship learning experience (Lam & Ching, 2007; Narayanan et al., 2010; Odio et al., 2014; Read et al., 2017). In the same vein, students did not report any journal writing or opportunities that allowed them to reflect on their learning experience. This practice is vital for students' learning throughout their internship because it helps them identify knowledge and skill gaps and think of actions to fill the gaps. Obviously, many students in this study could reflect on their learning, but it was spontaneous rather than structured. Thus, many students felt confused at the workplace as they had to manage their learning alone, with the academic supervisor some distance away and the mentor busy and possibly confused about his or her own role.

Conclusion

In short, this study showed that student interns held different beliefs about the internship and their employment outcomes, which seemed to affect their engagement throughout the internship. Nevertheless, the internship offered them a valuable opportunity to develop employability capital: consolidating their knowledge and skills, applying the acquired knowledge and skills into practice, identifying skills and knowledge gaps, developing new knowledge and skills, getting acquainted with new colleagues, identifying career paths and job opportunities, and even changing their learning approach and behaviors. However, these benefits varied between students, and were mostly positive for those engaged with the internship. The study also revealed that students' learning experiences with the internship were affected by their own beliefs and engagement, the mismatch between what the university taught students and what was required at the workplace, and a lack of collaboration between the university and industry in providing structure.

It is recommended that universities should improve their students' meta-cognition of the internship and of their learning so that students can engage with internship. Meta-cognition and self-directed learning abilities may help students explore their professional sector to develop their professional expertise and make well-informed decisions about their career paths. In addition, universities should collaborate with industry in designing their curriculum and the internship, making them align with each other so that student learning is well-structured. A tight connection between the university and industry can also facilitate the organization of internships, increasing the match between students' studies and where they undertake their internship. Moreover, university academics should also collaborate with industry mentors regarding providing internship supervision because internship mentorship is one of the significant factors that constitute a student's learning experience throughout an internship.

Note

1 KSAOs refer to knowledge, skills, abilities, and other characteristics.

References

Binder, J. F., Baguley, T., Crook, C., & Miller, F. (2015). The academic value of internships: Benefits across disciplines and student backgrounds. *Contemporary Educational Psychology*, 41(April), 73–82.

Borghetti, C., & Beaven, A. (2017). Lingua francas and learning mobility: Reflections on students' attitudes and beliefs towards language learning and use. *International Journal of Applied Linguistics*, 27(1), 221–241.

Bourdieu, P. (1989). Social space and symbolic power. *Sociological Theory*, 7(1), 14–25.

Bourdieu, P., & Wacquant, L. (1992). *An invitation to reflexive sociology*. Cambridge, UK: Polity.

Clarke, M. (2017). Rethinking graduate employability: The role of capital, individual attributes and context. *Studies in higher education*, 43(11), 1923–1937.

Elo, S., & Kyngäs, H. (2008). The qualitative content analysis process. *Journal of Advanced Nursing*, 62(1), 107–115.

Fugate, M., Kinicki, A. J., & Ashforth, B. E. (2004). Employability: A psycho-social construct, its dimensions, and applications. *Journal of Vocational Behavior*, 65(1), 14–38.

Gault, J., Leach, E., & Duey, M. (2010). Effects of business internships on job marketability: the employers' perspective. *Education + Training*, 52(1), 76–88.

Gilbert, B. L., Banks, J., Houser, J. H., Rhodes, S. J., & Lees, N. D. (2014). Student development in an experiential learning program. *Journal of College Student Development*, 55(7), 707–713.

Jackson, D. (2015). Employability skill development in work-integrated learning: Barriers and best practice. *Studies in Higher Education*, 40(2), 350–367.

Khalil, O. E. (2015). Students' experiences with the business internship program at Kuwait University. *The International Journal of Management Education*, 13(3), 202–217.

King, R., Findlay, A., & Ahrens, J. (2010). *International student mobility literature review*. Retrieved from: https://core.ac.uk/download/pdf/20458001.pdf

Lam, T., & Ching, L. (2007). An exploratory study of an internship program: The case of Hong Kong students. *International Journal of Hospitality Management*, 26(2), 336–351.

Lave, J., & Wenger, E. (1991). *Situated learning: Legitimate peripheral participation*. Cambridge, UK: Cambridge University Press.

Li, S., Whalley, J., & Xing, C. (2014). China's higher education expansion and unemployment of college graduates. *China Economic Review*, 30(Sep), 567–582.

McQuaid, R. W., & Lindsay, C. (2005). The concept of employability. *Urban Studies*, 42(2), 197–219.

Merriam, S. B. (2009). *Qualitative research: A guide to design and implementation*. San Francisco, CA: Jossey-Bass.

Montano, D. E., & Kasprzyk, D. (2015). Theory of reasoned action, theory of planned behavior, and the integrated behavioral model. In K. Glanz, B. K. Rimer, & K. Viswanath (Eds.), *Health behavior: Theory, research and practice* (5th edn, pp. 95–124). San Francisco, CA: Jossey-Bass.

Narayanan, V., Olk, P. M., & Fukami, C. V. (2010). Determinants of internship effectiveness: An exploratory model. *Academy of Management Learning & Education*, 9(1), 61–80.

Navarro, D., & Thornton, K. (2011). Investigating the relationship between belief and action in self-directed language learning. *System*, 39(3), 290–301.

Nunley, J. M., Pugh, A., Romero, N., & SealsJr, R. A. (2016). College major, internship experience, and employment opportunities: Estimates from a résumé audit. *Labour Economics*, 38(Jan), 37–46.

Odio, M., Sagas, M., & Kerwin, S. (2014). The influence of the internship on students' career decision making. *Sport Management Education Journal*, 8(1), 46–57.

Oliver, B. (2015). Redefining graduate employability and work-integrated learning: Proposals for effective higher education in disrupted economies. *Journal of Teaching and Learning for Graduate Employability*, 6(1), 56–65.

Read, P., Hughes, J. D., Blagrove, R., Jeffreys, I., Edwards, M., & Turner, A. N. (2017). Characteristics and experiences of interns in strength and conditioning. *Journal of Sports Sciences*, 35(3), 269–276.

Rothman, M., & Sisman, R. (2016). Internship impact on career consideration among business students. *Education + Training*, 58(9), 1003–1013.

Schmidt, M. K. (2017). Personal and professional development through internship engagement. In T. Newman & A. Schmitt (Eds.), *Field-based learning in family life education* (pp. 39–49). Cham: Springer.

Simiyu, R. R., Okaka, F. O., & Omondi, P. (2015). Geography students' assessment of internship experience at a Kenyan university. *Journal of Geography in Higher Education*, 39(3), 343–355.

Son, T. (2015). Vietnam to get tough on bribery for job, promotion: Officials. *Thanhnien News*, 30 January. Retrieved from https://bit.ly/2SArdZk

Tomlinson, M. (2017). Forms of graduate capital and their relationship to graduate employability. *Education + Training*, 59(4), 338–352.

Tran, L. H. N. (2018a). Game of blames: Higher education stakeholders' perceptions of causes of Vietnamese graduates' skills gap. *International Journal of Educational Development*, 62(Sep), 302–312.

Tran, L. H. N. (2018b). The skills gap of Vietnamese graduates and final-year university students. *Journal of Education and Work*, 31(7–8), 579–594.

Tran, L. H. N., & Nguyen, T. M. D. (2018). Internship-related learning outcomes and their influential factors: The case of Vietnamese tourism and hospitality students. *Education + Training*, 60(1), 69–81.

Tuoi Tre News (2012). *Corruption in Vietnam is serious, blatant, rampant*. Retrieved from https://bit.ly/2W1eGzS

Wenger, E. (2010). Communities of practice and social learning systems: The career of a concept. In C. Blackmore (Ed.), *Social learning systems and communities of practice* (pp. 179–198). London: Springer.

Wu, C.-C. (2011). High graduate unemployment rate and Taiwanese undergraduate education. *International Journal of Educational Development*, 31(3), 303–310.

Yorke, M. (2006). *Employability in higher education: What it is, what it is not*. Retrieved from https://bit.ly/22VzZS0.

9 Students' experience with developing soft skills via participation in extracurricular activities

Introduction

In response to employers' lament on the shortage of work skills in graduates (Bodewig & Badiani-Magnusson, 2014; Lindorff, 2011; UK Commission for Employment and Skills, 2016) and political moves requiring universities to develop students' employability skills (Tertiary Education Quality and Standards Agency, 2013; The Quality Assurance Agency for Higher Education, 2014), many universities have engaged with developing employability for their students, mostly with a focus on enhancing their non-technical skills, also known as soft skills (Al-Mahmood & Gruba, 2007; Barrie, Hughes, Smith, & Thomson, 2009). Skills subjects are inserted into the curriculum to develop learning skills and work skills for students. Unfortunately, higher education (HE) curricula are already crowded; therefore, inserting additional skills subjects into the curricula results in less time for specialized subjects (Al-Mahmood & Gruba, 2007; Barrie et al., 2009). If these skills subjects are designed as electives, students may disregard them and prioritize specialized subjects instead. Integrating soft skills into specialized subjects of a curriculum would mean that there would be radical changes in the way teaching and learning are organized, which may dishearten many academics (Barrie et al., 2009). For this reason, extracurricular activities (ECAs) have been used as an alternative option where soft skills can be developed for students with less pedagogy and curriculum-related issues. Several studies have found that ECAs are conducive to the development of students' soft skills and enhance their employment prospects (Al-Ansari et al., 2016; Hordósy & Clark, 2018; Lau, Hsu, Acosta, & Hsu, 2014; Thompson, Clark, Walker, & Whyatt, 2013). However, the contribution of ECAs and challenges in organizing them have been under-researched and thus need further investigation.

This chapter will report a mixed-methods study that investigated the effectiveness of the development of employability skills for students in Vietnamese universities via ECAs. Statistical analyses of 423 responses to a survey and content analysis of 18 semi-structured interviews with students consistently revealed that the Youth Union and its associates (YUA) of Vietnamese universities contributed greatly to the execution of soft skills in their institutions via organizing ECAs. Participants reported that these activities developed several employability skills, mostly soft skills, for them. However, this development appeared to depend greatly on student engagement, which was found to be associated with: (i) their beliefs about the relevance and possibility of developing employability via ECAs; (ii) their ability to balance formal education activities, part-time work, and ECAs; (iii) the availability of information about these activities; and (iv) the professional organization of these activities. This chapter contributes to a scarcity of studies that investigate the role of ECAs in developing employability skills for students both qualitatively and quantitatively. It will also point out obstacles that need to be removed so that ECAs can better develop employability for students.

Extracurricular activities and employability skills

Employability is "a set of achievements—skills, understanding and personal attributes—that makes graduates more likely to gain employment and be successful in their chosen occupations, which benefits themselves, the workforce, the community and the economy" (Yorke, 2006, p. 23). As such, employability not only helps graduates obtain a job but also enables them to function and thrive in that job (Yorke, 2006). Employability includes both technical and non-technical skills, also known as soft skills, such as communication and interpersonal skills, self-management skills, career-management skills, and lifelong learning skills. Research has found that soft skills significantly add value to graduates' employability package. A study conducted by the Stanford Research Institute and Carnegie Melon Foundation found that 75% of long-term job success depends on non-technical skills and only 25% on technical knowledge (Litecky, Arnett, & Prabhakar, 2004). In another study in the UK, Nickson, Warhurst, Commander, Hurrell, and Cullen (2012) surveyed 173 clothing, footwear, and leather retailers about what was important for their hiring decision. The results showed that job applicants' personalities (79.7%) and appearance (68.2%) were much more important for their decisions than the applicants' work experience (41.1%) and qualifications (4.6%).

Therefore, many universities have invested in developing soft skills for their students. It is observed that from East to West, universities have included ECAs into their strategies to improve students' soft skills (Al-Ansari et al., 2016; Hordósy & Clark, 2018; Lau et al., 2014; Thompson et al., 2013). As the name suggests, ECAs are separate from the disciplinary curriculum, and play a complementary role in consolidating students' knowledge and developing skills that may not be included in the main curriculum. ECAs may include but are not limited to participating in community services, volunteering programs, certain skills-focused clubs, non-compulsory internships, and field trips (Barrie et al., 2009).

Several studies have found that specific types of ECAs are conducive to the development of soft skills in students (Kalles & Ryan, 2015; Osman, 2011; Scarinci & Pearce, 2012). For example, Osman (2011) found that Malaysian students participating in service learning were able to understand their acquired knowledge at a deeper level and gain better communication skills in the multicultural context, better collaborative working skills, and a higher perception of gender differences. Similarly, Scarinci and Pearce (2012) studied the contribution of travelling on the development of soft skills with the participation of 326 undergraduate business students at Northwood University (Florida, USA). The results showed that students improved 18 soft skills from a moderate to a great extent. Independence, being open-minded, adaptability, feeling comfortable around all types of people, and understanding and awareness were found to improve the most.

In addition, recent studies have found that students' participation in ECAs as a whole positively correlates to the growth of their employability skills and employment outcomes (Al-Ansari et al., 2016; Hordósy & Clark, 2018; Lau et al., 2014; Thompson et al., 2013). For example, Lau et al. (2014) conducted a study that involved 28,768 business graduates in Taiwan about the impact of participating in ECAs and their employability. Based on participants' self-ratings, results showed that those who joined ECAs developed their communication, leadership, creativity, and self-promotion skills to a higher level than their peers. The study also found that different types of ECAs yielded different impacts on these graduates' employability. Involvement in sports clubs helped develop leadership skills the most, while creativity skills flourished from participation in music clubs. Communication and self-promotion skills developed moderately and did not vary much between students who participated in different types of ECAs. Surprisingly, participating in ECAs appeared to not help develop students' time-management skills. Similarly, Clark, Marsden, Whyatt, Thompson, and Walker (2015) conducted a study into the importance of participating in ECAs with 620 university alumni. The participants reported that ECAs helped develop their employability a great deal, enhanced their chances of obtaining their first job, and facilitated their work performance. The graduates who were working as recruiters also revealed that participation in ECAs was an important element that they sought from applicants when screening applications.

However, developing soft skills for students via ECAs is not easy. The first challenge is student engagement. As these activities are extracurricular, many students may not believe in the benefits that participating in them may bring (Roulin & Bangerter, 2013), or they may disregard participating in these activities when compared with the specialized knowledge taught in class (Tran, 2015). The second challenge is that some types of ECAs—such as being a research assistant, intern, or serving in a student committee—are limited to a small number of students (Barrie et al., 2009). Next, as most students have to study and work, there is little time left for them to truly engage in ECAs (Clark et al., 2015; Thompson et al., 2013). Furthermore, students' perceptions of the relevance of certain types of ECAs or the way these activities are organized may also influence student participation (Al-Ansari et al., 2016). Finally, as most ECAs are linked to local communities, the support of external stakeholders, such as local people, industries, or authorities, is essential. Without resources and support from these external stakeholders (Khan & Zhang, 2017; Sepahpanah, Zarafshani, Mirakzade, & Rosch, 2013), ECAs may only occur on campus, which hinders the development of soft skills in real-life contexts.

In short, ECAs are conducive to developing soft skills for students. However, stakeholders, especially students, have not adequately recognized their role and importance. Likewise, factors influencing the effectiveness of developing soft skills via these activities have not been sufficiently examined. Therefore, these issues need to be explored further by research.

Context for developing employability skills via extracurricular activities in Vietnamese universities

In Vietnamese universities, ECAs are often organized by the YUA. This union is a social-political organization of the youth in Vietnam. It was founded by Ho Chi Minh and is now led by the Communist Party, the only political party in Vietnam. Information on its website declares its three functions as below (Ho Chi Minh Communist Youth Union, 2019):

- Contributing to building the Party, inheriting and sustaining the legacy of the party and Ho Chi Minh.
- Creating an environment for young people to study and develop their personalities, and the skills of a worker suitable for societal need.
- Be a representative who cares about and protects the legal rights of young people.

As such, the YUA often organizes political education, and leads youth in community-engagement activities. For example, it organized the Green Summer Campaign for students to go to rural areas to teach poor children, help disadvantaged people, or transfer knowledge and technologies to farmers. Recently, the organization has been involved in training students with concrete skills that immediately enhance students' employment outcomes. In my personal experience as a YUA leader for five years, along with communication with YUA leaders of six universities, the YUA has been involved in developing employability skills for students via organizing skills classes and exposure to career options, recruitment days or career-consultation services. They also organize activities or competitions for students to strengthen specialized knowledge or develop specialized skills. These academic-related activities are often held at the school level to better fit into the characteristics of disciplines. For example, in the School of Education, there is a Teachers Club; in the School of Business, there is a Traders Club; in the School of Information Technologies, there is an IT Club. The YUA also organizes numerous recreational activities throughout the academic year, including sports competitions, singing or dancing performances, and cultural festivals. Finally, a number of clubs are organized to help students develop special talents such as painting, music composition, or handicrafts.

Although they are categorized as ECAs, in most Vietnamese universities, student participation in those activities is recorded and assessed against concrete criteria at the end of each semester to generate *điểm rèn luyện* or a self-improvement score. It is often used in conjunction with their academic achievements as a reference for student scholarship granting. Employers, especially those in the public sector, usually refer to such a rank to judge students' personality and even dignity. Therefore, the YUA has a significant influence on students' lives during their academic years as well as later on in their employment prospects.

The present study

As mentioned earlier, this chapter will examine the contribution of the YUA to developing employability for Vietnamese university students via ECAs. It is a vital matter because in many Vietnamese universities, it is the main channel through which students develop their employability skills, but these ECAs are often overlooked. This chapter answers the following questions:

- To what extent do ECAs contribute to developing employability skills for students in Vietnamese universities?
- What factors influence student engagement with developing employability skills via ECAs?

The study was conducted using a mixed-methods approach to take advantage of both qualitative and quantitative data (De Lisle, 2011). It was carried out as a quantitative study followed by a qualitative study. The process of data collection and analysis can be summarized as follows.

Stage 1: Quantitative study

Quantitative data were collected from April to July 2015. A total of 500 paper-based surveys were randomly distributed to students in the campuses of two public and four private universities in Can Tho and Ho Chi Minh cities, Vietnam; 423 responses provided enough information for the analysis in this chapter.

In the survey, participants were first asked to provide some demographical information. The second section invited students to rate the frequency of some ECAs organized by the YUA and the frequency they participated in these activities on a 5-point Likert scale, in which 1 denoted "very infrequently" and 5 "very frequently." In the third section, the participants were asked to rate the extent to which participating in the ECAs organized by the YUA contributed to the development of 35 employability skills on a 5-point Likert scale, in which 1 denoted "very little" and 5 denoted "very much." These 35 employability skills were identified from the literature and the researcher's experience as a YUA leader for more than five years at a Vietnamese university. Three YUA leaders helped validate this list of skills to ensure that they could be developed under YUA's activities. There was a short description after each skill so that participants could have a consensus of understanding of what the skills were.

The data were analyzed using SPSS. Among the 423 participants, 52.7% were male and 47.3% were female. The percentages of first-, second-, third-, and fourth-year students accounted for 23.9%, 23.2%, 31.7%, and 24.8%, respectively. In terms of disciplines, 20.3% of them were attending science, technology, engineering and math (STEM) programs, 23.2% social science programs, 31.7% business programs, and 24.8% teacher education programs.

Data in the second section were analyzed descriptively using means (M) and standard deviations (SD). Independent-sample T-tests were computed to find differences in the way the YUA of public and private universities organized ECAs.

Independent-sample T-tests and one-way ANOVA tests were also computed to find differences in participation patterns between groups of students (genders, attending universities, academic disciplines, and years of study).

The researcher decided to extract principal components, or the data set in the third section of the survey, because the 35 skills may be clustered together in some ways. To do that, he first checked the internal consistency of this data set. The reliability test result showed that Cronbach's alpha was relatively high; $\alpha = 0.80$. Item-total correlation values (r) ranged from 0.20 to 0.41. Eleven items had r-values smaller than 0.30. It is often advised to eliminate these before extracting principal components, but the researcher decided to keep these items because excluding the 11 items did not increase Cronbach's alpha. Next, the Kaiser-Meyer-Olkin (KMO) test was run to determine if the remaining set of data was adequate to extract principal components. Theoretically, if the KMO test result is above 0.70, it is suitable to perform factor analysis as correlations among items are sufficiently high (De Vaus, 2014). For this test, the KMO value was 0.78, signaling that the data set was to conduct factor analysis.

The researcher ran factor analysis using a varimax rotation to extract principal components with eigenvalues greater than 1. The result suggested that 11 components should be extracted, which together accounted for 60.52% of the variance in the item pool. However, this extraction solution was not practical for the purpose of analysis. Therefore, the researcher decided to extract principal components based on the scree plot because of the adequate sample size and high communalities (Williams, Onsman, & Brown, 2010). The extraction solution of four principal components, which explained 35.24% of the variance, appeared to have the best construct and face validity; therefore, it was chosen.

Traditionally, in social sciences, the threshold of 0.3 is used to determine the loadings (L) that should be retained for interpretation. In this study, the researcher chose the threshold of 0.5, which is relatively high in practice. Two items (critical-thinking skills and daily conversation skills) did not satisfy this criterion so they were excluded from the scale. The two skills were outliers possibly because participants disregard daily communication as an important soft skill and critical-thinking skills are not highly welcomed in a socialist and Confucian-heritage country like Vietnam, especially when ECAs are organized by the YUA, an agent of the Communist Party. At the 0.3 cut-off point, all items loaded uniquely on one of the four components (Table 9.1):

- Interpersonal and communication skills (14 items, $\alpha = 0.84$, variance explained 13.21%).
- Self-management skills (after excluding two items for loadings lower than 0.5 (rounded), seven items remained, $\alpha = 0.70$, variance explained 7.58%).
- Professional management skills (six items, $\alpha = 0.68$, variance explained 7.32%).
- Learning skills (six items, $\alpha = 0.66$, variance explained 7.12%).

After the 33 items were extracted into four components, descriptive statistics were run to find means (M) and standard deviations (SD). The means of the

Table 9.1 Contribution of extra-curricular activities participation to students' employability skills

Factor	M	SD	L
Interpersonal and communication skills	**3.92**	**0.60**	
Writing skills	3.93	1.09	.67
Visual-presentation skills	3.87	1.07	.65
Computer skills	3.91	0.99	.64
Information skills	3.90	1.11	.64
Reading skills	3.92	1.03	.59
Assertiveness	4.02	0.95	.59
Foreign-language skills	3.90	1.07	.58
Listening skills	3.92	1.11	.54
Teamwork skills	3.98	0.98	.52
Numeracy skills	3.76	1.08	.50
Socialization competence	3.97	1.04	.49
Oral-communication skills	3.95	1.07	.49
Creativity	3.82	1.10	.49
Leadership skills	4.02	1.04	.47
Self-management skills	**3.75**	**0.65**	
Being responsible	3.81	1.07	.64
Self-presentation skills	3.71	1.10	.63
Self-assessment skills	3.80	1.11	.59
Self-confidence	3.83	1.08	.56
Problem-solving skills	3.53	1.06	.54
Being proactive	3.73	1.09	.53
Being self-disciplined	3.81	1.07	.47
Professional management skills	**3.75**	**0.69**	
Awareness of consequences following a decision	3.77	1.18	.64
People-management skills	3.72	1.12	.62
Broad visions	3.82	1.13	.61
Organization skills	3.79	1.03	.61
Decision-making skills	3.79	1.10	.53
Awareness of employment opportunities	3.59	1.12	.51
Learning skills	**3.62**	**0.70**	
Skills for planning learning	3.55	1.17	.65
Skills for searching learning resources	3.51	1.16	.59
Skills for diagnosing learning needs	3.61	1.13	.58
Self-directed learning ability	3.68	1.12	.55
Skills for change adaptation	3.67	1.18	.53
Reflective-learning ability	3.72	1.09	.50

M = mean; SD = standard deviations: L = loading values in the extraction of principal component analysis contribution of ECAs to students' development of ES were interpreted using the following framework:

1.0 ≥ M > 1.8: very weak
1.8 ≥ M > 2.6: weak
2.6 ≥ M > 3.4: moderate
3.4 ≥ M > 4.2: strong
4.2 ≥ M > 5.0: very strong

Independent-samples T-test and one-way ANOVA tests were also performed to compare differences in the experience between groups of students over the contribution of attending YUA activities to the development of their ES.

Stage 2: Qualitative study

Qualitative data were collected after the analysis of quantitative data in mid-2016. The researcher invited 30 participants for interview via the email address or phone number that they provided on the survey. Eighteen of them agreed to join the interview via Skype, including six students who worked as YUA organizers. All of them were informed of the purpose of the study and were asked for their consent to use the information they provided for research purposes. Interviewees were invited to discuss: (i) their experiences with participating in ECAs throughout their university years; (ii) skills that they acquired from participating in these activities; and (iii) reasons why these activities were effective or ineffective in developing skills for them. All interviews, which lasted for about 13 to 21 minutes, were recorded and transcribed verbatim. The data were analyzed using a content-analysis approach (Elo & Kyngäs, 2008). The interviews were transcribed verbatim and read several times to understand the main points. Then each transcription was coded against the three themes mentioned earlier. Finally, codes of all 18 transcriptions were compared, and sub-themes were classified and compiled into the final report.

The contribution of ECAs to students' employability skills

Consistent with previous studies (Al-Ansari et al., 2016; Hordósy & Clark, 2018; Kalles & Ryan, 2015; Lau et al., 2014; Scarinci & Pearce, 2012; Thompson et al., 2013), this study also found ECAs had a positive influence on the development of students' employability. Results (see Table 9.1) showed that in students' experience, participating in ECAs helped develop four groups of work-related skills to a high level. More specifically, it facilitated the development of "interpersonal and communication skills" ($M = 3.92$, $SD = 0.60$) the most, followed by "self-management skills" ($M = 3.75$, $SD = 0.65$), "professional management skills" ($M = 3.75$, $SD = 0.69$), and "learning skills" ($M = 3.62$, $SD = 0.70$).

These results can be explained in two ways. First, Vietnamese parents are notoriously protective and willing to make sacrifices for their children's education (Mestechkina, Son, & Shin, 2014). Children in Vietnam are expected to be submissive to their parents, focus on their formal studies obediently, and are often discouraged from joining in other socialization activities. Thus, many young adults in Vietnam are found to lack basic skills for leading their life independently. When enrolling in university programs, for most students, it is the first time they have ever lived away from their family, independently planned their life, or truly socialized. Second, programs in Vietnamese universities focus primarily on transmitting knowledge, rather than training students in skills (Tran, 2018); hence, ECAs are where students could have opportunities to socially interact with peers, engage with local communities or to build awareness about their future career, especially via activities that teach them skills for job applications, interviews, and meeting with employers. It could also be where they are exposed to experiential learning, which is almost non-existent in classroom-based learning. All of these mean that ECAs can play a fundamental role in HE in developing learning skills, practical work skills, and an awareness of future career opportunities.

Specifically, five skills that developed the most via participating in ECAs were assertiveness ($M = 4.02$, $SD = 0.95$), leadership skills ($M = 4.02$, $SD = 1.04$), teamwork skills ($M = 3.98$, $SD = 0.98$), socialization competence ($M = 3.97$, $SD = 1.04$), and oral communication skills ($M = 3.95$, $SD = 1.07$). Five skills that involvement in ECAs helped develop the least were skills for seeking out learning resources ($M = 3.51$, $SD = 1.16$), skills for planning learning ($M = 3.55$, $SD = 1.17$), problem-solving skills ($M = 3.53$, $SD = 1.06$), critical-thinking skills ($M = 3.55$, $SD = 1.16$), and daily conversation skills ($M = 3.51$, $SD = 1.05$). The last two skills were excluded from the scale, as mentioned earlier.

Independent-sample T-test results showed that there were no statistically significant differences in the contribution of participating in ECAs to their employability skills development (i) between groups of male and female students, or (ii) between groups of students from public and private universities. However, the test results showed that student groups that participated in ECAs with the intent to develop skills ($M = 3.78$, $SD = 0.67$) could develop "professional management skills" significantly higher than those who were involved in ECAs for recreational purposes ($M = 3.50$, $SD = 0.79$); $t(421) = 2.74$, $p = 0.01$. Likewise, the former ($M = 3.66$, $SD = 0.69$) could develop "learning skills" significantly higher than the latter ($M = 3.35$, $SD = 0.71$); $t(421) = 2.99$, $p = 0.00$. This indicates that students' intention when they participate in ECAs could affect the development of soft skills, especially learning skills.

One-way ANOVA tests were conducted to check whether there were differences in the extent that participating in ECAs contributed to developing generic skills for students between groups of students of different years of study. The test results showed no statistically significant difference between these groups. However, one-way ANOVA test results indicated that there were statistically significant differences in the extent that participating in ECAs contributed to developing "interpersonal and communication skills" between groups of students of disciplines as determined by one-way ANOVA $F(3, 419) = 6.82$, $p = 0.00$. A Turkey post-hoc test revealed that students of Education ($M = 3.92$, $SD = 0.60$) developed "interpersonal and communication skills" via participating in ECAs more significantly than did STEM students ($M = 3.82$, $SD = 0.64$) $p = 0.00$, and social sciences ($M = 3.77$, $SD = 0.63$) $p = 0.00$. While there are no data to explain such differences, the results suggest that disciplinary characteristics may affect the development of interpersonal and communication skills.

Students' experience with the effectiveness of certain types of ECAs

The analysis showed that six groups of ECAs were organized to help develop employability skills for students in Vietnamese universities. The analysis also revealed that several factors influence the effectiveness of developing students' employability skills via ECAs.

Political-education activities

This type of activity was organized in different formats, including formal classes where students listen to talks given by political leaders about student-related policies, meetings where YUA leaders propagandize their work agenda, and events to commemorate historical events or political holidays. Interviewees held contrary perspectives about the benefits of these activities, as illustrated below:

> They gave me opportunities to understand the country's history, political perspectives and develop my patriotism and the responsibility of the young to our society. (Student of Education 1)
> Attending political-education activities are compulsory, but they fail to engage students. Students only participate physically but do not engage with these activities. (Student of Engineering)

As such, most interviewees agreed that students tended to participate in these activities only for the *điểm rèn luyện*. The YUA organizers believed that these activities were relevant for students whereas three students reported that they ignored these activities even though their self-improvement scores were deducted, because, in their belief, these activities were not relevant for them.

Activities that train specialized skills

These activities were often organized within a school to fit better with the characteristics of the discipline. All interviewees reported that they could consolidate their discipline-specific knowledge and skills by attending such clubs. However, five interviewees commented that these activities were not organized professionally, which demotivated them from continuing to attend. An interviewee described how the English-Speaking Club was run in her school as below:

> Some discussion questions were difficult; only leaders or good students could discuss these questions. They only picked members with good English skills to present answers to the questions or participate in some games, ignoring others, like first-year students. I felt there was a lack of organization so that all club members could engage in the discussion. (Student of Education 1)

Consistent with her viewpoint, three YUA organizers admitted that some of their activities were not organized professionally because YUA student organizers kept turning over as they graduated and new organizers took their positions.

Activities that train practical work skills

Interviewees reported that the YUA provided career-consultation services and organized classes to train students in communication skills, teamwork, job-interview skills, CV-writing skills, among others, and activities that connected students and employers, such as career expos, meeting with successful business people, and recruitment days. All interviewees recognized that by participating in these activities, they could develop skills necessary for their future career, increase their awareness of their career paths and employment opportunities, and especially gain skills that would enable them to obtain a job upon graduation; therefore, they sought out these activities.

> Career expos are beneficial for us to develop relevant skills for job applications [...]. For example, we can join in mock interviews, and then receive feedback about our performance, which helps us identify weaknesses and strengths. (Student of Biology)

An interviewee, also a YUA organizer, revealed that most of these activities were organized with the support of external stakeholders; therefore, they were professional and could attract many students. In contrast, six interviewees reported that they did not hear much about these activities or they found out about them too late, suggesting poor communication to students. Almost one-third of the interviewees mentioned that their class had to share a limited number of tickets to attend such activities because there was not adequate space for all students who wanted to attend. This suggested that the YUA could not meet the demand for such activities.

Social-engagement activities

In the interviewees' experience, the YUA's social-engagement activities were diverse. In addition to the Green Summer Campaign Education and other community-development activities, students also joined in activities such as blood donation, promoting environmental protection awareness in the community, and visiting and assisting orphanages or the elderly who lived alone. The interviewees admitted that through participating in these activities, they developed various skills and attributes. For instance, a female interviewee commented on the benefits of participating in social-engagement activities as below:

> Via these activities, my communication skills improved a lot. In high school, I did not have opportunities to socialize with strangers. When participating in these charity works, I had a chance to work with some young, like-minded foreigners, so I could understand differences in cultures, and different practices regarding doing charity work. I could develop communication skills remarkably, and develop many ethical attributes, build up positive attitudes to life, and become more willing to give help to disadvantaged people. (Student of English Studies)

However, three interviewees stated that some social-engagement activities lasted for a long time, such as the Green Summer Campaign that lasted for at least a month. For this reason, they could not leave their part-time jobs to join in such time-intensive activities. Many others suggested that some social-engagement activities were more effective than others due to the way these activities were organized and how students participated in them. These issues can be illustrated by the two comments below:

> Some students participated in these activities just because they wanted to get a "self-improvement" score. Others participated because they really wanted to help the elderly and orphans. [...] These activities are beneficial in terms of spiritual values rather than material ones. (Student of Engineering)

> Many YUA organizers are just students like us, but when they organize the activities, they act as if they were our boss ... they look so arrogant. They do not plan and organize the activities well enough, so when problems happen, they panic, get angry with each other and start to be grumpy. (Student of Bio-Technology)

Therefore, three interviewees reported switching to ECAs organized by external stakeholders. Meanwhile, the others tolerated the inappropriate attitudes of these YUA organizers, commenting that they joined in these activities for the sake of the benefits they would bring to the community.

Recreational activities

Sports activities were organized relatively often in the interviewees' experience, in the form of competitions between classes or schools. These activities were reported to improve students' physical health, and at the same time trained them in teamwork skills. Similarly, performing arts such as singing, dancing, and playing musical instruments were frequently organized. Most of the interviewees found that these activities helped them relax after learning and/or developed their self-confidence, teamwork skills, and patience, if they joined as performers.

The annual singing contest in my university is a time for reunion of class members. We feel a spirit of consolidation, teamwork and confidence. (Student of Education 3)

However, half of the interviewees stated that recreational activities were organized so frequently that they negatively affected their learning. This was because the YUA required each class to send a certain number of students to attend such events. Therefore, some students were forced to miss classes to attend, so that they or their classes would not be fined by the YUA. In these cases, students only participated to avoid penalties from the YUA, rather than out of their free will.

Special talents clubs

In interviewees' experience, these activities were limited to those with special talents (painting, dancing, handicrafts, music composition, etc.). A YUA student organizer also stated that in his university, students often founded and led these clubs with almost no support from the YUA. From interviewees' perspectives, these activities only benefited a small number of students, mostly to improve their skills in these talents, socialization, and a sense of belonging. Some interviewees revealed that these clubs dispersed soon after foundation, as members had study obligations, or due to a lack of leadership.

Finally, three interviewees revealed that they preferred to either participate in activities organized by external social bodies or to organize their own activities. The three reasons for this were that they could manage their time better, participate in activities of their chosen interests, and escape from the "control" of their university's YUA. For example, an interviewee stated that if she did not participate in the YUA's activities, her "self-improvement" scores would be deducted, but she did not care because she really wanted to do something that benefited herself and the people around her. Therefore, she sought after ECAs outside her university. She added that joining activities organized by external social bodies helped her and her friends develop many practical work and social skills.

Student engagement with extracurricular activities

Frequency in organizing extracurricular activities

Table 9.2 shows the frequency with which six types of ECAs were organized by the YUA in Vietnamese universities. On a 5-point scale, the means indicate that activities that trained students in specialized skills were organized moderately frequently (M = 3.24, SD = 1.24) whereas all the others were organized frequently. Activities that trained students in social-engagement skills (M = 3.89, SD = 1.11) were organized most regularly, followed by activities that trained work skills (M = 3.76, SD = 1.17), activities that nurtured special talents (M = 3.74, SD = 1.20), and recreational activities (M = 3.70, SD = 1.20). Political-education activities were organized just over the level of "moderately frequently" (M = 3.48, SD = 1.09).

Table 9.2 Frequency of organizing some types of extra-curricular activities and student engagement

ECAs	Frequency of organization		Student engagement	
	M	SD	M	SD
Political-education activities	3.48	1.09	3.76	1.13
Activities that train specialized skills	3.24	1.24	3.31	1.18
Activities that train work skills	3.76	1.17	3.64	1.18
Activities that train social-engagement skills	3.89	1.11	3.73	1.09
Recreational activities	3.70	1.20	3.67	1.04
Activities that nurture special talents	3.74	1.20	3.80	1.06

Independent-sample T-tests were conducted to check whether there were significant differences in the frequency of organizing ECAs between public and private universities. The results showed that in students' experience, private universities (M = 3.34, SD = 1.21) organized activities to help students develop specialized skills significantly more frequently than did public universities (M = 3.03, SD = 1.25), t(421) = 2.39, p = 0.02. Similarly, the results showed that private universities (M = 3.81, SD = 1.12) organized activities to help students develop specialized skills significantly more frequently than did public universities (M = 3.47, SD = 1.32), t(240.31) = 2.60, p = 0.01.

Level of engagement

The results (Table 9.2) showed that students engaged with participating in the five types of ECAs to different extents. They reported that they joined in activities that nurtured their special talents (painting, playing musical instruments, chess, martial arts etc.) most regularly (M = 3.80, SD = 1.06). It was surprising to find that although political-education activities were not organized the most frequently, students appeared to partake in this type of activity regularly (M = 3.76, SD = 1.13). Student engagement with recreational activities (M = 3.67, SD = 1.04), activities that trained them in social-engagement skills (M = 3.73, SD = 1.09), and work skills (M = 3.64, SD = 1.18) also fell in the category of "frequently." Students participated in activities that trained them in specialized skills at a moderate level (M = 3.31, SD = 1.18).

Results of an independent-sample T-test showed that there were no statistically significant differences in the engagement with ECAs between male and female students. However, results of another independent-sample T-test indicated that students from private universities (M = 3.75, SD = 1.16) engaged with activities that trained work skills more than those from public universities (M = 3.41, SD = 1.19), t(421) = 2.87, p = 0.00. Similarly, students from private universities (M = 3.80, SD = 1.01) engaged with recreational activities more than those from public universities (M = 3.41, SD = 1.05), t(421) = 3.74, p = 0.00.

One-way ANOVA tests were run to check whether there were significant differences in the engagement with ECAs between groups of students of different disciplines. The results revealed that there were statistically significant differences in student engagement with ECAs that trained students in specialized skills at the $p < 0.05$ level $[F(3,419) = 3.29, p = 0.02]$. A Turkey post-hoc test revealed that STEM students ($M = 3.57$, $SD = 1.11$) participated in these types of ECAs more regularly than students of other disciplines, but significantly more regularly than students of social sciences ($M = 3.04$, $SD = 1.30$), $MD = 0.53$, $p = 0.01$.

One-way ANOVA tests were run to determine whether there were significant differences in the engagement with ECAs between groups of students of different years. The results revealed that there were statistically significant differences in student engagement with ECAs that trained students in special talents at the $p < 0.05$ level $[F(3,419) = 3.39, p = 0.02]$. A Turkey post-hoc test revealed that fourth-year students ($M = 3.60$, $SD = 1.20$) participated in this type of extracurricular activity less regularly than students of other years, but significantly less regularly than second-year students ($M = 4.02$, $SD = 0.96$), $MD = 0.41$, $p = 0.02$.

Factors influencing student engagement

Despite recognizing the importance of ECAs in developing their employability, students did not seem to engage with these activities to a high extent. The analysis of qualitative data revealed that student engagement with ECAs was associated with four factors. Firstly, their disbelief in the benefits of participating in ECAs could influence their participation. For example, many interviewees disregarded political-education activities, whereas many others believed that the political attributes acquired from these activities would enable them to function better in the socialist country of Vietnam. Similarly, those who believed in the ability of ECAs to develop employability skills sought out information, selected, and participated in relevant activities to develop the skills they wanted to possess, while others did not. Others who did not join in ECAs could have been influenced by the common belief that formal education and credentials were important for securing a job. Thus, they disregarded participating in ECAs, or participated superficially for "self-improvement scores" rather than for improving their skills, as pointed out in Tran (2015).

Secondly, student engagement appeared to be influenced by formal education activities and their part-time jobs, which is consistent with findings in studies by (Clark et al., 2015) and Thompson et al. (2013). As the curriculum in Vietnamese universities is often crowded, students had to spend a great deal of time, both in class and out of class, on their formal learning, which left little time for ECAs (Tran, 2015). Likewise, as stated by many students, they had to work part-time to help their families fund their studies; therefore, they did not have time for ECAs that overlapped with their work schedule. Their experiences are illustrated below:

> We have to study many subjects, and each of which requires us to work in groups! Plus, we have to work part-time, so we cannot manage the time to participate in ECAs, especially for activities that are recorded for self-improvement scores. These activities are very time-consuming. (Student of English Studies)

Thirdly, the efficiency in organizing such activities could influence student engagement and determine the extent to which students' employability skills are developed, which has been pointed out by Al-Ansari et al. (2016). More than two-thirds of the interviewees pointed out that many ECAs were irrelevant or were organized formalistically. Some of them criticized that such activities wasted time and resources, did not develop employability for students, and demotivated students from participating in similar activities.

> Many of these activities were excessively formalistic; they brought little benefit to the community. (Student of Bio-Technology)

Most ECAs in Vietnamese universities were led and managed by YUA organizers, who were students selected by YUA leaders. In the interviewees' experience, these student organizers often lacked organizational, leadership, and management skills. The interviewed YUA organizers attributed this issue to the frequent turnover of YUA organizers when they graduated. This reduced the effectiveness in leadership and management of ECAs, which in turn affected the quality of developing employability for students via ECAs. These two issues suggest that Vietnamese universities need to sufficiently invest in YUA's personnel development to ensure these activities are led and managed professionally as part of the overall institutional strategy for soft-skills implementation.

Fourthly, student participation and engagement with ECAs were influenced by a lack of information about these activities. However, this issue appeared to result from both the YUA and students. Many interviewees complained about the YUA leaders or organizers announcing their activities too late for them to participate. In contrast, others argued that it was students who did not proactively seek out information about these activities, which was evidenced by the fact that the YUA leaders and organizers always sent emails to the students or posted on social media about their upcoming activities.

> The YUA sent emails to students to inform about their activities too late. For example, an activity is about to take place on the 20th, they sent an email on the 18th. (Student of Biology)
>
> A lack of information is just an excuse from those who don't like to participate in ECAs [...]. The Student Office has already informed students about the YUA activities and where to look for information related to these activities. (YUA organizer—Student of English Studies)

This is consistent with Tran (2015), who found that students did not proactively seek information about taking part in ECAs that would develop their employability. Hence, ECA organizers would need to strongly market their activities as well as the benefits of participating in them.

Conclusion

In summary, this study has found that ECAs could greatly contribute to developing employability skills for students. However, the contribution appeared to depend greatly on student engagement, which was found to be associated with: (i) their beliefs about the relevance and possibility of developing employability skills via ECAs; (ii) their ability to balance formal education learning activities, part-time work, and ECAs; (iii) availability of information about these activities; and (iv) professional organization of these activities.

Based on the findings, it is recommended that if universities would like to develop employability skills for students via ECAs, they should inform students of the relevance of participating in ECAs as well as the potential benefits that these activities may bring to students' learning and future employment opportunities. By improving students' awareness and beliefs about the usefulness of taking part in ECAs, universities could increase student engagement with these activities, which would in turn improve the learning outcomes via this type of informal learning. In addition, to increase student engagement, it is pivotal for ECA organizers to identify skills that students may need, as well as prioritize ECAs that students are interested in which will elevate students' participation rate and reduce waste of resources. Finally, these activities should be organized professionally, even though they are extracurricular, and students should be notified early so they can adjust their schedule if necessary to attend. This is significant in the context where more students have to undertake part-time work alongside their studies as well as heavy workloads from their curriculum-based learning activities.

This study has some limitations. Firstly, the list of skills included in the survey were selected by the researcher based on his experience as an ECA organizer; therefore, there may be some subjectivity in identifying this list of skills. Secondly, this study only examined the contribution of participating in ECAs to students' employability skills as a whole; however, participating in certain types of ECAs may help develop certain employability skills better than others. Thirdly, this study did not include ECA leaders' perspectives, which might have helped highlight organizational factors influencing their operation, such as leadership perspectives, funding, or networks with external stakeholders. Therefore, future studies should also address these limitations so that we can more thoroughly understand the relationship between participation in ECAs and students' employability-skills development and employment outcomes.

References

Al Ansari, A., Al-Harbi, F., AbdelAziz, W., AbdelSalam, M., El Tantawi, M. M., & ElRefae, I. (2016). Factors affecting student participation in extra-curricular activities: A comparison between two Middle Eastern dental schools. *The Saudi Dental Journal*, 28(1), 36–43.

Al-Mahmood, R., & Gruba, P. (2007). Approaches to the implementation of generic graduate attributes in Australian ICT undergraduate education. *Computer Science Education*, 17(3), 171–185. doi: 10.1080/08993400701538054

Barrie, S., Hughes, C., Smith, C., & Thomson, K. (2009). *The national graduate attributes project: Key issues to consider in the renewal of learning and teaching experiences to foster graduate attributes*. Sydney: The University of Sydney.

Bodewig, C., & Badiani-Magnusson, R. (2014). *Skilling up Vietnam: Preparing the workforce for a modern market economy*. Washington, DC: World Bank Publications.

Clark, G., Marsden, R., Whyatt, J. D., Thompson, L., & Walker, M. (2015). "It's everything else you do…": Alumni views on extracurricular activities and employability. *Active Learning in Higher Education*, 16(2), 133–147.

De Lisle, J. (2011). The benefits and challenges of mixing methods and methodologies: Lessons learnt from implementing qualitatively led mixed methods research designs in Trinidad and Tobago. *Caribbean Curriculum*, 18, 87–120. Retrieved from https://bit.ly/2JbhJUU.

De Vaus, D. A. (2014). *Surveys in social research*. Abingdon, UK: Routledge.

Elo, S., & Kyngäs, H. (2008). The qualitative content analysis process. *Journal of Advanced Nursing*, 62(1), 107–115.

Ho Chi Minh Communist Youth Union (2019). *Ho Chi Minh Communist Youth Union*. Retrieved from http://english.doanthanhnien.vn/.

Hordósy, R., & Clark, T. (2018). Beyond the compulsory: A critical exploration of the experiences of extracurricular activity and employability in a northern red brick university. *Research in Post-Compulsory Education*, 23(3), 414–435.

Kalles, S., & Ryan, T. G. (2015). Service-learning: Promise and possibility in post-secondary education. *International Journal of Progressive Education*, 11(1), 132–148.

Khan, S. A. R., & Zhang, Y. (2017). The effective role of visiting lecturers in the courses of supply chain management. *American Journal of Traffic and Transportation Engineering*, 2(6), 104–109.

Lau, H.-H., Hsu, H.-Y., Acosta, S., & Hsu, T.-L. (2014). Impact of participation in extra-curricular activities during college on graduate employability: An empirical study of graduates of Taiwanese business schools. *Educational Studies*, 40(1), 26–47.

Lindorff, M. (2011). Skills gaps in Australian firms. *Journal of Vocational Education and Training*, 63(2), 247–259.

Litecky, C. R., Arnett, K. P., & Prabhakar, B. (2004). The paradox of soft skills versus technical skills in IS hiring. *Journal of Computer Information Systems*, 45(1), 69–76.

Mestechkina, T., Son, N. D., & Shin, J. Y. (2014). Parenting in Vietnam. In H. Selin (Ed.), *Parenting across cultures* (pp. 47–57). Dordrecht, Netherlands: Springer.

Nickson, D., Warhurst, C., Commander, J., Hurrell, S. A., & Cullen, A. M. (2012). Soft skills and employability: Evidence from UK retail. *Economic and Industrial Democracy*, 33(1), 65–84.

Osman, K. (2011). The inculcation of generic skills through service learning experience among science student teachers. *Procedia – Social and Behavioral Sciences*, 18, 148–153. doi: 10.1016/j.sbspro.2011.05.022

Roulin, N., & Bangerter, A. (2013). Students' use of extra-curricular activities for positional advantage in competitive job markets. *Journal of Education and Work*, 26(1), 21–47.

Scarinci, J., & Pearce, P. (2012). The perceived influence of travel experiences on learning generic skills. *Tourism Management*, 33(2), 380–386.

Sepahpanah, M., Zarafshani, K., Mirakzade, A., & Rosch, D. M. (2013). Service learning processes and challenges in Iran: A case study. *NACTA Journal*, 57(3a), 36–39.

Tertiary Education Quality and Standards Agency (2013). Australian qualifications framework. Sydney: The Australian Qualifications Framework Council.

The Quality Assurance Agency for Higher Education (2014). *The frameworks for higher education qualifications of UK degree-awarding bodies.* Retrieved from: www.qaa.ac.uk/docs/qaa/quality-code/qualifications-frameworks.pdf

Thompson, L. J., Clark, G., Walker, M., & Whyatt, J. D. (2013). "It's just like an extra string to your bow": Exploring higher education students' perceptions and experiences of extra-curricular activity and employability. *Active Learning in Higher Education*, 14(2), 135–147.

Tran, L. H. N. (2018). Game of blames: Higher education stakeholders' perceptions of causes of Vietnamese graduates' skills gap. *International Journal of Educational Development*, 62(Sep), 302–312.

Tran, T. T. (2015). Is graduate employability the "whole-of-higher-education-issue"? *Journal of Education and Work*, 28(3), 207–227. doi: 10.1080/13639080.2014.900167

UK Commission for Employment and Skills (2016). Employer skills survey 2015: UK results. Retrieved from https://bit.ly/2PpNxFj

Williams, B., Onsman, A., & Brown, T. (2010). Exploratory factor analysis: A five-step guide for novices. *Australasian Journal of Paramedicine*, 8(3), 1–13.

Yorke, M. (2006). *Employability in higher education: What it is, what it is not.* Retrieved from https://bit.ly/22VzZS0.

10 External stakeholders' roles in developing soft skills in Vietnamese universities

Introduction

Soft-skills implementation in higher education (HE) requires collaboration from different groups of stakeholders: university leaders, academics, professional staff, students, and external stakeholders, among others (Al-Mahmood & Gruba, 2007; Barrie, Hughes, Smith, & Thomson, 2009). In Vietnamese universities, external stakeholders' support in carrying out the Ministry of Education and Training's (MOET) soft-skills policy appears to be a significant determinant for its success due to a lack of teachers, expertise for skills development, and the use of extracurricular activities (ECAs) as the main channel to develop soft skills for students.

However, external stakeholders' participation in soft-skills implementation cannot be taken for granted. Many issues may arise, regarding what implementation tasks they can take part in, the extent to which they can participate, how to ensure that they carry out the assigned tasks effectively, what benefits they will get from their contribution, etc. Likewise, in a HE system whose leadership, governance and management are still much centralized, as in Vietnam, involving external stakeholders in students' soft-skills development may not be easy.

Therefore, this chapter will feature how Vietnamese university leaders could involve external stakeholders for the implementation of soft skills and challenges related to their attempts, using two complementary studies. Drawn from a project on soft-skills implementation in six Vietnamese universities, the first study found that external stakeholders were involved in curriculum-based, extracurricular, and work-integrated learning (WIL) activities to help develop soft skills for students. The challenges that the universities faced in such a task included a lack of connection with industry, a lack of resources, and some issues related to governance, leadership, and management. The study also found that external stakeholders could pose some difficulties for the implementation, including their pedagogical practice, collaboration with academics, and their engagement with the academic community in the university. The second study explored the intentions and influential factors of Vietnamese university alumni, as representatives of external stakeholders, to help develop work-readiness for current students. The study suggested that alumni were willing to assist their university in a variety of tasks, but they were concerned about their expertise, the benefits they might get from such participation, and their perceived connectedness with the university's soft-skills implementation. The chapter discusses some ways to foster the contribution of external stakeholders, mostly alumni, in developing soft skills for current students.

External stakeholders' roles in developing students' soft skills

The landscape of HE worldwide has undergone rigorous changes in recent decades. Higher education was traditionally for the elite and focused on enlightenment and liberal education, but is now shifting towards mass and universal education (Hayhoe, Li, Lin, & Zha, 2012). This has resulted in an increase in the number of graduates, more intense competition in the labor market, and a decrease in the value of a university credential with respect to ensuring employment (Mok & Jiang, 2018; Yang, 2018). In addition, the operation of many HE institutions has been strongly affected by recent funding cuts by the government (Lebeau, Stumpf, Brown, Lucchesi, & Kwiek, 2012). Higher education institutions enroll full-fee-paying students, including international students, to tackle the issue of inadequate resources for their operation; yet this creates other problems. These students, along with their families, invest in HE studies and expect greater advantages for career prospects as a result (Choudaha, Chang, & Kono, 2014). This puts more pressure on HE institutions to improve the chances of employment for these students, and the pressure is becoming more pressing when employers repeatedly complain about graduates' work ability. Finally, the current trend of university ranking (Heffernan & Heffernan, 2018; Soh, 2017) also increases HE institutions' commitment to developing work-readiness for students. These league rankings often use employers' opinions of graduates' work performance as a ranking indicator, which may greatly affect future student enrolments at a university.

To address the mentioned changes in HE and to sustain its educational values, universities have launched some initiatives to equip their students with skills that enhance their chances to obtain employment upon graduation and thrive in their careers. Employers and other groups of external stakeholders are more frequently consulted to determine relevant work skills so that universities can integrate into the curricula accordingly (Chowdhury & Miah, 2016; Maxwell, Scott, Macfarlane, & Williamson, 2009; Singh & Jaykumar, 2019). For example, to help narrow the gap of the skills mismatch for Indian hospitality and tourism students, employers, alumni, and faculties were consulted to identify relevant skills to embed in the curriculum (Singh & Jaykumar, 2019). By doing so, they identified a list of ten core soft skills to develop for the students, which served as the basis for their curriculum renewal.

In addition, external stakeholders are also involved in designing programs and teaching these skills in many universities via guest lectures (Anthony & Garner, 2016; Khan & Zhang, 2017; Mason, Williams, & Cranmer, 2009). For example, Anthony and Garner (2016) analyzed the effectiveness of different pedagogical strategies used to teach soft skills, including self-analyses, interviews, guest lectures, journal articles, and soft-skills videos. Students rated that guest lectures were the most helpful and influential in their study of soft skills. Indeed, professionals, not necessarily high-profile business people, can offer students new content, new real-life learning situations, increase their understanding of how industries function, inspire students, and expand their professional network (Khan & Zhang, 2017; van Hoek, Godsell, & Harrison, 2011). However, using guest lecturers to impart soft skills may be challenging because they must be able to conduct their teaching as an integral part of the program rather than as an add-on element or a faculty substitution (Khan & Zhang, 2017). This suggests that guest lecturers must be trained or mentored in teaching methods. Likewise, it is difficult to recruit professionals and arrange a time that is convenient for both the university and these professionals (Khan & Zhang, 2017).

Moreover, under the WIL approach, students are sent out into industries to undertake work placements or internships, which will help them strengthen their existing knowledge and develop relevant work skills (Carter, Ruskin, & Cassilles, 2017; Jackson, 2015). External stakeholders participate in this WIL as mentors where they provide guidance to student interns throughout the internship and may assess students' work performance. Research has found that WIL can help students develop professional expertise and soft skills, change their learning behaviors, and identify possible career paths (e.g. Jackson, 2018; Tran & Nguyen, 2018). The issues with the WIL approach can include a lack of internship opportunities and difficulties in supporting students throughout the internship (Jackson, 2015). Mentors may not be able to help students to construct their learning and assess students' learning methodologically (Jackson, 2015).

Furthermore, external stakeholders, such as local authorities, employers, non-governmental organizations, and public services, could provide many opportunities for students to develop generic skills via service learning and ECAs (Kohlbry, 2016; Osman, 2011). Although liaising with external stakeholders to organize such learning activities is difficult given the tight budget and lack of connection with relevant external stakeholders, students often look down on ECAs compared to curriculum-based activities (Tran, 2013). Community-service learning is also facing many difficulties related to administrative, financial, educational, and evaluative areas for educational administrators (Sepahpanah, Zarafshani, Mirakzade, & Rosch, 2013).

Finally, alumni-mentoring programs have been set up to help current students connect with an alumnus who would support them in their studies and orient them for career development. Associating with a graduate in the same area of study would help current students gradually become accustomed to an industry related to their studies. For example, Murray, Ross, Blaney, and Adamson (2015) reported the outcomes of a graduate-mentoring program that involved 345 civil and environmental engineering student mentees, 83 graduate mentors, and 31 employers. The results showed that the student mentees were positive about what they learned from the graduate mentors or employers. On completion of their mentoring program, the majority of the students committed to changing their attitudes and behaviors toward continued professional development. The authors also reported a number of challenges related to such alumni-mentoring programs, including maintaining student mentees' motivation throughout the program and looking for graduate mentors who willingly engaged with it.

In short, the literature indicates that external stakeholders, especially employers, are playing increasingly important roles in HE. Having a solid network with people in industry is an advantage for educational and training activities of HE institutions, especially in developing soft skills for students. However, external stakeholders' roles in educational and training activities in Vietnamese HE have not been documented adequately by research; therefore, further investigations in this direction are necessary.

Study 1: Challenges for Vietnamese universities in involving external stakeholders in soft-skills programs

Research design

This study will highlight external stakeholders' roles in developing soft skills for Vietnamese university students and factors influencing their roles. This section will expand our insights into university-industry collaboration by investigating it in a non-Western HE system. More specifically, it answers the following questions:

- What are the roles of external stakeholders in soft-skills implementation in Vietnamese universities?
- What challenges do Vietnamese universities face when involving these stakeholders in soft-skills implementation?

This study was conducted as a qualitative multiple case study, which provided an opportunity to investigate the implementation in depth and within its real context, as well as allowed a comparison of soft-skills implementation across the cases to identify similarities and differences (Yin, 2009). Based on a maximum-variation sampling principle (Merriam, 2009), the researcher selected six universities with different institutional types (public versus private), locations (metropolitan versus regional city-based), and their history of establishment and development. Three of them were public universities and the remainder were private universities.

This study only focused on soft-skills implementation of the business administration program of the six universities in order to preserve disciplinary distinctiveness, analyze the research issues in more depth and reasonably compare results across the universities. The program was popular in Vietnamese universities, and there is more evidence of soft-skills implementation in the School of Economics (or an equivalent name) compared to other programs.

The participants in each of the selected universities were recruited using a snowball-sampling technique (Browne, 2005), which allowed the researcher to approach key informants of soft-skills implementation in a university based on the recommendation of another participant. A total of 69 interviewees were recruited (Table 10.1), including university leaders, school leaders, and teachers, as well as leaders and staff members of the Youth Union and its associates (YUA).

Data were collected via semi-structured interviews (Horton, Macve, & Struyven, 2004) in conjunction with relevant documents and policies that were available on the university websites or were provided by the participants. A qualitative

Table 10.1 A summary of participants and universities

University	Characteristics	Participants
University A	A public university Located in a regional city Less than 15 years old	4 leaders 7 teachers 1 YUA leader 1 YUA staff member
University B	A public university One of the key universities in Vietnam Located in a metropolitan city More than 50 years old	4 leaders 8 teachers 1 YUA leader
University C	A public university One of the top performing universities in Vietnam Located in a medium-sized city More than 50 years old	3 leaders 9 teachers 1 YUA leader
University D	A private university upgraded from a vocational college Has curriculum autonomy Has an extensive network with industry Less than ten years old (as a university)	4 leaders 5 teachers 1 YUA staff member
University E	A newly-established private university Located in a regional city Less than ten years old	3 leaders 6 teachers 1 YUA staff member
University F	One of the oldest private universities Located in a metropolitan city Less than ten years old	3 leaders 6 teachers 1 YUA staff member

content analysis was employed to analyze the data (Elo & Kyngäs, 2008). On a case-by-case basis, all relevant data were repeatedly reviewed for content. Passages relevant to roles of external stakeholders in association with tasks in the analytical framework were highlighted and coded. Then the codes were compared across the cases to find similarities and differences in external stakeholders' roles in soft-skills implementation between the universities. This step also involved evidence-based interpretation of factors influencing the roles and contribution of external stakeholders in developing soft skills for students across the six case studies. Finally, the results emerging from the analysis were organized into the final report.

Findings

What groups of external stakeholders are involved?

Chapter 4 presented soft-skills implementation models in Vietnamese universities. Although there are slight differences in these models, mostly due to institutional contexts, the universities fundamentally developed soft skills for students via curriculum-based, extracurricular, and WIL activities.

Within the curriculum of the business administration program, soft skills are embedded in a number of skills subjects, which can be delivered by teachers of the School of Business or an independent department that the university has set up for the provision of foundational education to all students in the university. Soft skills are also compulsorily imparted by disciplinary teachers in specialized subjects in the case of University D, but at these teachers' discretion in the other five universities. In this regard, external stakeholders were involved in two tasks. In all universities—except University B, which intentionally delayed the implementation to save resources and attention for other reforms that occurred at the same time this study was conducted—employers were consulted so that the university could select relevant skills for their students to develop. Also, consistent with practices in their universities in other countries (Khan & Zhang, 2017; van Hoek et al., 2011), universities D and E invited skills experts from industry to teach skills classes. Likewise, in all six universities, teachers of the business administration programs sometimes invited successful business people from industry to give a guest talk in their class, aiming to inspire students and to help impart certain skills such as presentation at the workplace, teamwork, and problem-solving skills. However, except for University D, the teachers did this at their discretion rather than following the university's policy. Another task that external stakeholders, especially employers, were involved in was completing a survey about their graduates' work performance, a source of data for the improvement of the programs they offered.

In addition, these universities also use internships, a form of WIL, to develop students' work-readiness and soft employability skills, just like in several counterparts around the world (Carter et al., 2017; Jackson, 2015). In University D, students of business administration are required to undertake two compulsory internships or an equivalent amount of part- or full-time work experience. In the other universities, the students are required to complete one internship only. In most cases, students are encouraged to look for internship opportunities by themselves, with some exceptional cases where the Student Support Service may assist in placing them in a company in a relevant industry. In this regard, the employer or a professional at the workplace was invited to collaborate with an academic to coordinate the student internships. These external stakeholders mentored students throughout the internship, showing them what and how to provide constructive feedback for their improvement, and providing a feedback form on students' work performance, which is used by the academic to decide students' internship results.

Resembling practices in other universities across the globe (Kohlbry, 2016; Osman, 2011; Sepahpanah et al., 2013), the six universities also used ECAs to develop soft skills for students. However, the YUA's extracurricular activities were included as an integral component of their soft-skills policy-implementation strategy. This is because the YUA has traditionally been in charge of political education and leading students in community-engagement activities. Activities that participants listed as contributing to students' soft skills, conceptualized as work-readiness in these universities, vary a great deal. They range from running classes that develop specific soft skills, CV-writing skills, and interview skills classes to organizing career fairs, charity work, environment-protection campaigns, or community-development activities. A diverse range of external stakeholders were involved in these activities: employers, human resource managers, alumni, skills experts, charity organizations, local authorities, etc., depending on the activities. Those people's roles also varied. In most cases, they led the activities, with the agreement of the YUA leader of the university. In other cases, they provided approval or resources for the YUA and students to conduct community-development activities.

Challenges facing the university in involving external stakeholders

Although external stakeholders are helpful and resourceful in supporting the universities in executing a soft-skills policy in their institutions, the involvement of these stakeholders was not a simple task. Institutional contexts strongly affected leadership decisions on the implementation, which in turn influenced how external stakeholders were involved for soft-skills implementation. At the time of research, there were several reforms concurrently happening, and each university involved in this study had a different level of institutional autonomy related to the curriculum, financial management, and staff appointments. Therefore, leaders of University B delayed soft-skills implementation, University C's leaders prioritized other reforms, and leaders of the Business Administration School of University F ignored it, despite their existing extensive connections with industry and convenient location. Consequently, in these universities, external stakeholders' participation in curriculum-based activities was very limited and informal. In universities A, D, and E, leaders attempted to involve external stakeholders in executing a soft-skills policy to different extents depending on how they could tackle a lack of autonomy in curriculum design and issues related to resources and staff appointment regulations. Therefore, the involvement of external stakeholders in curriculum-based activities in these universities was fragmented. In all six universities, external stakeholders were involved mostly in student internships and ECAs. Even so, they faced other difficulties, as reported below. These findings well reflect Tomlinson's (2018) finding that university–employer/external stakeholder relationships depend on contextual and cultural factors.

For universities that decided to engage with soft-skills implementation, the leadership was not effective enough for the involvement of external stakeholders. A lack of clarity in policy communication also limited the opportunities of involving external stakeholders in in-class teaching activities. For example, in University D, although all interviewed teachers knew that they were required to teach soft skills, not all of them knew that they could co-teach their subjects with a guest lecturer from an industry and the latter would be paid by the university. In addition, the university leaders also seemed to rely on teachers' initiatives to involve qualified skills experts or successful business people in teaching soft skills, except the university that had a clear policy to recruit teachers that had both academic qualifications and industry work experience. Moreover, a lack of resources also prevented the universities from employing external stakeholders in tasks related to soft-skills implementation. For example, the YUA leaders of University A had to closely consider their budget prior to inviting skills experts to organize a skills class, or organize community-engagement activities, an issue noted in (Sepahpanah et al., 2013). Most of their ECAs were being supported by their alumni; even so, keeping in contact with their alumni was limited due to a lack of personnel and it has not been considered an important mission in Vietnamese universities until now.

> The challenge is inviting a guest speaker within the allowed budget from the university. (Participant A12, YUA leader)
> Our skills development center can only operate with sufficient budget [...]. In the long run, we may not open classes for students because they cannot afford them [...] even though our participation fee is very low for them now. (Participant A11, YUA staff member)

Another major challenge that most of the universities in this study were facing was their lack of an extensive connection with industry. Therefore, it was hard for them to identify and recruit reliable people to involve in the implementation task, as noted in studies by Khan and Zhang (2017) and T. T. Tran (2013). Long-standing universities located in metropolitan areas seem to have less difficulty in this task than newly established institutions located in regional cities. For example, University D, with a long tradition of vocational education, had extensive industry networks, so they could organize two internships for students easily and invite skills experts to deliver skills subjects for their students. However, University D faced difficulties in recruiting experts to run their skills classes because the university was newly established and located in a regional city.

A number of challenges on the part of external stakeholders were also identified. First, aligned with findings in Khan and Zhang (2017), most of them did not have enough time to join in soft-skills development tasks as these skills would need a substantial amount of time to develop. Therefore, as reported by some leaders and teachers in this study, employers or professionals often turned down their invitations to join in soft-skills development tasks. It could be because teaching a subject throughout an academic semester would consume a lot of their time, which might affect their business badly.

Second, for those who are qualified to teach at the university, they seemed to struggle with pedagogical and assessment practices, and were often found to tell students about the skills rather than helping students develop these skills, as observed by academics in University E below:

> The university is employing people from local industries to teach some disciplinary subjects [...]. Employing a bank director or a head of a sales department is good in that they disseminate real experiences to students, but they do not teach generic skills. (Participant E6, academic)

There seemed to be a disconnection between these external teachers and academics. Academics might know about teaching and assessment methods, but they often refused to accept their role of imparting soft skills. External teachers knew the importance of these skills and could provide real-life situations for the application of these skills, but they might not be able to use teaching methods appropriately. A lack of collaboration between these groups failed to create a community of practice for soft-skills teaching and assessment, resulting in a huge waste of opportunities and expertise sharing, which disadvantaged both groups of teachers.

Third, regarding student internships, several participants reported that employers hesitated to provide internship opportunities to students. Where they did provide internships, mentors were found to be able to assist students with performing specific assigned tasks but often fail to help students develop a well-constructed experiential or social learning experience throughout the internship, as some academics suggested. Sometimes, their final report to the academic was not aligned with other internship-related assignments that students submitted to the academic, causing confusion in the assessment process. But this also seemed to result from a lack of collaboration between academics and mentors, as revealed by the statements of two academics below:

> We academics decided on scores for the student internship on a scale of ten [based on the assignments they submitted]. But that process needs to take into account their mentors' feedback. […] It is impossible to give a student a three or four if the mentor's feedback is so positive. (Participant F2, academic)
> Mentor's feedback is not always reliable. Students may undertake the internship in a company whose owner they know well, so students may write the feedback and ask for a seal. In such a situation, the feedback is not used as a proxy to assess students' skills. We just cannot certify whose feedback it is. (Participant B07, academic)

In short, the business programs of the six universities involved external stakeholders in soft-skills development tasks to different extents. Such an involvement appeared to be challenged by current institutional context, institutional leadership, a lack of connection with industry and some issues related to external stakeholders' timetable, teaching or mentoring experience, and collaboration between academics and industry mentors.

Study 2: Alumni's support for programs that develop soft skills

Research design

In 2019, a small-scale study was designed to follow up on Study 1 above. The main objective of this study was to explore whether university alumni's willingness to participate in activities could develop work-readiness skills for current students.

182 *External stakeholders' roles*

The study also aimed to identify obstacles that might prevent them from participating in these activities. The research questions were:

- To what extent are Vietnamese universities' alumni willing to participate in activities to develop work-readiness skills for current students? In what way can they contribute?
- What do they consider to make the decision on whether or not they will participate?

The study was conducted as a quantitative study to measure the variables. Data were collected by means of an online survey. The survey content was developed based on findings of the former study and on the researchers' experience. In the survey, participants were asked to provide some demographic information, then to select what activities they believed they could participate in to develop work-readiness skills. The survey also asked them to rate the frequency of their participation in the activities on a 5-point Likert scale in which 1 denoted "very infrequently" and 5 "very frequently," with an extra choice zero as "never participated." Finally, participants were asked to rate the influence of a number of factors that might discourage them from taking part in the activities mentioned in the previous sections, also on a 5-point scale in which 1 denoted "very little" and 5 "very much."

Participants were recruited by a snowball-sampling technique. The researcher sent the survey link to his colleagues in a number of Vietnamese universities, requesting them to forward the link to their former students who had graduated at least one year ago and were employed. The survey was open for only one month (March 2019). By the end of this period, a total of 154 responses from 20 provinces and cities, mostly in the south of Vietnam, were collected. Participants had a variety of jobs: doctors, dentists, human resource managers, teachers, office clerks, sales people, construction engineers, interpreters, tour guides, lawyers, accountants, IT technicians, and software developers, among others. The percentage of male participants was 56.5% and female was 43.5%. In terms of work experience, 41.6% had worked for less than three years, 23.4% between three and six years, and the remaining 35.0% over nine years. Those who were in a management position accounted for 27.2%, in a staff position 67.3%, and the remaining 5.5% were employers. Those who were working for a Vietnamese public organization, a private organization owned by a Vietnamese, a private organization owned by a foreigner, and a non-governmental organization were 26.6%, 50.6%, 21.4%, and 1.3%, respectively.

Data were descriptively analyzed using SPSS version 20. Frequencies were counted to determine activities where participants could contribute the most; means (M) and standard deviations (SD) were computed to determine the extent to which participants had participated in these activities.

The data set that explored the extent to which certain factors might prevent them from participation was analyzed for principal components which helped extract latent variables into main components. The internal consistency of this set of data, measured by Cronbach's alpha, was 0.84, item-total correlations varied from 0.37 to 0.67. The KMO test was run to measure sampling adequacy. The KMO value was 0.80, signifying that the samples were adequate for extracting latent variables into principal components. Using varimax rotation, the analysis suggested that three principal components should be extracted, which together explained 66.81% of the variance. The results were as below:

- Factor 1: The quality of alumni's contribution (including five latent variables, α = 0.81, variance explained: 42.23%).
- Factor 2: Benefits that alumni may gain (including three latent variables, α = 0.67, variance explained: 14.00%).
- Factor 3: Alumni's perception of their relation to soft-skills implementation (including two latent variables, α = 0.90, variance explained: 10.53%).

Independent-sample T-tests and one-way ANOVA tests were also conducted to compare differences in the influence of these factors between groups of participants.

Findings

In what activities can alumni help students develop work-readiness skills?

Data from the survey showed that alumni, at different stages of their career, appeared to be willing to contribute to helping current students to develop soft skills. Almost half of the participants (49.4%) believed that they could assist the university in identifying soft skills important for the workplace and for students in their journey to employment. However, when it came to designing learning activities or teaching these skills to students in the classroom, only 29.9% and 35.1% believed that they could help. Surprisingly, for a similar teaching role, but as a mentor to a student intern, 47.4% reported that they could undertake that role. More than one-third (36.4%) were also confident that they could be a personal coach to help an individual student or a group of students to build their career development step by step from the time they were at university to the graduation point. The percentage of those who would like to help current students develop soft skills via ECAs was 35.1%. Finally, only 16.9% of them believed that they could support the implementation by means of financial donation (see Table 10.2).

For the teaching activities, participants believed that they could contribute in various ways. For example, 12.3% of them could help students understand the current trends and realities of the labor market so that students could be prepared for the job-finding endeavor. Almost 30% of participants believed that they could help students to locate and access information about job opportunities, while 32.5% and 27.3%, respectively, would like to train students in CV-writing skills and job-interview skills. Also, 43.5% of them felt confident developing learning skills for students so that they could better develop their profession in this time of

Table 10.2 Activities that alumni can participate in

Activities	Frequency (N = 154)	Percentage (%)
Advising the university to choose relevant soft skills	76	49.4
Designing skills-development activities	46	29.9
Teaching soft skills	54	35.1
Assessing students' soft skills	56	36.4
Playing the role of an internship mentor	73	47.4
Coaching students to prepare for their future career	56	36.4
Organizing extracurricular activities	54	35.1
Contributing financial resources	26	16.9

fast-changing workplaces. Finally, 61.1% of the participants believed that they could train current students in the specific soft skills that employers or their future jobs would require

Alumni's actual participation in developing work-readiness skills for current students

However, when asked to rate the extent to which they had participated in activities related to developing soft skills for students, the participants revealed that they had not participated much in these activities. Accordingly, the three activities that participants took part in the most were playing the role of a mentor in student internships (61.04%), coaching students to develop their career (56.49%) and organizing extracurricular activities (55.84%). More than half of the participants had never been involved in other tasks such as consultation of the relevant soft skills for students to develop (60.39%), design of skills-development activities (54.55%), teaching soft skills (55.84%) or assessing students' soft skills (51.63%). In terms of contributing to soft-skills-development programs at Vietnamese universities, 56.49% of them admitted that they had never done so.

For those who had participated in the mentioned activities, the frequency of their participation was low, with mean ranging from 1.91 to 2.69 on a 5-point Likert scale. It was also observed that the standard deviations were relatively high, meaning that many of them participated very infrequently while others did so very frequently (see Table 10.3).

Factors influencing alumni's participation intentions

The study also attempted to explore the extent to which certain factors may influence alumni's participation in activities to develop soft skills for current students. The results (Table 10.4) showed that alumni seemed to be most concerned

Table 10.3 Alumni's participation in soft-skills-development activities for current students

Activities	Participation rate (%) (N = 154)				N	M	SD
	1	2	3	4			
Advising the university to choose relevant soft skills	60.39	24.03	11.04	4.55	60	2.28	1.06
Designing skills-development activities	54.55	25.33	10.39	9.74	70	2.43	1.11
Teaching soft skills	55.84	27.92	9.09	7.15	68	2.37	1.16
Assessing students' soft skills	51.63	31.17	11.04	6.50	75	2.27	1.12
Playing the role of an internship mentor	38.96	29.87	16.23	14.93	94	2.69	1.24
Coaching students to prepare for their future career	43.51	33.76	14.29	8.44	87	2.26	1.10
Organizing extracurricular activities	44.16	31.17	13.64	11.04	86	2.47	1.17
Contributing financial resources	56.49	32.47	7.79	3.25	67	1.91	1.00

Note: 1 = never; 2 = very infrequently and infrequently; 3 = average; 4 = frequently and very frequently

Table 10.4 The influence of certain factors on alumni's participation intention

Influential factors	All (N = 153)*		< 3 years (N = 64)	
	M	SD	M	SD
The quality of their contribution	**3.00**	**0.95**	**3.16**	**0.91**
A lack of experience in curriculum/program development	2.92	1.26	3.20	1.16
A lack of experience in teaching skills	2.97	1.27	3.19	1.19
A lack of experience in leading social activities	2.89	1.22	2.98	1.20
A lack of time to participate in these activities	3.20	1.23	3.20	1.25
Bureaucratic issues with the university	3.02	1.34	3.20	1.34
Benefits of their participation	**2.91**	**0.98**	**3.17**	**0.98**
Payment for participating in these activities	2.68	1.27	2.98	1.30
Invitation from the university	3.40	1.31	3.44	1.28
Restriction of personal financial problems	2.65	1.18	3.09	1.19
Perceived relation to soft-skills-development activities	**2.11**	**1.24**	**2.33**	**1.24**
Having no interest in helping the university	2.17	1.25	2.38	1.28
Developing soft skills for students is not their job	2.06	1.34	2.30	1.35

*One participant did not provide information for this set of data

about the quality of their contribution (M = 3.00, SD = 0.95), followed by concerns about the benefits they may get (M = 2.91, SD = 0.98), and finally their perception about their relation to soft-skills implementation in the university (M = 2.11, SD = 1.24). However, the means were quite low (on a 5-point Likert scale), suggesting that these factors in fact might not strongly influence their intentions and participation. In other words, although some participants may be affected by these factors to different extents, generally, alumni are willing to collaborate with the university to assist current students to develop soft skills.

Independent-sample T-tests were run to compare differences in the influences of these factors on participants' participation intention. However, the tests results showed that there was no statistically significant difference in the influence of these factors on participation intentions between male and female groups, or between management and staff groups.

One-way ANOVA tests were run for a similar purpose. At the level $p < 0.05$, the results showed that:

- There was no statistically significant difference in the influence of these factors on their participation intentions between groups of participants currently working for Vietnamese government agencies, private enterprises owned by a Vietnamese, and private enterprises owned by a foreigner.
- There was a statistically significant difference in the influence of "benefits that alumni may gain" on their participation intentions between groups of participants with different years of work experience $F(2,150) = 4.58$, $p = 0.01$. A post-hoc Turkey test showed that those having less than three years' work experience (M = 3.17, SD =1.00) were influenced by this factor significantly more than those who have between three and six years' work experience (M = 2.61, SD = 0.92), $p = 0.02$; but not significantly higher than those having more than six years' work experience (M = 2.79, SD = 0.92), $p = 0.09$.

The results above suggest that alumni consistently indicated their willingness to support the universities develop students' soft skills. Although they might experience some influential factors, there was no significant difference in the influence of these factors on participation intentions between most groups of alumni. The exception was new graduates (less than three years' work experience), whose concern was about the benefits they may get from their participation. This possibly could arise from the fact that this group are most disadvantaged in terms of employment. They might not have an established career; they might have to strive their best to advance in their career. Therefore, they would hesitate to spend time participating in soft-skills-development activities for current students without some promise of benefits.

Discussion and conclusion

The first study indicated that at the time of research, Vietnamese universities relied heavily on the contribution of external stakeholders for the implementation of soft skills in their institutions. Consistent with existing literature (Jackson, 2015; Khan & Zhang, 2017; Osman, 2011; Singh & Jaykumar, 2019), external stakeholders participated in several roles: (i) consulting with universities to select relevant soft skills to develop for students; (ii) participating in teaching soft skills via curriculum-based or extracurricular activities; (iii) providing, supervising, and assessing student internships; and (iv) evaluating soft-skills-implementation programs (for instance, via employer surveys). Different groups of external stakeholders were involved in these roles, including employers, skills experts who were based in industries, alumni, social organizations, and local authorities.

Among these activities, their roles related to ECAs appeared to be the most prominent, which was because external stakeholders involved in these activities were not subject to regulations about teaching qualifications. These ECAs were also less structured in terms of timetable, teaching methods, and student-assessment schemes. External stakeholders could participate as a one-off activity at a time convenient to them instead of having to conduct their activities bit by bit throughout a semester. Conversely, within-curricular activities required them to possess appropriate qualifications, have experience in using pedagogical and assessment practices, and follow a fixed timetable, which would not be suitable for their work in the industry. Therefore, this explained why some of the universities in this study found it hard to employ industry-based skills experts to deliver their skills curriculum or co-teach a specialized subject.

The study also indicated that leadership of each university appeared to strongly affect the involvement of these external stakeholders. Because leaders of the six universities conceptualized soft-skills implementation as developing work-readiness skills for students, they involved employers and work-skills development experts in implementation tasks more often than did other external stakeholder groups. In addition, university leaders decided the time (at the time of research or delayed until later), the channels (curriculum-based, WIL, or extracurricular), and the extent to which these groups could participate, as reported in the Findings section. In addition, a lack of connection with industry also caused several difficulties with regard to consulting relevant soft skills to develop for students, employing soft-skills teachers, placing student internships, and organizing the YUA's extracurricular activities. Moreover, external stakeholders' participation also depended on their willingness. In many occasions, they ignored the universities' invitations to participate in soft-skills-development tasks. This unwillingness could be ascribed to their busy work schedule, lack of confidence in teaching skills, or perception of gaining no immediate profits for their businesses. This unwillingness, foremost from employers, points out a paradox that, while employers want skilled employees, they do not actively collaborate with universities to develop work skills for students. This unwillingness was partially addressed in the second study.

The second study, which involved alumni (with employers included), generated some conflicting results with those in the first study. Unlike the perspectives and experiences of university leaders and academics, almost one-third to one-half of the participants demonstrated that they wanted to participate in soft-skills implementation tasks (Table 10.2). This means that there is always a source of external stakeholder out there willing to help Vietnamese universities execute a soft-skills policy. Unfortunately, the study showed that in contrast to alumni's willingness to assist the university, in reality, more than half of them had never been involved in soft-skills-development tasks, including the simplest way of suggesting what skills to develop for students via a survey. Three activities that they reported to have participated in the most were mentoring students during their internships, organizing ECAs, and coaching students to develop their career. It is noted that in the current context of Vietnamese HE, these tasks are not necessarily initiated by the universities. These stakeholders can mentor students to undertake a voluntary internship, not as part of their study; they can lead ECAs as part of a community-development project rather than under the YUA of a university; and they can coach students solely based on personal relationships with a student or a group of students rather than as part of a university's alumni–current student coaching program. All of these suggest that, while possibilities exist, Vietnamese universities have not made good use of these possibilities. This could be linked back to the leadership-related issues and contextual factors found in the first study.

The second study also found out the reasons why alumni participated (or not) in soft-skills-development activities. Despite low man scores, the three principal influential factors were their expertise, followed by the benefit they could gain from participation, and finally their general view about their relation to soft-skills implementation in the university. Among the sub-factors that constitute the three mentioned principal factors, not being invited by the university was the highest rated influential factor (M = 3.40, SD = 1.31), much higher than other factors. This once again suggests that members of university leadership need to explicitly communicate to their alumni their need for assistance with their soft-skills implementation. Otherwise, alumni feel unwelcome or perceive themselves as ineligible to participate.

In short, the findings of the two studies suggest that university leaders need to be more proactive in seeking help from external stakeholders in executing soft-skills-development programs in their institutions. While involving external stakeholders in curriculum-based activities may be restricted by regulations and external stakeholders' pedagogical expertise, there is plenty of room for them to be involved in ECAs and internship programs. The main issue here is that there should be signals from the universities inviting these external stakeholders. External stakeholders do not automatically approach the university to offer assistance as obviously it is not their job. The best and long-term strategy is to keep in touch with graduates who will become professionals and possible employers. These graduates could help the university to organize mentoring programs or provide/introduce internship opportunities, or even provide financial assistance for soft-skills-development programs. Gradually, when the alumni network grows, the university would have an abundance of connections to support all of their skills-development programs and related initiatives.

References

Al-Mahmood, R., & Gruba, P. (2007). Approaches to the implementation of generic graduate attributes in Australian ICT undergraduate education. *Computer Science Education*, 17(3), 171–185.

Anthony, S., & Garner, B. (2016). Teaching soft skills to business students: An analysis of multiple pedagogical methods. *Business and Professional Communication Quarterly*, 79(3), 360–370.

Barrie, S., Hughes, C., Smith, C., & Thomson, K. (2009). *The national graduate attributes project: Key issues to consider in the renewal of learning and teaching experiences to foster graduate attributes*. Sydney: Australian Learning and Teaching Council.

Browne, K. (2005). Snowball sampling: Using social networks to research non-heterosexual women. *International Journal of Social Research Methodology*, 8(1), 47–60.

Carter, L., Ruskin, J., & Cassilles, A. (2017). Three modes of work-integrated learning: stories of success. In L. N. Wood & Y. A. Breyer (Eds.), *Success in higher education* (pp. 203–215). Singapore: Springer.

Choudaha, R., Chang, L., & Kono, Y. (2014). International student mobility trends 2013: Towards responsive recruitment strategies. *World Education News & Reviews*, 26(2), 1–8.

Chowdhury, T. A., & Miah, M. K. (2016). Employability skills for entry-level human resources management positions: Perceptions of students and employers. *Australian Journal of Career Development*, 25(2), 55–68.

Elo, S., & Kyngäs, H. (2008). The qualitative content analysis process. *Journal of Advanced Nursing*, 62(1), 107–115.

Hayhoe, R., Li, J., Lin, J., & Zha, Q. (2012). *Portraits of 21st century Chinese universities: In the move to mass higher education (Vol. 30)*. Dordrecht, Netherlands: Springer Science & Business Media.

Heffernan, T. A., & Heffernan, A. (2018). Language games: University responses to ranking metrics. *Higher Education Quarterly*, 72(1), 29–39.

Horton, J., Macve, R., & Struyven, G. (2004). Qualitative research: Experiences in using semi-structured interviews. In C. Humphrey & B. Lee (Eds.), *The real life guide to accounting research: A behind-the-scenes view of using qualitative research methods* (pp. 339–357). Oxford, UK: Elsevier.

Jackson, D. (2015). Employability skill development in work-integrated learning: Barriers and best practice. *Studies in Higher Education*, 40(2), 350–367.

Jackson, D. (2018). Developing graduate career readiness in Australia: Shifting from extracurricular internships to work-integrated learning. *International Journal of Work-Integrated Learning*, 19(1), 23–35.

Khan, S. A. R., & Zhang, Y. (2017). The effective role of visiting lecturers in the courses of supply chain management. *American Journal of Traffic and Transportation Engineering*, 2(6), 104–109.

Kohlbry, P. W. (2016). The impact of international service-learning on nursing students' cultural competency. *Journal of Nursing Scholarship*, 48(3), 303–311.

Lebeau, Y., Stumpf, R., Brown, R., Lucchesi, M. A. S., & Kwiek, M. (2012). Who shall pay for the public good? Comparative trends in the funding crisis of public higher education. *Compare: A Journal of Comparative and International Education*, 42(1), 137–157.

Mason, G., Williams, G., & Cranmer, S. (2009). Employability skills initiatives in higher education: What effects do they have on graduate labour market outcomes? *Education Economics*, 17(1), 1–30.

Maxwell, G., Scott, B., Macfarlane, D., & Williamson, E. (2009). Employers as stakeholders in postgraduate employability skills development. *International Journal of Management*, 8(2), 13–23.

Merriam, S. B. (2009). *Qualitative research: A guide to design and implementation*. San Francisco, CA: Jossey-Bass.

Mok, K. H., & Jiang, J. (2018). Massification of higher education and challenges for graduate employment and social mobility: East Asian experiences and sociological reflections. *International Journal of Educational Development*, 63(Nov), 44–51.

Murray, M., Ross, A., Blaney, N., & Adamson, L. (2015). Mentoring undergraduate civil engineering students. *Proceedings of the ICE-Management, Procurement and Law*, 168 (4), 189–198.

Osman, K. (2011). The inculcation of generic skills through service learning experience among science student teachers. *Procedia-Social and Behavioral Sciences*, 18, 148–153.

Sepahpanah, M., Zarafshani, K., Mirakzade, A., & Rosch, D. M. (2013). Service learning processes and challenges in Iran: A case study. *NACTA Journal*, 57(3a), 36–39.

Singh, A., & Jaykumar, P. (2019). On the road to consensus: Key soft skills required for youth employment in the service sector. *Worldwide Hospitality and Tourism Themes*, 11 (1), 10–24. doi: 10.1108/WHATT-10-2018-0066

Soh, K. (2017). The seven deadly sins of world university ranking: A summary from several papers. *Journal of Higher Education Policy and Management*, 39(1), 104–115.

Tomlinson, M. (2018). Employers and universities: Conceptual dimensions, research evidence and implications. *Higher Education Policy*. doi: 10.1057/s41307-018-0121-9

Tran, L. H. N., & Nguyen, T. M. D. (2018). Internship-related learning outcomes and their influential factors: The case of Vietnamese tourism and hospitality students. *Education + Training*, 60(1), 69–81.

Tran, T. T. (2013). Limitation on the development of skills in higher education in Vietnam. *Higher Education*, 65(5), 631–644.

van Hoek, R., Godsell, J., & Harrison, A. (2011). Embedding "insights from industry" in supply chain programmes: The role of guest lecturers. *Supply Chain Management: An International Journal*, 16(2), 142–147.

Yang, L. (2018). Higher education expansion and post-college unemployment: Understanding the roles of fields of study in China. *International Journal of Educational Development*, 62(Sep), 62–74.

Yin, R. K. (2009). *Case study research, design & methods* (4th edn). Thousand Oaks, CA: Sage.

11 Students' participation and engagement with soft-skills development

Introduction

Previous chapters have reported the context and initiatives that Vietnamese universities have launched to help develop employability for students with a focus on soft skills. In brief, Vietnamese universities conceptualized developing soft-skills implementation as developing work-readiness for students. They have added skills subjects, serving as a co-curriculum or part of the main curriculum of a university program, and have these subjects delivered by skills teachers. They have encouraged or officially required teachers who taught specialized subjects to train students in soft skills alongside technical skills. Foremost, the majority of the universities have used extracurricular activities (ECAs) as the main channel through which students can develop relevant soft skills for themselves. These activities are organized by the Youth Union and its associates (YUA), with the support of external stakeholders such as employers, alumni, local authorities and non-governmental organizations. However, although these activities have helped students develop soft skills to different extents, they are facing several challenges in terms of governance structure, leadership, soft-skills expertise, stakeholder engagement, and resources.

Regardless of the availability of activities purposefully organized to develop soft skills for students, whether students engage with these activities is a critical issue. Without their engagement, organizing these activities becomes meaningless and wasteful. A limited number of existing studies have found that students may disregard developing soft skills due to their misconception of the importance of these skills (Tran, 2015) or their lack of awareness of soft-skills policies in their university (Barrie, Hughes, Smith, & Thomson, 2009). Teachers who disengage from teaching soft skills may also spread the belief that these skills are not important, resulting in student disengagement. Institutional factors such as availability of soft-skills development activities, leadership, and linkages with external stakeholders, and student-related factors such as motivation, timetable, and financial situation may also affect their engagement with developing soft skills. In the case of Vietnamese students, recent studies have indicated that they are lacking in several soft skills (Bodewig & Badiani-Magnusson, 2014; Nguyen, 2011; Nguyen, 2018; Nguyen, Ngoc, & Montague, 2019; Tran, 2018). However, while there is a limited number of studies on this issue (Tran, 2015), it seems that students are not engaged with developing soft skills.

Therefore, this chapter will report a study about student experience with soft-skills development implementation in their university and their engagement with such activities, and factors influencing their engagement will be examined. The chapter will help complete the picture of soft-skills implementation in Vietnamese universities using different stakeholders' perspectives and provide important implications for soft-skills implementation in higher education.

Student engagement: Concepts, dimensions, and influential factors

Student engagement has lately been a central research topic in teaching and learning in higher education because it is associated with students' learning outcomes. However, it has been viewed and defined differently by people in different positions in higher education. From leadership and management positions, student engagement is viewed as "the process whereby institutions and sector bodies make deliberate attempts to involve and empower students in the process of shaping the learning experience" (The Higher Education Funding Council for England (HEFCE), 2008). From the student position, it is defined as "the range of activities a learner employs to generate—sometimes consciously, other times unconsciously—the interest, focus, and an intention required to build knowledge and skills" (Toshalis & Nakkula, 2012, p. 16). Others attempted to strike a balance between the two mentioned views, positing that student engagement is "the time and effort students devote to activities that are empirically linked to desired outcomes of college and what institutions do to induce students to participate in these activities" (Kuh, 2009, p. 683).

Kahu (2013) critically reviewed the literature and identified three approaches to student engagement. Firstly, from the behavioral perspective, it is defined as the "time and effort students devote to educationally purposeful activities" (Radloff & Coates, 2010, p. 1). It has also been defined as students' participation in in-class and out-of-class educationally effective practices which results in different measurable outcomes (Kuh, 2007), and as "the extent to which students are engaging in activities that higher education research has shown to be linked with high-quality learning outcomes" (Krause & Coates, 2008, p. 493). The National Survey of Student Engagement (Kuh, 2001) was the well-known student-engagement measurement tool developed within this perspective. It has five engagement scales: academic challenge, active learning, interactions, enriching educational experiences, and supportive learning environment. Although it is often seen as a valid tool to measure student engagement, many studies also point out its limitations regarding the structure of the instruments, a lack of theories for to justify the development of items in the scales, etc. (Kahu, 2013).

Secondly, the psychological perspective views engagement as an internal and evolving psycho-social process whose intensity may vary over time and across different settings. For example, Hu and Kuh (2002, p. 575) define engagement as "the quality of effort students themselves devote to educationally purposeful activities that contribute directly to desired outcomes." Various overlapping dimensions of engagement have been proposed under this perspective, including behavior, cognition, emotion, and conation. Early researchers in this school of thought often considered student engagement within one of the mentioned dimensions, but their successors have considered student engagement more holistically. The behavior dimension, resembling the behavioral perspective reported earlier, has three elements: conducting and following rules, involving in learning, and participating in ECAs (Fredricks, Blumenfeld, & Paris, 2004). Cognitive engagement is "a student's psychological investment in and effort directed towards learning, understanding, or mastering the knowledge skills or crafts" (cited in Kahu, 2013, p. 761). This cognitive dimension is frequently described in association with students' self-regulation and effective use of deep learning strategies (Fredricks et al., 2004), as well as their personal characteristics such as motivation, self-efficacy, and expectations (Jimerson, Campos, & Greif, 2003). Affective or emotional engagement can be understood simply as "the feelings and beliefs held by those who are engaged" (Shuck & Wollard, 2010, p. 105). The affective dimension considers engagement in terms of students' attachment and their sense of belonging (Libbey, 2004), as well as immediate emotions, such as enjoyment and interest in the task (Furlong et al., 2003). The affective dimension distinguishes students with intrinsic motivations from those with extrinsic motivations. The former is motivated to engage cognitively and behaviorally out of their passion and interest in the learning whereas the latter is motivated to attain tangible results such as scores and certificates.

Thirdly, the sociocultural perspective focuses on examining the impact of the broader social context on student experience. Most remarkably, researchers who follow this perspective attempt to investigate student engagement by looking at its opposite, student disengagement or alienation (Johnson, 2005; Macfarlane & Tomlinson, 2017; Mann, 2001). This may occur in the form of students' refusal to comply with behavioral expectations such as coming to class punctually, politely accepting grades and feedback, or enthusiastically participating in in-class learning activities (Macfarlane & Tomlinson, 2017). Many studies have showed that social context contributes to student-engagement levels. For example, Mann (2001) identifies that disciplinary power, academic culture, and an excessive focus on performativity can cause student disengagement. Similarly, Thomas (2002) argues that institutional habitus, which is social and cultural practices that favor the dominant social groups in an institution, may lead to poor retention of non-traditional students. Initial experience with university learning culture may cause culture shock and learning shock to several students, which may also cause student disengagement (Christie, Tett, Cree, Hounsell, & McCune, 2008; Krause & Coates, 2008; Thomas, 2002). Moreover, Kahu and Nelson (2018, p. 59) propose an integrative framework, emphasizing that "individual student engagement occurs dynamically within an educational interface at the intersection of the student and their characteristics and background, and the institution and its practices." The framework also acknowledges the outcomes of engagement: it is through being engaged with their study that students learn and thus not only acquire skills and knowledge, but also experience academic success and personal growth. Furthermore, engagement is also examined in students' responses to contextual factors. For example, Linnenbrink-Garcia, Rogat, and Koskey (2011) related student engagement to their affect and behavior during collaborative group work. Reeve and Tseng (2011) and Filsecker and Kerres (2014) added another dimension of engagement, taking into account students' agency or will, showing that students' proactive contribution to the instruction teachers provide may affect their engagement.

Impact of student engagement on students' learning outcomes

Student engagement is a key contributor to learning and academic success. Research has provided increasing evidence that links student engagement to higher grades, and school completion rates, and their engagement appears to be associated with the perceived institutional or school context (Fredricks et al., 2004; Wang & Fredricks, 2014; Wang & Holcombe, 2010). For example, in a short-term longitudinal study, Wang and Holcombe (2010) examined the relationships among 1,046 middle school students' perceptions of school environment, school engagement, and academic achievement. They found three dimensions of school engagement: school participation, sense of identification with school, and use of self-regulation strategies. Students' perceptions of the school environment were found to influence their academic achievement directly and indirectly through the three types of school engagement.

Likewise, Konold, Cornell, Jia, and Malone (2018) tested whether the authoritative school climate, which has high structure and student support, can nurture student engagement and whether these factors are associated with higher academic achievement. Using a multilevel multi-informant structural model on a sample of 60,441 students and 11,442 teachers in 298 high schools, the researchers found that both structure and student support in authoritative schools were associated with higher student engagement. They also found that student engagement was directly associated with academic achievement.

Moreover, in a higher education setting, Kimbark, Peters, and Richardson (2017) found that participating in a Student Success Course could increase students' persistence, retention, academic achievement in English and mathematics, and student engagement. Additionally, participants claim that taking the Student Success Course not only altered their perceptions of the importance of the course, but their social and study skills as well. These findings suggest that student engagement is intervenable and that university context, such as a lack of student support services or learning skills courses, affects student engagement.

Furthermore, in a non-formal learning context, Klauda and Guthrie (2015) conducted a longitudinal study that compared the development of reading motivation, engagement, and achievement between two groups of adolescents with different levels of reading ability. The results showed advanced readers had stronger motivation and engagement with achievement than struggling readers. However, motivation predicted concurrent engagement and growth in engagement similarly for struggling and advanced readers. These results are interpreted as support for the hypothesis that cognitive challenges limit the relations of motivation and engagement to achievement for struggling readers.

All of these, despite not all being associated with higher education, show that student engagement is critical for students' learning outcomes, which will affect their employability. However, their engagement should not be taken for granted but needs intervention from teachers and school leaders by creating a favorable learning environment that stimulates personal factors such as motivation, interests, and a sense of belonging.

The present study

As mentioned earlier, this chapter will report on how students engage with developing soft skills in Vietnamese universities and what factors influence their engagement. It answers the following questions:

- In what ways and to what extent do Vietnamese students engage with developing soft skills?
- What factors influence their engagement with developing soft skills?

The study was conducted using a mixed-methods approach to better understand the issues under investigation (Lisle, 2011). Quantitative data were collected by an online and paper-based survey. The survey was developed based on a literature review and the researcher's former studies in soft-skills implementation in Vietnamese universities. On top of obtaining participants' demographic information, the survey used a 5-point Likert scale to measure:

- Section 2: Students were asked to rate the importance of certain soft skills in the Vietnamese context and the current workplace.
- Section 3: Students were asked to rate the frequency of their participation in a variety of soft-skills development activities.
- Section 4: Students were asked to rate their agreement on statements that describe their awareness, behaviors, and emotion when they participated in soft-skills development activities.
- Section 5: Students were asked to rate the influence of some factors that affected their engagement with participating in soft-skills development activities.

Quantitative data were collected from February to April 2019. The researcher sent the link to the survey to academics of six universities for dissemination to students in their universities. Within eight weeks, 466 responses from 11 universities were recorded. Five responses were excluded because the participants did not provide enough information. The demographic information of the 461 retained participants is summarized in Table 11.1.

Table 11.1 Participants' information

Classification		Percentage
Gender	Male	33.6
	Female	66.4
University type	Public	54.2
	Private	45.8
Year of study	Year 1	19.5
	Year 2	29.5
	Year 3	27.1
	Year 4	23.9
Discipline	STEM, education and health	20.7
	Social sciences and humanities	30.7
	Business and finance	48.6

The data were analyzed using SPSS. Descriptive statistics calculations were performed to generate the mean (M) and standard deviation (SD) for the data set in the second and third sections mentioned above. Data from the third and fourth sections were analyzed using principal component analysis, descriptive analysis with means and standard deviations, and inferential analysis with independent-sample T-tests and one-way ANOVA tests. The means were interpreted using the following framework:

Mean	Section 2	Section 3	Section 4	Section 5
$1.0 < M \leq 1.8$	Very unimportant	Very infrequent	Very low	Very weak
$1.8 < M \leq 2.6$	Unimportant	Infrequent	Low	Weak
$2.6 < M \leq 3.4$	Unsure	Moderate	Moderate	Moderate
$3.4 < M \leq 4.2$	Important	Frequent	High	Strong
$4.2 < M \leq 5.0$	Very important	Very frequent	Very high	Very strong

Qualitative data were collected simultaneously with quantitative data via semi-structured interviews with eight male and ten female students who were randomly selected from five Vietnamese universities. The students represented their peers from 13 programs, ranging from natural sciences to social sciences. Nine of them were in their final year, six were in their third year and three in the second year.

The participants were recruited using recommendations of the researcher's colleagues in the five universities. Students were informed of the purpose of the study, their roles and how their identities would be protected. They were also asked to consent to the researcher using the information they provided for the purpose of the study. The interviews, which lasted for about 13 to 21 minutes, were conducted via Skype or phone. In the interview, they were invited to discuss the following issues:

- Their perceptions of the most relevant soft skills.
- Their beliefs about the importance of soft skills for their work and life.
- How and how often they develop their soft skills.
- Factors that affect their participation in activities that develop soft skills.

All interviews were recorded and transcribed verbatim. The transcripts were read several times to understand viewpoints. Then the data were analyzed using a thematic analysis approach. The researcher coded the data on a case-by-case basis. Finally, the codes between interviewees were compared and classified into themes. In this chapter, however, the qualitative findings are used purposefully to illustrate the quantitative findings.

Results

Students' perception of the importance of soft skills

Section 2 of the survey asked students to indicate their perception of the importance of 15 soft skills for their future work and life. Among them, 10 were recommended as the most sought-after soft skills in 2018 and the other five were important soft skills for Vietnamese society. The results are summarized in Table 11.2. On a 5-point Likert scale, students rated that communication skills (M = 4.25, SD = 0.79) and

Table 11.2 Students' perception of the importance of soft skills

Soft skills	M	SD
Political qualities	3.34	1.04
Paying attention to details	3.40	1.00
Understanding cultural values	3.65	0.97
Leadership skills	3.70	0.87
Creativity	3.77	0.88
Teamwork skills	3.85	0.83
Vision of the future	3.85	0.94
Time-management skills	3.89	0.86
Adaptability	3.90	0.83
Collaboration skills	3.92	0.84
Negotiation skills	3.98	0.83
Computer skills	3.99	0.88
Professional ethics	4.04	0.88
Communication skills	4.25	0.79
Foreign-language skills	4.28	0.83

foreign-language skills (M = 4.28, SD = 0.83) were "very important" for their future whereas political qualities (M = 3.34, SD = 1.04) was a moderately important soft skill in the list. Political qualities also had the highest standard deviation, signifying that students' views on this varied significantly. The other 12 surveyed soft skills were rated as "important."

The qualitative findings also support the quantitative results. In the interviews, students listed an array of soft skills that they perceived to be important for them to secure jobs or work effectively. All of the skills could be identified in Table 11.2. The students also held different viewpoints on the importance of these skills. Yet, they seemed to emphasize the prominent roles of communication skills, English skills, computer skills, and teamwork.

> I believe that teamwork skills are important because we often work in teams. But I think English skills and computer skills are more important. (Khanh, male, Chemistry)

> I think upon graduation, communication skills would be vital for securing jobs because when the interviewer sees you communicate fluently and with confidence, they will have a good impression. And of course, a good-looking physical appearance is a plus. And at work, being responsible, creative, able to work under pressure are necessary to perform work duties effectively. In our modern life, creativity is needed to catch up with new trends. Enterprises now seem to stress continuous growth. (Tien, female, Marketing)

All of these findings suggest that students believed in the importance of soft skills for their future work and life. Such a belief can drive them to participate in and engage with activities organized to help them improve these skills, as many studies have found a positive correlation between one's beliefs and one's behavior (de la Harpe & David, 2012; de la Harpe & Radloff, 2008).

Students' participation in soft-skills development activities

Section 3 of the survey asked students to rate the frequency of certain activities that can develop soft skills organized by their university, including those "not organized." These activities were classified into three groups: (i) curriculum-based activities; (ii) extracurricular activities; and (iii) student services. The results are summarized in Table 11.3. On a 5-point Likert scale, students reported that the first was least frequently organized (M = 3.27, SD = 1.14), followed by the second (M = 3.39, SD = 1.14), and the third was the most frequently organized (M = 3.50, SD = 1.09). These findings indicated that Vietnamese universities have engaged with developing soft skills for their students via different activities, which would afford students the options most convenient to them.

Among the ten activities surveyed, students recognized that paid courses that trained students in soft skills such as English or computer skills were organized most frequently (M = 3.77, SD = 1.04), followed by on-campus ECAs led by the

Table 11.3 Availability of soft-skills development activities in Vietnamese universities

Activities	N	M	SD	Not organized
Curriculum-based activities		3.27	1.14	
Arranging internships in a relevant industry	427	3.18	1.12	34
Teaching soft skills as stand-alone subjects	437	3.31	1.14	24
Teaching soft skills in specialized subjects	425	3.33	1.15	36
Extracurricular activities		3.39	1.14	
Organizing classes on CV-writing or job-interview skills	424	3.17	1.23	37
Organizing career consultation with professionals	445	3.28	1.13	16
Organizing international student-exchange programs	426	3.31	1.20	35
Organizing community-engagement activities	455	3.53	1.10	6
Organizing on-campus extracurricular activities	452	3.65	1.06	9
Student services		3.50	1.09	
Providing part-time job service for students	434	3.22	1.13	27
Providing paid course on soft skills (e.g., English skills)	453	3.77	1.04	8

YUA (M = 3.65, SD = 1.06). Activities that students reported to be least organized were curriculum-based activities and a number of ECAs, at a moderate level.

The mean scores indicate that these activities were organized at a moderately frequent extent or just above this extent. The number of students who chose "not organized" and high standard deviations suggest that there were disparities in students' recognition of the availability of these activities. This also signifies that information about these activities could not have been effectively imparted to students.

Section 3 of the survey also asked students to indicate their frequency of participating in soft-skills development activities during the time they were at the university on a 5-point Likert scale. The results (Table 11.4) show that students participated in activities that were less likely to be organized by their university. Accordingly, they watched online soft-skills development video clips (M = 3.49, SD = 1.10), worked part-time (M = 3.44, SD = 1.18), or networked with experienced professionals to learn from these people (M = 3.44, SD = 1.11) at a "frequent" level. They also read know-how or skills-development books (M = 3.20, SD = 1.12) at a "moderately frequent" level.

Their participation in activities that were more likely to be organized by their university was often rated at a "moderately frequent" level. Among these activities, formal soft-skills classes such as English skills, computer skills, or other soft skills offered by the YUA or a service of the university (M = 3.25, SD = 1.17) appeared to attract students the most. These paid courses often provide students with a certificate of participation or completion that can be used for their job applications

Table 11.4 Students' participation in soft-skills development activities

I develop soft skills by …	N	M	SD
Participating in international exchange programs	454	2.70	1.26
Participating in community-service activities	458	3.04	1.12
Participating in curriculum-based learning activities	458	3.09	1.02
Participating in on-campus extracurricular activities of the YUA	458	3.17	1.03
Reading know-how or skills-development books	453	3.20	1.12
Attending paid soft-skills development classes	457	3.25	1.17
Networking with experienced professionals	457	3.44	1.11
Working part-time	456	3.44	1.18
Watching online soft-skills development video clips	458	3.49	1.10

in the future. Students also participated in extracurricular activities (M = 3.17, SD = 1.03), often organized by the YUA, more frequently than activities organized by their teachers while delivering formal classes (M = 3.09, SD = 1.02). Participating in community-service activities (M = 3.04, SD = 1.12) received a little less attention from students compared to formal learning activities. International student-exchange programs appeared to attract a lot of students, but not many of them could do them possibly due to cost and availability, demonstrated by a low mean score and high standard deviation (M = 2.70, SD = 1.26).

The findings above are consistent with students' comments in the interviews about activities organized in the classroom and those outside the classroom. The majority of students agreed that there was a lack of soft skills teaching in the classroom, or if there was, these activities were not conducive to their soft-skills development. Therefore, many of them chose to develop soft skills by participating in activities outside the classroom, be they organized by the university or by themselves.

> I selectively participated in some YUA activities, or activities organized by my class. It is because we have to study from morning to afternoon, and so we have no time left to join extracurricular activities. I often read books and magazines and try to develop soft skills via activities that fit my circumstances. (Lan, female, Business Administration)

> Soft-skills classes are just like other classes. Students come to those classes when they have time, but I do not see they are effective because they are theory-based and delivered in a short time, so we cannot grow these skills much. […] I find that my time-management skills and public-speaking skills are still limited. […] So, I have joined an English-speaking club to improve my speaking skills, and also work part-time for a tourism agency. Those are my ways to tackle the soft skills that I lack. (Khoa, male, English Studies)

It was also found that a number of students never participated in the mentioned activities. Although the number of students was small (less than ten out of the 461 students), it suggested that some students were not aware of the necessity of developing soft skills for their future work and life or that there were factors hindering them from participating in such activities.

Students' engagement with soft-skills development

Section 4 of the survey included 11 statements describing students' engagement with developing soft skills. Three statements were written to reflect their cognitive engagement (items 1 to 3), five to reflect their behavioral engagement (items 4 to 8) and three to reflect their emotional engagement (items 9 to 11). Students were asked to indicate their engagement level by rating whether these statements were true for their case on a 5-point Likert scale, ranging from "strongly disagree" to "completely agree."

The data were analyzed using principal component analysis. The internal consistency of this set of data was high (Cronbach's alpha $\alpha = 0.92$) and correlations between the 11 latent variables ranged from 0.58 to 0.76. The KMO test result was 0.90; therefore, it was appropriate to extract principal components.

The principal component analysis with a fixed three-factor solution using varimax rotation was run by SPSS version 20. This solution resulted in a scale that explained 74.12% of the variance. When looking closely, variable 5 did not satisfy the criterion that its loading values in the three factors should be at least 0.2 apart. Therefore, this variable was excluded, as suggested in Lessiter, Freeman, Keogh, and Davidoff (2001), and the principal component analysis procedure was repeated. This time, the resultant scale with 10 latent variables classified into three principal components explained 75.25% of the variance. The structure of the scale was as below:

- Factor 1: Behavioral engagement (5 items, alpha 0.87, variance explained: 31.02%).
- Factor 2: Emotional engagement (3 items, alpha 0.85, variance explained: 23.36%).
- Factor 3: Cognitive engagement (2 items, alpha 0.86, variance explained: 20.86%).

Descriptive statistical analysis results (Table 11.5) showed that students cognitively engaged with developing soft skills to a high level, almost reaching a very high level (M = 4.17, SD = 0.49). However, although their emotional engagement (M = 3.89, SD = 0.74) and behavioral engagement (M = 3.71, SD = 0.74) was still within the range of a high level, it was lower than their cognitive behaviors. These results indicate that there could be issues that prevented students from engaging with developing soft skills even though they recognized and felt that they needed to do so.

Independent-sample T-tests were conducted to compare the engagement between groups of male and female students; students from public and private

Table 11.5 Student engagement with soft-skills development

Components	M	SD
Behavioral engagement	**3.71**	**0.74**
I actively look for learning resources related to soft skills	3.71	0.89
I reflect on my progress in soft skills that I am not good at	3.61	1.01
I actively network with experienced professionals to learn soft skills from them	3.82	0.89
I regularly update information about relevant soft skills	3.54	0.92
I proactively look for opportunities to develop my soft skills	3.87	0.83
Emotional engagement	**3.89**	**0.74**
I feel pleased when I participate in soft-skills development activities	3.84	0.84
I am excited to develop certain soft skills by working with my friends	3.98	0.82
I gradually feel I belong to a profession when I have the soft skills they need	3.84	0.87
Cognitive engagement	**4.17**	**0.69**
I know that soft skills are vital for my securing employment opportunities	4.15	0.72
I know that I need to improve some of my soft skills	4.20	0.75

universities; first- and second-year students, and third- and fourth-year students. The results showed that:

- There are statistically significant differences in behavioral engagement between groups of male students (M = 3.90, SD = 0.67) and female students (M = 3.62, SD = 0.75), t(459) = 3.92, p = 0.00, MD = 0.28. There are statistically significant differences in emotional engagement between groups of male students (M = 4.02, SD = 0.67) and female students (M = 3.82, SD = 0.77), t(459) = 2.82, p = 0.01, MD = 0.20.
- There are statistically significant differences in behavioral engagement between groups of students from public universities (M = 3.60, SD = 0.77) and those from private universities (M = 3.84, SD = 0.67), t(459) = - 3.7, p = 0.00, MD = 0.23.
- There are statistically significant differences in behavioral engagement between groups of first- and second-year students (M = 3.79, SD = 0.76) and third-

and fourth-year students (M = 3.63, SD = 0.71), t(459) = 2.35, p = 0.02, MD = 0.16. There are statistically significant differences in emotional engagement between groups of first- and second-year students (M = 4.00, SD = 0.74) and third- and fourth-year students (M = 3.78, SD = 0.72), t(459) = 3.09, p = 0.00, MD = 0.21. There are statistically significant differences in cognitive engagement between groups of first- and second-year students (M = 4.24, SD = 0.71) and third- and fourth-year students (M = 4.11, SD = 0.67), t (455.63) = 2.00, p = 0.05, MD = 0.12.

A one-way ANOVA test was performed to compare the engagement between students of different disciplines. However, there was no difference in the engagement with soft-skills development between students of different disciplines.

Factors influencing students' engagement with soft-skills development

Section 5 of the survey comprised 16 statements describing factors that may affect students' engagement with developing soft skills. Four latent variables reflected their self-interest about the relevance of a soft-skills development activity (items 1 to 4), eight to reflect expectations or requirements of others on their engagement (items 5 to 12) and four to reflect control factors that might hinder them from engaging with a soft-skills development activity (items 13 to 16). Students were asked to indicate the extent to which these variables affected their intention to participate in a soft-skills development activity on a 5-point Likert scale, ranging from "very little" to "very much."

The data set in Section 5 was analyzed using principal component analysis. The internal consistency of this set of data was high (Cronbach's alpha α = 0.95) and correlations between the 11 latent variables ranged from 0.59 to 0.80. The KMO test was computed to check whether the samples were adequate to extract principal components, often suggested to be at least 0.70. The KMO test result was 0.90; therefore, it was appropriate to extract principal components.

A principal component analysis with varimax rotation based on eigenvalues greater than 1 was run by SPSS version 20. This solution resulted in a scale that explained 75.43% of the variance. When looking closely, variables 4 and 12 did not satisfy the criterion that their respective loading values in the three factors should be at least 0.2 apart. Therefore, after excluding these two variables, as advised by statistics experts (for example, see Lessiter et al., 2001), the principal component analysis procedure was repeated. This time, the resultant scale with 14 latent variables classified into three principal components explained 75.27% of the variance. With this solution, all primary loading values of a latent variable loaded uniquely in a principal component being at least 0.2 apart from the secondary loading value. The structure of the scale was as below:

- Factor 1: Influence of third parties (7 items, alpha = 0.92, variance explained: 33.23%).

Table 11.6 Factors influencing student engagement with soft-skills development

Principal component	M	SD
Influence of third parties	**3.48**	**0.84**
My teachers advise that the activity is useful for my employability	3.62	0.95
My friends believe that the activity will be useful for my job applications	3.47	0.96
Graduates of my discipline told me that the activity enhanced my job prospects	3.46	1.04
Employers often look with favor on those who participate in the activity	3.46	1.06
In Vietnam, students are expected to participate in the activity	3.46	1.00
Social media informs that the activity is useful for career development	3.62	0.96
The university requires us to participate in the activity	3.29	1.08
Controlling factors	**3.51**	**0.88**
Participating in the activity does not consume much time	3.53	0.97
Participating in the activity does not interfere with my learning timetable	3.56	0.96
Participating in the activity does not cost me much	3.54	1.00
Participating in the activity does not require much effort	3.40	1.04
Personal beliefs	**3.71**	**0.83**
That activity gives me a special interest	3.63	0.95
That activity is aligned with my hobbies	3.79	0.88
That activity is aligned with my personality	3.70	0.92

- Factor 2: Controlling factors (3 items, alpha = 0.91, variance explained: 10.57%).
- Factor 3: Personal interests (3 items, alpha = 0.89, variance explained: 8.13%).

Descriptive statistical analysis results (Table 11.6) showed that personal beliefs about the relevance of a soft-skills development activity affected their engagement the most (M = 3.71, SD = 0.83), followed by practical problems such as time, cost that may prevent them from participation (M = 3.51, SD = 0.88), and finally the expectations or requirement from others (M = 3.48, SD = 0.84).

In terms of latent variables, the top five most influential factors of student engagement were:

- The alignment between the activity and their hobbies (M = 3.79, SD = 0.88).
- The alignment between the activity and their personalities (M = 3.70, SD = 0.92).
- The alignment between the activity and their self-interests (M = 3.63, SD = 0.95).
- Their teacher's encouragement (M = 3.62, SD = 0.95).
- Attestation of the benefits of an activity by social media (M = 3.62, SD = 0.86).

These findings well reflect students' viewpoints in the interviews, as illustrated by the comments below:

> Everything would need to derive from your interests. If soft-skills development activities want to achieve effectiveness, they need to address students' interest because there are several students who have different interests. For example, I am introverted, so I prefer activities that align with my personality, and for those who are active, there should be active activities for them. […] Generally, throughout my studies, I participated in a number of student groups to improve my communication and teamwork skills, to be more confident in the crowd. I have not improved my English skills much because I do not have enough time, and money, to join such classes. (Khanh, male, Chemistry)

> I decided to undertake a volunteer internship because I found that the sooner I am exposed to the workplace, the better […]. During the internship, I learned many lessons and received advice from my seniors, and I found they are useful for me. (Vy, female, English Studies)

Independent-sample T-tests were run to compare the influence of principal components on student engagement between male and female students; students from public and private universities; first- and second-year students and third- and fourth-year students. The results showed that:

- There are statistically significant differences in the influence of third parties on student engagement in participating in soft-skills development activities between groups of males (M = 3.60, SD = 0.84) and females (M = 3.43, SD = 0.83), t(459) = 2.11, p = 0.04, MD = 0.17. Likewise, there are statistically significant differences in the influence of controlling factors on student engagement between groups of males (M = 3.43, SD = 0.78) and females (M = 3.60, SD = 0.91), t(354.58) = 3.64, p = 0.01, MD = 0.28.
- There are statistically significant differences in the influence of third parties on student engagement in participating in soft-skills development activities between groups of students from public (M = 3.41, SD = 0.85) and private universities (M = 3.57, SD = 0.81), t(459) = - 2.13, p = 0.03, MD = 0.17. Likewise, there are statistically significant differences in the influence of

controlling factors on student engagement between groups of students from public (M = 3.43, SD = 0.87) and private universities (M = 3.60, SD = 0.88), t(459) = - 2.06, p = 0.04, MD = 0.17.
- There are statistically significant differences in the influence of personal beliefs on student engagement in participating in soft-skills development activities between groups of first- and second-year students (M = 3.79, SD = 0.79) and third- and fourth-year students (M = 3.62, SD = 0.86), t(459) = 2.11, p = 0.04, MD = 0.16. There are statistically significant differences in the influence of third parties on student engagement between groups of first- and second-year students (M = 3.57, SD = 0.86) and third- and fourth-year students (M = 3.43, SD = 0.80), t(459) = 2.22, p = 0.03, MD = 0.17. There are statistically significant differences in the influence of third parties on student engagement between groups of first- and second-year students (M = 3.60, SD = 0.91) and third- and fourth-year students (M = 3.43, SD = 0.83), t(459) = 2.09, p = 0.04, MD = 0.17.

A one-way ANOVA test was run to compare the engagement between groups of students of different disciplines. The results showed that there was a statistically significant difference between groups of students of different disciplines as determined by one-way ANOVA ($F(2,458)$ = 10.45, p = .00). A Tukey post-hoc test revealed that personal beliefs affected the engagement of students of social sciences and humanities (M = 3.93, SD = 0.76) significantly more strongly than those of business (M = 3.54, SD = 0.87), MD = 0.39, p = 0.00.

Discussion and conclusion

The study reported in this chapter explored how students in Vietnamese universities are engaging with developing soft skills for their future work and life. The results show that while they appear to appreciate the importance of soft skills, they do not engage with developing these skills to a high extent, and there have been several factors affecting their engagement.

Among the three types of engagement, students' cognitive engagement was rated the highest (M = 4.17, SD = 0.69) whereas when it came to their behavioral and emotional engagement, the mean scores decreased remarkably (M = 3.71, SD = 0.74 and M = 3.89, SD = 0.74, respectively). On the one hand, this indicated that even when students had a high level of awareness of improving their soft skills, that cognition would not be translated into behaviors and emotion with the same level of cognitive engagement when they participated in soft-skills development activities. On the other hand, this suggested that there were factors hindering their behavioral and emotional engagement.

Indeed, several hinderers of student engagement with soft-skills development were identified. Among them, factors related to students' beliefs about the match-up of these activities with their self-interest appeared to be the most influential (M = 3.71, SD = 0.84), which resembled findings in (Tran, 2015). This result was also consistent with the fact that students chose to participate in non-curriculum-based activities for improving their soft skills, such as part-time work, watching online skills-development videos, or networking with professionals (see Table 3). These activities obviously provided them with more options to cater for their personal needs and interests. Conversely, curriculum-based activities such as independent skills subjects, soft-skills development activities in specialized subjects, international student-exchange programs, or even the non-curriculum-based but structured YUA extracurricular activities were not so welcomed by students. The mean scores showed that students engaged with such activities the least. International student-exchange programs were not affordable to most students in Vietnam due to high cost, and there were limited opportunities available. Skills development within specialized subjects were dependent on their teachers' discretion, as specifically reported in Chapter 6. Independent skills subjects and YUA activities are available, but students did not engage to the fullest, possibly because these activities were not well-aligned with their needs and interests, as partially depicted in Chapter 9 of this book. Thus, it is suggested that these activities should be re-examined for their relevance to students' needs. Otherwise, effort and investment for these activities would become a huge waste as students do not engage with them.

Likewise, student engagement was affected by several controlling factors such as time, overlapping timetables, cost, and participatory efforts. Because most soft-skills development for students in Vietnamese universities is organized by the YUA, they had to consider timetables overlapping between their formal education and these extracurricular activities (Tran, 2017). Unfortunately, the curricula of Vietnamese university programs are often heavy in terms of content knowledge (Tran, Le, & Nguyen, 2014), students having little time left for other activities. This group of factors also helps explain why students rated part-time work as their second-best choice for soft-skills development: they could gain authentic work experience, connect with professionals, and receive some extra earning for their studies within the tight time budget they had. Online video watching may be useful in terms of knowledge or awareness about soft skills, but it may not develop soft skills for students if they do not put the acquired knowledge into practice and practice frequently.

The study also found that student engagement with a certain type of soft-skills development was strongly influenced by third parties' endorsement, especially by their teachers and the media. As suggested in (Barrie et al., 2009) and consistent with teachers' perspectives in Chapters 6 and 7, this indicated that students might not know much about the policies, activities, and resources available in their university. Thus, they should be informed of the soft-skills policy, activities, and possible benefits by their teachers through other means of communication such as emails, noticeboards, student-learning systems, etc. If university leaders could enhance clarity in communication of policy and strategies for soft-skills development to students, preferably via teachers, this would increase both student and teacher engagement. As a result, these two key agents of the implementation at their best would hopefully collaborate to realize the policy.

The study also revealed that student engagement varied between groups of students. Male students' behavioral and emotional engagement was significantly higher than that of female students, although their cognitive engagement was almost the same. While it is difficult to thoroughly explain this discrepancy, it could be attributed to the fact that at present most soft-skills development activities in Vietnamese universities are ECAs that are organized outside the formal learning timetable and many of them are off campus. Therefore, female students cannot attend these activities due to family restrictions. Female students in a Confucian-heritage country such as Vietnam always have less freedom in participating in social activities than do male students, although there have been recent changes (for example, read Tsai, 2006). Likewise, students from public universities are less behaviorally engaged compared to students from private universities. This can be explained in terms of improving competitiveness for their future employment. Most public universities in Vietnam are considered prestigious and often enroll the best high school graduates. Thus, graduates of these universities are favored in the labor market, even though these universities often focus more on intellectual ability than work-readiness. Private universities, therefore, invest in improving their students' employment competitiveness by equipping them with soft skills. Students from these universities can also understand this issue, thus they engage in soft-skills development more than their peers in public ones.

Several factors also affected the engagement of groups of students to varying extents. First- and second-year students' beliefs more strongly affected their engagement than did those of third- and fourth-year students, but their engagement was more likely to be influenced by third-party endorsements than was the case for third- and fourth-year students. This again confirms the importance of informing students of soft-skills implementation from the beginning of their university education to enhance their belief in the importance of developing these skills. If their beliefs are enhanced by third parties, such as their teachers or other stakeholders within the university, they will engage more deeply with the implementation. Similarly, male students' engagement was affected by controlling factors less strongly than that of female students. This finding well reflects the explanation above about the freedom that male and female students have in partaking of social activities in the Confucian heritage culture of Vietnam. It was also influenced by third parties' endorsement more significantly than that of females, meaning that more intervention should be applied to male students so that they could engage with soft-skills development than to female students. Finally, public university students were less affected by both controlling factors and third parties' endorsement than private university students. These findings suggest that private universities should pay more attention to removing obstacles related to time, cost, and effort requirements as well as providing more information about the benefits that students may gain when organizing soft-skills development activities

In short, this chapter has showed that Vietnamese students believe in the importance of developing soft skills for their future work and life. However, when it came to participation, students appear to partake of non-curriculum-based activities more than curriculum-based ones. They cognitively engage with these activities much more than emotionally and behaviorally. Several factors were identified which affect their engagement, including their beliefs, controlling factors, and third-party endorsements. These findings suggest that soft-skills development activities should be well-aligned with students' needs and interests to maximize their participation and engagement. In that way, students' soft skills levels can be greatly improved, as can the efficiency of soft-skills implementation in each university, since organizing several types of activities consumes a great deal of time, financial, and human resources.

References

Barrie, S., Hughes, C., Smith, C., & Thomson, K. (2009). *The national graduate attributes project: Key issues to consider in the renewal of learning and teaching experiences to foster graduate attributes.* Sydney: The University of Sydney.

Bodewig, C., & Badiani-Magnusson, R. (2014). *Skilling up Vietnam: Preparing the workforce for a modern market economy.* Washington, DC: World Bank Publications.

Christie, H., Tett, L., Cree, V. E., Hounsell, J., & McCune, V. (2008). "A real rollercoaster of confidence and emotions": Learning to be a university student. *Studies in Higher Education*, 33(5), 567–581.

de la Harpe, B., & David, C. (2012). Major influences on the teaching and assessment of graduate attributes. *Higher Education Research & Development*, 31(4), 493–510.

de la Harpe, B., & Radloff, A. (2008). Developing graduate attributes for lifelong learning-how far have we got? Paper presented at the 5th International Lifelong Learning Conference, 16–19 June, Yeppoon, Australia.

Filsecker, M., & Kerres, M. (2014). Engagement as a volitional construct: A framework for evidence-based research on educational games. *Simulation & Gaming*, 45(4–5), 450–470.

Fredricks, J. A., Blumenfeld, P. C., & Paris, A. H. (2004). School engagement: Potential of the concept, state of the evidence. *Review of Educational Research*, 74(1), 59–109.

Furlong, M. J., Whipple, A. D., Jean, G. S., Simental, J., Soliz, A., & Punthuna, S. (2003). Multiple contexts of school engagement: Moving toward a unifying framework for educational research and practice. *The California School Psychologist*, 8(1), 99–113.

Hu, S., & Kuh, G. D. (2002). Being (dis)engaged in educationally purposeful activities: The influences of student and institutional characteristics. *Research in Higher Education*, 43(5), 555–575.

Jimerson, S. R., Campos, E., & Greif, J. L. (2003). Toward an understanding of definitions and measures of school engagement and related terms. *The California School Psychologist*, 8(1), 7–27.

Johnson, G. M. (2005). Student alienation, academic achievement, and WebCT use. *Journal of Educational Technology & Society*, 8(2), 179–189.

Kahu, E. R. (2013). Framing student engagement in higher education. *Studies in Higher Education*, 38(5), 758–773.

Kahu, E. R., & Nelson, K. (2018). Student engagement in the educational interface: understanding the mechanisms of student success. *Higher Education Research & Development*, 37(1), 58–71.

Kimbark, K., Peters, M. L., & Richardson, T. (2017). Effectiveness of the student success course on persistence, retention, academic achievement, and student engagement. *Community College Journal of Research and Practice*, 41(2), 124–138.

Klauda, S. L., & Guthrie, J. T. (2015). Comparing relations of motivation, engagement, and achievement among struggling and advanced adolescent readers. *Reading and Writing*, 28(2), 239–269.

Konold, T., Cornell, D., Jia, Y., & Malone, M. (2018). School climate, student engagement, and academic achievement: A latent variable, multilevel multi–informant examination. *AERA Open*, 4(4), 1–17.

Krause, K. L., & Coates, H. (2008). Students' engagement in first-year university. *Assessment & Evaluation in Higher Education*, 33(5), 493–505.

Kuh, G. D. (2001). *The national survey of student engagement: Conceptual framework and overview of psychometric properties*. Bloomington, IN: Indiana University Center for Postsecondary Research. Retrieved from https://bit.ly/2HRUHAq.

Kuh, G. D. (2007). How to help students achieve. *Chronicle of Higher Education*, 53(41), B12–B13. Retrieved from www.chronicle.com/article/How-to-Help-Students-Achieve/31980

Kuh, G. D. (2009). What student affairs professionals need to know about student engagement. *Journal of College Student Development*, 50(6), 683–706.

Lessiter, J., Freeman, J., Keogh, E., & Davidoff, J. (2001). A cross-media presence questionnaire: The ITC-Sense of Presence Inventory. *Presence: Teleoperators & Virtual Environments*, 10(3), 282–297.

Libbey, H. P. (2004). Measuring student relationships to school: Attachment, bonding, connectedness, and engagement. *Journal of School Health*, 74(7), 274–283.

Linnenbrink-Garcia, L., Rogat, T. K., & Koskey, K. L. (2011). Affect and engagement during small group instruction. *Contemporary Educational Psychology*, 36(1), 13–24.

Lisle, J. D. (2011). The benefits and challenges of mixing methods and methodologies: Lessons learnt from implementing qualitatively led mixed methods research designs in Trinidad and Tobago. *Caribbean Curriculum*, 18, 87–120.

Macfarlane, B., & Tomlinson, M. (2017). Critiques of student engagement. *Higher Education Policy*, 30(1), 5–21.

Mann, S. J. (2001). Alternative perspectives on the student experience: Alienation and engagement. *Studies in Higher Education*, 26(1), 7–19.

Nguyen, M. T. (2011). Vietnamese students' employability skills. *International Education Studies*, 4(4), 175.

Nguyen, N. D., Ngoc, N. B., & Montague, A. (2019). Enhancing graduate work-readiness in Vietnam. In S. Dhakal, V. Prikshat, A. Nankervis, & J. Burgess (Eds.), *The transition from graduation to work* (pp. 221–237). Singapore: Springer.

Nguyen, T. N. (2018). Issues in soft skills development for Vietnamese students in current undergraduate programs. *Tạp chí Khoa học*, 15(7), 114–124. Retrieved from https://bit.ly/2ZHlMNc

Radloff, A., & Coates, H. (2010). *Doing more for learning: Enhancing engagement and outcomes: Australasian survey of student engagement: Australasian student engagement report*. Camberwell, Australia: Australian Council for Educational Research (ACER).

Reeve, J., & Tseng, C.-M. (2011). Agency as a fourth aspect of students' engagement during learning activities. *Contemporary Educational Psychology*, 36(4), 257–267.

Shuck, B., & Wollard, K. (2010). Employee engagement and HRD: A seminal review of the foundations. *Human Resource Development Review*, 9(1), 89–110.

The Higher Education Funding Council for England (HEFCE) (2008). *Tender for a Study into Student Engagement*. Bristol: Higher Education Funding Council for England.

Thomas, L. (2002). Student retention in higher education: The role of institutional habitus. *Journal of Education Policy*, 17(4), 423–442.

Toshalis, E., & Nakkula, M. J. (2012). *Motivation, engagement, and student voice*. Retrieved from: https://studentsatthecenterhub.org/wp-content/uploads/2012/04/Exec-Toshalis-Nakkula-032312.pdf

Tran, L. H. N. (2017). Developing employability skills via extra-curricular activities in Vietnamese universities: Student engagement and inhibitors of their engagement. *Journal of Education and Work*, 30(8), 854–867.

Tran, L. H. N. (2018). The skills gap of Vietnamese graduates and final-year university students. *Journal of Education and Work*, 31(7–8), 579–594.

Tran, L. T., Le, T. T. T., & Nguyen, N. T. (2014). Curriculum and pedagogy. In *Higher education in Vietnam: Flexibility, Mobility and practicality in the global knowledge economy* (pp. 86–107). London: Palgrave Macmillan.

Tran, T. T. (2015). Is graduate employability the "whole-of-higher-education-issue"? *Journal of Education and Work*, 28(3), 207–227.

Tsai, C. T. L. (2006). The influence of Confucianism on women's leisure in Taiwan. *Leisure Studies*, 25(4), 469–476. doi: 10.1080/02614360600898177

Wang, M.-T., & Holcombe, R. (2010). Adolescents' perceptions of school environment, engagement, and academic achievement in middle school. *American Educational Research Journal*, 47(3), 633–662.

Wang, M. T., & Fredricks, J. A. (2014). The reciprocal links between school engagement, youth problem behaviors, and school dropout during adolescence. *Child Development*, 85(2), 722–737.

12 Building soft skills for employability
The way ahead

Introduction

This book focused on investigating the implementation of soft skills in Vietnamese higher education (HE) as a strategy to build students' employability and identify challenges facing the implementation. The book began by establishing why soft skills are essential in the current workplace and why HE should focus on helping students develop these skills. A review of the literature on this topic and an overview of the context of soft-skills implementation in Vietnamese HE generated the theoretical background for the book. Chapters 4 to 11 reported empirical studies that feature different aspects of soft-skills implementation, ranging from conceptualization of the implementation, leadership and management, to delivery and assessment, and collaboration between stakeholders.

This final chapter will summarize the key findings across the empirical studies and link them with relevant issues in the West. Four key issues related to soft-skills implementation will be discussed: the influence of contextual factors on different tasks of soft-skills development for students, the influence of institutional leadership on teacher engagement, the contribution of the Youth Union and its associates' (YUA) extracurricular activities (ECAs) to the development of students' soft skills, and university–industry linkages. The chapter ends with practical recommendations for advancing soft-skills implementation in HE.

The influence of contextual factors on soft-skills implementation

Vietnamese universities' response to MOET's soft-skills policy

Vietnamese universities are at different stages in their execution of MOET's soft-skills policy. Their responses appear to be associated with the extent of curriculum autonomy they have, their experience with policy implementation, the priority of soft-skills implementation compared with other institutional reforms, and an absence of national drivers for the implementation.

MOET's tendency to grant privileges differently to different institutions and exert control over the curriculum were found to make the six universities respond differently with regard to developing students' soft skills. As reported in Chapters

4, 5, 6, and 7, University D, with the tradition of a vocational college, made good use of its curriculum autonomy to modify the curricula, add skills subjects, and employ a work-integrated learning (WIL) approach to train students in work-readiness skills relevant to the labor market. Leaders of University B intentionally delayed the implementation until they received autonomy in finance and student recruitment. The other four universities, which did not have curriculum autonomy, struggled to balance skills and disciplinary subjects to fit with the 120–140 credits for a university program, as specified by MOET. They resolved this issue either by cutting out certain disciplinary subjects to save credits for some soft-skills subjects or by having these skills imparted via YUA's extracurricular activities. It was interesting to note that at the time of research (2012–2016), the Higher Education Law (Vietnamese Government, 2012) granted Vietnamese universities curriculum autonomy. However, in practice, university leaders hesitated to use this autonomy due to the vague definition of autonomy in the law (Vu, 2014). Commonly, small universities would often wait, observe, and then replicate the moves of larger, prestigious universities. Hence, MOET's tight control over the curriculum content and structure not only limited its universities' capacity for innovating with their programs but also hindered their flexibility to address labor-market demands (Tran, Le, & Nguyen, 2014). Therefore, curriculum autonomy seems to be an important prerequisite for universities to effectively execute their soft-skills policy.

University leaders' experience with policy implementation also affected their response to MOET's soft-skills policy. Unlike previous policy, which was often accompanied by a detailed guideline, Guideline 2196/BGDĐT-GDĐH (MOET, 2010a) did not provide details on how Vietnamese universities should execute the soft-skills policy. This condition both facilitated and inhibited the execution of MOET's soft-skills policy. On the one hand, university leaders could freely select soft skills relevant to their institutional missions and visions, because the Guideline did not concretely define but only suggested examples of soft skills. On the other hand, they were confused due to their lack of experience with implementing changes related to the curriculum (Nguyen, 2013). In such a centralized HE system (Do, 2014), university leaders often rely on MOET's decisions and guidance for their institutional operation. Consequently, unlike their Western counterparts, this lack of guidance and inadequate leadership experience slowed down the implementation (see Chapters 5, 6, and 7).

Furthermore, soft-skills implementation had to compete with many other institutional reforms or priorities occurring simultaneously. As reported in Chapter 4, University C prioritized building a credit-based curriculum and management system plus shifting to using student-centered pedagogical practice. Their choice appeared to be associated with the institutional objective of receiving quality accreditation and making their programs comparable with others in the ASEAN University Network. Likewise, University F focused on finalizing procedures to transform its institutional status from a "people-founded university" to a non-public university, which also facilitated their operation regarding legitimate matters. Similarly, leaders of University E had to split their attention to upgrading teacher qualifications and teaching capacity as well as building their campus. As a newly established university, these issues were prerequisites for their operation, and also influenced their future enrolment quota (MOET, 2010b). All of these activities would enhance their institutional status and competitiveness; thus, it was not surprising to find that soft-skills implementation was not as highly prioritized.

Finally, the universities' slow response to MOET's soft-skills policy appeared to be linked with a lack of national drivers for the implementation. At the time of research, there had been no inspection, no standardized soft-skills assessment test, no reward scheme or sanction that compelled Vietnamese universities to execute the soft-skills policy. Resembling what happened in Western universities, a lack of such drivers would result in slow or fragmented implementation (Barrie, Hughes, Smith, & Thomson, 2009). In reality, Vietnamese universities prioritized other institutional reforms or objectives instead, as mentioned above. The delivery of these soft skills relied mainly on the voluntary work of individual teachers and the YUA. Still, in response, most universities chose to comply with the policy by including some soft skills in the statements of learning outcomes. Such a compliant attitude meant soft-skills implementation in Vietnamese universities would largely remain only rhetoric or yield minor improvements on students' generic learning outcomes.

Conceptualization and selection of soft skills

Findings in the current book resemble those findings of studies conducted in other countries where universities selected soft skills according to their perspective of the purpose of HE (Danish Government, 2008; Thai Government, 2006) and the missions and visions of their institution (Pitman & Broomhall, 2009). In Vietnam, the purpose of HE is to prepare highly skilled human resources whose duty is to build up the country, sustaining the socialist socioeconomic and political system (Tran, 2015; Vietnamese Government, 2012). Therefore, it was unsurprising to find in this study that all six universities chose to train students in socialist political qualities and work-readiness skills.

However, there were distinctions between the public and non-public universities in selecting which soft skills to develop for their students. The three non-public universities and newly established universities appeared to prioritize soft skills that would enhance graduates' success with obtaining their first job and their performance in the workplace. The three public universities and long-standing universities seemed to focus more on training students in civic engagement. This distinction is understandable as the public universities are state-run institutions, so they also focused on training students in competencies that contribute to sustaining the socialist system, on top of work-readiness skills. Non-public institutions are often vocation-oriented, so they prioritized training students in employment-related skills. For both groups, their selection of soft skills seemed to align with the purpose of Vietnamese HE that primarily produces a workforce to support and develop the country rather than for personal growth (Vietnamese Government, 2012).

Differences in selection of soft skills suggest that, like their Western counterparts, Vietnamese universities were concerned about the purpose of contemporary university education: how to train students to be employable and capable of contributing to civil society. This issue was pointed out a long time ago, but has yet to be fully addressed, at a roundtable discussion between businesses and university leaders in Australia (B-HERT, 2003). It is also noted that conceptualizing and selecting relevant soft skills is an essential step in the implementation because it will influence the adoption of strategy, pedagogical approach, and staff development that would come at a later stage. However, selecting and integrating soft skills into the curricula does not mean that they will be imparted to students automatically. That would need further investment.

Developing the implementation strategy

The term "implementation strategy" used in this section refers to the approach that a university selected to coordinate its schools and departments, and the design of curriculum models to develop students' soft skills. Pedagogical practice could be considered part of the implementation strategy, but it did not prominently emerge as part of the implementation strategy in this study; therefore, it will be discussed independently in the next section.

Unsurprisingly, all six universities were found to use a top-down approach for soft-skills implementation because such a leadership and management practice has been long-standing in Vietnamese universities, reflecting the nature of a centralized HE system (Do, 2014; Marginson, 2011). As stated by university leaders and senior academics in these universities, such an approach was adopted to make the implementation harmonious between schools and university departments. However, its deployment was noticeably different. In universities C, D, and E, university leaders—particularly the rector—appeared to direct all initiatives for the implementation. While universities A, B, and F employed the top-down approach, they seemed to blend in some features of a bottom-up approach for the implementation. In these universities, leaders only managed the progress of the implementation, but school leaders led the implementation to fit with their school context and nature of the discipline as well as to increase the awareness and engagement of teachers.

The six universities also executed the soft-skills policy with slight differences, as shown in Chapter 4. This could result from the fact that university leaders refer to the implementation strategy of other universities when developing their institutional implementation strategy, as suggested by many of them in the interviews. Commonly, they executed the policy by: (i) adding and delivering skills subjects as part of the curriculum; (ii) encouraging or requiring disciplinary teachers to integrate and teach these skills in specialized subjects; and (iii) organizing extracurricular activities (ECAs) to offer students more opportunities to develop soft skills. At the time of research, four universities reported having difficulties in teaching soft skills within the curricula, mostly due to the lack of curriculum autonomy and teacher capacity. Therefore, in all universities except University D,

ECAs were the main channel through which students could develop soft skills. The inclusion of the YUA's extracurricular activities as an integral component of the institutional strategy to execute soft skills is a distinction in soft-skills implementation in Vietnamese universities. This was because the YUA had a long tradition of providing political education and social engagement in Vietnamese universities. Their contribution to the implementation was significant, as demonstrated in Chapter 9 (to be discussed further in the subsequent section). This means that, in the Vietnamese HE context, the YUA's extracurricular activities are significant for nurturing the development of soft skills in students.

Pedagogical practice

Three tasks related to pedagogical practices for the imparting of soft skills to students included setting soft-skills learning objectives, teaching soft skills, and assessing soft skills. To put the concept of developing work-readiness skills for students into practice, generally a WIL approach was employed in Vietnamese universities. However, teaching and assessing soft skills was fragmented: there was no alignment of soft skills-learning objectives between subjects in the curriculum; the teaching faced several challenges; and there was no consensus on assessment criteria.

In the West, to ensure harmonious progress in teaching and assessment of soft skills between subjects in a curriculum, curriculum mapping has recently been introduced (Ang, D'Alessandro, & Winzar, 2014; Lawson et al., 2013). However, it was thought too complicated and time-consuming, and required a lot of additional effort (Ang et al., 2014; Lawson et al., 2013). Of the six qualitative case studies involved in this book project, four had not initiated this task (exceptions were universities D and F). University D completed curriculum mapping for its programs in 2014, as suggested by a top-level university leader. Although soft-skills implementation in the School of Business Administration of University F was obstructed by the dean, other schools in this university were found to have completed aligning learning objectives between subjects of the curricula. That two out of the six Vietnamese universities had moved forward in this respect is a good sign for the implementation regarding the challenges of the task. In the other four universities, a lack of national and institutional drivers could have resulted in formalistic implementation; thus, curriculum-mapping to align soft-skills learning objectives between subjects in a curriculum could have been ignored.

In terms of teaching, participants mentioned that they were using a student-centered approach, including WIL, to impart soft skills to students. As the findings in Chapter 6 showed, in-class student-centered teaching was facing several challenges such as students' self-learning abilities, large class sizes, and a lack of resources. Disciplinary teachers imparted soft skills to different extents using different methods or even ignored them completely. Their engagement with developing soft skills for students depended heavily on their beliefs about the relevance of this task for the students' future, their role at the university, their recognition of the expectations of others and their consideration of factors that may affect their teaching. Regarding WIL, most universities organized only one internship for students whereas University D organized two due to its vocational tradition and connections with industry. Many researchers have found the use of WIL conducive to developing students' soft skills (Jackson, 2017, 2018; Rowe & Zegwaard, 2017). However, the six case studies suggested that the success of using this pedagogical approach appears to largely depend on the following factors:

- **Leadership**: Deciding on how many internships students would undertake, who was responsible for looking for the internship and how students' performance during the internship would be assessed.
- **Location and linkages with industries**: Affecting the number of internships that students would take, and the extent to which the university can collaborate with industries in managing student internships.
- **Collaboration between the university and people in industry**: Affecting the quality of students' learning experience during the internship; the closer the collaboration is, the more meaningful students' learning experience will be.
- **Student engagement**: Determining the quality of their internship-related learning outcomes, including soft skills.

The use of internships and the student-centered teaching approach in the classroom to impart work-readiness skills to students was in progress in Vietnamese universities, although a traditional teaching approach is still dominant in the HE system (Tran, Phan, & Tran, 2018; Tran et al., 2014). It seemed that the introduction of a soft-skills policy triggered changes in teachers' pedagogical practices.

The assessment of soft skills in Vietnamese universities was fragmented and appeared to be hindered by the existing assessment convention. Teachers generally agreed on what soft skills were, but they had not gained a consensus on how to assess those skills and the assessment criteria. In most cases, teachers ignored this task due to their non-teaching of soft skills, or assessed students' levels of soft skills based on their "experience" or "intuition." Teachers rarely used assessment to cater for students' development of these skills, but only used assessment for summative purposes. Their universities' regulations on the score weighting and organization of midterm and final exams also hindered teachers from assessing students' soft skills, which needs to be conducted on a regular basis throughout a semester. These assessment-related difficulties resembled those found in Western universities (Chapman & O'Neill, 2010; Tremblay, Lalancette, & Roseveare, 2012). The difficulties in the Vietnamese case could be attributed to a lack of institutional and national drivers, resulting in teachers' ignorance of such a task. However, because assessment may drive students' learning behavior, and can generate data about the effectiveness of soft-skills implementation, it is necessary to improve soft-skills implementation in this respect, such as develop a standardized test that can be adaptive to different disciplinary contexts. Obstacles related to teachers' assessment expertise and existing assessment convention need to be considered and removed, if possible, to facilitate teachers' engagement in this task (Hughes & Barrie, 2010).

Teacher engagement: Causes and effects

Teacher engagement appeared to strongly influence the implementation of soft skills in Vietnamese universities. The evidence suggested that personal, organizational, and cultural factors, student disengagement, and several teaching practicality issues resulted in disciplinary teachers' disengagement. All these factors, to some extent, are linked to university and school leadership.

Several studies suggest that the teachers' perception of their role, attitudes towards soft skills, and their expertise in soft skills can influence their confidence and the extent to which they engage with teaching the skills (Barrie, 2007; de la Harpe & David, 2012; de la Harpe & Radloff, 2008; Jones, 2009). Consistent with existing literature, studies in this book showed that teachers' perception of the relevance of teaching soft skills appeared to have a strong effect on their engagement with teaching these skills (see Chapters 6 and 7). Those who chose to teach soft skills shared a common belief that teaching soft skills was important for their students' futures, relevant to their subjects, and part of teachers' inherent responsibility. Those who chose not to teach soft skills believed that teaching soft skills was not part of their duties, even though they knew these skills were important for students' futures, or they claimed that the existing conditions in their universities were not favorable for teaching soft skills. Several disciplinary teachers did not engage because there was a lack of clarity in the communication of the soft-skills policy, including its incentives and drivers. Therefore, leadership needs to be exercised in order to gain their buy-in, develop their confidence, and remove obstacles for their teaching and assessing of soft skills.

Unfortunately, like their counterparts in Western countries (Al-Mahmood & Gruba, 2007; Barrie, Hughes, & Smith, 2009), studies in this book indicated that several organizational factors related to leadership affected teacher engagement with developing soft skills for students. First, soft-skills policies and institutional strategies were not clearly communicated to disciplinary teachers (see Chapters 5, 6, and 7). With the exception of University D, several disciplinary teachers in the universities thought the policies and implementation strategy were for skills teachers and the YUA. They believed that university leaders only "encouraged" them to teach soft skills; however, the interviews with university leaders revealed that they expected their disciplinary teachers to teach these skills as best they could. In addition, a lack of incentives for soft-skills teaching discouraged teachers from enacting the policy. Consistently across the six qualitative case studies, teachers complained that teaching soft skills was "hard" and "time and effort consuming," but the universities did not incentivize. Therefore, they felt demotivated and only showed a compliance attitude toward teaching soft skills. Moreover, in most universities, a lack of effective management tools to regulate teachers' delivery of soft skills resulted in disciplinary teachers' disengagement. The use of a student experience questionnaire failed to engage them because it was designed to obtain students' general experience with a course, not with soft-skills learning. Several teachers directly admitted that they did not teach soft skills because nobody controlled their teaching.

Another organizational factor that strongly influenced disciplinary teacher engagement was a shortage of activities to build teacher capacity for soft-skills teaching and assessment. Traditionally, disciplinary teachers' primary role is to prepare students with disciplinary knowledge (Jones, 2009), so they may have different attitudes and responses when asked to impart these skills (Barrie, 2006, 2007). On top of gaining their buy-in, it is necessary to develop their pedagogical expertise so that they can embark on the implementation process at the subject level with confidence (Barrie et al., 2009). The studies in this book suggested that Vietnamese universities did not provide sufficient or relevant training to their teaching staff. Thus, they were not confident and were discouraged from conducting the teaching task. Apart from a lack of training, a lack of community of practice also worsened this shortage of soft-skills teaching expertise among the teaching staff. Teachers' ignorance of teaching and assessing soft skills as well as fragmented implementation demonstrated that there was a lack of shared understanding and practice, which can be addressed by a community of practice. The analysis suggested three organizational culture factors behind this lack of a community of soft-skills teaching and assessment practice:

- First, the distance in relationship between novice and senior teachers is relatively large due to Confucian educational values embedded in the organizational culture of Vietnamese universities (Marginson, 2011; Napier & Hoang, 2013; Tran et al., 2018). In this organizational culture, novice teachers are expected to approach senior teachers with appropriate manners and behaviors; seniors tend to expect that their juniors will be at their beck and call (Napier & Hoang, 2013). The fact that many Vietnamese universities recruit and train their graduates to become lecturers seemed to make the existing distant relationship between teachers more marked.
- Second, in some universities, the distance in relationship also occurred between full and part-time teachers. For example, in University E, university leaders employed skills experts to teach soft skills together with other teachers in the university, expecting them to collaborate and learn from each other. Contrary to the expectations of leaders, the teachers did not work closely with these skills experts. This dichotomy between the two groups of teachers would be an obstacle for harmonious implementation.
- Third, there was a lack of leadership in teaching soft skills at the faculty or school level. In the interviews, disciplinary teachers could easily identify at least one colleague who had soft-skills expertise, but they were hesitant to identify someone that could be a role model for their teaching of soft skills. Novice teachers were confused with their teaching of these skills because their seniors, in their observation, did not teach the skills.

Therefore, it is important to develop a community of practice for teachers to build their soft skills teaching and assessment expertise. This can be done by enhancing the ability of senior teachers, especially those in management positions such as deans or heads of department, to lead the teaching of soft skills in their school or department. Their leadership is a "vital ingredient in creating a climate and culture in faculties that is conducive to staff members engaging in the teaching and curriculum development work that is required to achieve [soft skills]" (Barrie et al., 2009 p. 20). Their leadership would bring people together to build a shared understanding about soft skills, implementation strategies, and concrete expertise to execute the policy in their class using appropriate pedagogies.

Studies in this book revealed that students' disregard of soft-skills learning also triggered teacher disengagement. Resembling their Western counterparts, Vietnamese universities adopted a student-centered approach, including WIL, to develop soft skills for students (for example, Brodie, 2011; Jackson & Collings, 2018; Shek & Chak, 2019; Vogler et al., 2018). One of the key factors for the success of employing such a pedagogical approach was students' active participation (Attard, Di Iorio, Geven, & Santa, 2010; Tran et al., 2018). However, data collected from both students and teachers consistently indicated that Vietnamese students hesitantly participated in curriculum-based activities to develop soft-skills (see Chapter 11). Teachers asserted that such students' non-participation discouraged them from developing soft skills for students (see Chapter 6). From teachers' perspectives, students' non-participation was caused by students' low academic abilities, personal characteristics, and superficial learning attitudes. From students' perspectives, they disengaged from curriculum-based soft-skills-learning activities due to a mismatch between their interests and the activities organized, or a lack of communication from stakeholders, and limited time (see Chapter 11). Thus, initiatives need to be organized to increase students' awareness and engagement with developing these skills.

Finally, several teaching practicality issues were identified that prevent teachers from teaching and assessing soft skills, as reported in Chapters 5, 6, and 7. Teachers involved in the studies asserted that there were a large number of students in Vietnamese universities, so most of them had to conduct an excessively heavy teaching workload in their institution. Owing to low salaries (Anh, 2014), they had to moonlight to make ends meet, and thus did not have sufficient time for effective teaching of soft skills, which require ongoing evaluation and feedback. Adding to this challenge was large class sizes of about 50–100—or even more—students. This situation forced many teachers to choose to ignore teaching soft skills or only superficially engage, such as telling students to develop those skills or directing students to online learning resources rather than teaching these skills. A lack of teaching resources and facilities due to financial constraints also disheartened many teachers. Interviews with university leaders and teachers suggest that this situation was caused by soft-skills implementation having to compete with other institutional priorities for limited resources (see Chapters 5 and 6).

YUA's extracurricular activities and soft-skills implementation

Studies in this book indicate that the use of ECAs can be beneficial for students' development of soft skills. In particular, ECAs meet students' diverse learning needs better than do curriculum-based learning activities.

The YUA has been leading Vietnamese students in socialist political-education and social-engagement activities for many years (Ho Chi Minh Communist Youth Union, 2019). Different from Western universities, where ECAs were an adjunct part, the YUA's extracurricular activities have recently been involved as an integral part of the implementation of soft skills in Vietnamese universities because of their traditional roles and MOET's restriction of credits for a university curriculum. The YUA conducted five major activities to develop soft skills for their students as follows:

- **Training political qualities**: Conventionally, this is the main duty of the YUA. Knowing and possessing political qualities were believed to help them survive better in a society with such a high level of flexibility.
- **Coordinating skills classes**: The YUA frequently organized classes to help students develop communication skills, job-interview skills, CV writing, presentation skills, and career-planning skills. These classes were either free or paid for by students.
- **Providing career consultation**: The YUA provided a career-consultation service where students could come and request advice about their career path relevant to the discipline they were studying. This also included matching students with an alumnus for personal coaching of career development.
- **Linking students with employers**: The YUA also organized some career fairs where students could meet potential employers to inquire about the skills employers need, and participate in mock job interviews.
- **Social-engagement activities**: The YUA has a long tradition in organizing these activities. Students were led to join in activities that contributed to the development of nearby communities. Students could go to rural areas to teach children, transfer new technologies to farmers, improve the irrigation system, and propagandize civilized lifestyles. Recently, they also organized international exchange programs for students to develop a worldview and inter-cultural competence.

Despite their leading role in soft-skills implementation, the extent to which they could contribute to the implementation varied between the universities. It seemed their contribution was affected by: (i) university leadership; (ii) student participation; (iii) support of external stakeholders; and (iv) YUA leadership.

The YUA's contribution to soft-skills-policy implementation seemed to be influenced by the university and school leadership. As an integral part of the institutional implementation strategy, YUA had to organize activities to develop soft skills aligned with those selected by the university. Such an alignment was to ensure the soft-skills-development agenda via curricular-based and extracurricular activities progressed in harmony. In addition, university or school leaders' perception of the YUA role also determined the extent of the YUA's contribution. In some cases, the YUA was seen to support students, whereas in other universities it was seen to lead students. In the supporting role, the contribution of the YUA to soft-skills implementation was largely dependent on students' proactivity. In the leading role, the YUA had more authority in organizing ECAs to develop soft skills for students. In addition, institutional acknowledgement of the role of the YUA in soft-skills implementation to relevant stakeholders also affected the YUA's contribution. Unfortunately, according to several interviewed YUA leaders and staff members, many teachers, administrative staff, and the public in general did not know about the role of the YUA in this regard. Therefore, they tended to reject supporting the YUA's activities, which affected the YUA's activities for soft-skills development for students.

The effectiveness of the YUA's activities also depended on the participation of students. As showed in Chapter 9, most students joined in the YUA's activities enthusiastically because they recognized the benefits of improving their soft skills. Simultaneously, like many stakeholders, many students considered ECAs as play instead of learning. Therefore, many only participated because they did not want to receive bad scores for "self-improvement," which could influence their academic ranking or scholarship opportunities. Consistent with findings in previous studies (Tran, 2015), this suggests that Vietnamese students often overlooked ECAs, which could have been because they were not well-informed about the importance and purpose of the YUA's extracurricular activities in developing their soft skills.

Furthermore, support of external stakeholders was significant for the YUA to organize soft-skills-development activities, either on or off campus. As shown in Chapter 5, although the YUA was acknowledged for its significant contribution to students' soft-skills development, sometimes it was not financially supported for this work. Much of its small grant was allocated to training students in political qualities and the rest was used with careful consideration for prioritized activities. To organize social engagements or job-oriented activities, the YUA had to look for other sources of funding and support from external stakeholders (see Chapter 10). In this respect, the YUAs of well-known universities, which had an extensive network with industry, seemed to receive more financial support from external stakeholders, such as employers, alumni, and local authorities. In contrast, University E's YUA mostly organized ECAs on the campus due to not having a network with external stakeholders, possibly because of being a new university.

Finally, the YUA leaders obviously influenced the effectiveness of the YUA's operation in implementing soft skills. They are often the ones who decided which activities are prioritized, which skills experts are to be invited, and the location that social-engagement activities would take place. All of these were associated with their perception of the importance and relevance of soft skills for students in the university, their experience in operating the YUA, and their networking with external stakeholders such as alumni, local employers, skills experts, or local authorities. However, as pointed out by students in Chapter 9, some YUA leaders appeared not to have effective leadership skills in organizing ECAs, which discouraged students from participating. Therefore, it is essential to align YUA leaders' perception of soft skills with that of the institution and foster them by developing leadership skills and social networks to enhance the quality of their contribution to soft-skills implementation.

University–industry linkages and soft-skills implementation

In recent years, there has been an increase in collaboration between universities and industry, not only in research but also in teaching activities, particularly the adoption of the WIL approach (Dollinger, Coates, Bexley, Croucher, & Naylor, 2018; Lam, 2011; Rampersad, 2015). Despite some challenges, collaboration with external stakeholders appears to contribute to the implementation of the soft-skills policy. The qualitative case studies showed that external stakeholders contributed to the implementation of soft skills in Vietnamese universities in four ways.

- **Consultation of relevant soft skills**: Local employers or local industries were asked for advice in regard to choosing relevant soft skills to develop for their students. However, they were involved in this role at different levels of the university, dependent on the chosen implementation strategy. In universities A, B, and F, they were consulted for soft skills at both school and subject levels. In universities D and E, they were consulted at university levels. At the time of research, only individual teachers in University C had consulted with local employers.
- **Teaching soft skills**: Experts from industries also took part in training students in soft skills. In all six cases, these experts were invited to organize skills-training sessions by the YUA. In most cases, some disciplinary teachers reported that they invited their contacts that had soft-skills expertise to visit their class and collaborate with them to teach some sessions. Universities D, E, and F explicitly invited skills experts to deliver a skills subject to students. Particularly for University E, these experts were expected to help train teachers at the university in pedagogical practices conducive to developing such skills for students.
- **Providing internships**: Employers help develop soft skills for students by providing internships. In the case of students of the business administration programs in this study, they were expected to take from one to two internships as a compulsory part of their degree. During the internships, students were trained with disciplinary skills, applying their disciplinary knowledge to the authentic context of the organization where they took the internships. At the same time, while exposed to real-life contexts, they were expected to polish the acquired soft skills and continue to develop skills they recognized to be relevant and important for their future career.
- **Assessing soft skills and evaluating the soft skills implementation program**: Although soft-skills assessment is still limited in the studied universities, employers appeared to be involved in assessing graduates' work performance,

including soft skills. This also means that employers help evaluate the success of the soft-skills-implementation program of a university. Unfortunately, as reported consistently in the six cases, employers did not participate in this role eagerly and the universities had only just taken the initial step toward utilizing this type of assessment or evaluation.
- **Financial support**: External stakeholders also provided some financial support, in terms of donation or sponsorship, for the YUA to organize certain ECAs, especially community-development ones.

Irrespective of the multiple roles they might have been involved with in soft-skills implementation in Vietnamese universities, it appeared that the extent to which employers and local industries participated in the aforementioned roles was directly influenced by the location, prestige, and type of university. Well-known metropolitan universities can attract support from external stakeholders, especially from businesses, more than newly established regional ones. While non-public institutions were keen on making connections with employers and industries for teaching soft skills, public institutions hesitated, possibly due to their attempts to preserve their status as public institutions whose primary mission was to train citizens to sustain the socio-political system. In contrast, the non-public institutions were vocation-oriented and aimed to produce graduates that met labor-market demands. Not receiving funding from the central government means these institutions must develop a strong connection with local industries and make good use of these connections for their institutional operation.

However, it was noted that external stakeholders hesitated to cooperate with the universities in some areas of the implementation. For example, local industries were not willing to support teachers of University A with authentic materials for teaching soft skills or did not respond to the employers' survey of graduates' work performance sent out by all six universities. This was in line with the findings of a study by (Tran, 2015), who argued that a lack of collaboration from employers and businesses was one of the causes for Vietnamese university graduates' lack of work skills. Still, this study documented some collaboration between the universities and local employers and businesses in developing soft skills for students, particularly University D. Based on what University D had been doing to successfully use WIL to develop work-readiness skills for students, and what others had not, it suggests that university-industry cooperation is closely associated with the leadership efforts and strategies or initiatives used by each institution.

Conversely, studies in this book (Chapter 10) also found that Vietnamese universities did not proactively reach out to external experts for soft-skills implementation. Universities had not paid adequate attention to building the linkage between their institution and local industries and employers, even with their alumni who would become professionals in industries. While alumni expressed a high level of interest in contributing to developing soft skills for current students, they did not receive invitations, notifications, or involvement in such activities. This was a huge waste of available human resources for a successful implementation of a soft-skills policy in HE. As a consequence of this, the use of WIL was not effective as there were limited internship opportunities for students, or industrial experts for co-teaching or guest-teaching of skills or specialized subjects. Likewise, the YUA's extracurricular activities were also affected. For example, the YUA of University E had to suspend its community engagement programs due to a lack of financial support (Chapter 5).

Implications for soft-skills implementation in higher education

Curriculum autonomy

As shown in the case studies, most of the universities struggled with the implementation as a result of MOET's regulation of the curriculum. This suggests that the universities need autonomy in designing their programs as a prerequisite for implementation. Such autonomy would enable them to add skills subjects and adopt a suitable pedagogical practice for their institution. Curriculum autonomy must be accompanied with other forms of autonomy in student enrolment and finance, which would allow them to select students who are suitable for the offered programs and would enhance flexibility in the operation of their institution. Although at the time of research, the new Higher Education Law allowed the universities to design their own curriculum, vagueness in defining autonomy and a lack of experience meant that many institutions did not dare embark on reforming their curricula. This will take time to change, but MOET can in the meantime enhance soft-skills implementation in universities by detailing what they can do with their curricula to ease worries about repercussions as a result of any mistakes within curriculum design. This would help the universities advance more quickly with soft-skills implementation in their institutions.

However, curriculum autonomy should go hand in hand with accountability. What and how to deliver programs must meet regulatory bodies' standards, such as quality assurance standards, and be subject to public scrutiny. If a program fails to comply with quality standards or stakeholders' expectations, it needs to be audited and closed if necessary. In this way, curriculum autonomy for soft-skills implementation in particular and for other curriculum-related reforms in general would be more effective.

Enhancing the role of extracurricular activities

The YUA's extracurricular activities have contributed a great deal to developing soft skills for students in Vietnamese universities. This indicates that ECAs should not be overlooked compared to curriculum-based activities.

Unfortunately, despite their contribution, in Vietnamese universities, the YUA's extracurricular activities are disregarded by both teachers and students as well as insufficiently supported by university leaders. To enhance the work of the YUA, it is important to communicate its role in soft-skills implementation with clarity in the institutional implementation strategy to all stakeholders in the university and to the public. This will change the public and stakeholders' ingrained beliefs that the YUA's extracurricular activities are "play" activities and it would enhance both internal and external stakeholders' support to the YUA when needed.

YUA leaders also need to be trained in their leadership skills and align their ECAs to develop the soft skills that the university select. Enhancing their leadership skills would help the organization of ECAs be more efficient and effective. YUA's student organizers also need to be recruited and trained carefully as they are the bridge between the YUA and students. Without appropriate preparation for these organizers, they may harm the reputation of the YUA and deflect focus away from the YUA's extracurricular activities, as indicated in Chapter 9.

Equally important is the need for a larger financial grant so that the YUA can organize a diverse range of activities for students rather than limit their activities on campus. At the moment, external stakeholders' contributions to soft-skills implementation are via the ECAs of the YUA. Without financial support from the university, the YUA would not be able to reach out to surrounding communities to organize community-engagement activities or to host skills experts to organize skills classes for students.

When Vietnamese universities begin to use curriculum autonomy in order to add a multitude of skills subjects into the curriculum, the role of the YUA in soft skills development should be maintained because the evidence suggests that it has already been successful and could support soft-skills development with authentic contexts to practice in, rather than just classroom study environments. These activities, in fact, can afford many opportunities for students to put soft skills taught in their class into practice within real-life situations. That is vital because soft skills always need substantial practice to grow.

Using institutional leadership to improve teacher and student engagement

Several teachers and students appeared not to engage with soft-skills implementation. Personal factors, organizational factors, and cultural factors, as well as teaching-learning practicality issues, were found to have influenced their engagement. All of these factors, to some extent, were associated with institutional leadership. Therefore, enhancing leadership to engage teachers and students with the implementation is essential, particularly considering the fact that Vietnamese HE is very centralized with all activities.

First and foremost, there should be initiatives to change teachers' and students' perceptions about the relevance and necessity of teaching soft skills in their subjects. Making the soft-skills policy visible and accessible is the first step in elaborating on the university's engagement with soft-skills implementation. The policy needs to clearly convey the purpose and objectives, as well as the responsibilities of each group of stakeholders university-wide. In addition, teachers and students should be involved in identifying relevant soft skills and developing the curriculum model to impart the selected skills. These activities would enhance their understanding of the nature of soft skills and develop their buy-in with the implementation (Barrie et al., 2009).

Second, teachers need to be trained in techniques to teach soft skills so that they can become more confident conducting this non-traditional role in the classroom. Teaching soft skills is not as simple as telling students what these skills are and how to develop them. There should be workshops or training courses to develop specific teaching skills for teachers to impart soft skills to students. These workshops or training courses could be coordinated by teachers with soft-skills expertise, or by external experts from an industry. It is also recommended that if a university adopts a specific pedagogical practice, such as WIL, for soft-skills development, its teachers should be carefully trained in that pedagogical approach. There should be teachers who play the role of key soft-skills implementers in each school and department, serving as the leadership of the implementation. A community of soft-skills teaching should be established to afford teachers with opportunities to motivate, share and learn soft skills teaching, assess experience, and build each other's confidence in this central task of the implementation. Similarly, in the first year, students would need to be trained in active learning skills that can enhance their transition to the university and facilitate their development of soft skills in subsequent years. When they are aware of the importance of soft skills and have sufficient active learning skills, they will better engage with the soft-skills development learning activities organized by their teachers.

Third, if a university wants teaching-learning of soft skills to be effective, it needs to provide these teachers with basic teaching practicalities (Barrie et al., 2009. The teaching system, facilities, learning resources, the teaching workload, and an appropriate number of students per class should be in place. With favorable teaching conditions, teachers would become motivated and engaged with teaching these skills and students would find it more compelling to engage with training in soft skills.

Finally, there should be institutional incentives and drivers to encourage teachers to engage with teaching soft skills. If teachers recognize that imparting soft skills is acknowledged or monitored by the university's policy and management tools respectively, they would tend to engage with it. For students, similar initiatives should be applied. For example, for students who successfully complete independent soft skills courses, they should be provided with a certificate which may serve as evidence of their employability to prospective employers and an encouragement for other students to exert more effort in completing such courses.

Forging university–industry linkages

External stakeholders have been found to contribute to soft-skills implementation in a variety of roles such as recommendation of relevant soft skills, teaching and assessing soft skills, providing internship opportunities and mentoring student interns, and participating in ECAs. However, it seems that Vietnamese universities, like their counterparts around the world, have not forged sufficient networks with external stakeholders, many of whom are willing to provide assistance, as shown in Chapter 10. Therefore, leadership need to be exercised to explicitly network and involve these stakeholders with the implementation. The author believes that alumni and students could and would help the university to close the current university-industry gap.

First, recent literature suggests that alumni can help connect and improve university–industry linkage (Schlesinger, Cervera, & Pérez-Cabañero, 2017; Sharda & Butler, 2004). Therefore, it is critical that universities stay in contact with their graduates and stress the mutual benefits of this relationship: alumni feedback, suggestions, and donations could help improve the reputation of their university, which may contribute to their future employment outcomes. Maintaining periodic communication with alumni would also help universities collect data on employment rates of the graduates, an index regularly used for assessing the quality of a university program, and extend their connection to the industry sectors that those students work for. Keeping in touch with them will nurture the growth of the connection between the university and industries because, in the long term, alumni will become professionals in their field, employers, or recruiters.

Second, student internships may foster university–industry linkages if organized effectively (Prabhu & Kudva, 2016). In many universities, students were in charge of looking for internship opportunities by themselves. In this sense, students have already acted as a bridge that connects the university and the internship provider. If the university can purposefully send its academic staff to the workplace to support students throughout the internship and require them to work closely with professionals in the workplace in supervising the students, that would help tighten the university–industry linkage. Such connections can be re-used in the future, and through time these connections would multiply.

Finally, university leaders need to openly express their interests in working with qualified or passionate professionals for soft-skills implementation. It would be a huge waste not to make good use of skills experts in industries. Due to these stakeholders' limited time, they can be invited to update changes in skills needs in the labor market, coordinate skills-development seminars under the YUA, independently teach a skills subjects or co-teach a specialized subject with an academic and provide guest lectures to inspire students. They can be invited to be trained in how to mentor student interns so that students can have a well-constructed learning experience. All of these activities would meaningfully enhance the alignment between what the university imparts and what the labor-market needs. However, these initiatives must be deployed with some reservations as not all professionals and skills experts can impart their expertise pedagogically. They should be properly oriented, trained with teaching skills, and regulated with effectual management tools; otherwise, they should not teach and assess soft skills, as University E experienced (see Chapter 5).

Conclusion

This book focused on exploring how soft skills are developed for students in a non-Western university context and identified challenges associated with the implementation. Taking Vietnam as the site of investigation, this book reveals that soft-skills implementation is strongly context-dependent.

Unlike most Western university leaders, Vietnamese university leaders often lack leadership and management skills as a result of depending too much on MOET or an equivalent regulatory body. In the case of soft-skills implementation, a lack of guidance from MOET has confused many university leaders in leading their institution to execute the policy. In addition, a lack of curriculum autonomy causes difficulties in modifying the curricula for executing the soft-skills policy. Moreover, soft-skills implementation was occurring amidst many other reforms, some of which were closely regulated and linked to future institutional privileges once completed. Being unlinked to any future institutional privileges, soft-skills implementation was either intentionally delayed, other reforms were prioritized over it, or it was formalistically executed to show compliance to MOET.

At the institutional level, the main concept for soft-skills implementation was developing work-readiness skills for students, which were aligned to the purposes of Vietnamese HE and increased concerns about the poor quality of work performance of Vietnamese graduates. The conventional centralized leadership and management was used to coordinate the implementation of soft skills in Vietnamese universities. Owing to the absence of curriculum autonomy, most universities included ECAs as an integral component of the institutional implementation strategy rather than an adjunct part, as in many Western universities. The use of these activities was facilitated because the YUA has traditionally led students' social-engagement and political-education activities.

At the subject level, to impart work-readiness to students, a student-centered approach, including WIL, was employed. However, the use of WIL was limited in many universities due to a lack of connection with industry or collaboration between the university and people in industry. This long-term unresolved issue reduced opportunities for student internship, employment of skills experts to teach skills classes, improvement of teacher expertise related to soft skills teaching and assessment, and the YUA's organization of ECAs. In addition, the teaching and assessing of soft skills was hindered by the disengagement of disciplinary teachers, which was associated with their institutional leadership. A lack of clarity in the soft-skills policy and implementation strategy, a shortage of teacher capacity, and an absence of incentives and management tools all contributed to teacher disengagement with the implementation. For those who taught soft skills, they faced difficulties such as large class sizes, heavy teaching workloads, and shortage of time.

Distinctively, the YUA's extracurricular activities were found to play a significant role in developing soft skills for Vietnamese students. This suggests that like curriculum-based activities, extracurricular activities have potential for nurturing students' soft skills; therefore, these activities should be promoted when implementing soft skills. However, the role of the YUA in soft-skills implementation was not communicated and acknowledged appropriately to university stakeholders. At the time of research, the work of the YUA relied on a very tight budget, the YUA leaders' proactivity in leadership, and volunteer support from external businesses and local authorities.

Conclusion

In conclusion, in investigating the implementation of soft skills in Vietnamese universities, this book found that contextual factors significantly influenced soft-skills implementation. The effectiveness of the implementation was associated with numerous factors, but foremost among them curriculum autonomy, leadership, and university–industry linkages. Therefore, every university, rather than "copying and pasting" an implementation model reported to be successful from elsewhere, must analyze the context in which it operates and its capacity so that they can appropriately conceptualize the implementation, and devise and deploy implementation strategies effectively. All of these require effective leadership to harness institutional capacity and engage stakeholders in the implementation.

References

Al-Mahmood, R., & Gruba, P. (2007). Approaches to the implementation of generic graduate attributes in Australian ICT undergraduate education. *Computer Science Education*, 17(3), 171–185.

Ang, L., D'Alessandro, S., & Winzar, H. (2014). A visual-based approach to the mapping of generic skills: its application to a marketing degree. *Higher Education Research & Development*, 33(2), 181–197.

Anh, H. (2014). University lecturers receive $183–368 monthly salary: Report. *Vietnamenet*. Retrieved from https://bit.ly/2W9Hcjy

Attard, A., Di Iorio, E., Geven, K., & Santa, R. (2010). *Student-centred learning: Toolkit for students, staff and higher education institutions*. Retrieved from https://bit.ly/2UCtDYG

B-HERT (2003).Developing generic skills: Examples of best practice. *B-HERT News*. Retrieved from https://bit.ly/2GAJ9QL

Barrie, S., Hughes, C., Smith, C., & Thomson, K. (2009). *The national graduate attributes project: Key issues to consider in the renewal of learning and teaching experiences to foster graduate attributes*. Sydney: The University of Sydney.

Barrie, S. C. (2006). Understanding what we mean by the generic attributes of graduates. *Higher Education*, 51(2), 215–241.

Barrie, S. C. (2007). A conceptual framework for the teaching and learning of generic graduate attributes. *Studies in Higher Education*, 32(4), 439–458.

Brodie, L. (2011). Delivering key graduate attributes via teams working in virtual space. *International Journal of Emerging Technologies in Learning (iJET)*, 6(3), 5–11.

Chapman, E., & O'Neill, M. (2010). Defining and assessing generic competencies in Australian universities: Ongoing challenges. *Education Research and Perspectives*, 37(1), 105.

Danish Government (2008). *Qualifications framework for Danish higher education*. Retrieved from https://bit.ly/2URzxtC.

de la Harpe, B., & David, C. (2012). Major influences on the teaching and assessment of graduate attributes. *Higher Education Research & Development*, 31(4), 493–510.

de la Harpe, B., & Radloff, A. (2008). Developing graduate attributes for lifelong learning-how far have we got? Paper presented at the 5th International Lifelong Learning Conference, 16–19 June, Yeppoon, Australia.

Do, H. M. (2014). Towards more flexible organization. In L. T. Tran, S. Marginson, H. M. Do, Q. T. N. Do, T. T. T. Le, N. T. Nguyen, T. T. P. Vu, T. N. Pham, H. T. L. Nguyen, & T. T. H. Ho (Eds.), *Higher education in Vietnam: Flexibility, mobility and practicality in the global knowledge economy* (pp. 54–85). New York, NY: Palgrave MacMilan.

Dollinger, M., Coates, H., Bexley, E., Croucher, G., & Naylor, R. (2018). Framing international approaches to university–industry collaboration. *Policy Reviews in Higher Education*, 2(1), 105–127. doi: 10.1080/23322969.2018.1424560

Ho Chi Minh Communist Youth Union (2019). *Ho Chi Minh Communist Youth Union*. Retrieved from http://english.doanthanhnien.vn/

Hughes, C., & Barrie, S. (2010). Influences on the assessment of graduate attributes in higher education. *Assessment & Evaluation in Higher Education*, 35(3), 325–334.

Jackson, D. (2017). Developing pre-professional identity in undergraduates through work-integrated learning. *Higher Education*, 74(5), 833–853.

Jackson, D. (2018). Developing graduate career readiness in Australia: Shifting from extracurricular internships to work-integrated learning. *International Journal of Work-Integrated Learning*, 19(1), 23–35.

Jackson, D., & Collings, D. (2018). The influence of work-integrated learning and paid work during studies on graduate employment and underemployment. *Higher Education*, 76(3), 403–425. doi: 10.1007/s10734-017-0216-z

Jones, A. (2009). Generic attributes as espoused theory: The importance of context. *Higher Education*, 58(2), 175–191.

Lam, A. (2011). University-industry collaboration: careers and knowledge governance in hybrid organisational space. *International Journal of Strategic Business Alliances*, 2(1–2), 135–145.

Lawson, R., Taylor, T., Fallshaw, E., Summers, J., Kinash, S., French, E., & Angus-Leppan, T. (2013). Hunters and gatherers: Strategies for curriculum mapping and data collection for assuring learning. Retrieved from https://bit.ly/2DqAWgk

Marginson, S. (2011). Higher education in East Asia and Singapore: Rise of the Confucian model. *Higher Education*, 61(5), 587–611.

MOET (2010a). *Công văn 2916/ BGDĐT-GDĐH hướng dẫn xây dựng và công bố chuẩn đầu ra ngành đào tạo*. Retrieved from https://bit.ly/2VlKS4I

MOET (2010b). *Quyết định: Quy định về việc xác định chỉ tiêu tuyển sinh, quy trình đăng ký, thông báo chỉ tiêu tuyển sinh, kiểm tra và xử lý việc thực hiện các quy định về xác định chỉ tiêu tuyển sinh đại học, sau đại học, cao đẳng và trung cấp chuyên nghiệp. (795/QĐ-BGDĐT)*. Retrieved from https://bit.ly/2ZI4DD4

Napier, N. K., & Hoang, V. Q. (2013). *What we see, why we worry, why we hope: Vietnam going forward*. Boise, ID: Boise State University CCI Press.

Nguyen, T. L. H. (2013). Middle-level academic management: A case study on the roles of the heads of department at a Vietnamese university. *Tertiary Education and Management*, 19(1), 1–15. doi: 10.1080/13583883.2012.724704

Pitman, T., & Broomhall, S. (2009). Australian universities, generic skills and lifelong learning. *International Journal of Lifelong Education*, 28(4), 439–458.

Prabhu, B. V., & Kudva, S. A. (2016). Success of student internship in engineering industry: A faculty perspective. *Higher Education for the Future*, 3(2), 164–182. doi: 10.1177/2347631116650550

Rampersad, G. C. (2015). Developing university-business cooperation through work-integrated learning. *International Journal of Technology Management*, 68(3–4), 203–227.

Rowe, A. D., & Zegwaard, K. E. (2017). Developing graduate employability skills and attributes: Curriculum enhancement through work-integrated learning. *Asia-Pacific Journal of Cooperative Education*, 18(2), 87–99.

Schlesinger, W., Cervera, A., & Pérez-Cabañero, C. (2017). Sticking with your university: The importance of satisfaction, trust, image, and shared values. *Studies in Higher Education*, 42(12), 2178–2194.

Sharda, H., & Butler, A. (2004). The role of alumni in increasing university/industry interaction. In *Creating Flexible Learning Environments: Proceedings of the 15th Australasian Conference for the Australasian Association for Engineering Education and the 10th Australasian Women in Engineering Forum*. Toowoomba, Australia: Australasian Association for Engineering Education.

Shek, D. T., & Chak, Y. L. (2019). Perceived changes and benefits of a service-learning subject for underprivileged children in Shanghai: Views of university students. In D. T. L. Shek, G. Ngai, & S. C. F. Chan (Eds.), *Service-learning for youth leadership: The case of Hong Kong* (pp. 33–47). Singapore: Springer.

Thai Government (2006). *National qualifications framework for higher education in Thailand*. Retrieved from: https://bit.ly/2DsbFSX

Tran, L. H. N., Phan, T. N. P., & Tran, L. K. H. (2018). Implementing the student-centred teaching approach in Vietnamese universities: The influence of leadership and management practices on teacher engagement. *Educational Studies*. doi: 10.1080/03055698.2018.1555453

Tran, L. T., Le, T. T. T., & Nguyen, N. T. (2014). Curriculum and pedagogy. In *Higher education in Vietnam: Flexibility, mobility and practicality in the global knowledge economy* (pp. 86–107). London: Palgrave Macmillan.

Tran, T. T. (2015). Is graduate employability the "whole-of-higher-education-issue"? *Journal of Education and Work*, 28(3), 207–227.

Tremblay, K., Lalancette, D., & Roseveare, D. (2012). *Assessment of higher education learning outcomes*. OECD. Retrieved from: https://bit.ly/2IRTRnB

Vietnamese Government (2012). *Luật giáo dục đại học*. Retrieved from https://bit.ly/2GNGV24

Vogler, J. S., Thompson, P., Davis, D. W., Mayfield, B. E., Finley, P. M., & Yasseri, D. (2018). The hard work of soft skills: augmenting the project-based learning experience with interdisciplinary teamwork. *Instructional Science*, 46(3), 457–488.

Vu, T. P. A. (2014). Tự chủ đại học ở Việt Nam: Thiếu thực chất. *Tia Sang*, 22 August. Retrieved from https://bit.ly/2IU59rC

Index

accountability 50, 225
accreditation 12, 19–20, 23, 36, 49–50, 213
Adamson, L. 175
adaptability 23, 140, 145, 156, 197
Africa 8
agriculture 41, 43, 103
Ajzen, I. 104–5, 112
alienation 193
alumni 156, 173–5, 179–88, 191, 221–2, 224, 228
Amaratunga, D. xiv
Al-Ansari, A. 169
Anthony, S. 174
ARWU World University Ranking 51
ASEAN Economic Community 41, 46, 62
ASEAN Qualification Reference Framework 49
ASEAN University Network 213
Asia-Pacific Economic Cooperation 41
Asian Development Bank 44
Asian dragons 41–4
assessment 4, 9, 11, 13, 20; and development models 64; and external stakeholders 175, 180–1, 184–5, 187; formative assessment 118, 128, 130; and implementation 22, 25–9, 32–4; and internships 150; leadership 78, 81–2, 86, 89, 91–2; peer assessment 13, 32, 118, 124, 129–30; self-assessment 32, 118, 124, 129–30, 147, 149, 160; of soft skills 117–34; summative assessment 118, 129; and teachers 97–100, 106, 110; and way ahead 212, 214, 216–20, 223, 227
Assessment of Higher Education Learning Outcomes (AHELO) 4, 8–9, 33, 119
Australia 1–2, 9–12, 22–4, 27, 30, 33, 35, 71, 119, 215

Australian Council for Educational Research (ACER) 33
Australian Qualifications Framework (AQF) 11
Australian Technology Network (ATN) 12, 23
autonomy 6, 49–51, 63, 66–8, 72–4; and external stakeholders 177, 179; and internships 139; and leadership 78–9, 83–4, 90–2; and teachers 96, 112; and way ahead 212–13, 215, 225–6, 229–30

B-HERT Project 12, 71
Baguley, T. 138
Barrie, S. 12–13, 21, 24, 27, 29, 31, 64, 91, 112, 120, 131, 207
Belgium 9
Berglund, A. 55
Binder, J.F. 138, 143
Blaney, N. 175
bottom-up approaches 13, 21, 215
Bourdieu, P. 79, 81, 89, 136
Bowden, J. 2
brain drain 50
bribery 148
Bridgstock, R. 104
British University Vietnam 49
British Virgin Islands 43
Brodie, L. 30
Broomhall, S. 12, 22
Brunner, B.R. xiii
Buddhism 11
bureaucracy 50, 185
Business Administration 44, 65–7, 69, 82–3, 87; and assessment 121, 123; and external stakeholders 176, 178–9; and internships 135, 139–41, 143–5, 149; and participation 200; and teachers 96, 100–1; and way ahead 216, 223

Can Tho University 51
Canada 10
capital forms 79, 81–2, 89–92, 136–7, 142–5, 148–50
capstone subjects 13, 33, 67, 119, 125, 129
career fairs 35, 68–70, 72, 80, 89, 164, 179, 221
career identities 136, 146–7
Carnegie Melon Foundation 155
CDIO concept 55
centralization 50–1, 78, 112, 173, 213, 229
Chak, Y.L. 30
cheap labor 44, 46
China 8, 11, 41, 43
Ching, L. 139
citizenship 8, 11, 52–3, 63
civil society 12, 215
Clark, G. 156, 168
class sizes 27, 32, 88, 92, 98; and assessment 127–8, 130–1; and teachers 100, 106, 108, 111–12; and way ahead 216, 220, 227, 229
co-curricular activities 18, 24–5, 34–5, 68, 83
collaboration 5, 7, 25, 29, 49; and assessment 124; and context 55; and external stakeholders 173, 176, 178, 181, 186–7; and extracurricular activities 155; and internships 135–6, 144, 149–51; and participation 194, 197, 207; and teachers 97–8, 100; and way ahead 212, 217, 219, 223–4, 229
Colombia 9
colonialism 41, 44, 46
Commander, J. 155
commercialization 50
communism 44, 78, 157, 159
communities of practice 81, 90–1, 138, 147–9, 181, 219–20, 227
community-service learning 13, 25, 30, 33, 80, 97, 119, 155, 175
competencies 1–2, 6–10, 12, 46, 52; and contexts 55; and extracurricular activities 160, 162; and internships 135, 140, 148; and leadership 85, 88, 90; and way ahead 213, 221
computer skills 52, 66–9, 74, 84, 90, 123, 137, 140, 160, 197–9
confidence 31–2, 68, 85, 96, 98; and assessment 124, 127; and external stakeholders 183; and extracurricular activities 166; and internships 137, 140, 142–3, 146; lack of 27, 106, 111–12, 120, 142, 148, 187, 219; and participation 198, 205; self-confidence 160, 165; and teachers 104, 108; and way ahead 218, 227
Confucianism 43–4, 46, 51, 62, 72, 91, 100, 145, 159, 208, 219
contexts 1, 3–4, 6, 8, 11–13; and assessment 117, 119–21, 127, 130; and development models 61–4, 72, 74; and external stakeholders 176, 178–9, 181, 188; and extracurricular activities 157, 170; and implementation 18–19, 22, 26, 28, 33, 41–60; and internships 139–40; and leadership 78–95; and participation 191, 193–5; and teachers 97, 99–100, 104, 107, 112; and way ahead 212, 215, 223, 226–7, 230
Cornell, D. 194
Crawford, A. 2166
critical thinking 4, 6–7, 9, 12, 22–3, 105, 136, 159, 162
Crook, C. 138
Cullen, A.M. 155
curricula 8–9, 11, 13, 20–1, 24–6; and assessment 117, 123, 129; and contexts 46–7, 49–50, 52, 54–6; curriculum design 22, 63–4, 179, 225; curriculum development 28, 78, 80, 220; curriculum mapping 28–9, 216; and development models 62, 66–74; and external stakeholders 173–5, 177–8, 185, 187–8; and extracurricular activities 154–5, 168, 170; and implementation 30–2, 34–6; and internships 147, 151; and leadership 79, 83–5, 87, 90–2; and participation 191, 198–200, 206–8; and teachers 96–7, 106–7, 113; and way ahead 212–13, 215, 221, 226, 229–30

Daniels, M. 55
Danish National Qualification Framework 11
Dao, K.V. 106
David, C. 98, 112
Davidoff, J. 201
Davis, B.D. 2
De la Harpe, B. 98, 112
Deakin University 32
Dearing Report 10
decision-making 6, 50, 160
Denmark 10–11
Department for Assessment and Quality Assurance 51

Department for General Education 68, 84
developing countries 32, 41, 56
development models 61–77
disciplinary knowledge 4, 10, 13, 22, 24–7; and assessment 126–7; and contexts 53–4; and development models 64, 68–70; and implementation 31; and leadership 88; and teachers 98, 106, 108; and way ahead 219, 223
drivers 19–20, 35–6, 79–80, 88, 108, 128, 212, 214, 216–18, 227
Duy Tan University 51

East 61, 155
Educational Development Strategy 52
Egypt 9
Eisner, S. xiv
elective subjects 66, 69, 72, 84, 87, 90, 154
employability 1–11; and assessment of soft skills 117–34; and development models 61–77; employability capital 136–7, 142, 149–50; employability skills 1, 12, 55, 62, 96, 117, 154–8, 160–3, 168–70, 178; employment outcomes 5, 61, 67, 86, 136–7, 140–1, 148, 150, 156–7, 170, 228; and engagement/disengagement 191–211; and external stakeholders 173–90; and extracurricular activities 154–72; and implementation 78–95; and internships 135–53; and leadership 78–95; and participation 191–211; and teachers 96–116; and way ahead 212–32
engagement/disengagement 19–20, 26, 28–33, 35–6, 47; and assessment 118–21, 128, 130–1; and development models 63–4, 66–7, 69–70, 72–3; and external stakeholders 173, 178, 180; and extracurricular activities 154, 156–8, 164–70; and internships 135, 140–2, 148–50; and leadership 79–81, 84–6, 88–92; and students 191–211; and teachers 96, 98–101, 104, 106–7, 109–13; and way ahead 212, 214–22, 225–6, 229
England 10
English language 13, 18, 52, 62, 66–9; and assessment 117, 121, 123, 127, 129; and extracurricular activities 164; and internships 143; and leadership 83–4, 87, 90; and participation 194, 198–200, 205; and teachers 101, 105–6, 110

epistemology 26
Europe 8
European Union (EU) 9
experts 21–2, 25–6, 28, 64, 66, 81, 87–8, 178–80, 187, 203, 219, 222–9
external stakeholders 62–3, 65–7, 74, 81, 104–5; and assessment 120; and extracurricular activities 156, 164–5, 170; and internships 135, 144; and participation 191; roles of 173–90; and way ahead 221–4, 226–7
extracurricular activities (ECAs) 18, 25, 34–6, 64, 66; and assessment 123; and development models 68, 70–4; external stakeholders 173, 175, 178–80, 183–5, 187–8; and leadership 79, 83–4, 86, 89, 91; and participation 191, 193, 198–200, 207–8; and student experiences 154–72; and teachers 103; and way ahead 212–13, 215–16, 221–3, 225–6, 229

feedback 32, 55, 79, 97, 105–6; and assessment 118–20, 124–7, 130–1; and external stakeholders 178, 181; and extracurricular activities 164; and internships 138–9, 144, 148, 150; and participation 193; and teachers 110; and way ahead 220, 228
feudalism 43, 46
Filsecker, M. 194
financial support 222, 224–6
Finland 9
Finley, D.A. 2
flexicurity model 11
foreign direct investment (FDI) 41–3, 56
Foreign Investment Agency 43
foreign languages 6, 44–5, 52–3, 63, 66, 71, 99, 127, 140
Framework for Higher Education Qualifications in England, Wales and Northern Ireland 10
France 10, 41, 44, 49
Freeman, J. 201
Fugate, M. 136
Fulbright Vietnam University 49
further research 13, 20, 28–9, 50, 55–6; and assessment 131; and development models 63, 74; and external stakeholders 176; and extracurricular activities 154–5, 157, 170; and internships 135, 138; and participation 191–2, 207; and teachers 113

Garner, B. 174
Gault, J. 138
Gayani Fernando, N. xiv
General Agreement on Trade in Services (GATS) 47, 62
General Statistics Office of Vietnam 47–8
generic skills 1, 4–5, 8–10, 12, 22–3; and assessment 119; and development models 69; and external stakeholders 175, 180; and extracurricular activities 162; and implementation 26–7, 31, 33, 35; and leadership 85, 88; and teachers 106–7
Germany 49
Gilbert, B.L. 137, 142, 144
globalization 44, 85, 99
Gonczi, A. 5
governance 50–1, 78, 173, 191
governments 3, 8, 10, 22–3, 41, 49–54, 56, 174, 186, 224
Graduate Skills Assessment (GSA) 33, 119
Grant-Smith, D. 34
Green Summer Campaign 35, 157, 164–5
Groh, M. 5
gross domestic product (GDP) 41–3
Group of Eight (Go8) 12, 22–3
Gruba, P. 13, 26, 92
Guideline 2196 53–5, 62, 71, 90, 213
Guthrie, J.T. 194

habitus 79, 81, 89, 193
Hager, P. 3, 104
Haigh, R. xiv
hard skills 2, 53–4, 63
Heckman, J.J. 2
Higher Education Council of Australia 2
Higher Education Development Strategy 52
higher education (HE) 1–11; and assessment 117–34; and development initiatives 8–13; and development of soft skills 46–56; and engagement/disengagement 191–211; and external stakeholder roles 173–90; and extracurricular activities 154–72; and internships 135–53; and participation 191–211; and teaching of soft skills 97–9; and way ahead 212–32
higher education institutions (HEIs) 8–9, 12–13, 18–26, 33–4, 44; and assessment 119; and contexts 47–50, 53; and development models 61, 63, 74, and external stakeholders 174, 176; and leadership 79

Higher Education Law 47, 78, 213, 225
Higher Education Reform Agenda (HERA) 49, 52, 68, 83
Higher Education Standards Framework (HESF) 11
Ho Chi Minh 47, 157
Ho Chi Minh International University 55
Holcombe, R. 194
Holland, S. 3, 104
Hong Kong 43, 139
Hong Kong Polytechnic University 30
Hu, S. 192
Hughes, C. 12
human resources 44, 47, 62, 179, 182, 209, 214, 224
Hunters and Gatherers Project 11, 29
Hurrell, S.A. 155

implementation 11–13, 97–9, 103, 106, 215–16; and assessment 118, 123, 127; and contexts 41–60; and development models 61–77; and external stakeholders 173–4, 176–80, 183, 186–8; and extracurricular activities 221–3; implications for 225–8; and leadership 78–95; and literature review 18–40; and participation 191–2, 195, 208–9; and teachers 109, 112–13; way ahead 212–14, 230
incentives 19–21, 31, 36, 51, 64; and assessment 126–8, 130–1; and leadership 79–81, 85, 88, 90, 92; and teachers 108–9, 111–12; and way ahead 218, 227, 229
India 174
Indiana University 137
industry 20, 22–3, 26, 35, 41; and assessment 119, 122, 129; and contexts 43, 45–6, 50–1; and development models 66, 68–9, 73; and external stakeholders 173, 175–81, 187; and extracurricular activities 156; industrialization 52, 56, 62; and internships 135–7, 143–7, 149–51; and leadership 79, 83, 85–92; and participation 199; and teachers 97, 100, 102, 108; and way ahead 212, 217, 222–5, 227–9
inflation 43
Information Technology (IT) 5, 135, 139–43, 146–7, 149, 157, 182
infrastructure 51, 53, 90, 100
Innovative Research Universities (IRU) Australia 12, 22–3
Institute for the Future 5, 7

institutional initiatives 12–13, 56, 61, 63–4, 72; and assessment 117, 121, 130; and development models 74; and engagement 226–7; and implementation 19–28, 36; and leadership 79–80, 84, 87–8; and participation 191; and teachers 112; and way ahead 229–30
international initiatives 8–10
internationalization 47, 49–50, 52, 56
internships 13, 24, 33–5, 66, 68–71; and assessment 119–20, 124–5, 129; contribution of 135–53; and development models 73; and external stakeholders 175, 178–9, 181, 183–5, 187–8; and extracurricular activities 155–6; internship.edn.vn 141; and leadership 80, 84, 86, 89, 91; and participation 199, 205; and way ahead 217, 223, 225, 227, 229
intuition 89, 106, 119, 126, 130, 217
Italy 9

Jackson, D. 147
Japan 9–10, 43
Jia, Y. 194
Jollands, M. 30
Jones, A. 26, 98
Jordan 5

Kahu, E.R. 192
Kaiser-Meyer-Olkin (KMO) test 159
Kautz, T. 2
Keogh, E. 201
Kerres, M. 194
Khalil, O.E. 137, 142, 145–6
Khan, S.A.R. 180
Kimbark, K. 194
Klauda, S.L. 194
Knight, P. 2
knowledge 2–3, 5–10, 13, 20, 22–7; and assessment 118–20, 125–30; and contexts 45–7, 53–5; and development models 62, 68–9; and external stakeholders 175; and extracurricular activities 155–7, 162–3; and implementation 31–5; and internships 135–8, 140–4, 146–50; knowledge economy 44, 52, 99; knowledge transfer 23, 97, 157, 162; and leadership 81–2, 87–8; and participation 192–4, 207; and teachers 98–9, 106, 108; and way ahead 219, 223
knowledge, skills, abilities and other characteristics (KSAOs) 136

Konold, T. 194
Koskey, K.L. 194
Krishnan, N. 5
Kuh, G.D. 192
Kuwait 9
Kuwait University 137

Labor Party 47
Laker, D.R. 3
Lam, T. 139
Latin America 8
Lau, H.-H. 156
Laura, R.S. 55
Lawson, R. 29
leadership 3, 20–1, 23, 28, 31; and assessment 117, 121, 124, 130–1; and contexts 43, 45, 50, 55, 78–95; and development models 62–5, 69, 72–4; and external stakeholders 173, 178–9, 181, 187–8; and extracurricular activities 156, 160, 162, 166, 169–70; and implementation 35; and participation 191–2, 197; and teachers 96, 98, 107–9, 112–13; and way ahead 212–13, 215, 217–21, 223–4, 226–7, 229–30
learning outcomes 8–10, 12, 19–20, 22, 24; and assessment 118, 128; and contexts 49, 53–4, 56; and development models 62, 67, 70; and extracurricular activities 170; and implementation 27, 30; and internships 138–9, 149–50; and leadership 85; learning objectives 11, 28–9, 36, 79–80, 106, 125, 216; and participation 192, 194–5; and teachers 97, 103–4; and way ahead 214, 217
legislation 52, 90
Lessiter, J. 201, 203
Li-yia, F. 120
lifelong-learning skills 4–5, 9, 11, 23, 61, 155
Lindsay, C. 136
linkages 22, 50–1, 92, 191, 212, 217, 223–4, 227–8, 230
Linnenbrink-Garcia, L. 194
literature reviews 11, 18–40, 55, 61, 118–21, 139, 175, 187, 192
local authorities 175, 179, 187, 191, 222, 229

McDonald, P. 34
McKenzie, D. 5
McMurray, S. xiii
McQuaid, R.W. 136
Al-Mahmood, R. 13, 26, 92

Index

Malaysia 10, 34, 155
Malaysian Institute of Higher Learning 3
Malone, M. 194
management tools 20–1, 31, 78–82, 108–9, 111–12, 124, 130–1, 218, 227, 229
Mann, S.J. 193
ManPower Group 45
market economies 41, 97
Marsden, R. 156
Marxism 47
Mayer, E. 12
media 44
mentorship 27, 119, 125, 129, 137–9; and external stakeholders 175, 178, 181, 183–5, 188; and internships 142, 144, 146, 148–51; and way ahead 227
meta-cognition 136, 138, 149–50
Metzger, C. 54–5
Mexico 9
Miller, F. 138
Ministry of Education and Training (MOET) 50–4, 56, 62, 66–9, 71–3; and assessment 117, 123, 129; and external stakeholders 173; and leadership 78, 83, 87, 90; and teachers 99, 103, 105–6; and way ahead 212–14, 221, 225, 229
Ministry of Labor, Invalids and Social Affairs (MOLISA) 44
missions/mission statements 12–13, 22, 33, 61–2, 97, 213–14, 224
Mitchell, G.W. 3
models 61–77
Muir, C. 2
Murray, M. 175

Narayanan, V. 147
National GAP Project 10–11, 24, 34
national initiatives 10–11, 18–19, 36
National Survey of Student Engagement 192
Nelson, K. 193
Nelson Report 33, 119
Netherlands 9
New Generation Universities (NGU) 12, 22–3
New Zealand 1, 10
Nguyen, M.T. 55
Nguyen, T.M.D. 138
Nguyen, T.N. 55
Nickson, D. 155
non-governmental organizations (NGOs) 175, 182, 191
non-technical skills 13, 154–5

Nordetrade 43
Norman, R. xiii
North Vietnam 41
Northern Ireland 10
Northwood University 34, 156
Norway 9
Nunley, J.M. 138

Odio, M. 138, 146–7
Organization of Economic Cooperation and Development (OECD) 6–7, 9
organizational culture 20, 22, 80–1, 219, 226
Osman, K. 155

parents 23, 35, 72, 104, 161–2
participation 154–72, 184–8, 191–211
patriotism 163
Pearce, P. 34, 155
pedagogy 13, 22, 27, 29, 31; and assessment 120, 127; and contexts 49, 51–2; and development models 61–4, 67–8, 70–1, 73; and external stakeholders 173–4, 180, 187–8; and extracurricular activities 154; and leadership 78, 80–1, 85, 88; and teachers 97, 106, 113; and way ahead 213, 215–17, 219–20, 223, 225, 227
performativity 193
Peters, M.L. 194
Pham Minh Hac 99
Pitman, T. 12, 22
political education 36, 79–80, 157, 178, 216, 221, 229
portfolios 13, 25, 32, 98, 119–20, 124–5, 129, 140
poverty 41
Powell, J.L. 3
private sector 47, 49, 51, 55, 65; and assessment 121–2; and development models 68–9; and external stakeholders 176–7, 182, 186; and extracurricular activities 158, 162, 167; and leadership 79, 83, 90; and participation 201–2, 205–6, 208; and teachers 102
privatization 51
problem-based learning 13, 30, 64, 80
problem-solving 3–4, 6–7, 9–10, 12, 23; and assessment 117, 125; and contexts 53–4; and development models 61, 63; and external stakeholders 178; and extracurricular activities 160, 162; and implementation 30–1; and internships

136, 143; and leadership 83–4, 87; and teachers 105
professional development 27, 80–1, 85, 87–8, 90; and assessment 118, 129–30; and internships 148; professionalism 52–3, 63, 145; and teachers 106, 108–9, 112; and way ahead 215
Program for International Student Assessment (PISA) 9
public sector 47, 51, 65, 69, 102; and assessment 121–2; and external stakeholders 176–7, 182; and extracurricular activities 157–8, 162, 167; and internships 148; and participation 196, 201–2, 205–6, 208; and teachers 108; and way ahead 213–14
public speaking 5, 200
Purdue University 137

QS World University Ranking 51
quality assurance 10–11, 18–19, 22–3, 36, 49–51, 97, 154, 225

ranking systems 43, 50–1, 89, 97, 174, 222
Read, P. 139
recessions 43
recommendations 11, 53–4, 63, 65, 69; and development models 71; and external stakeholders 176; and extracurricular activities 170; and internships 136, 150; and leadership 82; and participation 196–7; and teachers 100, 113; and way ahead 212, 226–8
Reeve, J. 194
Renovation Policy (*Doi Moi*) 41, 47, 62
Richardson, T. 194
Rivera, D. Jr. 2
Rogat, T.K. 194
role models 28, 219
Ross, A. 175
Rothman, M. 146
Royal Melbourne Institute of Technology (RMIT) 49
Russian Federation 9

Scarinci, J. 34, 155
Schmidt, M.K. 137, 142
Sepahpanah, M. 180
service learning 13, 25, 30, 33, 80, 97, 119, 155, 175
service sector 41, 43, 46–7, 62
Shaw, K. 55
Shek, D.T. 30

Simiyu, R.R. 137, 142
Singapore 43
Sisman, R. 146
situated learning theory 138, 143, 147–8
skill gaps 44–6, 100, 135, 143, 146–8, 150
Skinner, L.B. 3
Smith, C. 12, 31
social fields 79, 81–2, 89–92
social media 169, 204
social relations 78, 136, 140, 149
socialism 41, 44, 46–7, 51, 62, 91, 100, 159, 168, 214, 221
socialization 160, 162, 165–6
soft skills 1–17; and assessment 117–34; basic skills 5; business skills 7; community skills 7; conceptualization of 214–15; and contexts 99–100; current relevance of 5–7; deficit in 41–6; definitions of 1–3; and development initiatives 8–13; and development models 61–77; development of 1–11, 79–80; employability skills 1, 12, 55, 62, 96, 117, 154–8, 160–3, 168–70, 178; and engagement/disengagement 191–211; and external stakeholders 173–90; and extracurricular activities 154–72; and implementation 18–40, 63–4, 70–1, 74, 78–95; and internships 135–53; and leadership 78–95; nature of 3–5; and participation 191–211; people-related skills 5–6; personal skills/attributes 7, 23; selection of 214–15; and teachers 96–116; in Vietnamese HE 46–56; and way ahead 212–32
South Africa 10
South Korea 9–10, 43
Southeast Asia 41, 43, 99, 117
Soviet Union 41
specialized knowledge 35, 46, 62, 87–8, 106, 127–30, 156–7
staff development 27, 80–1, 85, 87–8, 90, 106, 108–9, 112, 118, 129–30, 148, 215
Stanford Research Institute 155
Statistical Package for the Social Sciences (SPSS) 103, 158, 182, 196, 201, 203
Stevens, M. xiii
Student Success Courses 194
Student Support Service 178
student-centeredness 29–32, 49, 64, 66–71, 73–4, 80, 97, 105–6, 213, 216–17, 220, 229
subject-level implementation 28–34, 36
superficial learning 85, 88–9, 220

240 *Index*

sustainable development 44, 52
Sweden 9
Swierczek, F.W. 55
Switzerland 10

Taiwan 43, 156
teachers 20, 25, 27, 29, 32–5; and assessment 117–20, 122–31; and contexts 43, 48–9, 51–2; and development models 63–7, 69–70, 72–3; and engagement 218–20, 226–7; and external stakeholders 176–7, 179–82, 187; and influential factors 96–116; and leadership 78, 80–92; and participation 194–5, 205, 207–8; and way ahead 212, 214, 217, 220, 222–3
teamwork 3–5, 30–1, 44, 53, 55; and assessment 117, 123–4, 129; and development models 61, 63, 71; and external stakeholders 178; and extracurricular activities 160, 162, 164–6; and internships 136; and leadership 84, 87; and participation 197–8, 205; and teachers 96, 99, 105
technical knowledge 2, 20, 22, 31–2, 142, 147, 155
technical skills 2–3, 8–9, 19–20, 22, 26; and assessment 125, 127–30; and contexts 45–6; and development models 62; and extracurricular activities 155; and implementation 31–2; and internships 142; and leadership 86, 88; and participation 191; and teachers 106, 111
Tertiary Education Quality and Standards Agency (TEQSA) 11
Thai National Qualification Framework for Higher Education 11
Thailand 10–11
Thomas, L. 193
Thompson, L. 156, 168
Tomlinson, M. 136, 179
Ton Duc Thang University 51
top-down approaches 21–2, 27, 29, 50, 63, 72, 78, 91, 215
tourism 43, 135, 139–40, 142–7, 149, 174, 200
Tran, L.H.N. 45, 138, 170
Tran, T.T. 55
Trung, T.Q. 55
Truong, H.T. 55
Truong, Q.D. 54–5
Tseng, C.-M. 194
Tuning Educational Structures in Europe 3–4, 7–9

Unaligned Universities (UU) 12, 23
unemployment 41–3, 46, 99, 138
United Kingdom (UK) 1, 10, 155
United States Collegiate Learning Assessment 9
United States (US) 1, 9, 41, 44
Universiti Malaysia Terengganu 34
universities *see* Vietnamese universities
University of Social Sciences and Humanities 99

Victorian Language and Learning Network 33
Viet-France University 49
Viet-Germany University 49
Vietnam 1, 3, 10, 18–19, 35; as Asian dragons 41–4; and contexts 41–60; and development models 46–56, 61–77; and external stakeholders 182; and participation 197, 204, 207–8; and skill gaps 44–6
Vietnam National University 56
Vietnamese universities 1–17; and assessment 117–34; and contextual factors 41–60, 78–95; and development models 61–77; and external stakeholders 173–90; and extracurricular activities 154–72; and implementation 18–60; and internships 135–53; and leadership 78–95; and participation 191–211; and teachers 96–116; and way ahead 212–32
Vietnamnet 43
Vishwanath, T. 5
Vo, H.-P. 55
Vocational Education and Training (VET) 10
Vogler, J.S. 30

Wales 10
Walker, M. 156
Wang, M.-T. 194
Warhurst, C. 155
Weber, M.R. 2
West 13, 44, 46–7, 51, 56; and assessment 117, 129; and development models 61–2; and extracurricular activities 155; and leadership 84; and teachers 96, 99, 112; and way ahead 212–18, 220–1, 229
White, B.J. 3
Whyatt, J.D. 156
work experience 44, 55, 68–9, 86–7, 90–1; and assessment 129; and external stakeholders 178, 180, 182, 186; and

extracurricular activities 155; and internships 136, 140, 143; and participation 207; and teachers 103, 108; work placements 13, 33–4, 119, 135, 175

work-integrated learning (WIL) 13, 30–1, 33, 64, 68–71; and assessment 120; and development models 73–4; and external stakeholders 173, 175, 178, 187; and internships 139; and leadership 80, 84–8, 91–2; and teachers 97, 100, 105; and way ahead 213, 216–17, 220, 224, 227, 229

work-readiness skills 62, 66, 68, 71, 74; and assessment 123; and external stakeholders 173–4, 178, 181–4, 187; and leadership 84; and participation 191, 208; and way ahead 213–14, 216–17, 224, 229

World Bank 44–5, 52, 56, 62

World Health Organization (WHO) 5–6

World Trade Organization (WTO) 41, 47, 62

Worsfold, K. 31

Ya-hui, S. 120

Yang, L. xi

Youth Union and Associates (YUA) 35, 47, 65–70, 72–3, 80; and assessment 121, 123, 126, 129; and external stakeholders 176, 178–80, 187–8; and extracurricular activities 154, 157–9, 161, 163–6, 169, 221–3; and implementation 221–3; and leadership 83, 86, 89, 91; and participation 191, 199–200, 207; and teachers 101, 107, 109–10; and way ahead 212–14, 216, 218, 225–7, 229

YouTube 5

Zhang, Y. 180

Printed in the United States
By Bookmasters